A Challenge for Living

Books of Related Interest

The Cancer Book
Geoffrey M. Cooper

Carpe Diem: Enjoying Every Day with a Terminal Illness
Ed Madden

*Dying, Death, and Bereavement: Theoretical Perspectives
and Other Ways of Knowing*
Inge B. Corless/Barbara B. Germino/Mary A. Pittman

Human Aging and Chronic Disease
Cary S. Kart/Eileen K. Metress/Seamus P. Metress

Life and Death: Grappling with the Moral Dilemmas of Our Time
Louis P. Pojman

Life and Death: A Reader in Moral Problems
Louis P. Pojman

Perspectives on Death and Dying
Gere Fulton/Eileen K. Metress

A Challenge for Living
Dying, Death, and Bereavement

Edited by

Inge B. Corless, R.N., Ph.D., F.A.A.N.
*MGH Institute of Health Professions
Massachusetts General Hospital
Boston*

Barbara B. Germino, Ph.D., R.N., F.A.A.N.
The University of North Carolina, Chapel Hill

Mary A. Pittman, Dr.P.H.
*President, Hospital Research and Education Trust
American Hospital Association
Chicago*

JONES AND BARTLETT PUBLISHERS
BOSTON   LONDON

Editorial, Sales, and Customer Service Offices

Jones and Bartlett Publishers
One Exeter Plaza
Boston, MA 02116
1–800–832–0034
1–617–859–3900

Jones and Bartlett Publishers International
7 Melrose Terrace
London W6 7RL
England

Library of Congress Cataloging-in-Publication Data
A challenge for living: dying, death, and bereavement / edited by
  Inge B. Corless, Barbara B. Germino, Mary A. Pittman.
      p. cm.
   "Companion volume to Dying, death, and bereavement"--Introd.
   Includes bibliographical references (p.) and index.
   ISBN 0-8672-817-1
   1. Thanatology. 2. Death. 3. Bereavement. 4. Terminal care.
  I. Corless, Inge B.   II. Germino, Barbara B.   III. Pittman, Mary A.
HQ1073.C464   1995
306.9--dc20   94-26561
                                                                   CIP

Editor: Joseph E. Burns
Project Coordinator: Joan M. Flaherty
Production Service: TKM Productions
Designer: Suzanne Pescatore, TKM Productions
Cover Designer: Hannus Design Associates
Printer: Edwards Brothers
Cover Printer: New England Book Components, Inc.

Photo Credits: p. xi, Grace Goldin; p. 37 (top, bottom), © 1991 Dan Rich; p. 159, The Tom Reynolds Studio; p. 241, Myron S. Wolf Photography; p. 313, © 1992 K. D. Zotter; p. 367, © Dan Crawford; p. 377, Fiona Good, A. I. I. P.; p. 393, Fisher Photo.

Printed in the United States of America
99 98 97 96 95   10 9 8 7 6 5 4 3 2 1

To all of our teachers:
those we have cared for,
loved, and mourned,
and especially
David Friendly,
Norma Micol,
and Thomas Pittman

Contents

Foreword

Dame Cicely Saunders

Trained as a nurse during the war and being invalided out, Dame Cicely Saunders obtained a war degree at Oxford and became a medical social worker. Concern for the pain control of dying patients and the distress of their families moved her to study medicine, and in 1958, she began work among the patients of St. Joseph's Hospice. The experience there was one of the roots of St. Christopher's Hospice, which she founded, together with a small group, and which opened in 1967. From the start, it was planned as a teaching center and a focus of research in the control of pain and other distress in terminal illness. This work has been recognized world wide and was the catalyst for the hospice movement.

Dame Cicely has received a number of honorary degrees, including Honorary Doctorate of Science from Yale in 1969, Lambeth Doctorate of Medicine from the Archbishop of Canterbury in 1977, Doctorate from the Open University in 1978, and Honorary Doctorate of Law, Columbia University, New York, in 1979. She has been a member of the Attendance Allowance Board since it started, and from 1973 to 1978 was a member of the Medical Research Council. Dame Cicely was awarded the Templeton Prize for Progress in Religion in 1981. Other honorary degrees have followed, including honorary doctorates in law and civil law from Oxford and Cambridge Universities in 1986.

She is an Honorary Fellow of the Royal College of Physicians, the Royal College of Surgeons, and the Royal College of Nurses. She was awarded the British Medical Association's Gold Medal for Distinguished Merit in July 1987 and was made a Freeman of the London Borough of Bromley in October 1987. In 1988, she was made an Honorary Fellow of the Royal College of Psychiatrists. In 1989, Dame Cicely was awarded the Order of Merit by Her Majesty the Queen.

Over 40 years ago, I had the opportunity and privilege of accompanying an isolated man who talked through his thoughts and feelings with me during the last two months of his life. A Jew from Warsaw, he had lost his family and believed that he had made no impact on the world during his short life of 40 years. The first ideas of hospice developed during our conversations and for me they are summed up in two of his phrases. The first referred to the fact that he would leave me a small legacy—a founding gift for a then nameless place. He said, "I'll be a window in your home." The second was a response to my offer to read him something from the Old Testament, as he was quietly returning to the faith of his fathers. His response was, "No, thank you. I only want what is in your mind and in your heart." At the time, it was a specific challenge to which I tried to respond but later I came to see it as a demand on us all for everything we could bring of thought, experience, and skill to the care of people facing death, to be offered together with personal concern. Setting these two demands together with the idea of a window challenged the beginnings of hospice to be open to many adventures and developments, focused always on close attention to individual people, their needs, and their potentials.

The story since February 1948 when David Tasma died "at peace," as he told me, has been one of surprising growth. This book brings together much of the experience of many workers during these years, all facing the demands on mind and heart in a spirit of openness. The original vision seems to have the capacity to keep us recognizably addressing the same concerns in our diverse cultures and settings. It appears that those of us who work in the whole field of death, dying, and bereavement have all tried to listen to those people who are facing their individual journey through this part of life. It is from them that we all continue to learn and find inspiration, whether we are concerned with researching and developing ever-improving symptom control, more understanding of psychosocial tensions and possibilities, or better ways of sharing in what surely has to be the work and support of an interdisciplinary team.

Seven years as an R.N. volunteer in one of the early Protestant Homes (St. Luke's Hospital, originally Home for the Dying Poor, opened in 1893) followed by another seven years as a physician in St. Joseph's Hospice (opened 1905) gave me opportunities to meet and listen to innumerable patients, to observe the regular giving of oral opiates at St. Luke's, and to introduce this method of giving analgesics to St. Joseph's Hospice. It enabled me to monitor our improving clinical practice and development with a retrieval system and to lay the medical foundations of St. Christopher's, opened in 1967 as the first home care and teaching hospice. A Christian as well as a medical foundation, its aim was "to express the love of God to all who come, in every possible way, in skilled nursing and medical care, in the use of every scientific means of relieving suffering and distress, in understanding personal sympathy, with respect for the dignity of each person as a human being, precious to God and man" (Aim & Basis, 1965). Emphasis was laid on the fact that all those working in the hospice would give their own contribution in their own way, in a spirit of freedom, while patients would seek *their* own way to peace without any pressure. It was emphasized, too, that it would be group work, open to further development.

It was not long before such a religious foundation was challenged by those wishing to enter this field without any such commitment. Certain of our own calling but concerned to open doors as well as windows, we refused to be dogmatic, concerned only that anyone in this field must expect his or her own philosophy to be challenged and to be faced with the difficult questions that may arise from people who are calling on their own resources in crisis. That the spiritual element of the "total pain" complex included far more than any form of personal religion became obvious as its physical, emotional, and social elements were also addressed with developing experience.

From the beginning, hospice learning and attitudes have formed bridges. First, the bridges between people as staff and volunteers have enabled these people to listen to their patients and families. The way forward must surely come in the same fashion. Patients are the true founders of the hospice movement and the field of related studies and development. Our moves into the future will be safeguarded if we go on listening, aware that the words of one individual or family may open up a whole new scene.

It has also been important to build a bridge to the researchers and in due course to enter this field ourselves. Early meetings with such pioneers as Beecher, Eddy, and Houde were followed by productive contact with Melzack and Wall. In an editiorial in the influential journal, *Pain*, Wall (1986) wrote, "The immediate origins of pain and suffering need immediate attention while the long-term search for basic care proceeds. The old methods of care and caring have to be rediscovered and the best of modern medicine has to be turned to the task of new study and therapy specifically directed at pain." The challenge to continue to look at all aspects of suffering still faces us, and we have to back up our demonstrations of effective relief with research studies that are widely published. Our teaching must be objectively based and we should be offering our patients continually improving understanding and therapy.

Workers in the field addressed in this comprehensive book also have a responsibility to build bridges into the community, both professional and general. That so many dying people all over the world are ineptly treated faces us with an almost overwhelming challenge, as does the isolation enforced on them and their bereaved families by the disregard of the public. Hospice is about living until the end, still as part of the community.

As we learned to demonstrate something of what could be done by what has come to be termed *palliative medicine*, we could begin to build effective bridges with the acute services. We have had to discover when and how to draw in other specialties and learn from them as well as educate from our standpoint. In no way are we to take the high moral ground, but we need to meet effectively as we come from our different professional backgrounds and across the disciplines.

We will often have appropriate treatment to offer between the two extremes of all life-prolonging intervention possible and the threat of legalized active shortening of life with all its social dangers. We have to earn the attention and respect that will draw us in for the right patients at the right time. The hospital support or palliative care team can have a central role in this area and is charting an important way forward.

Our whole field has not only been about need but, above all, about achievement. We are concerned that a person should live this part of life, whether in dying or in bereavement, to the maximum potential, not only in physical ease or activity but also in family relationships and in addressing the most important inner values. A time of crisis can be a time of growth, often at surprising speed, of resolving long-standing problems and of reconciliation, both with oneself and with those around. Hospice workers find that the freedom from distress they aim to give by their treatment and hospitality opens up new space for personal development. Bridges are built among the conflicted families who are more and more often referred to us in recognition of what we try to offer.

Good communication can facilitate unexpected sharing and responses and develop the growth through loss we see so often. Here, I believe we reach the central and most positive area of our concerns. We have all been inspired by those we have seen bringing unexpected gains out of loss, whether it be of health, life, or bereavement. It may come out of distress that is very painful to share as we try to maintain the bridge between us. The rewards come from the resolutions that happen surprisingly frequently—but not always. At times, we can only stay beside unresolved problems or, at best, trust that what we have offered is the best we can, hoping it is good enough. A lifetime's difficulties may remain unchanged and it would be unrealistic to expect anything else.

It is the individual's inner values that matter when there is only a limited time left or when the most important person has died. The spiritual dimension encompasses searches for meaning in many varied ways. We have never been concerned that the people we serve should see things our way; rather, they should discover or reinforce their own way, asking for help if they wish, in freedom from any pressure or obligation. We have found that not only is our own search for meaning continually stimulated by the often desperate situations we face but also that this constant challenge helps develop a climate of shared discovery and hope.

Reference

Wall, P. D. (1986). Editorial: "25 Volumes of Pain." *Pain*, 25, 1–4.

Introduction

A Challenge for Living: Dying, Death, and Bereavement with its focus on thanatological issues serves as a companion volume to *Dying, Death and Bereavement: Theoretical Perspectives and Other Ways of Knowing*. In the earlier volume, the emphasis was the presentation of a theoretical and experiential overview of dying, death, and bereavement. The acknowledgment of the value of cognition as well as affect can be observed in chapters that represent the authors' reflections on their experiences with the dying of family members and hospice clients. This same recognition of the importance of the "me" as well as the "I" is acknowledged in the second volume; particularly in the section on Issues for Caregivers.

A Challenge for Living: Dying, Death, and Bereavement has been developed at a time when individuals, by dint of geographical and circumstantial placement, are confronted by many problems not of their own making. Whether it be malnutrition created by the sequestering of food stuffs by rival war lords, the ethnic cleansing of former neighbors by individuals called to arms under the religio/political banners of leaders with xenophobic motives, or death by disaffection and neglect of the homeless in the inner city or the rural poor, modification of the external environment has a direct effect on the well-being of every individual.

When the source of the disability is chronic, long-standing disease, the manipulation of the external environment is less significant than the readjustment of the internal environment—whether by surgery, drugs, radiotherapy, or some other means. When such mechanisms are ineffective the individual and concerned others are confronted with a challenge for living—dying, death, and bereavement.

It is the more constrained, less problematic world condition, sans the chaos of military and political machinations, that is the context for the consideration of dying, death, and bereavement in this volume. All of the complexity of dying as a result of a chronic disease is magnified by poverty, homelessness, starvation, and fratricidal battle.

Perhaps it is only when the right to live is vouchsafed that the right to die can become an issue. Were the right to die taken for granted, there would be a need to rally for the right to live. Given murderous acts, the state has the right to deprive the individual of both liberty and life. Other than the immediate protection of life and limb, no individual has the right to deprive another of life. Such a right is reserved to the state in response to the determination of a jury of peers.

The sanctity of life undergirds a number of practices. The call for assisted suicide while recognizing the right of the individual to self-determination contributes to the erosion of the responsibility of the citizen and the state not to engage in life-depriving activities. Furthermore, the shift from determination by self to determination by others is subtle. Given that most individuals do not wish to burden family members, partners, or friends with the care required as a result of prolonged illness, assisted suicide may seem obligatory (even noble!) to the dying person.

These questions have been given renewed attention as a consequence of the efforts of Dr. Jack Kevorkian to assist suicides of individuals with various diseases, some in the early stages, others chronic rather than characterized by immediate decline. Although each of the individuals has died by her (or his) own hand while in Dr. Kevorkian's presence, he has provided presence as well as information and apparatus. Other individuals and organizations have concentrated on information and have not formally provided presence. The concern of persons who contemplate death by their own hands is one of doing an ineffective job of it and thereby not dying. Presence of a responsible individual assures completion but makes the, survivor vulnerable to prosecution if complicity involved assistance. These issues are not easily resolved, nor should they be. Qvarnstrøm addresses this question of euthanasia as the topic of her chapter. Both Churchill and Corless also touch on these issues, as does Degner in her chapter on treatment decision making. Related to these questions of control of the end of life is the concern that individuals neither be kept alive interminably in a persistent vegetative state nor resuscitated when there is no hope of recovery. Various mechanisms for advance directives have been instituted so that the individual's wishes may be heeded, thus relieving the family and health-care providers of concerns and litigation that either too much or too little was done. These directives, which Lund Person addresses in her chapter on regulatory issues, are a response to technological capability of life extension in situations without the capacity for meaningful interaction.

The impact of politics and economics as well as history on these issues is significant. These influences are present in some of the other subjects addressed in this book. The ever-present politics of care is explicitly addressed by Preston and McCorkle in their chapter on symptom management. The constraints imposed by shrinking resources aggravates some of the tensions between different professions. Issues resulting from reduced resources and different caregiving stances are discussed by Foster and Davidson.

Issues and approaches in working with the terminally ill and subsequently with the bereaved constituted the major focus of this book. Whether the topic is communication, life review, helping children, or the role of physiotherapy, the authors share their visions of how and what is helpful to those who are dying and those who are or will become bereaved.

Prognosticating is always a hazardous activity. The futures of thanatology and of palliative care are elaborated by Churchill and Doyle, a respected philosopher and a medical educator. If in fact their future becomes our present, we are likely not to remember their foresight. If, however, events unfold in ways considerably different from what was foretold, then these chapters are the most likely to seem out of step even though a number of the other chapters examine current and future issues. Thus Churchill and Doyle deserve special appreciation for their willingness to help us prepare for the future, along with Lund Person, who examines regulatory issues, and Wass and Corr, who discuss death education for children and for adults.

Indeed death education for children and for adults may enable us to meet the challenges of death and bereavement and our own dying with equanimity and grace, with hollering and bellowing, and with gratitude for the gift of life. All of this presumes a life fully lived and not foreshortened by acts of personal violence, war, or the scourge of disease. That is not to say that individuals who have not lived long have not lived fully. Rather that the challenge for the dying person and the bereaved is greater than under more sanguine circumstances. Whatever the circumstances, dying, death, and bereavement constitute a challenge both to and for living. *A Challenge for Living: Dying, Death, and Bereavement* has the immodest aim of equipping individuals to confront these challenges effectively. Fortunately, we do so together with other concerned individuals in the context of an increasing interest in meeting these challenges.

Acknowledgments

We acknowledge all of those who have contributed to this book directly and indirectly. We are gateful for the ongoing support of our families— Inge's daughters Theresa and Patricia; Barbara's husband Vic, daughter Laurie, son Michael, and granddaughter Talia; Mary's husband David and sons Mark and Scott. Our editor, Joe Burns, graciously gave us the space to develop this project and the ongoing support to complete it. Amina Sharma, editorial assistant, with her pleasant demeanor eased the production of the manuscript. Joan Flaherty, with her other ways of knowing, took our collective product and transformed it into a book, and with it all has become a valued friend and colleague. We appreciate the cover design by Dick Hannus, whose artistry contributes visual beauty to the theme.

Contributors

Thomas Attig, PhD
Professor and Chair
Department of Philosophy
Bowling Green State University
Bowling Green, Ohio

Paula G. Balber, RN, MA
Lecturer/Chronic and Terminal
  Illness Therapist
Durham, North Carolina

Larry R. Churchill, PhD, MDiv
Professor and Chair
  Department of Social Medicine
Adjunct Professor
  Department of Religious Studies
University of North Carolina
Chapel Hill, North Carolina

Charles A. Corr, PhD
Professor
School of Humanities
Southern Illinois University at
  Edwardsville
Edwardsville, Illinois

The Reverend Roderick Cosh
Vicar
St. Augustine of Canterbury
Whitton, Twickenham
London, England

Kay W. Davidson, DSW
Associate Professor
School of Social Work
Hunter College
New York, New York

Betty Davies, RN, PhD
Professor, School of Nursing
  University of British Columbia
Investigator, Research Division
  British Columbia's Children's
  Hospital
Vancouver, British Columbia,
  Canada

Lesley F. Degner, RN, PhD
Professor, Faculty of Nursing
University of Manitoba
Winnipeg, Manitoba, Canada

Lynne Ann DeSpelder
Instructor
Cabrillo College
Aptos, California

Derek Doyle, OBE, FRCP
Medical Director
St. Columba's Hospice
Edinburgh, Scotland

Zelda Foster, MSW
Chief, Social Work Service
Department of Veterans Affairs
Brooklyn, New York

Elizabeth P. Lamers, MA
The Lamers Medical Group
Malibu, California

Judi Lund Person, MPH
Executive Director
Hospice for the Carolinas
Raleigh, North Carolina

Ruth McCorkle, RN, PhD, FAAN
Professor, School of Nursing
Director, Center for Advancing
  Care in Serious Illness
The University of Pennsylvania
Philadelphia, Pennsylvania

Joseph T. Mullan, PhD
Assistant Adjunct Professor
Human Development and Aging
  Program
University of California
San Francisco, California

Patrice O'Connor, RN, MA, CNA
Palliative Care Consultant
St. Luke/Roosevelt Hospital
New York, New York

Betty O'Gorman, MCSP, SRP
Superintendent Physiotherapist
St. Christopher's Hospice
Sydenham, London, England

Leonard I. Pearlin, PhD
Professor
Human Development and Aging
  Program
University of California
San Francisco, California

Vanderlyn R. Pine, PhD
Professor of Sociology
State University of New York
The College at New Paltz
New Paltz, New York

Fredrica A. Preston, RN, MA
Director
Nursing Resource Development
Fox Chase Cancer Center
Philadelphia, Pennsylvania

Ulla Qvarnstrøm, PhD
Professor of Nursing Science
University of Bergen
Bergen, Norway

Gail Egan Sansivero, RN, MS, OCN
Clinical Nurse Specialist
Oncology/Hematology/Bone
  Marrow Transplant
Albany Medical Center
Albany, New York

Phyllis R. Silverman, PhD
Professor
Institute of Health Professions
Massachusetts General Hospital
Boston, Massachusetts

Marilyn M. Skaff, PhD
Research Psychologist
Human Development and Aging
  Program
University of California
San Francisco, California

Albert Lee Strickland
Writer
Santa Cruz, California

Hannelore Wass, PhD
Professor Emerita
Educational Psychology
University of Florida
Gainesville, Florida

Morris A. Wessel, MD
Clinical Professor of Medicine
  Yale University
Consultant Pediatrician
  Clifford Beers Guidance Clinic
New Haven, Connecticut

Part One

Issues in the Care of the Dying and Bereaved

One

Treatment Decision Making

Lesley F. Degner

Dr. Lesley Degner is professor at the Faculty of Nursing, University of Manitoba; adjunct professor in the Department of Psychology, University of Manitoba; and Nurse Scientist-in-Residency at St. Boniface General Hospital in Winnipeg. Her primary role is that of nurse-scientist in cancer and palliative care. She has an ongoing program of research that focuses on patient roles in medical treatment decision making, and is coauthor of the book Life-Death Decisions in Health Care. *She also conducts a clinical practice at the St. Boniface General Hospital Oncology Unit where she is applying the findings of her research with women with breast cancer.*

Choices about treatment present challenges during the last phases of life. Treatment choices affect all those involved in care of the dying patient. For those individuals who remain conscious as their disease advances, seeking alternative forms of treatment—whether it be experimental therapy, unorthodox remedies, or palliative care—offers a final chance to affect their destiny. When the individual is no longer able to exercise choice, the family often has to assume decisional responsibility, projecting what their loved one would have wanted. Health professionals providing the care have a tremendous influence on the process of decision making, because they control the flow of information about treatment alternatives. All of these people converge to play out their roles as the patient's illness enters its final stage, and each will influence the process of treatment decision making.

This chapter discusses some common problems that arise during the decision-making process. Understanding these problems provides the basis for an intervention model for nurses and others who wish to facilitate the transition from curative to palliative care, when that is appropriate. Finally, this chapter provides a perspective that can be used to judge the effectiveness of the process of therapeutic decision making, as opposed to judging the effectiveness of a medical intervention in accomplishing a therapeutic goal. Taken together, these elements of treatment decision making provide a way of clarifying issues that might ordinarily appear complicated and unsolvable.

Common Problems in Treatment Decision Making

The issues in treatment decision making discussed in this chapter were identified as a result of a four-year observational study that addressed a general question: How are treatment decisions made for patients with life-threatening illnesses? Participant observation occurred in fourteen health-care settings that ranged from an isolated northern settlement, through neonatal, pediatric, and adult intensive care units, to general wards and outpatient clinics. Field notes were recorded as treatment decisions were being made, and interviews occurred with as many participants as possible in each situation. These conversations included patients and families as well as health professionals. Information was also extracted from the patient's health-care record. The qualitative data were analyzed using a method of content analysis called constant comparative analysis (Glaser & Strauss, 1967), and major factors that affect treatment decision making were identified and described (Degner & Beaton, 1987). The problems we identified as usually associated with each of the major factors in treatment decision making form the basis of the following discussion.

Should Patients and Families Participate in Decision Making?

Assumptions are often made about the ability of patients and family members to participate in decisions about their treatment. Two prevalent assumptions are that patients and families do not have the knowledge required to participate in making critical choices, and that even if they did, they might suffer psychological harm if the outcomes of the decision they made were negative. There is little empirical evidence to support these beliefs.

Indeed, several studies have found that patients encouraged to assume an active role in treatment decision making experienced benefits. They understood their treatment better, and achieved better therapeutic responses (Greenfield, Kaplan, & Ware, 1985; Merkel, Rudisill, & Nierenberg, 1983; Robinson & Whitfield, 1985; Schulman, 1979). Recent studies of women with breast cancer found that both women and their husbands who were offered choice of treatment (lumpectomy versus mastectomy) had lower anxiety levels, irrespective of the choice they made, when compared with patients whose surgeon made the choice (Fallowfield, Hall, Macguire, & Baum, 1990; Morris & Royle, 1988).

While the results of these studies challenge prevailing assumptions, there has been no long-term follow-up of the consequences of active participation in treatment decision making in the final stages of life. For example, do family members who want to influence treatment decision making for the dying patient but are unable to do so, experience any problems in the bereavement period? Evaluation of a bereavement follow-up program (Hildebrandt, 1987) suggested that family members who felt uninvolved in the decision-making process experienced guilt and anger they were unable to translate into any effective action. As one family member stated: "I knew he wasn't getting the best care, so I should have forced them to listen to me and then they would have made better decisions." The family members reported more discomforting hallucinations and had more difficulty connecting with their social networks. These findings emphasize the importance of further study of family participation in treatment decision making for the dying.

What Is the Knowledge Base of the Patient and Family?

Another potential source of problems is the knowledge that the patient and family is using to guide its decision making. This knowledge is most frequently drawn from the family's previous experience with the treatment of serious illness. If, for example, a relative or even neighbour had an experience with using morphine for pain control that was less than effective, the patient or family may also assume that this intervention will be ineffective in their own case. Usually this "knowledge" is unspoken and is not systematically elicited by those caring for the patient. The result is that decisions which make perfect sense from the family's perspective may seem irrational to the caregivers. Unless health personnel clarify with the patient and family what they already "know" about the treatment alternatives being offered, misunderstandings and conflict can easily arise.

A study of 210 family members of the dying found that their most important need was for information (Kristjanson, 1989). The families wanted information about how to manage the patient's pain at home, about the patient's tests, and about the prognosis. They also wanted the physician to arrange a family conference to discuss the patient's illness, and wanted caregivers to be straightforward when answering questions. All of these strategies would enable family members to become more informed participants in treatment decision making.

Similar strategies are required to help patients become and remain informed participants in their care. Several studies have indicated that, in spite of a strong preference for information about their disease and treatment, patients ask very few spontaneous questions when interacting with physicians (Robinson & Whitfield, 1985). As Beisecker and Beisecker (1990, p. 27) noted: "Patients take cues about appropriate role behavior from doctors and others with whom they interact." Their study found that longer interactions were associated with increased asking of questions by patients. Nurses and other professionals need to communicate their willingness to respond to patient questions so that patients feel comfortable in assuming a more active role. However, one descriptive study of nurse and physician interactions with patients found that both groups of caregivers made statements that reflected a shared decision-making approach less frequently than statements of command (Taylor, Pickens, & Geden, 1989). Command statements would reinforce the patient's expectation that the only appropriate role in treatment decision making is a passive one, in which few questions are asked.

What Health System Structures Affect Decision Making?

A variety of structures in the health-care system can either interfere with or facilitate treatment decision making for the dying. Most decisions are made during medical rounds when family members are not present, and as a result their ability to control the treatment plan may be limited. Confusion may exist as to who is actually responsible for the patient's care when multiple consultants are involved. Responsibility can quickly become diffused, with no one on the treatment team assuming the task of informing the patient and family about the current decision making. Alternately, several caregivers may communicate conflicting information about treatment plans, such that the family's confidence in them is eroded.

Within large tertiary referral hospitals, even finding space for a dying patient can become problematic. Family members may understandably consider that transferring their loved one from a unit where they know the staff to another area in the hospital just because the bed is needed, is a dehumanizing decision. The structure of the health-care system creates many obstacles so that at times families feel they are traversing a mine field in their efforts to get effective care for their dying loved one. The family's lack of control over decision making when the patient is hospitalized may be so stressful that they resist admission even when symptoms are severe (Chekryn, 1989).

Who Controls Treatment Decisions?

The issue of who actually makes treatment decisions is central to how the process of decision making is subsequently perceived. While most treatment decisions continue to be made by health professionals, there are many patients who wish to assume this responsibility themselves or at least share this responsibility with professionals. These patients tend to be younger, more highly educated, and female (Cassileth et al., 1980; Blanchard et al,, 1988). How to identify which patients prefer to play a more active role in treatment decision making remains problematic, although progress is being made in this effort (Degner & Russell, 1988; Neufeld, Degner & Dick, 1993).

At present it is difficult to estimate how many dying patients wish to play an active role in making decisions about their medical care. Among adults newly diagnosed with cancer and being treated in a tertiary referral center in Canada, we estimate that one in ten patients wants to play an active role in selecting his or her own treatment; three in ten want to play collaborative roles; and six in ten prefer to let the physician make the decisions (Degner & Sloan, 1992). Our study of 436 patients found no differences in role preferences by stage of disease, so these estimates may also hold for patients with advanced disease who are dying. Sutherland et al. (1989) found a similar distribution of role preferences among sixty radiotherapy patients at various stages of their disease and treatment who were being treated at a regional cancer center in Toronto.

However, both Blanchard and Cassileth found in their American samples totalling 658 cancer patients that approximately two-thirds preferred to participate in decisions about their treatment rather than leaving decisions to their physician. While cultural factors may explain these conflicting findings, differences in access to health care probably provide a stronger explanation. In Canada, all patients have access to the tertiary referral system, illustrated by the finding that about one-third of patients in our samples have had less than grade ten education. In the United States, where an increasing proportion of the population has no health insurance (Freeman, 1989), this segment of the society may not be able to afford tertiary care and as a result may be excluded from American studies conducted in tertiary settings.

Gender is another variable that has been found to be associated with preferences about roles in treatment decision making. Blanchard et al. (1988) found that men, particularly older, sicker men, preferred a less active role. These investigators ascribed this finding to the traditional role that wives play in negotiating with health-care professionals on behalf of the patient. The findings of our study of 436 cancer patients were consistent with this result, in that women, particularly those with cancer of the reproductive system, preferred the most active roles in treatment decision making. This finding helps to explain why American women with breast cancer lobbied successfully in several states to obtain legislation that requires physicians to discuss all the treatment options with women newly diagnosed with this disease.

Caregivers should use these findings to guide their practice with the following caution. Not all young, highly educated people want to make their own decisions; not all elderly people with less than high school education want to delegate decisional responsibilities; and not every woman with reproductive cancer wants to participate in decisions about her treatment. Indeed, two recent studies have found that only 15 percent of the variance in preferences about roles in decision making is accounted for by sociodemographic variables (Degner & Sloan, 1992; Ende, Kazis, Ash, & Moskowitz, 1989). Assessment of each individual patient's preferences remains the best approach. Health professionals are as much at risk of overestimating the amount of control a patient wants as they are of underestimating it (Strull, Lo, & Charles 1984). As Ende and colleagues (1989) noted: "Just as the principle of autonomy guarantees each patient the right to make decisions, each patient also has the right to forego decision making. Each patient's preference is his or her own and depends upon individual factors, modulated by illness."

Is There Effective Communication?

Failure to communicate about how the decisions are being made and about the resulting treatment plans are a major source of conflict in treatment decision making. If, for example, the health professionals are using one approach to think through and weigh the advantages and disadvantages of treatment alternatives, while the family is using a totally different approach to decision making, problems are inevitable. Once a decision has been reached, clear communication to all members of the health-care team and family is essential. Patients may be unnecessarily resuscitated or exposed to other stressful treatments unless decisions are expressed both verbally and in written documents.

What Is the Impact of Participation?

Finally, the psychological impact of participating in life–death situations is so intense that many people are unable to respond effectively. This includes health professionals as well as patients and families. The sight of wasting limbs, disintegrating flesh, and bodily excretions provides vivid images that influence the perspective each participant brings to treatment decision making. It is sometimes difficult to separate the intense personal reactions these images evoke from the need to decide what is best for the dying person. As my colleague Janet Beaton wrote in our book, "The wonder is not that nurses sometimes fail to act in this manner, but rather that they succeed as often as they do" (Degner & Beaton, 1987, p. 87).

An Intervention Model

For most patients whose disease cannot be cured, we need to develop an alternative perspective on how to provide help (Brickman et al., 1982; Northouse & Wortman, 1990). In the traditional medical approach to helping, caregivers assume that they can prescribe a solution to the patient's problems. This approach is inadequate for the dying because there are no solutions. Rather, help needs to be provided in a context where the helper is doing for the patient what he would do for himself, were he able. This involves the ill individual in defining goals that are appropriate for him at this stage of his life. This approach to helping is called "compensatory" because it involves caregivers in compensating for the patient's dwindling resources. The compensatory approach to helping was used to develop an intervention model that provides guidelines to nurses and others on how to facilitate the transition from curative to palliative care, when this transition is appropriate.

The questions in Table 1.1 are meant to be raised at critical moments when treatment decisions are being considered. This approach can be extremely effective in influencing the course of treatment, although nurses frequently hesitate to use it. One physician described a nurse who used this approach very effectively. He was considering putting chest tubes into a patient who had pleural effusion as a result of advanced cancer. The therapeutic goal was to reduce the patient's discomfort. One nurse came to him and said she was uncomfortable about

Table 1.1   Treatment Decision Making for the Dying

Nursing Questions	Alternative Answers
1. What is the intent of the treatment being proposed?	Cure, control, or palliation
2. What role does the patient/family want to play in treatment decision making?	Active role, collaborative role, or passive role that delegates decisions to others
3. What are the risks and the potential benefits of the treatment being proposed?	High risk–high benefit Low risk–low benefit High risk–low benefit Low risk–high benefit
4. Have these risks/benefits been clearly communicated to the patient/family?	Yes/No
5. How are the patient/family making their decision about selecting, accepting, or declining further treatment?	Risk–benefit calculation Feeling better–feeling worse calculation
6. What is the time frame for decision making?	Short–Prolonged

his decision, even though she was aware this was his standard approach. She asked him one question, "How effective has this intervention been in accomplishing your goal?" He was troubled by her question, did a chart review, and found that the intervention had indeed not been achieving the therapeutic goal. As a result, he changed his approach with subsequent patients. Nurses should never underestimate the importance of being in the right place to ask the right question at the right time.

Clarifying Treatment Intent

The first useful question related to decision making is, "What is the intent of the proposed treatment?" Interventions may appear to be curative in intent (such as chemotherapy), when they are really intended to provide palliation (such as shrinking a tumor that is compressing a body structure). Unless the intent of the therapy is clearly communicated, misunderstandings can easily arise. Nurses are often caught between physicians who leave treatment orders without specifying the therapeutic intent, and family members or colleagues who automatically assume that any active intervention must be curative.

This problem has been explored through research. Mackillop and colleagues (1988) studied patient and physician perceptions of treatment intent. Of 48 patients who were receiving treatment that physicians intended to be palliative, 16 thought that the doctor's aim was to cure them. Forty of the 48 patients significantly overestimated the probability that the treatment would prolong their lives. These investigators concluded that patients who seriously misunderstand their situation almost always pass unrecognized. Making the intent of the proposed treatment explicit could go far toward correcting this problem.

Eliciting Preferences about Participation

Defining the role that the patient or family wants to play in treatment decision making is a useful approach. Patients may prefer more or less active roles with respect to different types of treatment decisions, such as decisions about surgery or chemotherapy, versus decisions about postoperative care or pain management. They may also change their preferences to participate over time, and in response to significant events such as improvement or deterioration. We have been using a set of five statements about roles in treatment decision making (see Figure 1.1) to help patients identify their preferred role with respect to specific types of decisions that need to be made in their care. These are presented on cards that are illustrated with cartoons and the patient selects the role that is

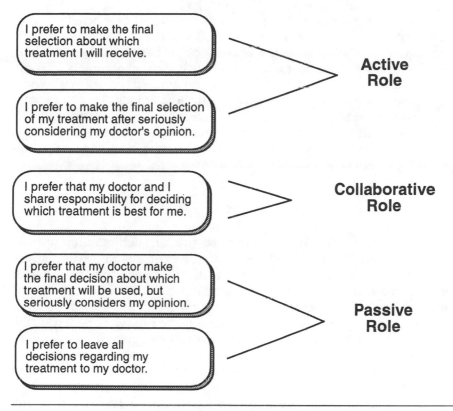

Figure 1.1   Statements on the role preferences card sort

best for him. Subsequent interactions about treatment decisions are guided by the patient's stated role preference. Whatever approach is adopted, it is important to elicit patient/family preferences explicitly, and to do this each time significant treatment decisions need to be made during the illness trajectory.

Clarifying the Risks and Benefits

The risks and benefits of the proposed treatment, whether it be curative or palliative, need to be clarified for all participants in the decision-making process. In some circumstances decisions about whether to pursue the treatment are simplified because the benefit is clear and the risk is low. Frequently radiotherapy treatments for pain control in advanced cancer fall into this category. Similarly, if the risks associated with the intervention are significant and the potential for benefit is low, the treatment option may not even be offered to the patient or family. Difficulties arise when there is a chance the treatment could offer some hope but there is significant toxicity (as with some experimental drugs), or when there is no proven benefit but no side effects (as with some unorthodox treatments). Feelings may run high among the participants in decision making when either of these alternatives is considered. The nurse can do much to defuse potential problems by helping participants identify the risks and benefits of each alternative from their own perspectives, and to communicate them to each other.

Clarifying the Decision-Making Criteria

Often patients and families do not use the decision-making process favored by health professionals. Although physicians in particular are trained to examine the risks and benefits of treatment alternatives before even raising them with patients, the decision making of nurses, patients, and families is frequently dominated by judgments as to whether the patient is getting better or worse. Making these estimates is part of the daily routine with dying patients. Difficulties can arise if one group of participants in the decision making is using a risk–benefit approach, while the other participants are using a getting better–getting worse approach.

Such difficulties can occur even when participants are using the same process of decision making. For example, family members sitting by the dying patient may be astounded to hear the physician come in and say, "I think he's a little better today," when the patient can no longer talk with them. But the physician has just come from the x-ray department where he found that the pneumonia in the patient's chest is clearing, and so he considers the patient "better." Similar conflicts can occur within families, particularly when there is disagreement about whether the patient will get better or worse with further treatment. Caregivers can play an important role in clarifying the criteria that both they and family members use in making their getting better–getting worse judgments. Disagreement often arises from the use of differing criteria.

Clarifying the Time Frame

Finally, the time frame that is available for making the therapeutic decisions needs to be specified. Does some decision need to be made within the next 24 hours if the patient is to experience any benefit? Or can some time be spent considering the alternatives at length? Patients or families may feel they have been rushed into making what is for them a momentous decision that they will have to live with for the rest of their lives. On the other hand, health professionals may feel the pressure of time weighing heavily as they watch the chance of a good outcome slip away. Decision making becomes less stressful in a context where all the participants can consider their options and attain some degree of comfort with the proposed course of action. Even a hastily convened family conference can do much to facilitate the transition in thinking about what is appropriate treatment for that patient.

The six questions outlined in Table 1.1 provide a clinical guide for caregivers. The purpose of asking these questions is to reduce the stress associated with life–death decision making for all those involved, including the nurse. Silence can often be more stressful than speaking out. Questions that are constructive are usually well received, and provide a sense of achievement when they improve the quality of care for the dying patient and his or her family.

The Goal: Effective Decision Making

The goal of this intervention model must always be kept in mind: it is effective decision making. This goal is distinct from considering the biological outcomes of the therapeutic decision. The process of decision making may be the best that could have been accomplished at that time, and still the patient deteriorates, pain is unrelieved, or the family is in distress. Good decision making does not guarantee a successful outcome, but it should increase the probability of the best possible outcome given the circumstances of the patient, the family, and the health-care environment.

Effective decision making requires a skilled decision maker. Such a decision maker knows what constitutes the minimum data set; that is, those pieces of information that are absolutely essential to an informed decision. This type of knowledge may appear somewhat mysterious to novices in a profession, but it is usually acquired through long experience in making difficult choices. As a result, professionals who are skilled in decision making may be called in to assist in difficult cases, even when these fall outside their formal field of specialization. The presence of such a skilled decision maker can result in the identification of one critical piece of information that is missing but essential to making an appropriate decision. Once this information is available, a confusing situation can be quickly simplified. Health professionals need to identify the skilled decision makers in their own agencies, and to make use of their talents.

O'Connor (1989) defined an effective decision as one that is informed, consistent with personal values, and acted upon. Clarifying the intent of treatment and the risks and benefits associated with alternative interventions can do much toward ensuring that a decision is informed. Eliciting the role that patients and families wish to play in treatment decision making at least provides a basis for ensuring that decisions are consistent with their values. However, patients frequently assume that by delegating decisional responsibility, usually to the physician, they will benefit from a value-free decision that is based on perfect knowledge. Physicians, on the other hand, are the first to admit that their personal values influence the decisions they make, and that the knowledge available to them is often imperfect in both scope and accuracy. Choices by patients or families to delegate decisional responsibility to professionals may lead to decisions that are ultimately inconsistent with their values and troublesome after the death of the patient.

For a decision to be effective, it must be carried through in practice. However, it is certainly the case that many health-care decisions are carefully considered, discussed, recorded, and never actualized. One source of this inconsistency is the complexity of the health-care system, which results in decisions being made in one location that are to be carried out in another location. Mislaid documents, misscheduled appointments, and lost telephone messages are day-to-day realities in any complex organization. For the dying patient, however, these minor errors of bureaucracy can be major sources of distrust and discomfort. Perhaps one of the most important roles that nurses play today is to shepherd the dying patient and his family through this complex system, ensuring that they actually achieve the benefits of effective decision making.

The diversity of the health-care system and the wide range of treatment alternatives available sometimes appear to make the chances of effective decision making seem increasingly remote. However, having a way of thinking about the problems created by this complexity as well as a way of seeking solutions can do much to improve the experience of the dying patient during treatment decision making. Effective decision making could have significant long-term benefits for the survivors as well as short-term benefits for the dying patient. The nature and extent of these benefits need to be defined in future research.

References

Beisecker, A. E., & Beisecker, T. D. (1990). Patient information-seeking behaviors when communicating with doctors. *Medical Care, 28,* 19–28.

Blanchard, C. G., Labrecque, M. S., Ruckdeschel, J. C., & Blanchard, E. B. (1988). Information and decision-making preferences of hospitalized adult cancer patients. *Social Science in Medicine, 27,* 1139–1145.

Brickman, P., Rabinowitz, V. C., Karuza, J., Coates, D., Cohn, E., & Kidder, L. (1982). Models of helping and coping. *American Psychologist, 37,* 368–384.

Cassileth, B. R., Zupkis, R. V., Sutton-Smith, K., & March, V. (1980). Information and participation preferences among cancer patients. *Annals of Internal Medicine, 92,* 832–836.

Chekryn, J. (1989). Families of people with AIDS. *Canadian Nurse, 85,* 30–32.

Degner, L. F., & Beaton, J. I. (1987). *Life–death decisions in health care.* New York: Hemisphere.

Degner, L. F., & Russell, C. A. (1988). Preferences for treatment control among adults with cancer. *Research in Nursing and Health, 11,* 367–374.

Degner, L. F., & Sloan, J. A. (1992). Decision making during serious illness: What role do patients really want to play? *Journal of Clinical Epidemiology, 45,* 941–950.

Ende, J., Kazis, L., Ash, A., & Moskowitz, M. A. (1989). Measuring patients' desire for autonomy. *Journal of General Internal Medicine, 4,* 23–30.

Fallowfield, L. J., Hall, A., Macguire, G. P., & Baum, M. Psychological outcomes of different treatment policies in women with early breast cancer outside a clinical trial. *British Medical Journal, 301,* 575–580.

Freeman, H. P. (1989). Cancer in the socioeconomically disadvantaged. *CA—A Cancer Journal for Clinicians, 39,* 266–288.

Glaser, B. G., & Strauss, A. L. (1967). *The discovery of grounded theory: Strategies for qualitative research.* Chicago: Aldine Atherton.

Greenfield, S., Kaplan, S., & Ware, J. E. (1985). Expanding patient involvement in care: Effects and patient outcomes. *Annals of Internal Medicine, 102,* 520–528.

Hildebrandt, T. (1987). Evaluation of the effectiveness of a bereavement follow-up program. Unpublished Master of Nursing Thesis, University of Manitoba, Winnipeg, Manitoba, Canada.

Kristjanson, L. J. (1989). Quality of terminal care: Salient indicators identified by families. *Journal of Palliative Care, 5,* 21–30.

Mackillop, W. J., Stewart, W. E., Ginsburg, A. D., & Stewart, S. S. (1988). Cancer patients' perceptions of their disease and its treatment. *British Journal of Cancer, 58,* 355–358.

Merkel, W. T., Rudisill, J. R., & Nierenberg, B. P. (1983). Preparing patients to see the doctor: Effects on patients and physicians in a family practice center. *Family Practice Research Journal, 2,* 147–163.

Morris, J., & Royle, G. T. (1988). Offering patients a choice of surgery for early breast cancer: A reduction of anxiety and depression in patients and their husbands. *Social Science and Medicine, 26,* 583–585.

Neufeld, K. R., Degner, L. F., & Dick, J. A. M. (1993). A nursing intervention to foster patient involvement in treatment decisions. *Oncology Nursing Forum, 20,* 631–635.

Northouse, L. L., & Wortman, C. B. (1990). Models of helping and coping in cancer care. *Patient Education and Counselling, 15,* 49-64.

O' Connor, A. (1989). Decisional conflict. In M. J. Kim, G. K. McFarland, & A. M. McLane (Eds.), *Pocket guide to nursing diagnosis* (pp. 17–18, 125). St. Louis: Mosby Year Book.

Robinson, E. J., & Whitfield, M. J. (1985). Improving the efficiency of patients' comprehension monitoring. *Social Science in Medicine, 26,* 583–585.

Schulman, B. A. (1979). Active patient orientation and outcomes in hypertensive treatment. *Medical Care, 17,* 267–280.

Strull, W. M., Lo, B., & Charles, G. (1984). Do patients want to participate in medical decision making? *Journal of the American Medical Association, 252,* 2990–2994.

Sutherland, H. J., Llewellyn-Thomas, H. A., Lockwood, G. A., Tritchler, D. L., & Till, J. E. (1989). Cancer patients: Their desire for information and participation in treatment decisions. *Journal of the Royal Society of Medicine, 82,* 260–263.

Taylor, S. G., Pickens, J. M., & Geden, E. A. (1989). Interactional styles of nurse practitioners and physicians regarding decision making. *Nursing Research, 38,* 50–55.

Two

Philosophy, Principles, and Politics of Symptom Management for the Terminally Ill

Fredrica Preston
Ruth McCorkle

Fredrica A. Preston, R.N., M.A., is Director of Nursing Resource Development at Fox Chase Cancer Center in Philadelphia. She received her B.S.N. from Georgetown University and her M.A. in nursing from New York University. Ms. Preston is an active member of the Oncology Nursing Society and has practiced oncology nursing since 1975 in clinical, administrative, and educational roles.

She is the mother of a daughter, Kara Allyson.

Ruth McCorkle, Ph.D., F.A.A.N., is an American Cancer Society Professor at the University of Pennsylvania School of Nursing where she is Director of the Center for Advancing Care in Serious Illness. Her career began as an oncology clinical nurse specialist in Iowa. Subsequently, she has established a nationally recognized graduate program in cancer nursing. She is internationally known for her research with patients with progressive cancer and the measurement of patient and family outcomes to improve the quality of their lives.

Living with a terminal illness is a challenging life experience for the person, family members, and professional caregivers. To enhance the quality of the person's experience within the context of continuing medical treatment and supportive services requires a coordinated effort among the parties involved. The prevention and management of symptom distress in terminal illness are essential parts of palliative care. For purposes of this chapter, the disease cancer is used as a prototype to illustrate the essential components of symptom management. We will discuss factors that directly and indirectly affect the health professional's ability to manage symptoms of terminally ill patients. Included in the discussion will be the philosophy, principles, and politics of symptom management.

Curative versus Palliative Approach

Scanlon (1989) defines the goals of palliative care as "the ameliorization of symptoms and disease-related problems and the promotion of the patient's well being and comfort". Palliative care used here is defined as the active, compassionate care of the terminally ill at a time when their disease is no longer responsive to the traditional aims of cure and prolongation of life, and when the emphasis of care is on comfort and quality of life until death (Caring Together, 1987). It embraces principles founded in the physical and social sciences and requires ongoing assessment, planning, intervention, and evaluation of the physical and psychosocial symptoms inherent in terminal illness. It is not enough to minister physically to the dying, to give a pill or injection and feel confident the discomfort is relieved. This action supports the belief that patient care is a unidimensional phenomenon, requiring treatment of physical symptoms only. If the focus of palliative care is to be on the person and not the symptom, a multidimensional approach is mandated. Benoliel (1976) has advocated that a balanced perspective on care and cure requires that healthcare providers be attentive to the impact of disease on the person as well as the body.

Though it seems obvious that palliation is the treatment of choice in terminal illness, there are some diseases where the choice is not clearcut. For example, in situations where the goal of treatment for cancer is not well defined, the individual's goals should direct the focus of care. Cure is a realistic treatment goal for many people with cancer. Hodgkin's disease, testicular cancer, and childhood leukemias are only a few of the cancers considered curable with aggressive, multimodality therapy. The emergence and continued growth of cancer survivorship groups is testament to the fact that with earlier diagnosis and multimodal therapy cancer is a curable disease in many cases. However, cure is not always a realistic goal. The American Cancer Society (1994) predicts 538,000 people will die of cancer in 1994. For these patients, treatment and care goals need to be shifted from cure to palliation. Benoliel and McCorkle (1977) have defined quality of life in palliative care as having to do with the opportunities available to the ill person for the achievement of personal goals during whatever period of time the individual has available.

Symptom Management: Broadening the Scope

Traditionally, the management of symptoms has been restricted to the physical dimensions of the ill person's problems. With the development of palliative care as a subspecialty of all health-related disciplines, the field has broadened to include the emotional and family dimensions as well as the physical ones.

Physical Dimensions

We know from clinical experience that some of the major personal problems associated with terminal illness result from the physical symptoms of disease and from the progressive deterioration of the body. Terminal illness is often accompanied by distressing symptoms such as nausea, anorexia, dyspnea, and pain. These physical changes and resultant functional limitations lead to a state of social dependency where the person becomes literally dependent for intimate activities not ordinarily performed by other people (bathing, toileting, feeding, etc.). As physical deterioration occurs, terminal illness is often accompanied by social isolation, a feeling reported by people with terminal illness. They describe that people withdraw from them and information is controlled that may have implications about the ill person's future (Holland, 1982).

Emotional Dimensions

When family members and healthcare providers withhold information about the disease and treatment, the individual is rather effectively cut off from talking about his or her fears and other concerns (Quint, 1966). Patients are confronted with multiple fears, including fear of pain, of recurrence, of increased dependency, and of death (Wortman and Dunkel-Schetter, 1979). Patients with cancer often feel as if their own bodies are out of control (Fiore, 1979). They feel helpless because they are unable to affect the course of their own disease. Yet talking with receptive family members and health providers about the person's prognosis, the future, concerns, and fears may not be easy to do even when full information is provided about the illness and its predictable future. Among the reasons frequently reported by professionals for not talking to patients about their condition is the concern that the patients will thereby become depressed and unduly concerned (Brewin, 1977; McIntosh, 1974). Not talking with patients about the meaning of their experiences and their understandings of what is happening only adds to their sense of helplessness, psychological tension, and fear of abandonment (Krant, 1976).

Family Dimensions

In addition to the patient, family members experience the stressors imposed by terminal illness and the multiple, difficult problems it introduces (Maguire, 1981; Oberst & James, 1985). Family communication patterns may change as family members try to protect themselves and others from painful feelings. Hiding feelings is a process many families go through to withhold their emotional concerns from one another; as a result many family members often bear their emotional pain alone (Northouse & Northouse, 1987).

Living with terminal illness means restructuring family styles to deal with the demands of medical treatment and the impingement of the disease on usual roles and relationships (Stetz, 1987). If terminal illness is prolonged, it puts extreme pressure on existing social support systems within the family, including depletion of financial and social support resources. Extended illness may cause further breakdown in patient and family relationships (Northouse, 1984; Kristjanson, 1989; Germino, 1991).

Philosophy of Symptom Management

We believe that the ultimate goal in palliative care is to help each person maintain his or her integrity by giving attention to that person's stated goals, wishes, and needs. We believe that the person and family must be informed about what is happening, who is involved, and the range of services available to assist them. We believe the family in which the ill person is a member is the unit of care. Family means one or more persons identified as important by the ill person; the person may or may not be related by birth or marriage. All members of the family require information and ongoing opportunities for questions and discussion of alternatives to facilitate their understanding and participation. Patients and family members need access to information and emergency services on a 24-hours-a-day basis. Services recommended to patients need to be coordinated and planned through the cooperative efforts of all parties involved. Successful management is best achieved when there is congruence of expectations among patient, family, and provider and mutually understood and accepted goals.

Diagnosis of a terminal illness can be conceived as catastrophic in nature because it produces major changes in living for the individual and the family. Over the last 25 years, reports describing the degree of symptoms and pain experienced by patients with terminal illness have varied widely. Certainly not all patients who are terminally ill have symptoms that require management. We believe symptoms that the person perceives as distressing can and should be managed. We also recognize that some patients' goals, such as mental alertness, may be incongruent with the goals of symptom relief if large doses of analgesics are needed. We believe that management decisions must always be guided by the patient's wishes.

Principles of Symptom Management

Symptom management is based on several principles that guide clinicians in the delivery of holistic, palliative care.

Symptom management is an ongoing process of assessment, intervention, and evaluation.   Symptoms vary in their etiology, intensity, duration, and response to treatment. Variations occur not only among persons but also for individuals over time. Many people experience changes in their symptoms as their disease progresses. Ongoing thorough assessment is needed to identify the etiology of the symptom and to achieve efficacy of treatment. For example, constipation can be caused by narcotics, diet, bowel obstruction, or chemotherapy, each requiring a different management strategy. Administering a laxative without further assessment could be harmful to the patient with a bowel obstruction. Pain that was once controlled with MS Contin 30 mg every 12 hours may now require a dose escalation to achieve the same effect. Assessment and intervention alone, without evaluating their effects, will lead to ineffective symptom management.

The patient has the ultimate choice in what symptom management strategies will be utilized.   We can explain the reasons for the symptoms, offer suggestions about how they might be managed, and teach patients and families how to implement these management strategies. However, if patients believe that treatment of the symptom would further disrupt their lives, it is their right to reject or accept our suggestions. An example is the patient who, despite having been instructed on the importance of and rationale for a round-the-clock analgesic schedule to prevent the recurrence of pain, will not take medication when he doesn't have pain and only takes it when the pain escalates to the point of incapacitating him. The analgesic effect of the medication takes longer to be achieved and the patient is at greater risk for the nonanalgesic effects of narcotics on demand, such as nausea and sedation. The obvious frustration this can cause caregivers can be tempered by the realization that the patient's autonomy and sense of control have been maintained.

Symptoms are best managed using an anticipatory approach. Both didactic and experiential lessons provide us two bases upon which the course of a disease or the effects of a treatment can be generally predicted with a reasonable margin of error. We know that the majority of patients on round-the-clock narcotic therapy will develop constipation if a bowel regimen is not instituted at initiation of narcotic therapy. We know that a patient with end-stage esophageal cancer may soon develop dysphagia and will need parenteral pain medication available for that time when he is unable to tolerate the oral medication. Anticipation of patients' needs and provision of resources to meet them prior to their actual occurrence maximize patients' comfort with minimal interruptions in care.

Symptom management requires a multimodality approach. Symptoms are multidimensional composites of physical, emotional, and social dimensions. Adopting the traditional unidimensional disease-oriented approach to symptom management negates the interdependence of these dimensions. The first priority in symptom management is to relieve the physical discomfort. This goal is best achieved through concomitant use of pharmacological and nonpharmacological measures. For example, antianxiety medications and narcotics may be ordered for treatment of dyspnea in conjunction with oxygen therapy and positioning. These interventions treat the symptoms but not necessarily the person experiencing the symptom. For this, the focus must shift to the emotional and social sequelae the symptom has for the patient and family. Are they fearful the patient may suffocate? What are their coping mechanisms for dealing with an obvious deterioration in the patient? Do they feel more assured when someone is with them? Do they have someone with whom to express their existential and spiritual concerns? These are but a few of the questions that demand further exploration and the utilization of a multidisciplinary approach that includes nurses, physicians, social workers, and clergy.

Common Symptoms

Symptoms may not always be directly caused by the cancer. Symptom etiology must be established because management is related to etiology, and routinely attributing symptoms to the cancer can result in inappropriate treatment. Symptoms can be caused by direct tumor involvement resulting in compression of nerves, blood vessels, and lymphatics (parasthesias, edema, pain, hemorrhage) obstruction of vital organs (pain, constipation, nausea, dysphagia, choking) or invasion into any body part as evidenced by site-specific symptomatology. For example, tumor invasion of the femur could produce symptoms of pain, decreased mobility, deformity, and edema. Symptoms may be secondary effects of disease treatment. Palliative radiation therapy to relieve an esophageal obstruction can cause gastrointestinal alterations such as nausea, esophagitis, and dysphagia. Metabolic imbalances secondary to poor nutrition can lead to nausea, drowsiness, and parasthesias. Correction of the imbalance with supplements often leads to some relief of the symptom. See Table 2.1 for a list of common symptoms experienced in terminal illness, their etiology, and potential pharmacological and nonpharmacological management strategies (Turnbull, 1986; Twycross & Lack, 1984; and Yasko, 1983).

Pain

Pain is a multifaceted phenomenon that affects a person's total being—physical, emotional, social, and spiritual. It is estimated that 60 to 90 percent of patients with advanced cancer experience pain at some point in their illness (Foley, 1985). The actual or potential relief of pain is a major concern for patients and their families. Unfortunately this concern is not unwarranted, for a void still exists in the individualization of pain assessment and management. We have become too comfortable with a "cookbook" approach to pain management, so diligently looking at equianalgesic tables and drug dose escalation charts that we can lose sight of the person experiencing the pain and a basic tenet of pain management: *Pain is a subjective, multidimensional experience and each patient is unique in his/her pharmacological and nonpharmacological needs, tolerance, and effects.*

Successful pain management begins with the belief that the person has pain. Obvious as this statement may be, patients are often challenged to "prove" their pain exists before appropriate interventions are initiated. Assessment of pain is best conducted using a methodological approach. Miaskowski (1988) lists five critical-pain assessment criteria:

1. description of the pain;
2. location and radiation;
3. severity (numerical scales are often utilized for rating pain, i.e., 0 = no pain, 5 = worst pain to allow the individual to rate his or her own pain while providing consistency in criteria for comparison);
4. aggravating and relieving factors;
5. previous treatment modalites and their effects.

Table 2.1   Common Symptoms, Their Etiology, and Management Strategies

Symptom	Etiology
Anorexia	pain nausea & vomiting sore mouth uremia emotional concerns
Constipation	dehydration narcotics chemotherapy immobility
Diarrhea	fecal impaction obstruction diet medications inflammation
Dysphagia	esophageal obstruction monilial infection
Dyspnea	anemia pulmonary edema pulmonary obstruction metabolic acidosis
Fatigue	disease progression depression anemia bextroamphetamine
Fungating Growths (usually breast or neck area)	anaerobic infections necrosis
Hiccoughs	irritation of phrenic nerve steroids tumor infiltation uremia
Nausea & Vomiting	medications obstruction constipation increased intracranial pressure treatment side effects metabolic abnormalities
Airway Secretions	fluid accumulation in lungs
Seizures	tumor cerebral edema metabolic alterations hemorrhage
Sore Mouth	monilial infection poor dentition malnutrition

Table 2.1 (continued)

Pharmacological	Nonpharmacological
steroids antiemetics (if nausea is a problem) Megace (Megastrol acetate) Periactin (Cyproheptadine HCl) alcohol	frequent small meals do not force foods frequent oral hygiene supplemental feedings
stool softeners laxatives Senna	establish prophylactic bowel regimen increase dietary bulk increase fluid intake increase activity as tolerated
antidiarrheals narcotics steroid enemas	increase fluid intake meticulous perianal care dietary modifications sitz baths
antifungals steroids change route of medications to liquid or parenteral	soft foods dietary supplements esophageal dilitation radiation therapy (if due to tumor compression)
antianxiety medications diuretics narcotics steroids bronchodilators	thoracentesis oxygen therapy reassurance correct acidosis position of comfort radiation therapy (if due to tumor compression)
antidepressants steroids	modify activities of daily living assure sleep at night and rest periods during day
cleocin rinses silvadine ointment dakins solution flagyl generic (metronidazole hydrochloride) chemotherapy	frequent dressing changes odor control keep area dry
chlorpromazine haloperidol amitriptyline metoclopramide	rebreath into paper bag relaxation oropharyngeal stimulation with safe ureter catheter
phenothiazines corticosteroids dexamethasone lorazepam metoclopramide triethyleperazine	assess & treat underlying causes provide adequate hydration

anticholinergics
  morphine
  atropine
	suctioning
	reassurance to family
	position of comfort

steroids anticonvulsants diazepam	assure open airway protect patient from harm correct metabolic imbalance

antifungal agents
viscous xylocaine and
  diphenhydramine rinses
	frequent oral hygiene
	oral irrigations
	avoid alcohol or mouth rinses
	  containing alcohol
	dietary modifications

Pharmacological Management

Pharmacological management remains the keystone to successful pain control. Multidrug regimens utilizing narcotics and nonnarcotics are employed to enhance pain control. Narcotics work on the central nervous system altering the perception of pain; nonnarcotics directly affect the peripheral nervous system. Factors to be considered in the choice of analgesics include age, route, type and severity of pain, and clinical status. Elderly patients metabolize medications more slowly and may need a dose modification to prevent drug accumulation and resultant toxicities. The other end of this age-related spectrum is the younger patient who may require increased doses or increased frequency of analgesics because of a higher metabolism (Duffy et al., 1990).

The preferred route for analgesics is oral, and scheduling is round the clock, not simply on demand. The trend is to utilize sustained-release narcotics (MS contin, Roxanol) available in the oral form and administered every eight or twelve hours. Patients on these long-acting narcotics should also have immediate-release analgesics available for treatment of breakthrough pain. When the oral route is contraindicated, parenteral narcotics provide optimal pain relief. Continuous parenteral infusions of narcotics provide effective pain control and fewer side effects and eliminate the "peaks and valleys" of bolus injections (Dickson & Russell, 1982).

Narcotics have the potential for contributing to the development of side effects, which usually diminish with continued administration and are responsive to interventions. The side effects include: sedation, nausea and vomiting, constipation, and respiratory distress. See Table 2.2 for a list of commonly used narcotics. Naloxone is a drug used routinely for narcotic-induced respiratory distress, but it is usually contraindicated in terminal care (Bruera, et al., 1988; Ventafridda, et al., 1990).

Fear of addiction remains a prime factor for undertreatment of pain. This fear is expressed by patients, family members, nurses, and physicians. Understanding the difference between addiction and tolerance is essential. Tolerance occurs when a medication dose must be increased over time to achieve the same relief. Tolerance to the analgesic effect of narcotics usually occurs in tandem with tolerance to the nonanalgesic effects (nausea, sedation, respiratory depression) offering little risk of increased toxicity with increased dosage. Addiction occurs with psychological dependence on a drug, an all-encompassing craving for the drug's psychological effect. Suboptimal dosing may in fact produce this craving, thereby creating a situation it intended to prevent.

Adjuvant treatment of pain includes the use of medications traditionally utilized for other purposes. These include the tricyclic antidepressants, steroids, phenothiazines, and antihistamines. Nonpharmacological methods of pain control include: radiation therapy, heat/cold massage, positioning, transcutaneous electrical nerve stimulator (TENS), distraction, relaxation, and hypnosis. Selection of one or more of these methods must be individualized.

Politics of Symptom Management

The term *politics* is used here to mean the connections related to the health-care system and its administration. Politics in the context of symptom management has to do with the operations of the members of the health-care team in systems, the policies and philosophies of the institution, and the competency of health professionals in the science of terminal care and art of symptom management. Health professionals need to recognize the mission of their individual institutions because palliative care is not always a priority. Professionals must balance their palliative care approaches with the goals of medical treatment. Unless professionals keep in mind the politics of their organizations, it is difficult to meet patient and family needs systematically. Political issues related to symptom management must be approached with "savvy" and thoughtfulness even though the issues are highly charged and emotionally laden.

Educational Directives for Symptom Management

Overall, the evidence suggests that the majority of health professionals has not been adequately trained to manage patient symptoms in palliative care (Goodell, Donohue, & Benoliel, 1982). In fact, there is much to suggest that education in general still emphasizes traditional roles organized around a hierarchical model of acute medical care (Sinacore, 1981). Curricula for health professionals fail to include the special clinical skills and knowledge associated with palliative care and the preparation of teamwork in the context of complex organizations. Benoliel (1987–1988) states that death education for health professionals requires more than introduction of new content into already crowded courses or curricula on palliative care, it requires ongoing opportunities to grapple with the complexities of choice and decision making affecting the lives of others in profound ways. There have been a number of individuals and groups who have systematically introduced courses or programs in death education into their schools (Benoliel, 1982; Bertman, Greene, & Wyatt, 1982; Degner & Gow, 1988; Goodell, Donohue, & Benoliel, 1982); but clearly educational standards are needed so that all professionals are exposed to essential palliative care content, especially pain and symptom management.

Table 2.2   Narcotics Commonly Used for Pain Management

Drug	Dose=10 mg MS$_{04}$ IM	Onset in minutes	Duration in hours
Meperidine (Demerol)	300 mg PO 75 mg IM	30–50	2–4
Morphine	10 mg IM 60 mg PO	30-60	4–5
MsContin	120 mg PO	90	8–12
Oxycodone (in Percodan and Percocet)	30 mg PO	15–45	3–6
Codeine	200 mg PO 130 mg IM	30–60	3–4
Dolophine (Methadone)	20 mg PO 10 mg IM 5 mg IM	30–60	4–6
Hydromorphone (Dilaudid)	7.5 mg PO 1.5 mg IM 1.0 mg IV	15–30	3–4
Levorphanol (Levodromoran)	4 mg PO 2 mg IM 1 mg IV	60–90	4–6

ASA = acetylsalicylic acid
CNS = central nervous system
PO   = by mouth
IM   = intramuscular
IV   = intravenous
GI   = gastrointestinal
mg   = milligrams

Table 2.2   (Continued)

Side Effects	Comments

Nausea & vomiting
Respiratory depression
CNS disturbance
Orthostatic hypotension
Constipation
	Poor PO: IM ratio
	Not for chronic pain
	May cause accumulation of
	  Normeperedine, resulting in
	  CNS excitation (seizures,
	  tremors)

Nausea & vomiting
Respiratory depression
Orthostatic hypotension
Constipation
Urinary retention
CNS disturbance
	Contraindicated in patients
	  with severe respiratory
	  impairments, asthma,
	  hepatic failure or increased
	  intracranial pressure

Nausea & vomiting CNS disturbance Constipation	PO form only with ASA=Percodan with acetaminiphen = Percocet
Nausea & vomiting Constipation Respiratory depression CNS disturbance Orthostatic hypotension	Do not use IV Additive effect with ASA
Nausea & vomiting Urinary retention CNS disturbance	Good oral absorption Long plasma half-life Caution re: cummulative nature of drug
Respiratory depression Orthostatic hypotension Urinary retention Circulatory depression CNS disturbance	Suppresses cough reflex
Respiratory depression Orthostatic hypotension CNS disturbance	Less GI toxicity than morphine Good oral effect

Congruency of Goals

A major task of palliative care is the establishment of communication of mutually acceptable goals for the patient, family members, and professional caregivers. Ultimately, the patient's goals can and should shape the care they receive, establishing parameters of aggressiveness (i.e., medical intervention) and providing caregivers a basis upon which to formulate interventions. While the patient's goals remain paramount, consideration must also be given to the other members of the care triad, the family and care providers.

Goals must be clearly stated and never assumed. For example, when the patient's goal is for a peaceful death with no heroics but this has never been communicated, life support measures may be initiated and the family and health-care providers subsequently left to make decisions without knowledge of the patient's wishes.

A Supportive Environment

Resources to provide support for patients and families have not evolved in tandem with the changing care environment for the terminally ill. We have discharged patients to home assuming continuity and even improvements in care, yet we cannot ensure the availability of all services needed to manage symptoms on a 24-hour basis. Family members are placed in a dual position of provider and recipient of care. Their new role of care provider may exacerbate the disequilibrium experienced with the role changes that accompany a family member's terminal illness. A balance must exist between relieving the patient's physical and emotional distress, with equal attention to the family's psychosocial needs and concerns. Interventions that help the family achieve a sense of control over the environment may decrease their sense of helplessness (McGuinnis, 1986). These interventions include the provision of concrete care instructions in conjunction with ongoing guidance and support.

Value and Cost of Terminal Care

The present financial climate of health care has shifted the care of terminally ill patients away from the hospital. No longer are dying patients admitted to hospitals where care is delegated to professional caregivers, and families maintain a silent vigil with little or no direct care involvement. Many terminally ill patients are now cared for in their homes where their families and community health nurses assume the role of primary caregivers. While this transition from hospital to home offers obvious benefits to patients, such as personal comforts, maintenance of autonomy, and increased presence of family and friends, the care can be overwhelming for families and for community nurses.

In the past, community nurses have focused on health maintenance and education. Patients with complex care requirements were admitted to hospitals where they were cared for by the hospital staff until they stabilized or died. This scenario has changed with the implementation of Diagnostic Related Groupings (DRGs), an increase in consumer awareness, and the institutional turmoil many hospitals are experiencing. Patients are not only discharged "sicker and quicker" but some are not even admitted, thereby requiring complex levels of care be instituted in the home. There is undeniable evidence that cost factors are dictating the type of care received, by whom, and for what period of time (Baird, 1987).

Ideally, patients with complex problems are referred to a home health agency or hospice for provision of professional care, a large component of which is nursing. As a result, the acuity of home-care clientele has increased dramatically (Mulhern, 1987). Community nurses are now administering narcotic infusions, managing complex symptoms, and providing a range of physical and psychological support to patients and families. Insurance reimbursement for these home nursing visits is based primarily on skilled nursing care (such as wound care, infusions, ostomies, nutritional feedings, etc.) and often is limited to a specific number of visits. This process has changed the focus of community nursing from maintenance and education to crisis intervention and nurses are often faced with juggling complex patient care needs with everchanging reimbursement regulations. Government cost-containment efforts have also put pressure on home health agencies to discharge patients as quickly as possible (Coleman, 1988). Current eligibility and benefit structures are so restrictive that only a narrow range of services will be paid for, with significant constraints placed on the intensity and duration of care (Reif, 1987).

Given these financial and nursing constraints, management of the physical distress of the symptoms may become the only goal that appears financially compensated. The challenge is to maintain a holistic patient management focus when extrinsic forces limit the level of professional involvement.

One way to achieve the successful management of patient symptoms at home is the provision of continuous support to family members. If mechanisms for communication are ongoing and well established between the primary caregiver in the home and the home health nurse, problems can be anticipated and crises prevented. Often nurses avert complications by monitoring patient's symptoms over the telephone, reporting changes in patient status to the physician, and securing treatments such as medications before symptoms become incapacitating (McCorkle et al., 1989).

Concerted efforts are needed to expand reimbursement regulations to include telephone calls and case management activities rather than limiting them to fee-per-visit schedules. In addition, a reevaluation of payment of services for patients whose conditions are changing is needed. Patients are frequently discharged from home health agencies once their condition becomes stabilized. Alternative, cost-effective programs need to be developed to monitor the maintenance of their status.

A Model of Care for Successful Symptom Management

Innovations in palliative care that will facilitate shared decision making among patients, family members, and health professionals are needed. We propose a model of care that ensures quality of life by assisting members of the patient's support network to maximize the capacity of living day to day. The model's major feature includes a focus on management of symptoms, provision of continuity of care, and the formation of partnerships with patients and their support networks (Saunders & McCorkle, 1985). Patients and family members manifest multiple physical, emotional, and social problems that are best resolved through a collaborative, multidisciplinary team effort. The most commonly identified team members in palliative care include physicians, nurses, and social workers. We propose that the nurse is in an ideal position to coordinate and manage services as the patient's needs change from acute, chronic, and progressive within terminal situations.

There is tremendous potential among nurses for leadership in the creation and maintenance of palliative care services for patients and families. Nurses, as a collective, must be willing to engage in the politics of negotiation for reallocation of health-care resources toward individualized services. Nurses must be able to establish a power base for influencing decisions within various organizations offering health-care benefits, such as the American Association for Retired Persons (AARP), at the local, state, and national levels of government. As individualized services are established, nurses must also move toward formalizing emergent practices into standards of care. In keeping with the adoption of standards of practice is the need to develop a consistent, universal nomenclature for assessing, monitoring, and evaluating patients' symptoms. Standardized scales for measuring symptoms (McCorkle, 1988) need to be incorporated routinely into the patient's plan of care.

We believe that the successful development and implementation of palliative care services depends on the support of administrators in all disciplines and across all settings. Administrators and key leaders in their individual practice disciplines need to recognize the complexity of

Table 2.3   Barriers to Successful Symptom Management

1. Fear of addiction to medications
2. Fear of untoward side effects from medications
3. Lack of ongoing consistent evaluation of symptoms
4. Incomplete assessment of etiology of symptoms
5. Lack of individualized treatment plans
6. Knowledge deficit regarding pharmacological and nonpharmacological strategies for symptom management
7. Ineffective communication among patients, families, and members of the health-care team
8. Incongruent goals among patients, families, and members of the health-care team
9. Lack of institutional policies to ensure a balance of priorities between cure and palliative care
10. Lack of administrative support within institutions to develop palliative care practice standards
11. Restrictive interpretation of reimbursement regulations
12. Lack of reimbursement for a variety of palliative care services

problems and lead the way to breaking down the barriers to successful symptom management. See Table 2.3 for a list of potential barriers.

Once the problems are recognized, palliative care services may be fostered through skilled negotiations with those in positions of power (Benoliel, 1978–1988). To promote interdisciplinary teamwork, social mechanisms need to be created within organizations. The inclusion of palliative care within mainstream health care requires a radical reordering of priorities and a strong commitment to collaborative practice. At the very heart of the matter, health professionals must be willing to confront continuously the demands of conflicting goals, cure versus palliative care. Mechanisms that support the patient's right to participate in care and to make the final decisions about treatment are essential. As demands for services increase and resources become scarce, it is imperative that health professionals keep pace and develop systems and regulations that ensure the continued development of the subspecialty of palliative care. Patients, family members, and potential consumers may be the most powerful group to safeguard the future of palliative care by insisting that the quality of their living is as important or more important than aggressive therapies to prolong their lives.

References

ACS 1993 Cancer Facts and Figures. (1994). *Ca: A Journal for Clinicians*. Atlanta, GA: American Cancer Society.

Baird, S. (1987). The changing economics of cancer care: Challenges and opportunities. *Proceedings of Fifth National Conference on Cancer Nursing*. Atlanta, GA: American Cancer Society.

Benoliel, J. Q. (1987–1988). Health care providers and dying patients: Critical issues in terminal care. *Omega, 18*(4):341–363.

Benoliel, J. Q. (Ed). (1982). Death influence in clinical practice: A course for graduate students. In *Death education for the health professional*, Washington, DC: Hemisphere.

Benoliel, J. Q. (1976). Overview: Care, cure and the challenge of choice. In Earle, A., et al. (Eds.), *The nurse as caregiver for the terminal patient and his family*. New York: Columbia University Press.

Benoliel, J. Q., & McCorkle, R. (1977). Ethical considerations in treatment. In *Proceedings of the Second National Conference on Cancer Nursing*. New York: American Cancer Society.

Bertman, S. K., Greene, J., & Wyatt, C. A. (1982). Humanistic health career education in a hospice/palliative care setting. In Benoliel, J. Q. (Ed.), *Death education for the health professional*, Washington, DC: Hemisphere.

Brewin, T. B. (1977). The cancer patient: Communication and morale. *British Medical Journal, 2*:1623–1627.

Bruera, E., Brenneis, D., McDonald, N. et al., (1988). The use of the SC route for the administration of narcotics in patients with cancer pain. *Cancer, 62*:407–411.

"Caring Together", (December, 1987). The report of the expert working group on integrated palliative care for persons with AIDS. Ottawa, Ontario: Health and Welfare Canada.

Coleman, S. (1988). Discharge planning from the home health agency. In O'Hare, P. & Terry, M. *Discharge planning: Strategies for assuring continuing of care* (pp. 175–180) Rockville, MD: Aspect.

Degner, L. F., & Gow, C. M. (1988). Preparing nurses for care of the dying. A longitudinal study. *Cancer Nursing, 11*(3):160–169.

Dickson R. J., & Russell, P. S. B. (1982). Continuous subcutaneous analgesics for terminal care at home. *Lancet, 1*(2):165.

Duffy, C. M., Pollock, P., Lerey, M., Budd, E., Caulfield, L., & Koren, G. (1990). Home-based palliative care for children, Part 2: The benefits of an established program. *Journal of Palliative Care, 6*(2):8–14.

Fiore, N. (1979). Fighting cancer—one patient's perspective. *The New England Journal of Medicine, 300*(2):284–289.

Foley, K. M. (1985). *Management of cancer pain* (p. 25) New York: MsKee.

Germino, B. (1991). Cancer and the family. In Baird, S., McCorkle, R., & Grant, M. (Eds.). *A comprehensive textbook: Cancer nursing.* Philadelphia: W. B. Saunders.

Goodell, B. W., Donohue, J. I., & Benoliel, J. Q. (1982). Death education in medical school: A seminar on terminal illness. In Benoliel, J. Q. (Ed.) *Death education for the health professional.* Washington, DC: Hemisphere.

Holland, J. C. (1982). Psychologic aspects of cancer. In Holland, J. F. S., & E. Frei, III (Eds.). *Cancer medicine.* Philadelphia: Lea S. Febiger.

Krant, M. J. (1976). Problems of the physician in presenting the patient with the diagnosis. In Cullen, J. W., Fox, B. H., & Isom, R. N. (Eds.) *Cancer: The behavorial dimensions.* New York: Raven Press.

Kristjanson, L. J. (1989). Quality of terminal care: Salient indicators identified by families. *Journal of Palliative Care,* 5(1):21–28.

Maguire, P. (1981). The repercussions of mastectomy on the family. *International Journal of Psychiatry,* 1:485–503.

McCorkle, R. (1988). The measurement of symptom distress. *Seminars in Oncology,* 3:248–256.

McCorkle, R., Benolicl, J. Q., Donaldson, G., Georgiadou, F., Moinpour, C., & Goodell, B. (1989). A randomized clinical trial of home nursing care for lung cancer patients. *Cancer,* 64:199–206.

McGuinnis, S. (1986). How can nurses improve the quality of life of the hospice client and family? *The Hospice Journal,* 2(1):23–33.

McIntosh, J. (1974). Processes of communication, information seeking and control associatcd with cancer: A selective review of the literature. *Social Sciences and Medicine,* 8:167–182.

Miaskowski, C. (1988). *Supportive care for the cancer patient* (p. 4) Valley Cottage, NY: A. H. Robbins.

Mulhern, P. J. (1987). High-tech nursing in the home and community. *Proceedings of Fifth National Conference on Cancer Nursing.* Atlanta, GA: American Cancer Society.

Northouse, L. (1984). Preventive intervention with the recently bereaved. *Arch. Gen. Psychiatry,* 34(12):1450–1454.

Northouse, P. G., & Northouse, L. (1987). Communication and cancer: Issues confronting patients, health professionals and family members. *Journal of Psychosocial Oncology,* 5:17–46.

Oberst, M., & James, R. H. (1985). Going home: Patient and spouse adjustment following cancer surgery. *Topics in Clinical Nursing,* 1:46–57.

Quint, J. C. (1966). Communication problems affecting patient care in hospitals. *JAMA,* 195:126–127.

Reif, L. (1987). The real victims of the crisis in home care: Patients and their families. *Home Health Care Services Quarterly,* 8(1):1–4.

Saunders, C. (1982). Principles of symptom control in terminal care. *Medical Clinics of North America, 66*:1169.

Saunders, J. M., & McCorkle, R. (1985). Models of care for persons with progressive cancer. *Nursing Clinics of North America, 20*:365–377.

Scanlon, C. (1989). Creating a vision of hope: The challenge of palliative care. *Oncology Nursing Forum, 16*(4):491–499.

Sinacore, J. M. (1981). Avoiding the humanistic aspect of death: An outcome from the implicit elements of health professions education. *Death Education, 5*:121–133.

Stetz, K. (1987). Caregiving demands during advanced cancer. *Cancer Nursing, 10*:260–268.

Turnbull, R. (Ed). (1986). *Terminal care.* Washington, DC: Hemisphere.

Twycross, R. G. & Lack, S. A. (1984). *Therapeutics in terminal cancer.* London: Churchill Livingstone.

Ventafridda, V., Ripamonti, C., DeConno, F., & Tamburini, M. (1990). Symptom prevalence and control during cancer patients' last days of life. *Journal of Palliative Care, 6*(3):7–11.

Websters New Collegiate Dictionary. (1977). Springfield, MA: G&C Merriam.

Wortman, C. B., & Dunkel-Schetter, C. (1979). Interpersonal relationships and cancer: A theoretical analysis. *Journal of Social Issues, 35*:120–155.

Yasko, J. M. (Ed.) (1983). *Guidelines for cancer care symptom management.* Reston, Virginia: Reston.

Three

Communicating about Death and Dying

Albert Lee Strickland

Lynne Ann DeSpelder

Albert Lee Strickland is a writer whose multidisciplinary interest in thanatology is reflected in his coauthorship of The Last Dance: Encountering Death and Dying, *a college text now in its third edition. He is a former editor of* The Forum *newsletter, published by the Association for Death Education and Counseling. His recent work includes* The Path Ahead: Readings in Death and Dying, *an anthology coedited with Lynne DeSpelder. A member of the Authors Guild, he is currently at work on a screenplay involving religious fanatacism, political antics, and nuclear Armageddon.*

Lynne Ann DeSpelder is an educator, author, and counselor. A faculty member at Cabrillo College, she developed and taught one of the first interdisciplinary courses on death and dying in California. Certified by the Association for Death Education and Counseling as a death educator and grief counselor , she was instrumental in developing that organization's Education for Certification program. Her first nationally published popular writing on death appeared in the November 1977 issue of New Age *magazine. She is coauthor of* The Last Dance: Encountering Death and Dying, *3rd edition, and is a member of the International Work Group on Death, Dying, and Bereavement.*

Waiting to speak with a patient who has just completed a series of diagnostic tests, a physician ponders how to break the news of a potentially fatal diagnosis. A parent wonders how to tell her small child that a beloved relative has died. The editor of a network news program sorts through videotaped coverage of an airliner crash, choosing the footage that will be shown on the evening news. On the job, the death of an associate's spouse raises anxious questions in the minds of coworkers about how to express their sympathy. A nurse hesitates before entering the room of a patient who is near death, hoping to find the right words that will convey sensitivity without revealing her own discomfort and uncertainty. Such encounters with dying and death present special challenges to us as communicators.

In most situations, communication is a two-way, interactive, and transactional process (Williams, 1984, p. 11). To say that communication is interactive means that messages can be readily, or even simultaneously, exchanged between the parties to the communication. To say that it is transactional refers to the evolving nature of the process, in which the present exchange of messages influences subsequent exchanges. Fundamentally, communication can be seen as a process involving a source, a message, and a receiver (Littlejohn, 1983, p. 118; Rubin, 1984, pp. 41–65; Williams, 1984, pp. 26–29). It is a process of give and take, an ongoing activity between persons who function alternatively as the source and the receiver of messages.

It has been said that one cannot *not* communicate (Bavelas, 1984; Watzlawick, 1984; Williams, 1984, p. 15). The truth of this statement becomes evident as we consider the range of nonverbal as well as verbal modes of communicating. Sight, touch, smell, taste, and sound correspond to the visual, tactile, olfactory, gustatory, and auditory modes of sensing and communicating. We communicate visually by means of facial displays, including changes in eye gaze and pupil dilation; body posture, gestures, and movement; costume and adornment; and physique. The tactile mode conveys information about pressure, pain, and temperature. Body odors, fragrances, and tastes convey olfactory and gustatory information. Auditory information is conveyed through vocalizations as well as incidental sounds present in the environment.

Nonverbal communication is typically divided into three components (Littlejohn, 1983, pp. 86–94; Rubin, 1984, pp. 78–93, 111, 115, 126–156; Williams, 1984, pp. 56–58): paralanguage (features of speech beyond the basic language symbols, including tone of voice and rate of speech), kinesics (gestures, facial expression, and body posture), and iconics (objects that convey meaningful information, such as clothes and jewelry). Labels such as M.D. and R.N., as well as titles such as doctor, nurse, and patient, are examples of symbolic identifiers that influence the process of communication. Space and time can be added to our catalog of nonverbal cues. Consider, for example, the time it takes a caregiver to respond to a patient's request for assistance or the physical distance established when a physician stands behind a desk while conversing with a patient. Nonverbal cues form a significant, though often unconscious, part of interpersonal communication.

Effective communication requires attention to the maintenance of the communication process (Williams, 1984, pp. 194–198). Especially important for successful communication are developing the requisite trust, achieving clarity about motives, and establishing an appropriate context. An individual's attitudes, beliefs, values, preferences, goals, capabilities, experience, communication style, and needs all influence how he or she will send or receive a particular message (Kaplan 1989; White & Robillard, 1989). Effective interpersonal communicators possess a positive self-concept and positive assertiveness, open-mindedness, the ability to feel empathy, and the ability to use various communication strategies appropriately.

As an example, consider the case of a young widow who was referred for counseling by her physician because she was reportedly "not doing too well." When the young woman entered the counselor's office for her initial session, she sat down rigidly on the couch, bracing herself with legs extended and her arms crossed. The counselor opened the session by saying, "I understand you've experienced a big change in your life recently." Through clenched teeth, the young woman said, "Yeah, my old man ate it on highway 17." Matching the young woman's language and communication style, the counselor said, "It sounds like that really pissed you off."

Exploding out of her rigid position, the young woman let go with a volcanic torrent of expletives: "Yes, I'm damned angry; he was drunk and ran off the road, leaving me alone with four kids under the age of five and no insurance or any kind of security." Then, breaking down into tears, she sobbed, "God, I must be going crazy; how can I be furious at someone who's dead?" Matching the young woman's language allowed the counselor to establish a rapport that facilitated opening the communication process. It readily became clear that she was very much in touch with her feelings about the circumstances of her husband's death, even when those feelings were contradictory and emotionally confusing. Attention to the communication process allowed these feelings to achieve expression, a crucial step on the path to resolving her grief.

The language we use when talking about the process of dying or the fact of death is rarely direct (DeSpelder & Strickland, 1992, pp. 22–23). Instead, we use euphemisms. Usually this means substituting mild, vague, or indirect expressions for ones considered harsh or blunt: The deceased person has "passed away" and is "laid to rest." Euphemisms are not always mild, of course, as in the case of the young widow. The military has added to our lexicon of euphemisms by citing "body counts" or "collateral damage" and by describing a person as "being wasted" by an adversary. Paying attention to the way language is used gives listeners an indication of the belief system and emotional state of the speaker. When we become aware of the metaphors, euphemisms, and other linguistic devices that people use when talking about dying and death, we come to appreciate more fully the range of attitudes toward death, thus allowing greater flexibility in communication.

Dysfunctional communication has been cited as one factor in the incidence of violence (Kastenbaum & Aisenberg, 1976, pp. 296-297). The use of prejudicial, dehumanizing, or derogatory labels can heighten the tension in inherently violent situations, whereas emphasizing similarities and common goals can help promote communication and contact between potential adversaries. This dynamic in language usage can be seen at the level of interpersonal relationships as well as at the level of international relations where political leaders sometimes employ derogatory language to portray adversaries as subhuman or "evil" (Keen, 1988).

Language is employed another way in the realm of humor, which can provide relief from the serious and somber matters of death (DeSpelder & Strickland, 1992, pp. 24–27; Hall, 1985; Hall & Rappe, 1994). Laughter can defuse some of the anxiety we feel toward death. Humor about death comes in many forms, from ironic epitaphs to so-called black or gallows humor, which often reflects a thumbing of one's nose at death, as if attempting to minimize the power of death and gain a sense of mastery over it. Caregivers find that humor provides relief and release from stressful duties involving contact with death. At a teaching hospital, doctors avoided using the word "death" when a patient died because of their concern that other patients might be alarmed if the news were communicated openly (DeSpelder & Strickland, 1987, p. 20). One day, as a medical team was examining a patient, an intern came to the door with information about another patient's death. Knowing that the word "death" was taboo and finding no ready substitute, the intern stood in the doorway and announced, "Guess who's not going to shop at Woolworth's anymore?" Soon, this phrase became the standard way for staff members to convey the news that a patient had died.

Newspapers, magazines, books, movies, and television have become the secondhand sources from which many people learn about death. The day's news usually includes an assortment of accidents, murders, suicides, and disasters involving death (Nimmo & Combs, 1985). With events such as the the disaster of the spaceship *Challenger* or the death of President John F. Kennedy, television provided a focal point for a nation's grief; some observers likened it to a "national hearth" around which viewers were symbolically gathered as they witnessed tragedy and contemplated its meaning. On the other hand, media coverage of events involving death may seem an intrusion on the bereaved. For example, during the memorial service for the *Challenger* crew, which was viewed on television by millions of Americans, the astronauts' grieving families were shown in close-up shots. The distinction between public event and private loss is not always easily drawn. The journalistic impulse to "capture the experience" for viewers or readers may result in a "second trauma" for survivors, restimulating or possibly amplifying the pain brought about by the event itself. Nor can the brief reports shown on television or reported in the daily newspaper do justice to the full range and depth of the human response to loss.

This incomplete picture of what death means in the lives of human beings is perpetuated also by entertainment programs, which seldom deal with how people actually cope with a loved one's death or confront their own dying. Instead, we are given a depersonalized image of death, an image often characterized by violence (Gerbner, 1980; Tate, 1989). Consider, for example, the western or detective drama, which glazes over the reality of death and suggests that death is an event that need not be mourned. Or recall the Saturday morning cartoon: Daffy Duck is pressed to a thin sheet by a steamroller, only to pop up again a moment later good as new—reversible death! When told of his grandfather's death, one modern seven-year-old asked, "Who did it to him?" The understanding of death usually offered by the media is that it comes from outside, often violently. The message being communicated is that death is an accidental rather than a natural process.

The attitudes toward death reflected by the media and elsewhere in society play a major role in the socialization of children relative to dying and death (DeSpelder & Strickland, 1992, pp. 109–118). Sometimes parents or other adults communicate this information directly: "This is how we behave in relation to death." One woman recalled her mother's message that she shouldn't look at the dead animals on the highway—"Put your head down; children shouldn't see that."—a clear communication about what constitutes appropriate behavior toward death. At other times, the message is indirect: "Let's not talk about it...." Or the message may be communicated unconsciously, as with the notion of replaceability. A child's pet dies and the parent says, "It's okay, dear, we'll get another one." Such messages may have unintended consequences, as when a woman recently bereaved by her husband's death was approached by her child who said, "Don't worry, Mommy, we'll get you another one."

In communicating with children about death, honesty is foremost. Second, children should be introduced to the topic of death before a crisis occurs. When a close death precedes the discussion, the explanation is charged with all the emotions generated by the crisis, making it more difficult to achieve a clear explanation. Third, it is important to set the level of explanation to the child's powers of understanding. By using the child's interest and ability to comprehend as a guide, an explanation can be provided that is appropriate to the child's circumstances.

When talking with children about death, it is important to verify what they think you've told them by asking them what they learned or what they heard you saying. Young children especially tend to be very literal-minded and concrete (Koocher, 1973, 1974; Lonetto, 1980; Speece & Brent, 1984; Stillion & Wass, 1979). Recognizing this, it is helpful to try to keep communication free of associations that might cause confusion in the child's mind. Although metaphorical explanations can provide a child-sized picture that aids understanding, unless fact is clearly separated from fancy, the child may grasp the literal details instead of the underlying message the analogy was intended to convey. A child told that her goldfish "went to heaven" may make an elaborate picture of the pearly gates and different sections of heaven—"Here is goldfish heaven, this is cat heaven, and over here is people heaven"—an organized concept that makes sense to a young child. If you tell a four-year-old that someone who has died is "up there" and you also say that Santa Claus lands on the roof, he may decide that Santa Claus and the person who has died are great buddies. Children are apt to point out any inconsistencies in what we tell them about death.

Communication in the Context of Bereavement and Grief

A death occurs. First to learn about it, after the attending medical team, are usually members of the immediate family. Those with closest relationships to the deceased are notified first, followed by those with less intimate relationships. This process of notification—taking in a gradually widening circle of relatives, friends, and acquaintances—continues until virtually everyone affected by the death is notified (Sudnow, 1967, pp. 153–168).

Death notification also takes place by means of notices published in the newspaper. We expect death announcements to appear in a timely fashion. When they do not, the results can be upsetting. The person who learns about a death only after the final disposition of the body may regret not having been a participant in the communal ceremonies marking the death. Because the mutual support of the community of bereaved persons is not likely to be as available after the initial period of mourning, the belatedly notified person may feel alone in dealing with his or her grief.

The process of death notification also helps to set apart the bereaved during the period of mourning. In some societies, the black armband, mourning colors and garb, as well as various other signs and symbols, are used to distinguish the bereaved person. Although most traditional signs of mourning have vanished from modern societies, people still feel that the bereaved deserve special consideration. A woman involved in an automobile accident just days after the death of her child said that she wished she could have had a banner proclaiming her status as a "mother whose child has just died." With no outward symbol of bereavement, she was subjected, as any of us would be, to the strain of waiting around and filling in seemingly endless forms. Death notification and symbols of mourning communicate a need for social support that is helpful to survivors in dealing with their loss.

When people learn about the death of someone significant to them, they tend to gather together, closing ranks to provide support and comfort in their mutual bereavement. The very act of coming together in this way is itself symbolic communication that gives reassurance and attests to the reality that we are part of a community (Young, 1978, p. 255). Gathering to support and comfort the bereaved continues throughout the events surrounding the funeral. This pattern of social interaction has important psychological implications for the bereaved. It serves to corroborate the fact that a loved one has died, and it expresses the notion that the community of family and friends has undergone a change of status: one of its members is dead. Such social interaction also facilitates the expression of grief.

During the period immediately following a death, the survivor's perceptions may be disorganized; events may seem unreal. Survivors may talk incessantly about the deceased, or they may seem to talk about everything but their loss and the circumstances surrounding the death. Often, survivors exhibit a general restlessness marked by considerable variability in emotions. In addition to sadness, longing, loneliness, and sorrow, there may be guilt or anger (Bugen, 1977; Lindemann, 1944; Osterweis, Solomon, & Green, 1984). Such feelings are normal, and movement toward healing after the experience of such a crisis can be facilitated by skillful communication that is cognizant of the bereaved's changing moods and circumstances.

Because a person's experience of loss is conditioned by his or her model of the world—that is, by his or her perception of reality and judgment about how the world works—issues relating to the survivor's personality, social roles and expectations, relationship to the deceased, and personal value structure all have a place in determining how best to provide social support (Jackson, 1957). Permission to have and express feelings is especially important. A survivor's response to death is complex, encompassing a multitude of personal, family, and social factors. By becoming aware of the vast range of responses that can be present in the experience of loss and grief, we increase our choices for dealing with loss in our own lives as well as for giving care to others in their bereavement. Grief can become a unifying rather than alienating human experience, and the loss can be placed in a context of growth, integrating what was lost into one's own life energies (Schneider, 1984). A perspective that allows for the notion that bereavement can be an opportunity for growth allows room for movement toward resolving the loss.

Communication in the Context of Terminal Care

Physicians and other health-care providers have traditionally occupied a place of honor in society. Aesculapius, the first physician according to Greek legend, was elevated to the pantheon of gods. As an activity closely associated with the elemental human experiences of birth, life, and death, medicine carries high symbolic importance (Hingson, Scotch, Sorenson, & Swazey, 1981). Both caregivers and patients may unwittingly conspire to perpetuate paternalism in health care, whereby the caregiver assumes a parentlike authority over decisions affecting the patient (von Raffler-Engel, 1989; West, 1984). The distinguishing uniforms of the nursing staff and the laboratory coat of the attending physician are examples of symbols that nonverbally communicate this sense of the caregiver's authority and power.

What happens after a physician diagnoses a patient's illness as life threatening? The communication during this critical period can significantly influence the patient's response to treatment, attitude toward the illness, and ability to cope with it. The physician should provide general information about the disease, giving as much detail as the patient wishes, so that the patient is informed about what to expect and the options that he or she may exercise as treatment proceeds (Rosenbaum, 1978). Sufficient time should be allowed to explore the patient's questions and concerns. An atmosphere of openness and trust should be established so as to help mobilize the patient's will to live, a key element in any therapeutic effort (Gray & Doan, 1990a, 1990b; Hans, 1988; LeShan, 1969). If appropriate, the physician may suggest some type of group counseling or social support program, in which the patient can share his or her concerns with others, thus relieving the sense of isolation that often accompanies a diagnosis of terminal illness.

It is a truism in medicine that hope and positive attitudes play a key part in a patient's ability to cope with illness (Bessinger, 1988). Physicians have sometimes withheld facts about serious illness, fearing that a full and open disclosure might lessen the patient's chances of recovery. There is a difference, however, between glossing over or neglecting a full disclosure of the facts because of a paternalistic desire to protect patients and framing one's communication about the situation in a way that corresponds to a particular patient's willingness to learn the truth. The latter course of action is based on cooperation and a sense of partnership between physician and patient.

Although surveys indicate that most people would want to be told if they were diagnosed with a life-threatening illness, the questions of *when* and *how* to tell are difficult to answer (President's Commission for the Study of Ethical Problems in Medicine and Biomedical and Behavioral Research, 1982a, 1982b). To present the news in a way that serves the best interests of each patient, it is necessary in each situation to consider factors of personality, emotional constitution, and capacity for continued function under stress. Most doctors are guided by their experience. Sometimes it is a member of the family who learns the truth first. Those who know then have a burden of responsibility, for they must decide what to tell the patient.

Most physicians acknowledge a responsibility to inform a patient about the facts of a life-threatening condition, although the climate of such truth-telling has changed markedly in recent decades. A survey conducted in the early 1960s revealed a strong and general tendency to withhold information (Oken, 1961). When patients were informed about a diagnosis of cancer, descriptions of the disease were often couched in euphemisms. The patient might be told that he or she had a "lesion" or a "mass," or might be given a more precise description such as "growth," "tumor," or "hyperplastic tissue." Adjectives were used to temper the impact of the diagnosis or to suggest that the cancer was benign. The tumor was "suspicious" or "degenerated." In short, these physicians explained the medical situation in the most general terms while still eliciting the patient's cooperation in the proposed course of treatment. Today, a patient diagnosed with a terminal condition is likely to learn the truth about his or her illness, and to learn sooner, than was usual in the past (Novack, Plumer, et al., 1979). Nevertheless, the full extent of an illness may not be disclosed until the patient or a family member exhibits a readiness to be told. Details that might be depressing news to the patient are often withheld unless the patient takes the initiative by asking specific questions. Furthermore, although physicians may be willing to frankly disclose medical facts related to diagnosis, they are generally more reticent when it comes to speculating about prognosis or outcome, matters that tend to involve much less certainty (Novack, Detering, et al., 1989).

The present tendency toward greater disclosure is related to the increased importance placed on obtaining a patient's informed consent to a proposed plan of treatment. It is generally recognized that the potential for litigation increases when physicians or other caregivers behave in a paternalistic manner that abrogates an individual's right to determine his or her treatment. The tendency toward greater disclosure of medical facts can also be seen as simply part of a broader social concern with the exercise of individual autonomy, or the right of self-governance. In the context of health care, such autonomy requires that there be a partnership or spirit of cooperation between patient and caregiver.

Informed consent is based on three principles (President's Commission, 1982a, 1982c): First, the patient must be competent to give consent. Second, consent must be given freely and voluntarily. Third, consent must be based on an adequate understanding of what is involved in the treatment program. Ideally, a physician will inform the patient about the risks of the proposed therapy, about alternative methods of treatment, and about the likely outcome of no treatment. The values underlying informed consent include serving the patient's well-being and respecting his or her right to self-determination. To make this a reality, attention must be paid not only to the patient's capacity to make decisions about his or her care, but also to the communication between patient and practitioner.

Although coercive treatment is rare, caregivers can unwittingly exert undue influence on patients by means of subtle or overt manipulation. Much routine care is provided without a patient's explicit consent. Once a patient has entered a health-care facility, cooperation with those who provide care is expected. The tacit communication may be that the patient has no choice. Thus, the communication process itself may determine whether informed consent is indeed present. Modern advances in medical care have raised our expectations about what can be achieved and have made medical practices more esoteric, a paradoxical situation given that the patient must sufficiently understand the medical realities to make informed decisions about treatment.

When a patient is treated as a whole person and his or her preferences are respected, the patient's sense of self-worth and dignity is elicited. Certainly, patients do vary as to the degree of disclosure with which they feel comfortable. The desire of a patient to "let the doctor decide" is no less worthy of respect than the desire of another to seek esoteric knowledge by obtaining primary citations in the literature regarding a treatment plan. In the end, patient autonomy and informed consent does not mean inundating patients with facts; rather, it means respecting the unique preferences of persons insofar as possible. The capacity to maintain a healthy self-concept, to set goals and strive to meet them, to exercise choice out of an awareness of one's power to meet challenges, to engage in active interactions with one's environment—all of these reflect a "coping capacity" that sustains the will to live in the face of death (Weisman, 1984).

Contact that spans the usual professional distance can reduce the sense of alienation that patients sometimes feel in the institutional setting. A century ago, physicians and nurses did perhaps as much to console as to cure the patient. Indeed, consolation and palliative measures were sometimes all the medical practitioner could offer the patient. A nurse who steps into the room, sits down by the patient's bed, and demonstrates a willingness to listen is more likely to be successful in providing comfort than one who merely breezes in, remains standing, and quips, "How're we doing today? Did we sleep well?" Skillful communication is a key to health care for the whole person.

When an attitude of caring and support is communicated to patients, it fosters trust and feelings of self-worth and value in the patient as well as the caregiver. Those who care for the dying must have confidence in their methods of caregiving and must believe that the care being provided is appropriate and beneficial, in the best interests of the patient. Establishing continuity of care between at least one caregiver and the patient is one way to elicit the trust and confidence required for a satisfactory outcome (Donovan & Pierce, 1976; Quint, 1967). Everyone who confronts the reality of dying—whether as patient, family member, or health professional—needs a supportive environment nurtured by openness, compassion, and sensitive listening. Caring is not always synonymous with doing. Despite the value we place on knowledge and action, it is also important to be open to not knowing. This approach reflects the awareness that learning can occur only when something is not yet understood.

Most people feel somewhat uncomfortable in the presence of a person who has been diagnosed with a life-threatening illness. What can we say? How ought we to act? It seems that anything we might think of to express our feelings is little more than a stale platitude. We may avoid eye contact or engage in other behaviors that reveal a shying away from real communication. We let ourselves off the hook while still managing to acknowledge our concern by directing our questions to a member of the patient's family rather than directly to the ill person. Our discomfort and uncertainty may be demonstrated by excessive sympathy or by obsessive avoidance.

There are no formulas for how to behave. Neither is there any special qualification for being sensitive to the situation as it actually presents itself and responding with care and understanding. Because there is no single "correct" way to behave, we can simply be ourselves, uncertainty and all. Being with someone who is dying does not mean that we must be comfortable; rather, we learn to accept our discomfort. What we can offer is ourselves as we are, including our uncertainty and fear and anxiety. Indeed, that is perhaps as close as we can come to "correct" behavior in all our intimate relationships, whether or not the context involves the immediate experience of dying or death.

In a community where patients are supposed to get well, the dying patient may be treated as a deviant. Death seems less a natural event than a medical failure. In such a cultural context, biological death may be preceded by social death (Blauner, 1966; Cassell, 1974). In some instances nurses have taken longer to answer the bedside calls of terminally ill patients than they took to answer calls of patients who were less severely ill (Bowers, Jackson, Knight, & LeShan, 1964, pp. 6–7). This pattern of avoidance may also be seen in the responses of caregivers when the topic of death is raised by dying patients. Such responses include reassurance ("You're doing fine"); denial ("You've got nothing to worry about"); changing the subject ("Let's talk about something more cheerful"), and fatalism ("We all have to die sometime"). In contrast to these evasive responses, caregivers can exhibit a willingness to enter into discussion with the patient ("What is happening to make you feel that way?").

Whereas the death of the body is a physical phenomenon, the passing of the person is a nonphysical (social, emotional, psychological, spiritual) one; yet, these aspects tend to become confused. Effective communication skills enhance not only care of the person as physical entity, but also care of the person with respect to the nonphysical dimensions that are no less important. An awareness of nonverbal as well as verbal modes of communication can facilitate discussion and the therapeutic flow of feelings. Actions, as well as words, can be used to meaningfully demonstrate support. Sensitive, caring communication is an essential complement to physical care. It is only with such communication that the dying person is enabled to live unto death.

References

Bavelas, J. B. (1984). *Reviewing pragmatics sixteen years later.* Paper presented at the meeting of the International Communication Association, San Francisco, CA.

Bessinger, C. D. (1988). Doctoring: The philosophic milieu. *Southern Medical Journal 81,* 1558–1562.

Blauner, R. (1966). Death and social structure. *Psychiatry 29,* 378–394.

Bowers, M. K., Jackson, E. N., Knight, J. A., & LeShan, L. (1964). *Counseling the dying.* New York: Thomas Nelson & Sons.

Bugen, L. A. (1977). Human grief: A model for prediction and intervention. *American Journal of Orthopsychiatry 47,* 196–206.

Cassell, E. J. (1974). Dying in a technological society. In P. Steinfels & R. M. Veatch (Eds.), *Death inside out: The Hastings Center report* (pp. 43–48). New York: Harper & Row.

DeSpelder, L. A., & Strickland, A. L. (1992). *The last dance: Encountering death and dying* (3d ed.). Mountain View, CA: Mayfield.

Donovan, M. I., & Pierce, S. G. (1976). *Cancer care nursing.* New York: Appleton-Century-Crofts.

Gerbner, G. (1980). Death in prime time: Notes on the symbolic functions of dying in the mass media. *Annals of the American Academy of Political and Social Science 447,* 64–70.

Gray, R. E., & Doan, B. D. (1990a). Empowerment and persons with cancer: Politics in cancer medicine. *Journal of Palliative Care 6* (2), 33–45.

Gray, R. E., & Doan, B. D. (1990b). Heroic self-healing and cancer: Clinical issues for the health professions. *Journal of Palliative Care 6* (1), 32–41.

Hall, M. N. (1985, April). *Laughing as we go.* Paper presented at the meeting of the Forum for Death Education and Counseling, Philadelphia.

Hall, M. N., & Rappe, P. T. (in press). Humor and critical incident stress. In L. A. DeSpelder & A. L. Strickland (Eds.), *The Path ahead: Readings in death and dying.* Mountain View, CA: Mayfield.

Hans, P. (1988). When the patient doesn't die. *General Hospital Psychiatry 10,* 367–372.

Hingson, R., Scotch, N. A., Sorenson, J., & Swazey, J. P. (1981). *In sickness and in health: Social dimensions of medical care.* St. Louis: Mosby.

Jackson, E. N. (1957). *Understanding grief: Its roots, dynamics, and treatment.* Nashville: Abingdon Press.

Kaplan, T. (1989). An intercultural communication gap: North American Indians vs. the mainstream medical profession. In W. von Raffler-Engel (Ed.), *Doctor-patient interactions* (pp. 45-59). Philadelphia: John Benjamins.

Kastenbaum, R., & Aisenberg, R. (1976). *The psychology of death: Concise edition.* New York: Springer.

Keen, S. (1988). *Faces of the enemy: Reflections of the hostile imagination.* San Francisco: Harper & Row.

Koocher, G. P. (1973). Childhood, death, and cognitive development. *Developmental Psychology 9,* 369–375.

Koocher, G. P. (1974). Talking with children about death. *American Journal of Orthopsychiatry 44,* 404–411.

LeShan, L. (1969). Mobilizing the life force. *Annals of the New York Academy of Science 164,* 847–861.

Lindemann, E. (1944). Symptomatology and management of acute grief. *American Journal of Psychiatry 101,* 141–148.

Littlejohn, S. W. (1983). *Theories of human communication* (2nd ed.). Belmont, CA: Wadsworth.

Lonetto, R. (1980). *Children's conceptions of death.* New York: Springer.

Nimmo, D., & Combs, J. E. (1985). *Nightly horrors: Crisis coverage by television network news.* Knoxville: University of Tennessee Press.

Novack, D. H., Detering, B. J., Arnold, R., Forrow, L., Ladinsky, M., & Pezzullo, J. C. (1989). Physicians' attitudes toward using deception to resolve difficult ethical problems. *Journal of the American Medical Association 261*, 2980–2985.

Novack, D. H., Plumer, R., Smith, R. L., Ochitill, H., Morrow, G. R., & Bennett, J. M. (1979). Changes in physicians' attitudes toward telling the cancer patient. *Journal of the American Medical Association 241*, 897–900.

Oken, D. (1961). What to tell cancer patients: A study of medical attitudes. *Journal of the American Medical Association 175*, 1120–1128.

Osterweis, M., Solomon, F., & Green, M. (Eds.). (1984). *Bereavement: Reactions, consequences, and care.* Washington, DC: National Academy Press.

President's Commission for the Study of Ethical Problems in Medicine and Biomedical and Behavioral Research. (1982a). *Making health care decisions: The ethical and legal implications of informed consent in the patient-practitioner relationship: Vol. 1, Report.* Washington, DC: U.S. Government Printing Office.

President's Commission for the Study of Ethical Problems in Medicine and Biomedical and Behavioral Research. (1982b). *Making health care decisions: The ethical and legal implications of informed consent in the patient-practitioner relationship: Vol. 2, Empirical studies of informed consent.* Washington, DC: U.S. Government Printing Office.

President's Commission for the Study of Ethical Problems in Medicine and Biomedical and Behavioral Research. (1982c). *Making health care decisions: The ethical and legal implications of informed consent in the patient-practitioner relationship: Vol. 3, Studies on the foundations of informed consent.* Washington, DC: U.S. Government Printing Office.

Quint, J. (1967). *The nurse and the dying patient.* New York: Macmillan.

Rosenbaum, E. (1978). Oncology/hematology and psychosocial support of the cancer patient. In C. A. Garfield (Ed.), *Psychosocial care of the dying patient* (pp. 169–184). New York: McGraw-Hill.

Rubin, B. D. (1984) *Communication and human behavior.* New York: Macmillan.

Schneider, J. (1984). *Stress, loss, and grief: Understanding their origins and growth potential.* Baltimore: University Park Press.

Speece, M. W., & Brent, S. W. (1984). Children's understanding of death: A review of three components of a death concept. *Child Development 55*, 1671–1686.

Stillion, J., & Wass, H. (1979). Children and death. In H. Wass (Ed.), *Dying: Facing the facts* (pp. 208–235). Washington, DC: Hemisphere.

Sudnow, D. (1967). *The social organization of dying.* Englewood Cliffs, NJ: Prentice-Hall.

Tate, F. B. (1989). Impoverishment of death symbolism: The negative consequences. *Death Studies 13*, 305–317.

von Raffler-Engel, W. (1989). Doctor-patient relationships in the 1980s. In W. von Raffler-Engel (Ed.), *Doctor-patient interaction*. Philadelphia: John Benjamins.

Watzlawick, P. (1984). *Self-reference and world views*. Paper presented at the meeting of the International Communication Association, San Francisco, CA.

Weisman, A. (1984). *The coping capacity: On the nature of being mortal*. New York: Human Sciences.

West, Candace. (1984). *Routine complications: Troubles with talk between doctors and patients*. Bloomington: Indiana University Press.

White, G. M., & Robillard, A. B. (1989). Doctor talk and Hawaiian 'talk story': The conversational organization of a clinical encounter. In W. von Raffler-Engel (Ed.), *Doctor-patient interaction* (pp. 197–211). Philadelphia: John Benjamins.

Williams, F. (1984). *The new communications*. Belmont, CA: Wadsworth.

Young, J. Z. (1978). *Programs of the brain*. New York: Oxford University Press.

Four

Dying in
the Hospital

Patrice O'Connor

Patrice O'Connor has been the director of the Palliative Care Program of the St. Luke's/Roosevelt Hospital Center since 1980. She has developed and implemented programs in the areas of the administrative aspects of palliative/hospice care and spirituality. She has lectured nationally and internationally on administration, spirituality, place of death in society, and humor as part of living and dying. She has planned research and published an attitudinal study of hospice workers in providing spiritual care, the effects of Medicare regulations on access to hospice care, and effects of an inner-city palliative care service on inpatient utilization. Ms. O'Connor established and chairs the Metropolitan Hospice/Palliative Care Administrators of New York City. She has received three American Cancer Society grants.

Introduction

There is a season for everything, a time for every occupation under heaven.[1]

It's not that I'm afraid to die, I just don't want to be there when it happens.[2]

It is a reality that we will all die. This is a fact of life. How, when, and where this event will happen is more of an uncertainty. It is clearer that, of the three—how, when, where—the where is the most predictable.

According to the Office of Technology Assessment Task Force Report of 1988, 80 percent of the 2 million Americans who die each year do so in hospitals.[3] The shift of place of death from home to medical setting is due to the advances in medical care and the philosophy of doing all that is medically possible to forestall death. Denial of the event of death has been facilitated by scientific developments and a sense that death is failure by caregivers. Death is no longer a family event, even though most people express the desire to die at home.[3]

The question then arises, how equipped are hospitals to handle the proceses of death and dying? What are the obligations of the medical personnel to patients, families, and themselves in meeting needs of the dying in these institutions? Has education for the professional addressed these critical issues of caring for the dying patient and his or her family?

These questions, along with the shrinking health-care dollar, evoke more concerns in the ethical, legal, and moral arenas about such issues as Do Not Resuscitate orders, Living Wills, and the right to die. Humanistic responses have not kept pace with the rapid technological developments, creating some very difficult death-related issues. With medical technology, the body can be kept alive, but what about the quality of life? How many times can a body "die" and then be restored to be maintained by machines? Who defines life? Do the wishes of patient, family, or hospital prevail? If there is conflict in the life and death decisions, what once were medical decisions become legal events and are now settled in the courts. The meeting of all these forces have made this a challenging time in health care.

Place of Death

With the increase in the proportion of deaths that occur in hospitals, there has been an increasing debate about appropriateness of the place of death. Death, in the opinion of many, should be a family affair and occur at home. It is increasingly institutionalized and hidden from public view. As people become less familiar with the process of death, they may increasingly assume that terminally ill patients receive better care in the hospital. However, this need not be the case. Most people want to die at home, but do not do so for social rather than medical reasons.[4,5]

Society is being challenged to change in order to meet the needs of a population in which the elderly are the fastest growing segment and in which medical technology has made it more difficult for patients to die. The increase in the number of people with AIDS, the increases in the elderly population, and the Gross National Product at 12%, raise the question of just how much can be spent on health care, let alone on care of the dying.[6,7,8]

Callahan has raised difficult questions concerning the medical goals in our aging society.[9] In particular, he examines the issue of resources being spent on the elderly and, therefore, being unavailable for future generations. As an example, he compares the expenses of high-technology care for an elderly terminal patient and the limited resources allocated for prenatal care. Callahan continues his argument offering an alternative that makes care rather than cure our societal priority.[10]

Patient and Family Expectations

Dying persons and families may represent a particularly vulnerable group, especially those dying in an acute care/cure-oriented setting. Benoliel notes that studies of family members in the hospital have consistently reported that relatives define support in two ways: 1) honest information and clear explanation about the patient's condition and what is being done; and 2) assurance that the patient is being kept comfortable. These findings also give evidence that nonsupportive behavior includes efforts to encourage them to cry, remove them from the bedside of the patient, and remind them that the suffering will be over soon.[11] The Assumptions and Principles Underlying Standards for Terminal Care emphasize that the patient and family have the right to expect that the hospital will respect their philosophy of life and death, assist them in maintaining their rights to set goals, and treat the patient and family as the unit of care.[12]

Wright and Dyck found that when relatives were asked to share concerns uppermost in their minds during the present hospitalization, four concerns were identified most frequently:

1. problems created by the symptoms of the illness,
2. fear of the future,
3. waiting, and
4. difficulty with obtaining information.[13]

Molter, in her study of needs of relatives of critically ill patients, states that the need to feel there is hope was the number one concern even when the relatives were acknowledging the impending death.[14] Hampe's research on grieving spouses of chronically ill oncology patients showed that the spouse had eight needs: to be with the dying person; to be helpful to the dying person; to be assured of the comfort of the dying person; to be informed of the mate's condition; to be informed of the impending death; to ventilate emotions; to receive comfort and support of family members; to receive acceptance, support, and comfort of health professionals.[15] Hull, in her review of nursing research on families during the terminal phase of a family member, found that families regarded information about their relative's conditions and interventions directed at their relative's comfort as most supportive. Families regarded as least supportive interventions that encouraged families to ventilate their own emotions. Being physically near their dying relatives was very important to families whose relatives were hospitalized.[16]

Persons and families have the right to expect that staff members in the hospital will be aware of and assist with their needs as indicated in these studies. To meet these concerns, administrators may consider forming an ethics committee to assist in addressing some of the difficult medical, legal, and moral issues around dying and death. Family members as well as staff should be encouraged to attend these meetings because open communication is an essential part of decision making.

Death is a natural part of the life cycle and the handling of the circumstances of the death in hospital settings should be done in a concerned manner with the full realization that death is not a failure.

Caregivers and Dying

"A good death is one a person would choose for himself."[17] Because most people would choose to die at home, free of pain, surrounded by loved ones, this statement implies a conflict between the ideal and the reality.[18] McCorkle has applied this notion to the role of the health-care professional and notes that "the presence of a knowledgeable caregiver is not enough, the caregiver must also be respectful of the dying person's right to choose and have deep respect for the person's choices especially when they differ from his or her own values and goals."[19]

Increasingly, death takes place in a hospital where the dying person is surrounded by sophisticated technological equipment and professionals whose task structures center on curing diseases and routinizing emergencies. Within this organizational context, dying carries with it the "curse" of failure.[20] What is the role of the health-care professional in this situation?

Recent medical literature describes how difficult it is for new, young medical students, interns, and residents to deal with dying patients.[21] Their experiences indicate they must respond to a wide range of situations in dealing with dying patients and families. The difficulty arises when they know the patient and feel they have been a failure if death occurs or if they come in "cold" to pronounce a patient dead and must communicate this knowledge to the family. In addressing these situations, physicians do not want to deny their humanity but need assistance in maintaining perspective.[22,23,24]

Issues of dealing with dying patients are not sufficiently addressed in medical schools and residency programs. The interest of patients and physicians alike are best served when decisions about life and death are made jointly. Medical students and residents need help in learning both attitudes and skills in this area. Medical educators have recommended that these specific topics be included as curricula are revised.[25]

The process of dying can trigger overwhelming emotions not only in the person and family, but also in their professional caregivers. Perhaps as a result of their education and socialization, physicians often feel helpless in the face of devastating illness and are afraid to project hopelessness to their patients.[26] Professional caregivers need assistance in expressing their feelings when the disease does not respond to the treatment. They need to be realistic in their expectations and communicate this to the patient and family and at the same time not abandon the patient in the dying process. Patients need to be related to as human beings and not as diseased entities that have failed treatment.[27]

Nursing publications contain many articles asking questions similar to those in medical journals. "Can a patient die with dignity in an acute care hospital?" and "What is the role of the nurse?" and "Has the nurse's education equipped her for this task?"[28-32] Degner and Gow have shown that nurses who have had classroom and clinical exposure to death-related issues and a required course that included clinical practice have significantly better attitudes toward caring for the dying.[33,34] They and others recommend that such experiences be required for all nurses and would benefit both caregivers and patients.

Acute care hospitals in the United States are generally oriented toward providing aggressive treatment aimed at curing or controlling disease. The reality of dying in the hospital setting may not be addressed in reference to patient or family let alone the professional caregiver. Stresses in dealing with the dying process may be manifested in many ways including:

- Role ambiguity—role expectations are not clearly communicated,
- Role conflict—expectations of various professions are incompatible or are in conflict, and
- Role overload—extent beyond which any person is capable of meeting multiple expectations.[35]

Administrators can reduce the stress by being aware of those needs during staff selection (such as identifying coping mechanisms, exploring unresolved grief, and questioning the presence of social support systems), staff training and orientation (adopting a role model buddy system, and offering continuing education programs) and including as part of the hospital program support systems such as support groups at work, and continuing peer support using formal and informal methods.[36]

The cumulative effect on staff of multiple patients' deaths may lead to emotional depletion and spiritual exhaustion. Attitudinal behavioral and social factors may manifest themselves in expressions of unresolved grief, the need to be perfect, projection of one's own needs, over-seriousness, lack of sharing, inappropriate sharing at home, norms of solemnity, lack of structured opportunities for sharing, and administrative nonresponsiveness.[37] Workshops on death awareness can reduce anxiety about death. Interestingly, it was observed that older nurses or those who had some clinical experience benefited more from these programs.[38]

Administrators can help staff members explore the option of leaving work without this decision being considered an admission of failure. With administrative authority, supervisors can help caregivers who develop serious maladaptive symptoms, by decreasing exposure to stressors by temporary work modification, by removing them from the job situation, and by providing professional support.[39] One of the most important challenges facing administrators today is finding ways to motivate and adequately support front-line staff.

The dying person and family have changed the implications of death in the hospital. The advances of medical technology have raised serious and difficult questions about the delivery or withholding of life support procedures. In the media, almost monthly, are specials that bring to the public such topics as "How doctors decide who shall live, who shall die."[40] The public can read in the Sunday paper that they now have the following freedoms:

- to ask questions
- to see records
- to demand emergency treatment
- to demand politeness, respect
- to say no to X rays, laxatives, excessive examinations
- to ignore advice
- to demand that care continues
- to have most illnesses kept secret
- to refuse medication
- to die.[41]

Yet, when a person is dying, the person and family, upon entering the hospital, relinquish control over the person's course of dying. The attitudes and behavior of staff determine, to a large degree, the social context in which the dying occurs.[42] Open communication among doctor, nursing staff, relatives, and patient is enhanced if all are told of the impending death.[43] Some of the major issues surrounding the dying process may include decisions about continuing aggressive treatment, telling other significant persons of the impending death, settling unfinished business, and discussing place of death.[44] The patient and family can be helped if they know what options are available. Although every patient has the right to full disclosure, he or she also has the right to be treated with compassion and common sense.[45] Although some patients may want to leave all medical decisions to their physician, the doctor's role is not one of paternalism. Patients and families may need encouragement in order to participate fully in the decision-making process and look for a cue from the professional caregiver in this matter.

Legal Influences on Care

Increasingly, the legal system is becoming part of the debate. Cases such as that of Nancy Cruzan will assist in determining the rights of patients' families to influence health-care delivery in certain illness situations.[46] Yet no matter what the courts rule, and despite all the changes in medicine, the place where doctors and patients with families will struggle over the right to die and chance to live will remain rather simple and familiar—the patient's room, doctor's office, solarium, or hallway of the hospital. Family conferences are one of the most powerful tools for assisting patients' families and caregivers with understanding the concerns of all involved. As a forum for educating patients and their families, the conference can furnish reliable, accurate medical information, set realistic and reasonable expectations, clarify health-care choices and provide instructions for treatment and caregiving from the professional caregiver.[47]

There was a candid tale of a mercy killing reported by a young doctor who was called at 3 A.M. to see a patient he did not know, who was dying of ovarian cancer. After he assessed the situation, he proceeded to give her an injection of morphine sulfate, which depressed her respiratory center, and she died. This story might have had a different ending if a family conference had been held earlier with staff who knew her and her family and that palliative care treatment offered a more peaceful experience in living and dying.[48]

One issue that is mandated as part of hospital policy is the wishes of patients and families about resuscitation. Each patient, at the time of admission, is required to indicate their choices if emergency resuscitation becomes necessary. Personnel (admission clerks, medical students, nurses, residents, or attending physicians) who discuss this issue with patients may vary from institution to institution, and may have varied backgrounds, skills, and expertise. The response of the patient is likely to be influenced by the manner in which it is presented and by whom. Patients have expressed the fear that if they sign a Do Not Resuscitate order that medical care will not be as good as if they did not sign. "Maybe the Doctor will not try hard enough." The hospital personnel, who must ask the patient their wishes about resuscitation, must be sensitive to the seriousness of the process and deal with each situation in a personalized and individual way. Examples of different situations might include a woman having a baby, a person having elective surgery, and a patient who is terminally ill. The new mother and the patient who is having elective surgery would probably want resuscitation efforts undertaken. The patient who is terminally ill may perceive that not all care will be given to him, and it may be the first time he was asked about resuscitation status since he became terminally ill. Different emotions can be expected from people in each situation.

Another area of stress for caregivers and families is in the telling that death has occured. Caregivers, no matter their profession, seem to show a strong dislike for the task of delivering such news, referring to the problematic and uncertain nature of each situation. Along with telling of the death may come the responsibility to ask for an autopsy and to request organs for transplantation. Although rare, this is also an uncomfortable part of delivering the bad news because it has to be done immediately after death. The issue of training for death telling would appear to be an important dimension of medical and nursing education.[49]

Implications for Dealing with Death in the Hospital

Because most Americans are dying in an institutional health-care setting, both administrators of these institutions and practitioners would be prepared better to deal with death issues if they had the opportunity to examine and understand a variety of perspectives and responsibilities in this matter. Policies and procedures might then reflect these concerns.

Death can occur in many ways in the hospital, such as sudden death on arriving at the emergency room, terminal illness on a floor for acute care, neonatal death, suicide, and death due to a hospital "mistake." Each of these circumstances is very different and each response will be different, but the common thread is that they all occurred in the hospital and were responded to by hospital personnel. Support is needed in all situations for family members and all too often forgotten for the caregivers themselves. Administrators can address some of these concerns in the following ways.

Selection of Staff

Quenneville reported that no major stress among staff members on a palliative care unit across a twelve-month period was ascribed to the careful selection of staff in combination with effective support sessions.[50] Some departments in the hospital, such as the emergency room, will deal with death more frequently than others. In screening candidates for employment, inquiries should be made about their feelings and experiences of handling situations in which persons are dying, and valuable information may be obtained as to how they have assisted patients and families in these circumstances. This is not to rule out new or inexperienced staff, but to alert them to the realities of the employer's expectations and make them aware that administrators perceive this function as part of their job performance. During the selection process, some inquiries should be made as to recent experiences with death. A person seeking employment in a cardiac unit who has just lost a family member with heart disease may need to be directed to another department during the grief and bereavement period.

Orientation of Staff

Campbell found that when physicians and nurses were compared on their attitudes toward death and terminal care, nurses associated death with tranquility and rebirth and physicians characterized death as cold and alone.[51] Therefore it would seem beneficial to address, during the process of orientation, the attitudes of all staff members on the topic of the dying patient and death. It may be helpful to have current employees share their experiences with new staff since this topic may have been handled only in an academic setting, if at all. Initial clinical experience for new staff members and daily exposure to dying patients can affect staff differently. Price and Murphy have indicated that staff, based on experience and education, may respond in a negative manner to multiple deaths.[52] A session on death awareness may be helpful. The methods covered as part of a death awareness session may vary from Worden and Proctor's Death Awareness Questionnaire[53] to a video or role-playing. This should depend on the needs of the department and the frequency of dealing with dying patients and death. The new staff members need to feel that death is not viewed as a failure of the health-care system, but a natural part of the life cycle. The skill of caring with compassion is needed in caring for all patients but especially when the patient is dying. The caregiver learns that interaction with the dying person can continue to be fruitful by relating as one human being to another.

In-Service Support for Staff

Eddy indicated that health-care professionals seeking to cope with the personal and social problems involved in the care of the dying will be more effective if they are able to reduce their own anxiety in the face of death.[54] Further, Murphy's study using two groups, one experiencing a death awareness workshop while the other did not, measured the effect of the death awareness workshop on the death anxiety of 150 nurses. The result indicated that the workshop did decrease the death anxiety level.[55]

Therefore addressing the topic of the dying person and death would benefit health-care professionals. This may be done on a departmental level, but since the dying patient and death can affect many departments within the institution that have served the same patient, some thought should be given to interdisciplinary in-service sessions. These sessions could focus on having staff share their reactions and feelings about a certain patient or the circumstances of the patient's dying. For departments where death is dealt with on a frequent basis, additional sessions may be useful. Administrators may offer these sessions, but an outside person should lead the session because this will give the formal and informal leaders of the group the opportunity to be full participants instead of putting energy into group process and outcome.

These sessions may include, but are not limited to, covering areas such as exercises in word association, life lines, time lines, Personal Death Awareness Index, and How I Want to Die, with case studies as examples, writing one's own obituary and eulogy.[53] It's also helpful to complete some open-ended sentences such as:

- My experience with death was...
- The reason I am working with this type of patient is...
- A positive experience with a dying patient and family was...
- A negative experience with a dying patient and family was...
- I am affected by my patient's death in the following ways...
- I express these feelings a) at work... b) at home...
- I feel most comfortable working and talking with someone who is dying when I know...
- I wish there were some way that families could be helped to...
- Ways that I can help other staff working with dying patients and families are...
- Ways that others can help me work with dying patients and families are...

The last session could be a memorial service that the staff develops with readings from different religious traditions or meaningful passages from literature. A passage used during a session for AIDS patients was "We cannot judge a biography by its length, by the number of pages in it, we must judge by the richness of the contents...Sometimes the 'unfinished' are the most beautiful symphonies..."[56]

Staff members react differently to each session. During one series, writing the obituary and eulogy were given as a homework assignment. Twelve staff members were participating in the workshop. Only two of these completed the request and returned with the assignment. Some participants stated they had completed the forms but forgotten the papers and one or two said it was too difficult to complete. At this point, new obituary forms were distributed. Allowing some time for completion, staff members were asked to communicate their responses if they felt comfortable. By the end of this session, all staff members had shared their obituaries.

It has proven helpful to have all questions and statements in handouts allowing time for each participant to write his or her response before sharing verbal responses. This gives time for introspection. The leader should fully participate in all exercises to re-enforce the idea that we all have feelings and reactions and need to explore them for ourselves and to benefit patients and families and support other team members. These sessions can help team members confront the facts about themselves and ways to support one another in dealing with the dying process and how it affects the patients and families.

One insight that becomes apparent in these sessions is how beyond education and clinical experience, past experiences and religious traditions can affect behavior. It assists staff in understanding one another's frames of reference when dealing with the dying process.

After the memorial service, a group of night nurses working with persons with AIDS expressed their concern for a number of patients who were alone and have no one to plan a formal memorial service. The night nurses decided to have a tape with some music ("Amazing Grace," "You'll Never Walk Alone") and a few Psalms (Psalm 23, "The Lord is my Shepherd...") ready so they could have a remembrance at the bedside.

By having the service on a tape, it could be played even if only one person could be present and it gave them a feeling of closure for the patient and for themselves. This in no way imposes a religious element to the death, but declares that the patient's life had meaning and needed to be acknowledged in a formal manner.

Peer Support Groups

Administrators should be aware that staff members have death in their personal lives. Through such programs as the Employee Assistance Program, peer group support could be offered to staff during this period. These groups may be open ended or scheduled in a discrete time frame.

Memorial Services and Bereavement Follow-up

Some departments in the hospital, such as AIDS centers and hospice, may have as part of their operations memorial services and bereavement follow-up. These services may be available to all staff as well as families. On a timely basis, the hospital may also have a memorial service for all who have died in the institution and invite families and significant others along with staff to express their feelings about the dead person. This time of remembrance can offer the family the opportunity to meet the staff who had taken care of the patient and express their gratitude for the care and concern that was given during the dying process.

At times, when staff members die, the hospital needs to acknowledge these deaths in a formal manner. This may be done at a formal memorial service or at the department where the person worked. In one hospital, the director of nursing was killed in an auto accident and administrators went to each nursing station to share the news and had follow-up meetings with the staff to encourage them to express their feelings.

During the construction of new facilities, consideration should be given to providing some private areas in the hospital's critical care units that would give patients, family, and staff a quiet place to express their feelings during the dying process and the death. The rooms do not have to be large but should have quiet colors, comfortable furniture, and a telephone. Those areas should be available in times of crisis so that interactions of a serious and emotionally painful nature do not have to be held in hallways or solariums with others present. Consideration should also be given to having staff available who can address these issues. This can be done by the social worker, chaplain, clinical liaison nurse, or administrator who has skills in dealing with situations such as a death in the emergency room, maternity ward, or any area of the hospital.

Conclusions

While biomedical technology in U.S. health care is rapidly changing, psychosocial aspects are similarly changing, although not so rapidly. A more humanistic approach is apparent at the beginning of life, evidenced in the increased numbers of birthing rooms around the nation, and at the end of life, with the continued development of hospice programs. It is becoming clear that individuals are gradually seeking to control more of their own health care. Perhaps the desire for more control over our own lives is a response to a universal threat of death.[57]

Hospitals, though life-affirming, need to address the fact that patients are dying in the acute care setting. Hospital administrators have no choice but to address issues concerning dying, and to create an environment for patient, family, and health-care professionals that will foster mutual support in the process of living and dying.

Notes

1. *The Jerusalem Bible.* (1966). (Ecc 3:1–3.) NY: Doubleday.
2. Allen, W. (1972). *Without feathers,* (p. 106). NY: Warner Books.
3. Allen, C. L. (July 23, 1990). In Medicine, ethics by committee. *Insight in the News,* pp. 52–53.
4. Bowling, A. (1983). The Hospitalization of death: Should more people die at home? *Journal of Medical Ethics, 9*: 158–161.
5. Mor, V., & Jeffrey, W. (1983). Determinants of site of death among hospice cancer patients, *Journal of Health and Social Behavior, 24*: 375–385
6. Thurow, L. C. (June 10, 1988). "Perspectives on health care from the economic viewpoint" presented at the 3rd annual leadership meeting of Allegany Health System, Rochester, NY.
7. Bayer R., Callahan D., Fletcher J., et al. (1983). The care of the terminally ill: Mortality and economics, *N Engl J Med,* 309: 1490–1494.
8. Scitovsky, A. (1989). The high cost of dying: What do the data show? *Milbank Mem Fund Q 62*: 591–608.
9. Callahan, D. (1987). *Setting limits.* NY: Simon & Schuster.
10. Callahan, D. (1990). What kind of life? NY: Simon & Schuster.
11. Benoliel, J. (1988). Health care providers and dying patients, critical issues in terminal care, *Omega, 18*: 341–363.
12. Wald, F. (Feb 1979). Assumptions and Principles, Underlying Standards Work Group on Death and Dying. *Am J Nurs,* 296–297.
13. Wright, K., Dyck, S., (Oct 1984). Expressed concerns of adult cancer patients' family members, *Cancer Nurs,* 371–374.
14. Molter, N. (1979). Needs of relatives of critically ill patients, *Heart and Lung, 8:* 332–339.
15. Hampe, S. K. (Mar April 1975). Needs of the grieving spouse in a hospital setting, *Nurs Res, 24:* 113–120.
16. Hull M. (1989). Family needs and supportive nursing behaviors during terminal cancer: A review, *Onc Nurs For, 16:* 787–792.
17. Weissman, A. D. (1972). *On dying and denying* (p.4). NY: Behavioral Publications.
18. Bowling, Op. cit.
19. McCorkle, R. (1981). A good death, *Cancer Nurs, 4:* 247.
20. Stoller, E. (1980). Effect of experience on nurses' responses to dying and death in hospital setting, *Nurs Res, 29:* 35–39.
21. Dickinson, G. E., (1988). Death education for physcians, *J Med Ethics, 63:* 412.
22. Smith, C. (1989). Learning to deal with death, *JAMA, 262* (21):3073.
23. Morse, D. (1990). When to touch, *JAMA 263* (16):2225.
24. Katz, M. (1988). On not growing accustomed to death, *West J Med,* 149: 488.
25. Wagner, S., et al. (1989). The physicians' responsibility toward hopelessly ill patients, *New Engl J Med, 320* (13): 844–849.
26. Seravalli, E. (1988). The dying patient, the physician, and the fear of death, *New Engl J Med, 319:* 1728–1730.

27. Cassell, E. (1976). *Healer's art*, NY: Lippincott.
28. Trevelyn, J. (1990). A Matter of life and death, *Nurs Times*, *86:* 36–37.
29 Wilson, V. (May 1990). How can we dignify death in the ICU, *Amer Jour Nurs*, *38:* 42.
30. Young, C. (1988). Afraid of death, *Jour of Ped Nurs*, *3:* 295.
31. Read-Sute, D. (July/Aug 1990). A Dream dies, *Amer Jour of Maternal/Child Nursing*, p. 258.
32. Nordberg, M. (1990). When patients die: Handling grief in the dialysis unit, *Dialysis & Transplantation*, *19:* 164–168.
33. Degner, L., & Gow, C. (1988). Evaluation of death education in nursing, *Cancer Nurs*, *11:* 151–159.
34. Degner, L., & Gow, C. (1988). Preparing nurses for care of the dying, *Cancer Nurs*, *11:* 160–169.
35. Vachon, M. (1986). Losses and gains. In McCorkle & Hongladaron (Eds.) *Issues and topics in cancer nursing*, (pp. 41–59). Norwalk, CT: Appleton-Century-Crofts.
36. Vachon, M. (May 1979). Staff stress in care of the terminally ill, *Qual Rev Bulletin*, 13–17.
37. Price, D., & Murphy, P. (1985). Emotional depletion in critical care staff, *Amer Ass of Neuroscience Nurses*, *17* (2): 114–118.
38. Murphy, P. (1986). Reduction in nurses' death anxiety following a death awareness workshop, *Jour of Continuing Ed in Nurs*, *17*(4): 115–118.
39. Vachon, M., Lyall, W., & Freeman I. (1978). Measurement and management of stress in health professionals working with advanced cancer patients, *Death Ed 1:* 365–375.
40. Buckley, J. (Jan 22, 1990). How doctors decide who shall live, who shall die, *U.S. News and World Report*, 50–58.
41. Hunt, M. (March 5, 1989). Patients' rights–body and mind, *The New York Times Magazine*, 55–56.
42. Stoller, E. (1980). Effect of experience on nurses' responses to dying and death in the hospital setting, *Nurs Res*, *29* (1): 35–38.
43. Hinton, J. (1980). Whom do dying patients tell? *Br Med J*, *281:* 1328–1330.
44. Pachow, R., et al. (1989). Attitudes of medical personnel toward informing the terminal patient, *Med and Law*, *8:* 243–248.
45. Jeret, J. (Winter 1989). Discussing dying, *Pharos*, *52:* 15–20.
46. *Cruzan vs Director*, (1990). Missouri Department of Health, 497 U.S.–111 L. Ed. 2d 224, 100s.Ct.: 2841.
47. Streim, J., & Marshall, J. (Nov 1988). The dying elderly patient, *Amer Family Physician*, *38:* 175–183.
48. Young, R. (Jan 8, 1988). It's over, Debbie, *JAMA 259* (2): 272.
49. Clark, R., & LaBeff, E. (1982). Death telling, managing the delivery of bad news, *J Health and Social Behavior*, *22:* 366–380.
50. Quenneville, M. (1982). Evaluation of staff support system in a palliative care unit, *Omega*, *12:* 355–358.
51. Campbell, T. W. (1984). Do death attitudes of nurses and physicans differ?, *Omega*, *14:* 43–49.
52. Price and Murphy, Op. cit., note 37 above.

53. Worden, W., & Proctor J. (1982). *Breaking free of fear to live a better life now*, NJ: Prentice-Hall.
54. Eddy, J., & Wesley, A. (1983). Death education, St. Louis: C. V Mosby.
55. Murphy. Op. cit., note 38 above.
56. Frankl, V. (1950). Man's search for meaning, NY: Simon & Schuster.
57. O'Connor, P. (Summer 1986). Spiritual elements of hospice care, *Hospice Jour*, 2 (2): 99–108.

Five

Dying at Home

Barbara B. Germino

Barbara Germino has had a 30-year career in nursing that includes hospital staff nursing, academic nursing, and assorted unique "Alaskan nursing adventures," such as teaching village health aides, in-service education in a 25-bed hospital, and public education for the village alcoholism treatment program. Her interests in life-threatening illness and death and dying evolved from critical experiences early in her career. Her doctoral training was mentored by Jeanne Quint Benoliel, whose work has inspired her for many years. Her research focuses on individual and family responses to life-threatening illness, initially and over time. She holds the Carol Ann Beerstecher-Blackwell Chair of Thanatology at the School of Nursing, University of North Carolina at Chapel Hill where she teaches an interdisciplinary graduate course in death, dying, and bereavement.

Introduction

In the United States, the place for dying has come nearly full cycle from what occurred before the turn of the century to the present. In the late nineteenth century, death at home was the norm. The first 80+ years of the twentieth century was a period of time when more than 90 percent of dying occurred in hospitals. We have begun to see a change where the place of death is increasingly once again in the home, especially for the elderly, those who have been ill for a long period of time, and those receiving hospice care (McCusker, 1983; Moinpour & Polissar, 1989).

A number of issues influence whether a dying person chooses (or the choice is made by others) to die at home. Some factors have been studied systematically; other influences are inductively derived from related research and reported observations and commentaries. *Health-care system or contextual factors* including health-care costs and efforts toward cost containment as well as third-party reimbursement are environmental factors that seem to influence the place of death for many dying persons (McCusker, 1983; Moinpour & Polissar, 1989). Who, if anyone, makes and communicates a *decision* about the place of death and the *timing of that decision* are factors that may reflect the interaction of environment, person/family, and illness on the probability of dying at home. The *availability, ability, and willingness of family or significant others to care for the dying person* and to commit to being with that person in the face of uncertainties about the future influence individual and family choices about where to live the final period of life. Dying persons' and families' or significant others' *experiences, values, and feelings* would also seem profoundly important in such choices, as would the *availability of supportive and care delivery services* that meet the needs of the person and family at home. The *trajectory of the illness*, in particular the length of illness and the intensity of demands on the ill person and those caring for him or her, may influence the ability of caregivers to persevere in providing care at home. Caregiving certainly takes its toll on physical and mental health. This chapter will discuss each of these influences in an effort to clarify those forces, both environmental and personal, that help to shape the events at the end of life, and in particular, the place of death.

Health-Care Environment

To a very great extent, the structure and functioning of the larger health-care system will influence the probability that an individual who is dying will die at home. There is documentation that home death is associated with the availability of hospice programs and the type of hospice programs (Gray, Macadam, & Boldy, 1987; Greer et al, 1986; Moinpour & Polissar, 1989; Mor & Birnbaum, 1983; Mor & Hiris, 1983 Torrens, 1985). It has also been suggested that system factors such as case mix and federal policies associated with prospective payment and the Medicare hospice benefit may influence not only length of stay in hospitals and hospice but also may affect the place of death (Moinpour & Polissar, 1989). Research indicates that hospice participation is the variable most strongly related to whether or not a cancer patient will die at home, but it is unclear whether hospice care is causally related to home death or if people who prefer to die at home tend to select hospice care (Moinpour & Polissar, 1989). In addition to hospice care, studies indicate that "patients age 85 and older, and those diagnosed close to death are more likely to die at home than would be predicted by age at death, time from diagnosis to death, and hospice alone" (Greer et al., 1986; Moinpour & Polissar, p. 1550).

Decisions and Timing of Decisions

Whether a clear personal decision is made about where the terminally ill person wants to die and whether that decision is communicated to family and professional caregivers are powerful factors in influencing whether the dying person stays at home or returns home if hospitalized at some point. A number of scenarios characterize such decision-making processes in the United States of the 1990s. If self-determination is held as the ideal in our culture, the "ideal" scenario is one in which a person, before ever being identified as terminally ill, formalizes in advance his or her decision to die at home in one or more directives, preferably more. After the identity as a dying person is clarified, if that person is still coherent and able, the decision to die at home may still be made, formally or informally, and communicated to family and professional caregivers. In situations where neither of these scenarios has occurred, where for instance, the dying trajectory is short and the declining person becomes unable to make such a decision, or where the awareness is such that the idea of this decision is not enabled, the opportunity for the dying person to direct his or her final days may be lost.

In a litigious society struggling with conflicts between secular and traditional Judeo–Christian values, if a dying person does not make a clear decision and communicate it, decisions about the course of dying as well as the place of death may be made as often by institutions and physicians as by those closest to the person who is terminally ill. Ethical dilemmas have become legal battlegrounds, as evidenced by the Cruzan and other "cases" and the legal precedents being set.

Caregivers' Experiences, Values, and Feelings

The dying person's and family's values, experiences, and feelings about the past as well as the current illness all help to shape the choice of dying at home or elsewhere. For many dying persons and their families, the benefits of being cared for at home outweigh those of being in an institution. These include privacy and control and active family participation in care, which may be part of the separation process and extremely important to the outcome of bereavement for survivors (Bohnet, 1986; Craven Wald, 1979). Wanting to be at home during the dying process does not preclude wanting the place of death to be elsewhere. Consider Woody, a 52-year-old man with esophageal cancer who, after a year of multiple hospitalizations and treatment regimes, chose to go home for the time remaining. He wanted his wife and daughters, sister and brother, nieces and nephews, and cousins to be around often. His favorite activity, when he was feeling up to it, was reminiscing and telling stories with his large extended family. He spent his days and nights on a large sofa in the living room, and those close to him would come and go, talking and laughing with him until he fell asleep. Home was special to Woody and that's where he wanted to be dying. However, in an effort to protect his daughters and his wife, he asked that, when it was clear there were only a few days left in his life, they take him to the hospital to die so that memories of him dead would not destroy the joy of home to his surviving family. He and his family were able to carry out his plan and his wife and daughters, a year later, dwell on his life and living rather than on his death.

For other families, giving care to a dying member may be precluded by fears, poor health, limited energy, inability to assume an open-ended responsibility, other family and work demands, or by family relationship issues. If the family caregivers are elderly or in poor health, they may be willing but unable or fearful of being able to care for a dying member, even though they might wish to do so. Lack of confidence in ability to handle the demands of care may be a factor as well.

Unresolved family relationship issues may be exacerbated by the knowledge that a family member is terminally ill and may influence the choice of dying at home. An adult child who might be the only family caregiver may never have developed an adult relationship with the dying parent; both family members may be aware on some level of that unresolved struggle and may choose to resolve their unfinished business through the process of caregiving or to leave it unaddressed. The dying person's and family's choice of where to die may reflect, at least in part, the dynamics of family relationships.

Patient and family value systems are another factor in the complex equation that represents the possibility of dying at home. In some families and in some subcultures, not having a person who is dying in a hospital where "everything, the best of everything, can be done, right up until the last" is less than what is considered the best care. For others, not caring for one's own goes counter to what is most important and strongly held. In the traditional Appalachian Mountain white subculture, for instance, hospice workers may have to struggle to convince people and their families to accept their services before a crisis occurs or symptoms are out of control. The response that "we care for our own" is a common one and calls for understanding of values that include suspicion of outsiders and rejects their intrusion into the home.

Finally, consideration must be given to the patient's and family's attempts to find some meaning in the dying and in their participation in that process. The anticipation of loss of the dying person to the family and to each family member is part of the struggle to find meaning. Much of what occurs for families either in the decision to care or continue to care for a dying person at home is a reflection of that family's relationships in the past. Krant's (1974) chapter on families of the dying describes eloquently the dynamics of both mature and ambivalent relationships and how these relationships continue to be reflected during the dying process. He notes that one key to the problem of continued and ongoing living and the resolution of grieving is the manner and meaning of the dying. Although these do not alleviate the pain of loss, there are far greater problems when family conflicts and tensions characterize a family member's dying, and the strains characteristic of such situations can lead to serious problems for surviving family members. The decision to care for a family member at home and the likelihood that family members can persevere in this decision if the dying is particularly difficult or prolonged is likely to be influenced by the nature of family relationships and the meaning of caregiving during the dying process.

Availability and Fit of Support Services

For the person without family and without a significant other willing to support the person's choice to die at home, the choices may not include dying at home unless their personal resources including third-party reimbursement are extraordinary, or unless health-care resources can be obtained and coordinated in a continuing manner. Hospices providing home-care services have often required that there be a primary caregiver in the home and other agencies have tended to be hesitant to provide care to those living alone once they reach a point where constant care and/or monitoring is required. In such situations, especially since hospitalization is no longer always an option, the dying person, if resources are available, may end up in a nursing home to live out his or her final days. That may not be a satisfactory solution for the dying person or for those attempting to provide that person services at home, but may be the only option that fits the need of constant observation and care.

Even where family members and significant others are available and willing to provide care at home, those persons often need services that may or may not be available. Specifically, research has indicated that family members often need education related to home-care management skills, in particular related to helping patients move from bed to chair and ambulate safely, and related to comfort care and symptom management (Grobe et al., 1981; Kirschling, 1986). Other services for which family members commonly feel the need include in-home medical monitoring, assistive equipment, transportation, personal care, household upkeep and chores, financial assistance or counseling, and respite care (Grobe, Ahmann, & Ilstrup, 1982).

Services required may or may not be available, depending on where the dying person and family live. In many rural areas of the United States, for instance, the availability of such educative and support services is extremely limited, if available at all. The fit of a person's and family's wishes for care at home, and the supportive services that might make that possible may be very poor. Options that do tend to be available, such as nursing home care (often at a distance), may create problems such as isolation of the dying person from the family; the demands of adjusting to a new environment at a time when energy to meet such demands is very limited; transportation problems and costs; and the difficulty of dealing with feelings of disappointment and guilt that personal and family goals could not be achieved.

Trajectory of the Illness

In a classic and often quoted study, Glaser and Strauss (1968) introduced the concept of dying trajectory—the length, course, shape, and pattern of the final portion of a dying person's life as well as the work it requires both of the dying person and of those caring for that person. They observed that patients and professionals may have very different perceptions of trajectories and that different types of trajectories create different kinds of work and different kinds of problems for those involved.

As difficult as sudden, unexpected death may be, the slow lingering process of dying may be most distressing in our culture because "dying is the inexorable and visible eradication of culturally stated personal meanings and concepts" (Krant, 1974, 340). A prolonged and difficult dying trajectory, with death at an uncertain future time, and with loss of bodily functions, loss of independence, and loss of the ability to do things that are important to the dying person, is difficult for many dying persons to accept and for many families to manage as well. Many dying persons fear becoming a burden to those they love, losing their ability to care for themselves and having to depend more on others (Krant, 1974). In his poignant discussion of dying and dignity, Krant (1974) notes that for many, dying is a series of losses of body functions, control over one's life, feelings of self-esteem, and loved and important aspects of life. Such losses bring suffering and may alter individual behavior in ways that cause family and others to withdraw because of the pain of their own losses. Prolonged and difficult dying at home may have the further effect of isolating the family caregivers as well as the patient from vital interaction with others and the support drawn from such relationships. Lack of support and the physical and emotional demands of caregiving endanger the health and well-being of even young and healthy family members. Family caregivers who have health problems and whose age may predispose them to health problems are at particular risk. Morbidity and mortality rates for widows and widowers have been known to be higher within the year following the spouse's death. Examinations of morbidity and mortality rates for other family caregivers in relation to the demands of caregiving and to resources for assistance and support are badly needed.

In contrast, the work of the most difficult and demanding of dying trajectories may in fact be buffered by the opportunity for the dying person to be cared for at home. With the opportunity for continuing contact with a caring professional or team of professionals and access to support and respite services, the difficulties arising in a prolonged dying trajectory may be anticipated, acknowledged, and addressed. Central to dying at home as an advantage, whatever the dying trajectory, is the opportunity for personalized care and the sense of being in control of one's living while dying.

Summary

It is clear from even a brief examination of factors that may influence the opportunity, quality, and outcomes of dying at home that while each focuses our attention on particular issues, all are part of the context for dying and interact with one another to shape the decisions and experiences related to the place for dying. Social and health-care system factors may place powerful constraints on choices about where to be cared for while dying. The availability of specific kinds of information and services fitted to the needs of the person and family cannot be assumed and may be the most significant factor in situations where services are very limited. The dying person's family's personal experiences, meanings, and personal resources for facing this situation are crucial, as is the unfolding of the dying trajectory. The choice of a place to be cared for while dying is one of a set of final important choices that may help bring meaning to a life nearing its end.

References

Glaser, B. G., & Strauss, A. L. (1968). *Time for dying*. Chicago: Aldine.

Greer, D. S., Mor, V., Morris, J. N., Sherwood, S., Kidder, D., Birnbaum, H. (1986). An alternative in terminal care: Results of the National Hospice Study. *Journal of Chronic Diseases 39* (9), 9–26.

Grobe, M. E., Ahmann, D. L., & Ilstrup, D. M. (1982). Needs assessment for advanced cancer patients and their families. *Oncology Nursing Forum 9* (4), 26–30.

Grobe, M. E. , Ilstrup, D. M., & Ahmann, D. L. (1981). Skills needed by family members to maintain the care of an advanced cancer patient. *Cancer Nursing 4* (5), 371–375.

Kirschling, J. M. (1986). The experience of terminal illness on adult family members. In B. M. Petrosino (Ed.). *Nursing in hospice and terminal care: Research and practice.* New York: Haworth Press.

Krant, M. J. (1974). *Dying and dignity: The meaning and control of a personal death.* Springfield, IL: Charles C. Thomas.

McCusker, J. (1983). Where cancer patients die: An epidemiologic study. *Public Health Reports 98* (2), 170–175.

Moinpour, C. M., & Polissar, L. (1989). Factors affecting place of death of hospice and non-hospice cancer patients. *American Journal Of Public Health 79* (11), 1549–1551.

Mor, V., & Birnbaum, H. (1983). Data watch. Medicare legislation for hospice care: Implications of National Hospice Study data. *Health Affairs 2,* 80–90.

Torrens, P. R. (1985). Hospice care: What have we learned? *Annual Review of Public Health 6,* 65–83.

Six

A New Decade for Hospice

Inge Baer Corless

Inge Baer Corless, a graduate of the Bellevue School of Nursing in New York City, attended Hunter College and graduated from Boston University with a bachelor's degree in nursing, the University of Rhode Island with a master's degree in sociology, and from Brown University with a Ph.D. in sociology. As a Robert Wood Johnson Clinical Scholar, Dr. Corless did postdoctoral study at the University of California, San Francisco. She has held academic positions at Russell Sage College, the University of Michigan, the University of North Carolina, Chapel Hill, as well as her current position at the MGH Institute of Health Professions at the Massachusetts General Hospital. Dr. Corless served as program director of St. Peter's Hospice in Albany, New York, and as a short-term consultant for WHO at the Western Pacific Regional office. A Fellow of the American Academy of Nursing, Dr. Corless has written on hospice and HIV disease and is co-editor with Mary Pittman-Lindeman of AIDS: Principles, Practices and Politics, *and with James T. Corless is co-author of* Theresa Iola and Patricia Irene.

Introduction

The modern hospice movement arose when the concern that something more *should* be done for terminally ill persons was transformed into the conviction that something more *could* be done. Supporters of the movement perceived that fragmented isolated activities might be organized into coordinated comprehensive care provided by an interdisciplinary team whose focus was the patient and the family (Lack, 1977). Crucial to this transformation have been the work of Dame Cecily Saunders and Dr. Elisabeth Kübler-Ross, the former in symptom management and spiritual care and the latter in the psychosocial sphere (Saunders, 1960, 1979; Kübler-Ross, 1969). Saunders in particular, with her clinically oriented studies, has led the movement of science in the service of terminal illness care. Thus the choice became not one of cure versus care, nor of care devoid of scientific underpinnings, but a recognition of the current limitations of scientifically based cure and an emphasis on scientifically based care (Twycross, 1983; Melzack, et al., 1976).

In addition, a model of care based on episodic illness was perceived to be inadequate for the multifaceted requirements of those dying after a lengthy chronic illness. Although many similarities exist between acute intensive care and chronic care, notably the need for coordination, those who are terminally ill following a chronic illness such as cancer also have distinctive needs (Corless, 1982).

The choice to participate in hospice care has become an option for those who have access to a program for which they meet the admissions criteria. Not every terminally ill person has such access, however, even though a publication by the National Hospice Organization (1991, p. 3) states: "If you receive Medicare benefits, you're entitled to hospice care." Furthermore, even if a program is geographically accessible, an individual may not be deemed eligible by the hospice program. The conundrum of entitlement—access and eligibility—is explored in this chapter, which examines some of the questions currently facing hospice and palliative care programs in the United States.

Background

The rapid development of hospice and palliative care programs in the United States as well as throughout different countries of the world has occurred, for the most part, in the last two decades. Hospice has been described as a concept of care, a program of care, and a place for care (Corless, 1984). As a concept of care, hospice was inextricably bound to the activities of the death awareness movement (Feifel, 1959). Changing attitudes legitimizing death and dying as a subject for scholarly inquiry have brought into sharp relief the contrast between dying in a hospital enshrouded in technology and dying at home surrounded by those one loves (Feifel, 1994). Hospice as a concept of care provides a mechanism to span the chasm of the modern and traditional visions of dying. In particular hospice espouses: choice with regard to the place of one's dying; attention to the comfort of the individual; a consideration of spiritual, social, and psychological concerns, as well as the physiological and functional manifestations of the disease process; a focus on the family as well as on the patient; an emphasis on dying, death, and the bereavement that follows; the provision of interdisciplinary care (not simply the attention of professionals from multiple disciplines); and the implementation of coordinated care across care settings.

These attributes are incorporated into hospice as a program of care. Wald (1994) describes the foundational steps that led to the program of care in the United States known as the Connecticut Hospice. The history of this period has been depicted by Mount (1976), Stoddard (1978), Foster, Wald, and Wald (1978), Lack and Buckingham (1978), Osterweis and Champagne (1979), Davidson (1978), Walter (1979), Hillier (1983), Corless (1983b, 1983c, 1985), Cohen (1979), and Saunders (1978, 1986).

Hospice as a program of care is not setting bound and may be independent or affiliated with another organization such as a hospital or home-care agency. Care is provided to individuals in the home, hospital, or extended care facility. Hospice as a place for care is *the* place for care and is setting oriented, whether as a freestanding structure or as part of another facility.

Beyond such conceptualizations, however, most definitions of *hospice* fail to capture the sense of mission of what has taken on many of the attributes of a social reform movement in health care. As with the early days of any such movement, there were moments of excess. The passion for hospice began in a decade marked with hopes for social reform and racial equality, the elimination of poverty, the despair over the assassination of political leaders and protracted civil and military conflict. The hope for societal transformation yielded to the denial of a generation torn between choices of Viet Nam or Canada and a reifying of the choice between cure and care. The battle cry of the foot soldiers of the hospice movement—"we care"—was hurled against the stalwarts of cure-oriented therapy, thus dichotomizing approaches that should be complementary rather than alternative. The movement also needlessly impugned the motives of many health-care practitioners, creating enmity toward hospice.

The hospice movement, in striving to change approaches to care of the dying, was itself changed when efforts to secure reimbursement for care emphasized the potential for cost savings. However, this attempt to secure a firmer financial foundation for hospice programs was made at the cost of limiting the mandate of hospice to those with the resources to remain at home. More significant, the price of becoming part of the system was to lose the charismatic elements of a social movement and become tamed, albeit legitimized, by the system. The hospice movement was co-opted by the federal establishment. The cost of such bureaucratization was to limit access to hospice to those who might have been sustained at home by traditional home-care agencies (Corless, 1984; Rhymes, 1990).

Traditional home-care compensation is provided on a per-visit basis with reimbursement limited to "skilled" nursing care (including teaching and assessment), physician's visits, and other prescribed and circumscribed modalities such as physical therapy. Psychosocial concerns and other nonphysically oriented care and support are not reimbursable in traditional home care. Proposed hospice funding, on the other hand, provided reimbursement on a capitation basis incorporating such levels of care as routine home care, continuous home care, inpatient respite care, and general inpatient care. The importance of capitation from a federal standpoint was as a means of controlling the costs of care. From a hospice perspective, the new approach to funding provided reimbursement for the aspects of terminal illness care not captured by traditional home-care funding mechanisms, aspects such as psychosocial visits, family care, medications, and out-of-pocket expenses. However, the boon of stability of funding was purchased at a cost of restricted access to care (Corless, 1983a). McCann (1988) notes: "Without national support of a definition of hospice care which goes beyond the parameters of reimbursement and addresses access to quality care for patients and families, we fail to support the right of any patient in America to have equitable access to hospice services and high quality care."

A Question of Access

McCann's statement addresses the heart of the argument about hospice, that is, the right of any citizen to have access to hospice care. The structure of the Medicare hospice benefit assumes that a lay caregiver will be present for the recipient of the hospice benefit. The reimbursement schedule was originally calculated on that assumption (Corless, 1985). It is amazing, therefore, that the hospice benefit has not been challenged successfully in the courts as being discriminatory to terminally ill individuals without the requisite caregiver. This argument has been propounded previously, notably that "single persons, those with a partner in frail health, or individuals from a family where there are multiple problems all are disenfranchised" (Corless, 1987–1988).

Access is also of paramount concern to hospices across the United States (Corless, 1990). However, is the access being contemplated one of access by individuals representing a greater spectrum of society, or is it access by more of the individuals and families who meet the characteristics congenial to the Medicare model? Saunders and McCorkle (1985) observe rightly that families are partners in the provision of care. Unless a family assessment and family plan of care are developed, it is arguable whether the family is part of the unit of care prior to bereavement (Saunders, 1993). Families facilitate care in the home, which is why individuals without such support may not receive hospice care.

If access implies attracting individuals with the requisite support structure, then the question of access is one of advertising. The Medicare message to the disenfranchised (those without a caregiver) is that they are not eligible for a premium product. The difference in access is between a system designed for the care of the terminally ill that is the standard of care and one whose resources have been preempted for lack of an alternative and that is standard care.

The question of access for minorities and other underserved populations is in part one of marketing when individuals with social support are sought as the potential recipients of care (Harper, 1990). Clearly, however, access involves more than marketing. It involves sensitivity to the cultural values of potential recipients of care (Beresford, 1990a), and it involves care provided with respect and concern for the lives of those affected. It is culturally sensitive, and better yet, it is humanly sensitive. It is what hospice care purports to be.

Access for minorities and all underserved populations is limited further by a benefit structured to ensure care at home. Inpatient care, in the Medicare hospice benefit, serves as a back-up and not as an alternative to home care. Beresford (1989, p. 12) speaks to this distinction: "Residential hospice care should be differentiated from inpatient hospice care which is intended primarily for the short-term acute medical needs of hospice patients or for brief periods of respite for exhausted family members." Residential care, a new setting inspired largely by the AIDS (Acquired Immune Deficiency Syndrome) epidemic, was the missing setting for which inpatient care was substituted in New York City's hospitals, in an effort to maintain access to hospice care for diverse populations (Corless, 1987–1988). Although the hospice benefit's financing is viable for serving the needs of the "haves," it is inadequate for the provision of service to the "have-nots." Furthermore, regulatory constraints placed on hospice programs that sought to serve their clients by providing inpatient care to individuals in the last stages of their lives were such that these programs (largely urban and institutionally based) no longer could call themselves hospices. As a result, their clients could not avail themselves of the hospice benefit and were restricted to the provision of care as outlined in traditional reimbursement mechanisms. And although nonreimbursed care could be provided by hospice or palliative-care programs, financial supplementation from other sources was required for a program to continue its services. Does the Health Care Financing Administration (HCFA) have a responsibility to either revise its regulations or provide federal dispensation so as to make hospice benefits available to all Medicare recipients?

Access also involves outreach. Stoddard (1990, p. 30) pleas for attention to the ghettos in the United States, stating that it is there that "hospice international outreach ought to begin. This is where the hospice concept is most desperately needed today with its attitudes, its skills, and its extraordinary power to rebuild fractured communities." She suggests placing demonstration hospice teams in storefronts or abandoned warehouses in New York and Los Angeles, bringing hospice to those in need of such care. Whether such individuals could be maintained at home or not, the presence of hospice teams near their clients would enhance outreach programs and access to care. A similar suggestion of course is not needed for Canada, Great Britain, and other nations that provide universal access to health care. In these nations questions of access have been replaced by questions regarding the rapidity with which access is obtained and restrictions related to age and condition.

Hospice programs in rural areas incur the costs of travel over great distances (Beresford, 1990b). The economies of aggregating clients in an easily negotiated area, usually within thirty minutes of the hospice program, are lost when clients are located at significant distances from one another and from the hospice office. Without the presence of a hospice program, however distant, the individual is deprived of access to the hospice benefit. Hospice programs that provide such access at a cost to their own financial probity recently have received special consideration by funding agencies. To the degree that federal or state regulations inhibit access to hospice programs, these regulations subvert the congressional mandate of legislation designed to enhance such access. As Congressman Leon Panetta stated (1981, p. 8542) in introducing hospice legislation: "The legislation that will be before the Congress is a beginning, a good solid beginning.... We can make the hospice story a reality—a fulfillment of the moral test of a nation dedicated to serving those in need. That is our bond. That is our pledge. That is our commitment. "

Access to Hospice Care for Those with AIDS

The strictures of hospice reimbursement also have had an impact on access to services for those infected with the human immunodeficiency virus (HIV) (Shietinger, 1986). Such limitations could have been predicted given the assumption of the presence of a caregiver by the regulations and the problematic availability of such an individual for the HIV-infected person. The resultant financial considerations may not be as significant as other factors in the failure to assume responsibility for the care of terminally ill persons with AIDS. Some hospice programs have failed to provide care as a result of fear related to the infectiousness of the disease, concern about stigma, and prejudice against those infected with HIV. All of these factors have been noted in the responses of other health-care providers (van Servellen, Lewis, & Leake, 1988, p. 6–8). A hospice program's financial concerns, however, can serve as a convenient screen to shield exploration of the real reasons for failure to provide care to HIV-infected persons.

Prejudice against HIV-infected individuals related to their lifestyles, whether sexual orientation or substance use, may result in inadequate and inappropriate care. If not explored prior to caregiving, it also may lead to consternation, if not chaos, among the caregivers. An expectation that a hospice program has a responsibility to provide care to HIV-infected persons, though laudatory, is not complete in itself. Caregivers need the opportunity to explore their fears and anxieties if they are to provide services to individuals who can benefit from hospice care. Informed discussion is recommended as well for the family members and friends of hospice care providers. Professionals have reported pressure by family members not to provide care to AIDS patients. In one instance a physician threatened to break his engagement to his fiancée, a nurse, if she provided such care. Although such an example is unusual, the concerns it demonstrates are expressed commonly and need to be addressed if the fears of caregivers and their loved ones are to be allayed.

Support also is required by the informal caregivers of terminally ill AIDS patients. Such support is all the more important given that the usual support from family, friends, and neighbors may not be available due either to prejudice against persons with AIDS or to an absence of support caused by a lack of knowledge of the gravity of the situation. The latter may occur as families attempt to protect themselves from stigmatization by not informing others of the severe problem facing them (Raveis & Siegel, 1991). Support also is needed when employed caregivers attempt to provide care and maintain an active occupational role (Pearlin, Semple, & Turner, 1989). Although legislation has facilitated leavetaking, some individuals may not abe able to avail themselves of such leave to care for a chronically or terminally ill partner or family member. Such individuals face the stress of work, the work of caring for a sick person, the loss of rest, and the stress of anticipated loss.

Lay caregivers and health-care workers also need instruction in infection control, safe disposal of contaminated sharp instruments and needles, and appropriate precautions for dealing with blood and other body fluids.

To be holistic, concern for the health-care worker requires attention to health-endangering practices in off-duty time; such practices include substance abuse and sexual behaviors in which the transmission of sexually transmitted diseases, including HIV, is likely. Although certain activities related to substance abuse may result in the loss of license to practice as a professional, other activities that may be perceived as stress reducing are in reality potentially illness producing. Invasion of privacy is a false issue when a colleague's health and life are at stake.

Health promotion for and by hospice professionals means a knowledge of condoms, their virtues and their defects. Frank and open discussion of sexuality and sexual practices are important for clients who have not resolved these matters previously. Prudery about examination of clients' sexual practices is not an appropriate professional attitude. The health-care worker whose personal predilections inhibit talking with a client may wish to seek the counsel or collaboration of a colleague so as to address sexual matters adequately,

Though not all hospice programs readily accept clients with AIDS, not all failure to do so is a result of prejudice. The illness trajectories of the person with cancer and the person with AIDS are different, with the latter requiring the use of acute care facilities to treat opportunistic infections as appropriate. Different trajectories may entail an increase in financial commitments. Such differences also involve modifications in caregiving (Brenner, Dennis, & Kaufer, 1990).

Persons living with AIDS have been reluctant to avail themselves of hospice care feeling that it implies "giving up." Brenner et al. (1990, p. 9) note that community health-care providers must be educated "to understand that the referral to hospice is not a surrender of hope and a giving up to the disease, but an empowerment which addresses the complex issue of how to live qualitatively and meaningfully in the terminal stage of disease. " This statement is valid for persons experiencing the terminal stages of any disease. Hope to live until a special event transpires, or hope for each day, is important for all engaged in hospice care. Hope is part of the spiritual environment for hospice care.

A Question of Spiritual Care

The hospice approach purports to encompass the physical, psychological, social, and spiritual needs of the patient. Saunders (1986), Wald (1986), and others have expressed concern that the spiritual aspects of care have been neglected. This neglect is not surprising given the perception by many caregivers that the spiritual concerns of a patient more properly belong to the patient and his or her religious counsellors. Publication of the *Assumptions and Principles of Spiritual Care for the Terminally Ill* provides a new and different perspective (Corless, et al., 1990, p. 80): "Caregivers should be aware that they each have the potential for providing spiritual care, as do all human beings, and should be encouraged to offer spiritual care to dying patients and their families as needed." The obvious danger is that an overzealous caregiver will attempt to impose his or her religious precepts or beliefs on a patient. The authors of *Assumptions and Principles of Spiritual Care* considered this possibility and state in Principle 18: "Caregivers should guard against proselytizing for particular types of beliefs and practices." (p. 79)

Spiritual care is important not only for patients and families but also for caregivers (Ley & Corless, 1988). A spiritual environment is an important resource for health-care workers confronted on a continual basis with the deaths of patients. Staff sessions with a psychiatrist, no matter how empathic, locate the difficulty within the individual rather than as a characteristic of a stressful situation in which much is demanded of the professional. That is not to say that work with a psychiatrist may not be beneficial. It is however to situate the problem in the caregiving environment.

Spirituality adds a dimension to life that connects an individual to a sphere beyond himself or herself. An environment that allows for spiritual expression changes the way in which interactions occur to one of greater acceptance of the other, regardless of individual beliefs. In such an environment, the loss of another can be acknowledged, and in so doing an individual's life is affirmed (Corless, 1986). Finding hospice professionals to be more spiritual in their personal lives than in their work, Millison and Dudley (1990, p. 76) speculate: "Perhaps there are deterrents or obstacles within hospice programs that prevent professionals from freely expressing their spirituality with patients."

Precepts regarding separation of church and state may have influenced hospice workers in subtle ways to maintain a distinction between work and spirituality. Equating religion with spirituality may compound the difficulties. Spirituality may also be perceived as solely a personal attribute rather than as a component of the environment.

Although hospice programs profess to provide spiritual care, the substance of such care may be illusory. Noting a patient's religious practice on an intake sheet is not equivalent to providing spiritual care; nor is the presence of a chaplain as a member of the team, although each may contribute to a positive outcome. Spiritual care implies integration not separation. Spiritual care is not the work of any one individual. It is the culmination of the efforts of all involved in hospice care to provide an environment where reflection on life and death and other issues is encouraged.

Saunders, as noted previously, was a pioneer in her insistence on both effective symptom control and the presence of a religio-spiritual environment at St. Christopher's Hospice. The incorporation of the arts at the Connecticut Hospice as described by Bailey (1994) is a secular expression of some of these same felt needs. The challenge of integrating the *sacred* with the scientific, though acknowledged to be important, may be viewed as secondary to the more pragmatic issues of hospice survival in an increasingly financially constricted environment, or may be denied in a highly technological curative atmosphere. Foster and Davidson, in chapter eighteen of this book, write about their despair that the latter is still commonplace in some health-care facilities. Thus spiritual care may be neglected because it is not seen to fit into the paradigm of cure-oriented patient care. Spiritual care also may be neglected because the press of financial concerns may be perceived as meaning the "life or death" of the hospice program.

A Question of Finances

Even though the reimbursement rates for the four levels of hospice care (home care, continuous home care, respite care, inpatient care) have been increased by the federal govemment, the imposition of budgetary control, including the question of whether particular modes of care will be reimbursed, has introduced additional constraints (Corless, 1990). Decisions by hospice care providers are being countermanded by third-party intermediaries who determine the appropriateness of care and the level of reimbursement for a given patient. Clearly, hospice teams are free to provide the care that is deemed appropriate. Reimbursement, however, is determined by the fiscal intermediary. This situation seems incongruous given the "cap" of dollars (for the total number of patients) already in place in order to curb governmental expenditures for hospice patients.

The problem of finances encompasses still other issues including those of "outliers," the need for acute inpatient care or continuous home care, and the responsibility of hospice programs for medications. Outliers are patients who use a disproportionate share of resources. Often this occurs as a result of a longer than expected stay in the program. Such individuals may skew the calculations (and expenses) particularly of small hospice programs, which by nature of their size do not possess the resilience to provide a counterweight to the intensive or extensive user of resources. Recognition of the outlier problem has resulted in modifications to compensate hospice programs more adequately.

The need for acute care or the provision of continuous care at home are decisions made by hospice care providers which, unless adequately documented, may be open to rejection by the fiscal intermediary. Such determinations are similar to those made in traditional home care in which the need for the service must be documented painstakingly if fee-for-service reimbursement is to occur. It was thought initially that per-diem rates would obviate the need for creative writing exercises in patient charts. Unfortunately, such is not the case.

Responsibility for the provision of medications and treatments has been a potentially explosive issue ever since palliative radiation, chemo-therapy, surgery, and other palliative procedures have become the financial responsibility of the hospice program. Developments such as total parenteral nutrition (TPN), a method of providing nutritional sustenance via a surgically implanted tube, are now being incorporated into the care of persons at home. Such approaches may require careful monitoring, as for example with TPN, to prevent metabolic intolerance (Newman & Capozza, 1991). The cost of one day of TPN at approximately $300 exceeds the hospice home-care per-diem rate.

Drugs such as Retrovir (Zidovudine) formerly called AZT (azidothymidine), ddI (2', 3'-dideoxyinosine), and ddC (2', 3'-dideoxycytidine) also might be considered palliative for persons living with AIDS, given that the underlying disease is not cured. Will hospice programs be financially responsible for these medications for their terminally ill AIDS patients? If so, will the costs of caregiving exceed reimbursement, particularly for geographic areas with high numbers of persons living with AIDS? Or will hospice teams determine that chemotherapy or radiation are not necessary, basing this decision on financial considerations or constraints rather than on palliative potential? And given the intensity of the psychosocial and physical needs of many persons living with AIDS (Clark, 1991), can hospice programs committed to caring for terminally ill AIDS patients survive as programs of care? It may be more to the point to ask whether society can afford to have these programs not survive.

A Question of Innovation

Innovative approaches to the provision of hospice care have entailed establishment of satellite hospice centers or teams to provide care to people living in large geographic areas, hospice arrangements with nursing homes, and mega-hospice programs such as Hospice Care, Inc. (HCI), which operates "comprehensive inpatient and home-care hospices in Boston, Chicago, Dallas, Fort Lauderdale, Fort Worth, Houston, and Miami" (HCI, 1990, p. 1). The key to the success of HCI is, in part, expert and centralized management. In addition to other economies, HCI participates in an electronic media claims (EMC) hook-up between HCI and Medicare. The result is a "cost turnaround of less *[sic]* than 30 days from date of service" (HCI, 1990, p. 6). Delays in reimbursement can spell financial gloom if not doom for hospice programs. And many programs with less electronic sophistication experience such delays.

Expansion of services to nursing homes by a hospice team whose members work with the patient, family, and nursing home staff is reflective of the model of hospice as a consultation team whose members go to the patient wherever he or she is located. The consultative approach was exemplified first by the Palliative Care Team at the Royal Victoria Hospital in Montreal, and by the Hospice of Marin in California. Such a model, particularly when the collaboration is with a nursing home or group home, obviates the concern about a caregiver. A study by Swan and Benjamin (1990) of AIDS patients in various stages of their disease notes that the average AIDS patient requires six and one-half hours per day of nursing time in a nursing home. A Vancouver hospital team reported a required nursing time of greater than eight hours for AIDS patients who were terminally ill (McLeod, Smith, & Willoughby, 1986). Such demands on nurses' time may require facilities to increase their staff to provide appropriate care. Any arrangements to provide care to HIV-infected patients at whatever stage of disease will need to address this issue, among others.

Hospice care may become available to a greater number of individuals when society and discrete communities solve the question of the financing of residential care for debilitated individuals who lack the necessary supports to remain at home, whether such care is given in a group home, by a host family, in a nursing home, or some other type of residence for care. Such innovative solutions will enhance access to hospice care, one of the major issues confronting hospice providers. Finances may undergird what is seen largely as an ethical issue involving a question of choice.

A Question of Choice

Hospice as a holistic concept of care providing attention to the physical, psychological, social, and spiritual needs of a patient has been perceived by its adherents as a countervailing force to those espousing the "right to die." Nevertheless, concerns about technology without restraint and well-known cases, such as those posed by Karen Anne Quinlan and Nancy Cruzan, have resulted in a continuing interest in living wills, the right to die, and euthanasia (Annas, 1990). Although Qvarnstrom addresses euthanasia in chapter ten of this book, it seems appropriate to raise some questions here regarding the right to die and hospice.

The goals of hospice care concern enhancing the quality of life of patients and their families. The usual methodology is to control troublesome symptoms and allow the person to live until he or she dies. But what of the small residual of patients for whom symptoms cannot be managed adequately? Is it part of the hospice mandate that they live in suffering until they die? Are there instances in which suffering continues unabated despite the best efforts of all concerned? Do some team members abandon these hospice treatment failures?

And what of the individuals who find themselves in such circumstances? What are their rights? What are their options? If hospice is concerned with giving clients control as Tuohey (1988) states, what are the parameters of such control? The very notion of "giving control," a notion applied to "patients" in a variety of settings, implies an inequity of power (Corless, 1991). The terms *patient* and *giving control* require further examination.

The term *client* implies a greater parity among the parties in the relationship than does the term *patient*, with its historic denotation of a dependent relationship in which the roles are superordinate and subordinate. Perhaps the time has come for a consideration of the implications of such labeling. *Giving control* usually refers to such things as choice of foods, when to engage in morning ablutions, or whether to engage in "social" activities. Patients, however, already have exhibited *choice*, if not *control*, by selecting hospice as a caregiving option. But the term *giving control* has an uncomfortable connotation. Perhaps it is a result of the aforementioned inequity of power implied between caregiver and care recipient and the ability of one party in the relationship to determine if and when control is to be shared.

A more congenial term is *choice*, not as in giving someone a choice, but as in choice inherent in the individual. Under such circumstances the expectation is one of the hospice client making choices about all aspects of his or her care. Not all persons will welcome the opportunities of such a model, but that too would be the client's choice rather than one that is imposed. Clients would determine the degree to which decision making is shared rather than automatically being the recipients of professional decision making.

The obvious question that follows such deliberations is, does choice include whether to maintain or relinquish life? Note that questions of *sustaining* life are those of caregivers. The question addressed here is, does the individual have the right to determine when to die? Care must be taken not to phrase this question as one of a determination of when an individual has suffered enough. Phrased in this manner, the issue becomes one of "earning" the right to make a choice.

If hospice programs presume to *give* clients control, should that control be limited to the trivial or does it concern reinforcing an individual's right to make choices regarding living and dying? Although the hope for adequate symptom control will be for a life fully lived, what approaches will be used when those hopes are not fulfilled and the patient concludes that enough is enough? The current discussions of living wills in acute-care facilities also apply to hospice programs. Specifications about not suffering may result in drug dosages that reduce the level of consciousness when suffering cannot otherwise be alleviated (Wanzer, Federman, Adelstein, Cassel, Cassem, et al., 1989).

Choices about life and death should not entail activities contrary to health-care workers' commitments to preserving life (Singer, & Siegler, 1990), nor should they entail actions that create liability for criminal prosecution—that is, a patient's right to choice does not include asking the care provider to engage in actions for which the provider may be penalized. Unassisted self-termination may be possible in a minority of cases. What if those individuals wishing to bring their lives to a close are too weak to implement their wishes? Further discussion of this issue is pursued by Churchill in chapter twenty-four of this book. It is clear, however, that hospice programs will need to reconsider issues in light of changing case law, state statutes, and values about living and dying.

Hospice: An Answer

The concept of hospice emboldened by the imperative that something more should be done for the dying person was created when something more could be done. Although much of the foregoing discussion concerns issues currently facing hospice programs, this chapter would not be complete without some reflections on the contribution of hospice to the death awareness movement.

Hospice programs have dramatized the potential for remaining at home to die, thereby taking dying out of the institutional closet. By once again anastomosing dying with living, the dying are no longer outcasts relegated to life on a back ward. The recognition by hospice leaders of this "back ward" approach as well as the changes that have ensued, have created new possibilities for how dying and death are perceived in our society. This is no mean accomplishment. Knowing that choices exist with regard to the manner of death from a chronic illness is liberating, whether one lives in the inner city or a rural area, and whatever the individual's race or style of living. To the extent that hospice care enhances the quality of living until death—no matter what the individual's self or cultural identity or living condition—to that extent will hospice have realized the vision of its founders. The choice is now ours. It is a new decade for hospice. Will access to hospice care be restricted or will it be available to all who wish it? The ultimate contribution of hospice to how living and dying are viewed in our society may be to facilitate a greater appreciation for living as the humane possibilities for dying are actualized.

References

Annas, G. (1990). Nancy Cruzan and the right to die. *New England Journal of Medicine, 323*, 670–673.

Bailey, S. (1994). Creativity and the close of life. In I. Corless, B. Germino, & M. Pittman (Eds.), *Dying, death, and bereavement: Theoretical prespectives and other ways of knowing* (pp. 327–335). Boston: Jones & Bartlett.

Beresford, L. (1989). Alternative, outpatient settings of care for people with AIDS. *Quality Review Bulletin, 15*, 9–16.

Beresford, L. (1990a). Creative approaches to minority outreach. *NHO Hospice News, 10*(3), 6, 11–12.

Beresford, L. (1990b). Hospice leader Jack Lee advises small rural hospices on issues of growth. *NHO Hospice News, 10*(9), 4–5.

Brenner, P. R., Dennis, J., & Kaufer, D. (1990). Admitting HIV patients: A distinct challenge for hospice. *Hospice, Spring*, 8–9.

Clark, J. (1991). HIV nursing management in the home health setting. *Journal of Home Health Care Practice, 3*, 1–16.

Cohen, K. P. (1979). *Hospice prescription for terminal care.* Germantown, MD: Aspen Systems.

Corless, I. B. (1982). Physicians and nurses: Roles and responsibilities in caring for the critically ill patient. *Law, Medicine, and Health, 10*, 72–76.

Corless, I. B. (1983a). A response to the evaluation of the NYS Hospice Demonstration Project. *Journal of the New York State Nurses Association, 14*, 6–9.

Corless, I. B. (1983b). Models of hospice care. In Chaska (Ed.), *The nursing profession: A time to speak* (pp. 540–550). New York: McGraw-Hill.

Corless, I. B. (1983c). The hospice movement in North America. In C. Corr & D. Corr (Eds.), *Hospice care principles and practice* (pp. 335–351). New York: Springer.

Corless, I. B. (1984). Hospice: The state of the art. *Proceedings of the Fourth National Conference on Cancer Nursing, 1983.* New York: American Cancer Society, 29–35.

Corless, I. B. (1985). Implications of the new hospice legislation and the accompanying regulations. *Nursing Clinics of North America, 20*, 281–298.

Corless, I. B. (1986). Spirituality for whom? In F., Wald (Ed.), *In quest of the spiritual component of care for the terminally ill* (pp. 87–96). New Haven: Yale University.

Corless, I. B. (1987–1988). Settings for terminal care. *Omega, 18*, 319–340.

Corless, I. B. (1990). The death, dying and hospice movement: The past and the coming decade (keynote address). *Tenth Annual Interdisciplinary Seminar Ten and Then.* Albany, New York State Hospice Association.

Corless, I. B. (1991). Review of Tuohey, caring for persons with AIDS and cancer: Ethical reflections in palliative care for the terminally ill. Toronto: *Journal of Palliative Care, 7*, 1.

Corless, I. B., Wald, F., Autton, N., Bailey, S., Cosh, R., et al. (1990). Assumptions and principles of spiritual care, developed by the Spiritual Work Group of the International Work Group on Death, Dying and Bereavement. *Death Studies, 14*, 75–81.

Davidson, G. W. (1978). *The hospice—development and administration.* Washington, DC: Hemisphere.

Feifel, H. (Ed.) (1959). *The meaning of death*. New York: McGraw-Hill.

Feifel, H. (1994). Attitudes toward death: A personal perspective. In I. Corless, B. Germino, & M. Pittman (Eds.), *Dying, death, and bereavement: Theoretical perspectives and other ways of knowing* (pp. 49–60). Boston: Jones & Bartlett.

Foster, Z., Wald, F. S., & Wald, H. J. (1978). The hospice movement: A backward glance of its first two decades. *The New Physician, 27*, 21–24.

HCI (1990). *Introducing Hospice Care, Incorporated*, to Dr. Inge B. Corless. Document.

Harper, B. C. (1990). Doing the right thing. *Hospice, Spring*, 14–15.

Hillier, R. (1983). Terminal care in the United Kingdom. In C. Corr & D. Corr (Eds.), *Hospice care: Principles and practice* (pp. 319–334). New York: Springer.

Kübler-Ross, E. (1969). *On death and dying*. New York: McMillan.

Lack, S. A. (1977). The hospice concept–the adult with advanced cancer. In *Proceedings of the American Cancer Society Second National Conference on Human Values and Cancer*. Chicago: American Cancer Society, 160–166.

Lack, S. A.,& Buckingham, R. W., III (1978). *First American hospice*. New Haven: Hospice, Inc.

Ley, D. C. H., & Corless, I. B. (1988). Spirituality and hospice care. *Death Studies, 12*, 101–110.

McCann, B. A. (1988). Hospice care in the United States: The struggle for definition and survival. *Journal of Palliative Care, 4*, 16–18.

McLeod, N. A., Smith, J., & Willoughby, B. (1986). Hospice care of AIDS patients. *Journal of Palliative Care, 2*, 1.

Melzack, R., Ofiesh, J. G., & Mount, B. M. (1976). The Brompton mixture: Effects on pain in cancer patients. *Canadian Medical Association Journal, 115*, 125–128.

Millison, M. B., & Dudley, J. R. (1990). The importance of spirituality in hospice work: A study of hospice professionals. *The Hospice Journal, 6*, 63–78.

Mount, B. M. (1976). *Palliative care service: October 1976 report*. Montreal: Royal Victoria Hospital/McGill University.

National Hospice Organization (1991). *About hospice under Medicare*. South Deerfield, MA: Channing L. Bete.

Newman, C. F., & Capozza, C. M. (1991). Home nutrition support in HIV disease. *Journal of Home Health Care Practice, 3*, 25–51.

Osterweis, M., & Champagne, D. S. (1979). The U.S. hospice movement: Issues in development. *American Journal of Public Health, 69*, 492–496.

Panetta, L. E. (1981). Presentation for National Hospice Organization, November 12, 1981. St. Louis, MO. Published in the *Congressional Record-House* (November 18, 1981) #8541–8542.

Pearlin, L., Semple. S. J., & Turner, H. (1989). The stress of AIDS caregiving: A preliminary overview of the issues. In I. Corless & M. Pittman-Lindeman

(Eds.), *AIDS: Principles practices and politics* (pp. 279–289). New York: Hemisphere.

Raveis, V. H., & Siegel, K. (1991). The impact of care giving on informal or familial caregivers. *AIDS Patient Care, February,* 39–43.

Rhymes, J. (1990). Hospice care in America. *JAMA, 264,* 369–372.

Saunders, C. M. (1960). *Care of the dying,* London: MacMillan.

Saunders, C. M. (1978). The evolution of the hospices. In R. Mann (Ed.), *The history of the management of pain: From early principles to present practice* (pp. 167–178). Carneforth, Lancashire: Parthenon.

Saunders, C. M. (1979). The nature and management of terminal pain and the hospice concept. In J. J. Bonica & V. Ventafridda (Eds.), *Advances in pain research and therapy* (pp. 635–651). New York: Raven.

Saunders, C. M. (1986). The modern hospice. In F. Wald (Ed.), *In quest of the spiritual component of care for the terminally ill* (pp. 41–48). New Haven: Yale University.

Saunders, J. M. (1993). Personal communication.

Saunders, J. M., & McCorkle, R. (1985). Models of care for persons with progressive cancer. *Nursing Clinics of North America, 20,* 365–377.

Shietinger, H. (1986). Hospice care needs of the person with AIDS. *Journal of Palliative Care, 2,* 31–32.

Singer, P. A., & Siegler, M. (1990). Euthanasia: A critique. *New England Journal of Medicine, 322,* 1881–1883.

Stoddard, S. (1978). *The hospice movement.* New York: Stein & Day.

Stoddard, S. (1990). Hospice: Approaching the 21st century. *The American Journal of Hospice and Palliative Care.* 7, 27 30.

Swan, J. H., & Benjamin, A. E. (1990). Nursing costs of skilled nursing facility care for AIDS patients. *AIDS and Public Policy Journal, 5,* 64–67.

Tuohey, J. F. (1988). *Caring for persons with AIDS and cancer: Ethical reflections on palliative care for the terminally ill.* St. Louis, MO: Catholic Health Association of the United States.

Twycross, R. G. (1983). Principles and practices of pain relief in terminal cancer. In C. Corr & D. Corr (Eds.), *Hospice care: Principles and practice* (pp. 55–72). New York: Springer.

van Servellen, G. M., Lewis, C. E., & Leake, B. (1988). Nurses' responses to the AIDS crisis: Implication for continuing education programs. *Journal of Continuing Education in Nursing, 19,* 6–8.

Wald, F. (1986). In search of the spiritual component of hospice care. In F. Wald (Ed.), *In quest of the spiritual component of care for the terminally ill.* (pp. 25–33). New Haven: Yale University.

Wald, F. (1994). Finding a way to give hospice care. In Corless, B. Germino, & M. Pittman (Eds.), *Dying, death and bereavement: Theoretical perspectives and other ways of knowing* (pp. 31–47). Boston: Jones & Bartlett.

Walter, N. T. (1979). *Hospice pilot project report.* Haywood, CA: Kaiser-Permanente Medical Center.

Wanzer, S. H., Federman, D. D., Adelstein, S. J., Cassel, C. K., Cassem, E. H., Cranford, R. E., Hook, E. W., Lo, B., Moertel, C. G., Safar, P., Stone, A., & van Erye, J. (1989). The physician's responsibility toward hopelessly ill patients: A second look. *New England Journal of Medicine, 320,* 844–849.

Seven

Stories of the Living-Dying: The Hermes Listener

Paula G. Balber

Paula G. Balber received a master's degree in psychiatric nursing in 1970 from New York University. Since that time, she has counseled both individuals and families in outpatient and inpatient clinical settings in psychiatry and oncology. She was clinical director of Triangle Hospice in Durham, North Carolina, for four years. Ms. Balber has lectured extensively on family dynamics and individual issues involved with cancer, chronic illness, and death and dying. She has published on care of the dying in Prevention and Treatment of Complications in Oncology for Physicians, *edited by John Laszco. The verbatim story material in this chapter comes from a two-part videotape project she directed, "Telling Times: Stories of the Living-Dying," funded by the North Carolina Humanities Council.*

Well, I was born in...I was born March 6, 1909 at that same...on that same night, there was a little white girl which my mother had worked there in the kitchen. They lived in the house and my daddy run the gin. This old man had a gin and his daughter was born on the same night I was. And, of course, her mother didn't have any milk at all and she asked the doctor and the doctor asked my mother...so they told me...her brother told me, if it hadn't been for my mother, his sister would have died. And I've heard her say, and I've heard so many people say...and of course she did that and this little girl, I seen her, I seen her myself as we grew up and we played together in the yard.
Brian S., 79 years old, one month before death

Stories are accounts. They are chronicles, descriptions, statements, narratives. Throughout our lives, particularly as we journey through transitions, we tell stories, if only to ourselves, about the experiences that form and shape us. As each of us becomes aware that our known life is

This manuscript was prepared with the editorial assistance of Steven Levine, Ph.D.

ending, the need to tell stories, "narrative hunger," named by Reynolds Price (Churchill 1988), often becomes more compelling as we face the transition to death. During this time in particular, people tell stories about their lives—past, present, and future—to family and friends, and to the health-care professionals who work with them. For the listener, personal stories, like that told by Mr. S., evoke powerful images of the "self" of the storyteller and his formative experiences, and in a profound way, reveal the familial, historical, cultural, and religious/spiritual forces that shaped that individual's life and how he approaches death. For a professional working with the living-dying—those with illnesses in which death is certain (Pattison 1967)— it is a privilege and responsibility to hear the stories of a person's life. They are a source of psychic education for the listener and teller both, and a means to enhance the quality of the life of the teller (patient) and the family.

This chapter focuses on people whose stories are stimulated by the knowledge of certain death. The population described was dying from cancer or AIDS. The words of the storytellers you read here are verbatim accounts unless otherwise noted. We will examine the personal stories of several people in the context of the living-dying process as it is traditionally conceived and as it can be framed within the universal story of the "Hero's Adventure," the monomyth of the archetypal journey to a renewed, transcendent self (Campbell 1968). This chapter also focuses on ways to facilitate the telling of the stories, to understand the possible meanings of the material for that individual, and to incorporate this information in working therapeutically with those who are living-dying and their families.

To begin, we will review briefly some cultural, familial, and intrapersonal aspects of living-dying.

> When I was in Vietnam, I was a fighter pilot; one day, we were on our third mission into the jungle and my best buddy was navigator. Suddenly, out of nowhere a rocket blew up the back end of my plane; I was on fire when I parachuted out of the burning plane and was rescued by some other guys, Americans. I had third-degree burns over half my body and was in the hospital for months…my buddy…was blown to Hell.
> (paraphrase) James R., 35 years old, immediately after being told he had weeks to live

Advances in medical technology and shifts in medical ethos mean that most people are told these days when they have a fatal illness. Knowledge that an illness will end in death catapults people and their families into a state in which the world is no longer familiar. Once they are told that they are facing temporal dissolution, people become aware that both their bodies and the reactions of those around them seem unpredictable and may remain unpredictable. For some, like James R., this information, abruptly delivered, exploded a carefully reconstructed life, blowing buried trauma up to the surface, and serving as a harbinger of things to come. For others, the sentence may be shocking, but not surprising, because they have experienced ongoing illness and increasing debilitation. In any case, for all, their lives are never quite the same; each becomes the living-dying, a marginal being.

In our culture, the sense of an isolated, marginal state of the living-dying is quite pronounced. As a society, we are so intent on progressing, achieving, and acquiring, that the dying who are only "being" and yielding have little place; indeed, many of us fear or feel helpless in the face of this inevitable state. From members of the medical establishment who regard them as treatment failures, to younger relatives who may despair the loss and know that with this death a "buffer" against their own deaths disappears, we encourage the dying to fight and hold on, and we support the ongoing lack of awareness that death is approaching. In addition, because so much of the dying takes place unattended in hospital rooms (May 1988), when we are dying we are deprived of a known path and role models to guide us through this experience. Thus an important form of psychic education as well as support is lost not only to those now dying but to all of us who will eventually face the same experience. This lack of education impoverishes us and renders us all more vulnerable to greater distress.

In a number of other cultures, however, by virtue of tradition or historical events, death is held in the individual and community consciousness long before the event, and preparation for it is an important task both for individuals and the community. For example, in Mayan Indian culture, death is a phenomenon for which one carefully prepares, in one way, by living with the coffin to get to know it; in addition, chosen members of the community are gathered around to hear recommendations for future behavior (Price 1988). In Ireland, elderly villagers look for premonitions that death is coming and pray that God will grant them a "'holy death,' a slow, gradual, even painful death, one that is met head on: alert, awake, aware, and with full faculties of sense and reason" (Scheper-Hughes 1983). Lifton (1976a) describes Hiroshima survivors, although isolated within the larger society, as having an acute awareness that death is within them, the sense of a permanent encounter with death.

Most Americans, by contrast, live their adult lives in the realm of awareness of "middle knowledge," first described by Avery Weissman and elaborated by Lifton "where we both *know* that we will die and resist and fail to act upon that knowledge" (Lifton 1976b). Even if people are aging and have already acknowledged that death is nearing in reverie, reminiscence, and in the preparations for disposing of belongings including their bodies, middle knowledge often prevails, in part because of our society's traditional response.

In addition, for most people, even when death is welcome, the disruption of the familiar (both internally and externally), the perception and treatment by others that demonstrate we are no longer "ourselves," and the threat of all the unknowns, provokes a rise in anxiety and fear, both for patients and families. Shneidman (1978) describes this as a dire situation in which the person will behave as he has in response to previous experiences of threat or failure. Loss (past, present, and future) and grief permeate this phase as well. Depression occurs in 20-50 percent of cancer patients (Goldberg 1988). Along with depression, fear, and anxiety, patients and families experience other psychic distress. Guilt and shame predominate when people believe that it is their behavior that has caused the disease, when they have many regrets about the past, or when they feel responsible for burdening their families financially, and for causing the reprioritizing of family time and the expenditure of physical and emotional energy necessary to meet their needs (Lewis, et al. 1986; Lewis, 1989; Welch-McCaffrey 1988). Some also experience guilt for abandoning family members who are dependent on them. In addition, anger, frustration, and exhaustion are equal partners for patient and family, as they all struggle with the "being" that no longer performs, health-care providers who may not take into account unique needs and requirements, and a world that moves along without consideration for them and their experience.

> We start dying the moment we are born. Death is woven into life and grows lives toward its own death and from the death of things it outgrows. But one day death in the real sense approaches. It means growing through and beyond this literal dying—the ultimate growing beyond self. (Durckheim 1990, p. 5)

Living-dying, unquestionably, is one of the most difficult stages that people and their families must endure, even if death per se is welcome. There are, however, other dimensions to the experience. These dimensions may be empowering for those dying and educational for people with whom they are involved. Many people seem to "live up" to the experience, rather than just accommodate to it or be destroyed by it, some to encompass and endure it, others to grow with and beyond it. They seem to acquire a recurring and thus enduring sense of grace (moral strength) and honor (personal dignity) in the ongoing process of yielding to death. In looking for clues as to how this evolves, one can review the literature that describes how people cope and who copes well, delimit the factors that offer support, detail what it is that helps to give meaning to the experience; it is valuable information, and this chapter will do some of that. However, there is a somewhat intangible, transcendent connectedness that threads the experience, surfaces periodically, and lends itself to the acquisition of attributes necessary for enduring and growing beyond pain of dying. This connectedness may be embodied even in those who disaffirm a personal spiritual/religious belief and sometimes occurs in those one would never expect to be able to move beyond lifestyle and personal problems. It is inherently present in many acts of creativity, but it is especially evident in the metaphors of myth and literature.

Since in this chapter we use myth to approach the transcendent relatedness, to encompass the spiritual/religious realm, and to frame the personal stories, it is important to define what we mean by *myth*. Many believe (especially pre-Joseph Campbell) that myth means tale, as in untruth, apocrypha. In fact, it is defined as "the expressions of the unobservable realities in terms of observable phenomena" (Leach 1967). "Mythology is poetry, metaphorical. It has been well said that mythology is the penultimate truth, penultimate because the ultimate cannot be put into words. Mythology pitches the mind beyond that rim to what can be known but cannot be told" (Campbell 1988, p. 163). "The aim of myths and symbols was to reach man's higher centers, transmit to him ideas inaccessible to the intellect and to transmit them in such forms as would exclude the possibility of false interpretations" (Ouspensky 1989, p. 4). Myths provide guiding images about ways to perceive the universe and order our experiences within it, often without our conscious knowledge of the ways they affect us. Because they aid us to move beyond every day and ordinary constructions, because they connect us to the ubiquitous mystery, myths are particularly prominent in times of momentous personal transition, such as in the living-dying process, when familiar ways of being and perceiving no longer exist, and what lies ahead is part of the mystery.

There lived an old priest-magician Hunnoes who had identical twin sons, Mo and Ho. According to custom, his elder son should succeed him; but which was the elder? 'To whichever brings back the Bitter-Rose, I shall hand on the great knowledge.' Mo climbed Mount Cloudy to search for this flower of discernment which retreats at the first hint of fear and is like 'looking for night in broad daylight.' Striking a rock with his hammer to place a screw ring, he accidentally kills a hollow man who lives in rock made of emptiness and who eats the void and drinks empty words. The next day they find Mo's empty clothes; he has been killed in revenge by the hollow men. Hunnoes tells Ho that he must kill his now-hollow brother; 'then Mo will live among us again.' Despite his bursting heart, Ho finds and strikes his brother's head and enters his body. With Mo's memories within him, now transformed,

Moho finds and retrieves the Bitter-Rose, and Hunnoes was able to leave the world peacefully, having passed on the great knowledge. (Daumal 1986, pp. 75–78, summary)

At the mythologic level, several (May 1988, among others) describe this liminal stage of living-dying as a kind of hero's adventure based in large part on the description of Joseph Campbell. He speaks of the "basic motif of the universal hero's journey—leaving one condition and finding the source of life to bring you forth into a richer or mature condition" (Campbell 1988, p. 163). Daumal's myth of the fractured soul bespeaks the rigor of this spiritual journey, which ends/begins in the birth of the transcendent being who can surpass surface dualities, and who commands great wisdom. By necessity, the first step in any hero's journey is the leavetaking of the familiar (Campbell 1968). For the living-dying, the call to leave the comfortable world comes from the messenger-physician who reveals the diagnosis and prognosis. It is then, or soon after, according to myth, that the hero encounters a protective figure, one who is a willing helper at critical times, a symbol of trust and guardianship, the conductor of the soul to the afterworld, a role such as Hermes, the Divine Herald, enacted in Greek mythology (Hamilton 1942). For the dying, this figure might be health-care professional, clergy, or one who in previous days was simply friend or family; in any case, the guardian is a wise being who lures the hero to the threshold and aids in the crossing, the second step of the journey. This step involves battling the hollow men, the powerful defenders of inscribed values and personal limitations that keep us from knowing important truths about our living and dying and about that which supports transcendence. The barrier is formidable, but must be overcome in order to reach the next stage of the journey, according to Campbell, the descent into confusion, fear, and grief-filled darkness.

The darkness may be seen as the unconscious (Campbell, 1968) and/or as the result of ongoing destruction of previously held internal and external guiding images. For the dying, the darkness is evoked by the trials of illness, the overwhelming losses and role transitions, by the unbidden eruption of pain-laden past events, and frightened projections onto an unknowable future. Finally, however, successful people come to terms with the darkness through transformation of consciousness and are held in the enfolding arms of a greater wisdom. This brings with it a tolerable sense of choosing death (Callan 1989), some measure of peace with the past and one's inevitable identity, and a sense of relative ease about what lies ahead.

One way many living-dying people traverse the necessary path of this journey, open to illuminating revelation, and gain new grace, integrity, and transcendence is by weaving personal stories, personal myths.

Influenced by hopes and wishes for the future, people interpret and symbolize moments of the past in order to serve present needs and to allay fears (Goodman, 1981; Hulbert, 1988; Molinari, 1984). These stories become the substance of "life review," a term designated by Butler (1963) and later described as "an attempt to come to terms with old guilt, conflicts and defeats, and to find meaning in one's accomplishments" (Lo Gerfo 1980, p. 42). People create these narratives about the present, especially about their illness experience and its impact; they compose stories about the future and what it holds. People search inward for stories of past, present, and future, but also reach outward to others, both past and present, to provide validating and affirming myth and accounts to guide the way. Personal, familial, cultural, and universal myth and symbol, history, and tradition inform each narrative. These personal myths and stories are cloaked in a myriad of forms, each unique to the individual and each bearing careful attending, but whether they are narrative of past, present, or future, they serve a number of more generalized functions. The functions of the narratives can be delimited as four: (1) to cope with the illness and its sequelae of fear, grief, and loss, (2) to chart and verify meaning in life, (3) to ensure the continuity of the self and valued images for the individual and those left behind, and (4) to mark a path through the darkness to transcendence, to renewed life. In their completeness and complexity, narratives may serve a number of functions at once; however, affirming the connectedness with the transcendent often forms the leitmotif throughout the stories of those who are living-dying.

Given the above, it is clear that listening well to stories is a complex and fertile encounter. As a health-care professional, if one listens and responds to story, one becomes part of the narrative. To listen with skill is to assume some part of the role of the willing helper, protective guardian, the "Hermes listener." This is the model described in death and dying literature as well as in myth, as the one who provides "safe conduct" (Benoliel 1985). If one wishes to help the traveler surmount the boundaries and mark a path through the darkness, rather than enact the polar opposite (to guard the surface boundaries and halt the journey), there is a necessary therapeutic framework within which to enact one's role. First, it is important to join in the journey with constancy, and without abandoning it, until the point at which people must proceed alone. One's professional work should be undergirded by the belief that the patient (and family) is the primary expert in understanding his or her needs, in evaluating the responses to intervention, and in making informed decisions about the care.

The structure is also supported by an attitude that embraces the Rogerian attributes of attentiveness, acceptance, and empathy, yet this framework is only an outward manifestation and is powered by a mythic force. The force that lies beneath and beyond is the silence within, "the primal silence in the tumult," (Durckheim 1989, p. 7) "the stillpoint...calm and strength in the face of threat...(proceeding from the belief) that one's internal and external environments are predictable and there is a high probability that things will work out as well as can reasonably be expected" (Jevne 1987, p. 1). From this stillpoint comes the energy to sustain concentrated, unbiased attention such that the observer disappears and enters wholly into the experience of being with the living-dying, moment by moment. This stance in particular, when encouraging and responding to story, "elicits unbidden insights and direction..." (and within which one becomes) "attentive simultaneously to multiple layers, the message beneath words, the histories behind events, the language of gesture and stance, as well as the subtle selectivity that must follow, combining the intuitive and the conscious" (Hejmadi 1990, pp. 70, 73). In the focused process of attending, one's skills in the therapeutic use of story may be applied with apt timing for the psychological moment.

In addition, if one assumes that the stories one hears will be enlightening for both teller and listener, and the prevailing attitude is one of receiving as well as giving, then listening and responding, de facto, become an act of genuinely enhancing a vulnerable self. Further, if one honors story as part of the unique journey of an individual and family, the style in which it is told is valuable in and of itself. The process of the telling with its dips backward and forward, in the end, provides much of the coherence and the meaning of the material to the individual and the therapeutic listener. Reifying story into a rigid, structured series of psychological episodes that one must do in order to have a good dying does violence to the narrator and to the coherence and meaning of the story. Finally, one must be aware in listening to story that it is "our own stories which give shape to what we hear...about the way we look at lives, which matters we choose to emphasize, which details we considered important, the imagery we use as we made our interpretations" (Coles 1989, p. 18).

One may ask many traditional questions to stimulate stories that evoke meaning from past, present, and future, such as, "What was your childhood like?" "Tell me about your family." "What did you do for a living?" "What do you think will happen next?" However, Doris Betts, a short story writer and teacher, suggests other, creative means to stimulate "that shiny trail of words like a snail would leave, all silver." She suggests such questions as, "Do you have any objects that you cannot throw away?" "What were your lucky breaks?" "Where were your life's turning points?" "What is your favorite memory?" "How was your life different from what you expected?" "In what family members do you recognize yourself?" "What would you like to have done instead of the work that you chose?" "How have you coped with the deaths of ones you've loved?" (Betts 1988). These questions are some that open the door to deepening and enriching accounts.

> Actually, lately, it's been pretty good...for the last couple of days. Last week, though, I was having real bad diarrhea and I had to wear diapers and little panty shields to protect my clothes. I'm real conscious of how I look... I wear shorts a lot; the only thing is with the shields, when I walk, I can hear the plastic kind of crinkle. It's real embarrassing, so I wear them only when I have on jeans, but then it makes me look like I have a big rear end.... For the last 6 months I've had mouth problems...it's the thrush, and something is eating little holes in the back of the palate of my mouth. It's gotten to the point where I brush my teeth with Novocain.
> *Michael M., 24 years old, diagnosed with AIDS*

As health-care professionals, more often than not we are told explanatory accounts of illness. These accounts initiate the journey and the relationship, and occur throughout. Indeed, they frequently form the majority of the stories of the present. They serve the first function of narrative, to cope with the illness and its sequelae. As such, they demand careful attention. To many health-care professionals who are told these accounts, it is tempting to remain within the folds of prescriptive response to the stories of the difficulties of the present. Yet in the Hermes relationship, one responds to them first as creations of meaningful narrative to which one attends to bear witness as well as to respond with prescriptions for intervention and care. If as witness and then caregiver, one does attend to the entirety of accounts such as Michael's, they will provide entree to a number of the explicitly difficult issues of living-dying: changes in body image; concerns about sexuality; the effect of loss of potency and self-control. By absorbing the whole and the flow, one can gain appreciation of the depth and power of the illness and its unique meaning to each individual. However, the Hermes listener also seeks to move the relationship beyond pain-filled accounts of physical and emotional difficulty, to narratives that evoke more implicit, deeper meaning and to stories of past and future. It is important to do so, for one reason, because these stories of other parts of the narrator's life and the exploration of deeper meanings of the present put the illness in perspective as part of a continuum, as only one segment of a larger whole. Thus the recent past and present, replete with suffering, does not remain imprinted as the entirety of a life, either for the patient or the family (Lewis 1989).

> We waited up for nights to see where the fire would blow next. The fire...it took all the woods behind my house...my neighbor's house

burned down...It was amazing, it skipped around; you couldn't predict where it was going to burn next. I got out there, made sure we put a barrier around the lawn; I was out all the time with the fire doing what I could...watching...We weren't sure we would have a house standing until the fire burned out...It was horrifying. Those days, they seemed like they lasted forever.

(paraphrase) David L., with a known prognosis of only a few months to live

If we return briefly to the monomyth of the hero's journey, the first step for the living-dying is the vault from the realm of the ordinary triggered by the news of impending death. Both David L. and James R. spontaneously reacted to the peripherally accepted news by employing the common metaphor of fire from which they both escaped, damaged, but alive. This metaphor powerfully captures the experience of hearing the news, and requires the careful attention of the Hermes listener. It bridges the connection with the mystery and it bespeaks the overwhelming force and unpredictability one feels when enveloped in it. In the eternal language of symbols, fire represents transformation by destruction, purification, and regeneration. It is the seed from which each successive life is reproduced (Cirlot 1962). It represents the beginning and the end of the journey, and helps mark the path to be traveled (the fourth function of narrative), looking at the entirety of the journey, not just its beginning.

Fire also represents a desire to annihilate time (Circlot 1962). When embarked on the journey and connected to the mystery, people often describe time as out of joint and at a standstill. Both ways of experiencing time represent the reality and the desire (for time to be at a standstill) of many of the living-dying for whom time, from the moment of being told, no longer marches evenly but instead lurches between timeless, everlasting seconds and foreshortened days (Feigenberg & Shneidman 1979). This alteration of time sense helps impel the crossing of the boundary into the darkness.

These stories, whether of fire or of other elements, also serve to support the narrator by providing some measure of control in response to the overwhelming stress of illness and its sequelae. Storytelling offers the kind of control or coping that involves self-regulation rather than behavior to alter external conditions. Active coping for the dying is often impossible because much is beyond their control (Shneidman 1978). For many, from the moment of being told or allowing in the awareness that he or she will die, the sense of days following one another in regular rhythm is destroyed. Telling stories, particularly such stories as these in which fire annihilates time, is an act that controls, in this case time, by "keeping the past available through memory and conquering the future in advance by anticipation" (Hulbert 1988, p. 297). It also provides a safe way to discharge the painful emotions, which are the constant companions of the illness journey, without endangering important social relations. In addition, while it is true that many avenues of active coping are closed to those living-dying, the stories can remind the narrator of active coping skills used in the past ("I was out all the time doing what I could") which are still feasible. Finally, these allegorical accounts provide a way of soliciting the listener to affirm that the narrator handled events as well as possible. A part of terminal illness is the responsive feeling of failure and lack of self-confidence; stories like David L.'s seek in fact, to validate, "I did the right thing," a theme commonly embedded in illness accounts (Price 1987).

When responding to stories such as these, it is often useful to remain within the metaphor, to highlight the coping skills still useful, and to reinforce the sense of control they offer to the individual, without necessarily taking note of the connection with the illness directly. Paradoxically, then, the therapeutic effect often can be achieved when the listener identifies with the narrator in experiencing the horrors of the fire and the feelings of awe it evokes, and without either of them ever directly mentioning that these same feelings are engendered by the illness and sequelae.

The most memorable example of this type of coping and response occurred with a black policeman dying of multiple myeloma. Almost devoid of emotion, he would recount very brief illness stories and say little else about himself. However, one could always locate how far he had progressed in his journey and determine just how he was feeling from his constant, vibrant stories about how he had integrated the upper echelons of the police department of this small southern city. In these symbolic accounts he related how he had dealt with authority, how he had bested a foe, how he had dealt with the ongoing stress of hostile undercurrents, and finally, how he had made alliances with old enemies, and had achieved a peace in his department. His somewhat unidimensional, metaphor-dependent style of coping reminds us that the capacity to cope openly with difficulty varies with each person, and that our ways of remembering and coping tend to run in grooves; we have a certain repertoire (Castelnuovo-Tedesco 1980). By allowing and encouraging his narratives (which were, in fact, enlightening), by focusing on the emotion they engendered, and by highlighting the coping skills he used to succeed in his department (which involved a great deal of self-regulation), he was able to maintain control throughout his illness, discharge his painful feelings, and achieve some sense of a journey complete. Most people, however, are not like this policeman. If one validates their feelings and their unique methods of coping within the symbolic experiences, it frees them to become more direct as needed. This, in turn, heightens the sense of experience profoundly shared, lessens the common fear of being unable to tolerate what lies ahead, and thus helps enable the living-dying to cross the boundary into the darkness.

Telling stories to a skilled, responsive listener provides just one part of the impetus to cross the threshold. Often, however, the illness experience itself and the reactions of people around will impel the crossing. As the dying are isolated from society and their inhibitions are burned away by that isolation and by the trials of illness, they often gradually develop an honesty that is less tempered than usual by fears of social reprisal. This encourages a freedom we do not usually experience and provides a path to, and then through, the darkness. The anthropologist, Langness, using Heidegger as his model, describes those facing death squarely as a being as whole, "who can thus act authentically, not leveled by the average mode which we adopt in order to live as social beings" (Langness 1981). If we turn to psychiatry, we can postulate that what is being introduced and exposed is the self as essence, the constant, unique self that resides at the deepest levels of the psyche, and is unchanging despite life's vicissitudes. This is the self that transcends death (Anscombe 1989).

The move toward the expanded realization of this self is made manifest in one way by Brian S. who, grinding his fist in his hand, can describe to the first white people to enter his house his anger at being called "boy" at the age of sixty. He can bitterly recount the times he was treated unfairly by a white foreman at his job in a tobacco plant.

> And he put me up there, I was getting on up in age there; he put me with the young men. But somehow or another I had done it so long that it wasn't no bother to me, and I was throwing off the sheets (of tobacco), and I was really tired. So he said, 'All right boys, jump down and get a quick drink of water and hurry back.' I says, 'Well, I wants a drink of water, but I can't do no running.' But I was tired, and I went and got this water, came back...and ever since then it was a push and a shove and something in the path.

Although Brian S.'s ability to recount the story in part reflects the greater freedom wrought by changes in our society in the sixties and seventies, clearly it also took personal courage and a leavetaking of imprinted culture to relate it to us, a group of seven white people. Many of his angry assertions ended in defensive undoing, "I love everybody, black, white, everybody," or "Lord, if I have done wrong, please forgive me," which signified the anxiety engendered by letting go. The same is true to a lesser extent of Ellen C. (p. 112), who eloquently describes beliefs about her afterlife, while noting that some may think her crazy.

If not censored, the narrator's move toward authenticity serves several functions. When told to the listener who acts to bear witness and who validates the meaning of the experience, it provides, once again, for discharge of painful emotion through which people can release attachment to past events and societally determined interpretations of one's life. For Brian S., it meant being able to partially lay to rest the bitterness and anger inherent in so much of his life and story. In addition, he was able to appreciate that for his family the times had changed enough that his sons and daughters had succeeded in their well-paying, higher status jobs. It became a source of pride to him (and to his listening family), through the storytelling, that he had paved the way for his children, his symbolic immortality, with his ability to remain in a hated job and provide for his family, while encouraging them to stay in school, church, scouts, and fight in the civil rights movement. The listener, in this case, served to suggest the expanded time frame for the experiences and encouraged the resulting shift in meaning for the narrator and his family. As such, through the narrated images created by him, the storytelling functions to support the continuity past death of an "enhanced self" of Brian S. It also moves both him and his family to appreciate themselves more as part of an ongoing whole, no longer just local, sui generis selves. Thus, in the end, paradoxically, the move toward authenticity and greater "is-ness" of the person act to pave the way for the final dissolution of the individual as such, and to provide the seeds for the assumption of a more universal, transcendent being.

For the listener, ongoing contact with this kind of authenticity has great value. Not only does it illuminate the ways in which historical, cultural, and familial forces operate and affect individuals, but it can also stimulate a responding authenticity in the willing participant. This teaches the professional much that is useful for the continued work with the living-dying, although it may make it somewhat more difficult to live as comfortably in ordinary society.

> The only time I think about religion…I kind of backslide and go back to bargaining when I'm scared and depressed and alone. According to a woman at work, this is Hell…whatever lies beyond must be better. (Is this what you feel, too?…Listener) I'm beginning to. It's been really hard being by myself. I've got my parents' financial support…I've got my friends, but I really have nobody. I've got lots of bodies, but nobody I can count on. When the time comes and I need somebody, I'm afraid there won't be that person. It's hard to be in a hospital bed and fall into a relationship.
> *Paul M., 24 years old, AIDS patient*

The confusing darkness descends as the living-dying disconnect from society and its imprint, spend more time in withdrawn musings of events gone by and portents of the future, and continue to face momentous shifts and losses. This forces a reevaluation of one's whole structure of meaning (Benoliel 1985). For some like Paul, "What was formerly meaningful may become empty of value" (Campbell 1968, p. 55). Studies by O'Connor et al. (1990) and Weissman and Worden (1976) point to the search for new meaning shortly after a diagnosis of cancer. In the ongoing upheaval of the world of the living-dying, especially in the time of darkness, value and priority are often reexamined, sometimes perceived to be outworn, and a reordering and redefinition of meaning often take place, yet again. In addition, when the diagnosis of cancer or AIDS is accompanied by an early death sentence, such as for David L. and for James R., the search for meaning is stimulated both by diagnosis and certain death and what remains to hold meaning is inevitably different than if death were not ineluctable. For the living-dying finding renewed meaning is important; it enhances quality of life and decreases anxiety and depression (Lewis 1989). It provides the undergirding for the transformed self.

> I barely made it last time...this time, I don't know...I retired right after I got home...Thank God I had the money...and I enjoyed every minute of my last year. I worried some about the leukemia coming back, but each day I did what was important...sometimes it was just sitting with my wife and fishing; it wasn't anything like I used to do, traveling and selling; I loved my job, but it didn't matter any more.
> *(paraphrase) David L., awaiting results of his bone marrow biopsy after two rounds of induction chemotherapy to treat his relapsed leukemia*

Storytelling is one way of reordering priorities and values, and demarking or validating new meaning in experience, for one's remaining life, which is the second function of narrative. For David L., as for most people, success at work loses importance, and primary relationships with caregivers, family, and friends assume new importance, as it must for the journey to be completed. One hospice patient frequently reminisced about his early life with his older brother whom he had not seen for many years after a fight whose details he could not remember. With each story, his regret grew over the loss of the significant relationship. The listener noted (to herself and eventually to him) that, for him, it no longer seemed as important to be right, no matter what the cost, as it had when he was younger, and there was instead a growing importance and value in spending his shortened time with family. As a result of these conversations, the patient decided to call his brother and make amends. A satisfying reunion was the direct outcome of his narratives and the therapeutic intervention.

The paraphrased story of David L., who retired to be at home with his wife, illustrates narrative's function as a mechanism of validation for already enacted shifts in consciousness and behavior. When helping to inscribe new meaning, the listener will find it useful to ask for descriptive detail. This makes vivid and palpable the satisfaction gained from the meaningful experiences ("Where do you go fishing?" "What's your favorite kind of fish to catch?"). The psychologists Bandler and Grinder note that for significant change to take place in behavior, it is essential to connect the client's model with experience and imbue the language that describes it with detail and richness (Bandler & Grinder 1975, p. 80). It is also helpful to continue to evaluate with people if the newly imprinted meanings are useful as they proceed in the journey ("You are at home all the time now; am I wrong or is that a good place to be?" or "Does X still keep you going?").

Paul's story of the Hell of his loneliness points the way for other work. Formerly content to have "many bodies," his consciousness has shifted and his priorities have been reworked. Unfortunately, there is no way to satisfy the new mandate for involvement with one who cares only for him. As the helping guardian, one can grieve the unfulfilled need with Paul and encourage those relationships that supply some measure of succor. In his work as a nursing assistant with AIDS patients, Paul described circumstances in which he gave and received affection. Helping him ascribe value and meaning to these interactions (the substitution of a more universal meaning of love) would be a helpful intervention. This, in essence, enlarges Paul's understanding of his experience and can thus decrease his sense of despair (Callan 1989). In addition, it is equally important to encourage and aid Paul to make concrete plans to attend to his stated need for a caregiver when he gets sick. Neither Paul nor David L. are unusual in their renewed emphasis on the wish to be cared for and cared about. The study by O'Connor et al. (1990) and the discussion by Martens and Davies (1990) of the needs of advanced cancer patients denote the importance of derived meaning from these significant relationships.

For many, there is a common shift to a renewed emphasis on faith, also noted by O'Connor et al. (1990). Faith and religious belief may provide meaning in the experience, mark the path of connection with the transcendent, and/or ensure the continuity of the self. For some, it provides the stimulus of fear. "Reflect upon three things and you will not come to sin: from whence you come...to where you are going...and before whom you are destined to give an account" (Spero 1981–1982, p. 39). These words from the Talmud provide a driving force behind the stories of a number of the living-dying as they atone before the fact of their approaching death and what they believe lies ahead. Paul's open lack of vital belief and uncertainty about an afterlife reflects another, somewhat common if often hidden, view held in this country where religious beliefs may have little meaning until death approaches. It is only then that people, grounded in desire or fear, may construct a belief in either a benevolent afterlife or condemnation to Hell.

For quite as many, like Brian S., faith in God provides the ever present meaning and sense of order in the past, present, and future. It was quite clear he felt he had nothing to fear on his judgment day. His words, which follow, reflect reliance on God's control and ultimate benevolence amidst the painful, meaningless, earthly darkness in which he had recently lived.

> Sometimes the Old Devil get busy and do everything he can to turn people against you. He'll do *everything* he can to turn people against you. You've got to watch as well as pray. You think you're doing good, and you think you're doing maybe better than you are. Sometimes you have to sit down and have a day's conversation with the Lord. But in my life I believe He will make a way for you. The devil and all his people can't do you no harm...The Lord, he suffered for Job to lose everything he had, but after a while he restored all of it back. Elijah was the same way, and I believe if he get ready for me, look for me somewhere in heaven, I'll be there.

Another way people find renewed meaning and a path through the disorienting darkness is by remembering the lustrous moments of the past. When possible, people continue to create events and subsequent accounts of these events to validate the newly enhanced self. In this way the living-dying can keep alive treasured images of the self to preserve their sense of a continuous identity (Castelnuovo-Tedesco 1980), and they can perpetuate important portions of that identity to provide their symbolic immortality, to help their families remember them in self-defined ways after death (Unruh 1983), which is the third function of narrative. In addition, people denote important memories that preserve family values and traditions. The very first story of this chapter, in which Brian S. reminisces about his mother saving the life of a white child, is a story meant, at least in part, to pass on his family value of color-blind generosity and goodness.

The story of Anne Marie, a middle-aged woman dying of lung cancer, evokes a sense of self quite opposite from that of Brian S. The ex-wife of a minister, she had always lived a determinedly independent lifestyle even when, in her own words, discretion might have been more prudent. She preserved her image of self-sufficiency in the face of the dependence of illness and dying by recounting many incidents citing her breaks with tradition. Anne Marie reached out for validation of her confrontive independence to the novels of Ayn Rand whose narrations celebrate unique and self-sufficient achievement.

The first thing he (her husband) came home with, they (his congregation) wanted me to wear a hat to church. He thought this was kind of trivial. There was no reason why, if they wanted me to wear a hat to church, I wouldn't wear a hat to church. I more or less told them, 'Hell No!' No way would I let someone else control my life to that extent.

In this episode, Anne Marie celebrates and preserves her triumph. Many times, however, memories inevitably evoke losses and defeats. These must be recalled, evaluated, and synthesized, which is the fourth function of narrative, as demonstrated earlier with Brian S.'s story of the tobacco plant (Webster & Young 1988). This then, is the substance of life review. In order to accept the reality of remembered loss or defeat and be able to move on emotionally, "every aspect is recalled and examined in detail" (Brown & Stroudmire 1983, p. 380). One must often be prepared to hear countless times the same story with variation. Anne Marie, for example, told endless symbolic versions of the account above (I didn't want to have my baby shower with church women, and I didn't; I refused to let my husband go to such-and-such seminary; I plugged in the church phone only when he was home; he was a minister; I was not a minister's wife.) Each was described as an episode of triumph, but all impelled the inevitable trajectory to divorce, ambivalently wished for, and in the end, actually sought by her husband who refused to continue counseling. The phenomenon of triumphal episodes reversing into tragedy over time or tragedy into triumph is not unusual as storyteller and listener contemplate the patterns in a life review. Noting the patterns and shifts at the psychologically apt moment helps the narrator perceive discrete events (especially the tragic/triumphal ones) with a new perspective. This ultimately aids the work of evaluation and synthesis; the narrator may come to appreciate, when the flow of discrete events merges into a whole, that each event contains seeds of the dualities of triumph and tragedy, sadness and joy. There is one caution, however: if tragedy becomes a major observed theme of a life, the Hermes listener must use acute clinical judgment when deciding if it is wise to make use of the information with the narrator and how to do so.

It is equally essential to be aware that anxiety and despair occur when defeats or losses are re-evoked even within discrete episodes (Molinari & Reichlin 1984–1985). With these, it is important to help the teller identify and express the inevitable feelings of anger, sadness, and guilt (Worden 1982). It is with this awareness that the protective guardian aspect of the Hermes listener especially emerges and symbolically holds the storyteller with more frequent visits and increased closeness to help him or her tolerate the inevitable despair. For one must face the despair and travel through it to achieve integrity (Rosel 1988) and transcendence.

In addition, it is important to note that when losses or defeats arise, the inevitable future loss eternally shimmers underneath and is being grieved in anticipation. For the living-dying, the path through the darkness always ends in death. One way people cope with this anticipatory grief is to project to a future reunion with loved ones who have died. Ellen C.'s story reveals such a belief and denotes her willing acceptance of, indeed longing for, death.

> I love him and I'm ready to go meet him at any time. I think about it a whole lot, most specially when you're laying in there by yourself and half dreaming and wishing, wishing I was with you right now or you were with me. Maybe it won't be too long now. As far as places I see him, it's places we've always been...it's not no strange place at all; it's at home or the store or in the country, just riding around. It's not no strange place at all. I think I'll meet him just like he left me, remembering everything, and I can't help but feel that way. Some people may think well, she's crazy, and I don't deny that...but when I know a thing, I know it...Fran said when I was in the hospital and she was holding me...they were trying to do something...and (she) said I looked right straight at her and I said would you please let me go; there is somebody waiting for me. I hope the children won't grieve and carry on. I hope they'll be just as happy in my death as I've been in life and expecting in death. So far, I've shedded no tears over it, and I don't think I will.
> Ellen C., 65 years old, two weeks before death

The reunion myths may be perceived not only as a means to cope with catastrophic loss of all that is known or beloved, but also as a revitalizing vision of what lies ahead. As people near death, many, not just Ellen C., from the haven of a happy marriage, experience visions of older family or friends who have already died, or of infinite God, beckoning to a world of light. The familial guides are one manifestation of the continued belief in the unbroken line of the human family (Pattison 1967). For others, such as one older man who had been newly diagnosed with widely metastatic lung cancer six months before, visions of approaching death are less literally linked to people or to God. He, who had been silent for days, sat up minutes before his last breath and in awe, describes approaching death as a wondrous opening, a doorway. Most people, of course, yield quietly with no words of description.

We leave this life richer for the journey, even those of us one would not ordinarily note as transformed. None of us ever really negotiates this journey and remains a "common man." This can be true of those we perceive as the least of us. To grieve and rejoice in the inheritance of the past (acknowledged to oneself or another), to live most fully through the pain and bittersweet pleasures of the present, and finally, to confront and release all of known future is, indeed, transformative. According to Campbell (1968), this occurs, in part, because:

> The unconscious brings forth life potentialities that we never managed to bring to adult realization. Those other portions of ourselves are there; those golden seeds do not die. If only a portion of that lost totality could be dredged up into light of day, we should experience a marvelous expansion of our powers, a vivid renewal of life.

Flawed as he was (and as we all are) and remains, yet spurred by impending death, Michael M. exemplifies the metamorphosing power of mastering the darkness; he achieved a kind of integrity. Born to the super-rich and status-conscious, he had been neglected and sometimes abused as a child. He left home at 17 to join the Navy, from which he received a dishonorable discharge. From then on, he lived with whomever would provide a bed and some semblance of concern for him. His drifter lifestyle (supported financially by his parents) stopped when he was diagnosed with AIDS. Although he had many upsetting quarrels and upheavals with others in the AIDS community, he endured to begin work with dying AIDS patients. He began as a volunteer, but then successfully completed the nursing assistant certification program and with pride maintained a job in the local hospital working with AIDS patients. He started psychotherapy when he began his volunteer work and spent many hours telling his story, attempting to come to terms with his demons from the past and ingrained habits that continued to haunt him. The following is his story about his work as a volunteer. It reflects his newly developed awareness of the needs of others, although the listener and Michael himself cannot help but be acutely mindful of his projections in the face of the coming role-reversal.

> I think a positive attitude helps. I give support; I stay with the patient when the families go out, like for groceries. I like it to be comfortable and smooth for the patient. If they're scared, it's going to be a miserable death. If you have really close friends, and you know they care for you, then I don't think the transition to the acceptance stage is so hard...that's why I throw myself into work and going out and making friends, and I've just started crocheting...to keep my time occupied so I don't keep thinking about it. I know it's there; I'll always know it's there. You know, but that I wanted to do what I could...and I guess it's my own guarantee that they'd be there for me when I needed it...I usually run away except for this; when it comes to this, I think it's because of such a personal effect. If I were to run away from it, I would be denying it.

Although Michael will never be the embodiment of what we usually think of as a hero, a truly transcendent being, few people actually are.

Like many of us, however, he matured throughout his illness, and he gained both grace and honor in the process. His ability to give and receive "universal love" with his patients was a gift he gave. In part, telling and reworking his story with a Hermes listener (exploring new meaning in his life; creating a budding self that he could treasure and from which would continue his symbolic existence; dealing with his past griefs and losses) was invaluable in helping him create a new being who found some peace in the past and in the inevitable future. From whence he came, he was transformed. In his unique fashion, as well as he could, he lived to represent the following wisdom from Ellen C., her reply when asked what she thought important to pass on to the next generation.

> Keep on living to the best of your ability and love everybody. Live a happy life and be kind to each other. Take care of each other and live for each other, not just for self. Love them and let them *know* you love them.

What emerges from the storytelling, for Michael, or for any of us, is the hero at peace with death, who has "died as the modern man, but as eternal man—perfected, unspecific, universal man—he has been reborn" (Campbell 1968, p. 20).

> Whatever can be Created can be Annihilated: Forms cannot:
> The Oak is cut down by the Ax, the Lamb fall by the knife,
> But their Forms Eternal Exist For-ever. Amen. Hallelujah!
> *William Blake (Powell 1982).*

References

Anscombe, R. (1989). The myth of the true self. *Psychiatry, 52,* 209–217.

Bandler, R. & Grinder, J. (1975). *The structure of magic.* Palo Alto, CA: Science and Behavior Books.

Benoliel, J. (1985). Loss and terminal illness. *Nursing Clinics of North America,* 20(2), 439–448.

Betts, D. (1988). Paper presented at the conference, *Telling Times Stories of the Living-Dying.* Chapel Hill, NC.

Blake, W. (1982). "Jerusalem." J. Powell, *In The Tao of symbols.* New York: Quill.

Brown, J. T., & Stoudemire, G. A. (1983). Normal and pathological grief. *JAMA, 250* (3), 378–382.

Butler, R. (1963). The life review: An interpretation of reminiscence in the aged. *Psychiatry 26,* 65–76.

Callan, D. (1989). Hope as a clinical issue in oncology social work. *Journal of Psychosocial Oncology, 7*(3), 31–46.

Campbell, J. (1968). *The hero with a thousand faces*. Princeton: Princeton University Press.

Campbell, J. (1988). *The power of myth*. New York: Doubleday.

Castelnuovo-Tedesco, P. (1980). Reminiscence and nostalgia: The pleasure and pain of remembering. In S. J. Greenspan & G. H. Pollak (Eds.), *The course of Life: Psychoanalytic contributions toward personality development*.

Churchill, L. (1988). Paper presented at the conference, *Telling Times: Stories of the Living-Dying*. Chapel Hill, NC.

Cirlot, J. E. (1962). *Dictionary of symbols*. New York: Philosophical Library.

Coles, R. (1989). *The call of stories*. Boston: Houghton Mifflin.

Durckheim, K. (1989). The call for the master. *Parabola, 14*(1), 4–14.

Durckheim, K. (1990). The voice of the master. *Parabola, 15*(3), 4–13.

Feigenberg, L., & Schneidman, E. (1979). Clinical thanatology and psychotherapy: Some reflections on caring for the dying person. *Omega, 10*,1–84.

Goldberg, R. (1988). Psychiatric aspects of psychosocial distress in cancer patients. *Journal of Psychosocial Oncology, 6*(1/2) , 139–162.

Hamilton, E. (1942). *Mythology*. New York: New American Library.

Hejmadi, P. (1990). Dhyana: The long, pure look. *Parabola,15*(2), 70–76.

Hulbert, R., & Lens, W. (1988). Time and self-identity in later life. *International Journal of Aging and Human Development, 27*(4), 293–302.

Jevne. R. (1987). Creating stillpoints: Beyond a rational approach to counseling cancer patients. *Journal of Psychosocial Oncology, 5*(3), 1–15.

Langness, L. L., Frank, G. (1981). *Lives: An anthropological approach to biography*. Novato, CA: Chandler & Sharp.

Leach, E. (1967). Genesis as myth. In Middleton, J. (Ed.), *Myth and cosmos (p. 1)*. Garden City, NY: Natural History Press.

Lewis, F. (1989). Attributions of control, experienced meaning, and psychosocial well-being in patients with advanced cancer. *Journal of Psychosocial Oncology, 7*(1/2), 105–119.

Lewis, F., Haberman, M., & Wallhagen, M. (1986). How adults experience personal control. *Journal of Psychosocial Oncology, 4*(4), 27–41.

Lifton, R. (1976a). Psychological effects of the atomic bomb in Hiroshima: The theme of death. In R. Fulton (Ed.), *Death and identity*. Baltimore, MD: Charles Press.

Lifton, R. (1976b). The sense of immortality: On death and the continuity of life. In R. Fulton (Ed.), *Death and identity* (p. 23). Baltimore, MD: Charles Press.

Lo Gerfo, M. (1980–1981). Three ways of reminiscence in theory and practice. *International Journal of Aging and Human Development, 12*(1), 39–46.

Martens, N., & Davies, B. (1990). The work of patients and spouses in managing advanced cancer at home. *The Hospice Journal, 6*(2), 55–73.

May, W. (1988). Sacred image in narrative. Paper presented at conference, *Telling Times: Stories of the Living-Dying*. Chapel Hill, NC.

Molinari, V., & Reichlin R. (1984–1985). Life review reminiscence in the elderly: A review of the literature. *International Journal of Aging and Human Development. 20*(2), 81–91.

O'Connor, A., Wicker, C., & Germino, B. (1990). Understanding the cancer patient's search for meaning. *Cancer Nursing, 13*(3), 167–175.

Ouspensky, P. D. (1989). The transparent veil of symbolism. *Parabola, 14*(2), 4–8.

Pattison, M. (1967). The experience of dying. *American Journal of Psychotherapy, 21*, 32–43.

Powell, J. (1982). *The Tao of symbols*. New York: Quill.

Price, L. (1987). Ecuadorian illness stories: Cultural knowledge. In Holland, D., & Quinn, N. (Eds.), *Natural discourse in cultural models in language and thought*. Cambridge: Cambridge University Press.

Price, L. (1988). Life review as a window on culture. Paper presented at conference, *Telling Times: Stories of the Living-Dying*. Chapel Hill, NC.

Rosel , N. (1988). Clarification and application of Erik Erikson's eighth stage of man. *International Journal of Aging and Human Development, 27*(1), 11–23.

Scheper-Hughes, N. (1983). Deposed kings: The demise of the rural Irish gerontocracy. In J. Sokolovsky (Ed.), *Growing old in different societies* (p. 140). Belmont, CA: Wadsworth.

Shneidman, E. (1978). Some aspects of psychotherapy with dying persons. *Psychosocial care of the dying patient*. New York: McGraw-Hill.

Spero, M. (1981–1982). Confronting death and the concept of life review: The Talmudic approach. *Omega, 12*(1), 37–43.

Unruh, D. (1983). Death: Strategies of identity preservation. *Social Problems, 30*(3), 340–351.

Welch-McCaffrey, D. (1988). Family issues in cancer care: Current dilemmas and future directions. *Journal of Psychosocial Oncology, 6*(1/2), 199–211.

Weissman, A., & Worden, W. (1976). The existential plight in cancer: Significance of the first hundred days. International *Journal of Psychiatry in Medicine, 7*, 1–15.

Worden, W. (1982). Grief counseling and grief therapy: *A handbook for mental health practitioners*. New York: Springer-Verlag.

Eight

Respecting the Spirituality of the Dying and the Bereaved

Thomas Attig

Thomas Attig received his Ph.D. in philosophy from Washington University (St. Louis) in 1973. Following a year as a visitor at the University of Pittsburgh, he joined the faculty of Bowling Green State University in 1972. Currently a full professor, he has served as chair of the department since 1983. Since 1974 he has been teaching courses on the philosophy of death and dying, and since 1979 he has regularly offered week-long intensive summer workshops on death and dying and on grief and bereavement. He is a life member of the Association for Death Education and Counseling, has served as its treasurer (1983–1987), on its board of directors (1989–1992), its second vice president (1993–1994), its first vice president (1994–1995), and its president  *(1995–1996). He is currently a member of the Board of Directors for the International Work Group on Death, Dying, and Bereavement. Since 1983 he has served the Ohio courts as an expert witness on grief and bereavement. His research interests include grief and bereavement, coping with personal mortality, suicide and suicide intervention, and death education. His book entitled* Grieving: Relearning the World *is forthcoming from Oxford University Press.*

When persons are dying, grieving or responding to others facing death, they are commonly challenged spiritually. It is perhaps then, more than at any other time, that they are prompted to wonder about the meanings of their lives, of the lives of those they love and care for, and of living in general. Confrontation with death casts life and its meaning in stark relief.

Persons' beliefs play an extremely important role in their spiritual lives. I have in mind beliefs about life and death, immortality, suffering, meaning and purpose, God, and the like. It is possible to ask what respect for the beliefs and for persons as believers requires while the validity of the beliefs is held in suspension. This question of respect is my concern here, with emphasis on respecting the dying and the bereaved. What does respect for the spirituality of persons require when they are struggling to make sense of and to find a way of sustaining meaning and purpose in living in the shadow of death?[1]

The Beliefs as Worthy of Respect

First, consider why beliefs about death and dying, life and its meaning, God and immortality are worthy of respect. By definition, beliefs we call spiritual are those that have bearing on persons' perceptions of the very meaning of their lives. Beliefs of such importance, understandably, are held as precious by their possessors. Minimally, respecting believers requires acknowledging the centrality of the beliefs in the person's self-definition and identity. Not only do persons often have firm convictions about spiritual matters, but they often think of these beliefs as defining their deepest selves. To profess "I am a Christian," "I am a Jew," or "I am Hindu" is often to speak volumes concerning perceptions of place and purpose in the universe, heritage, place in the community, personal integrity, orientation or posture in the face of challenge, fond hopes and aspirations, personal destiny, and the like. All of these matters are intimately related to persons' most cherished values, that is, what they care about most fundamentally. To the extent that persons are what they care about and these beliefs importantly define what they care about, personal identity is intimately connected with personal spiritual belief.

Moreover, many derive self-esteem, both in the sense of self-confidence and in the sense of self-worth, from the understandings of themselves, their experiences, and their place in the world that the beliefs provide. Their beliefs can be a principal source of the confidence required to (a) affirm the meaning of their lives and of living a human life in general, (b) carry on day to day, (c) maintain hope for the future, (d) sustain faith in the face of adversity, and (e) meet life's greatest challenges without despairing. When life is most difficult and the temptation to conclude that it is of little worth is the greatest, spiritual beliefs can support people in believing that individual human lives cannot be reduced to insignificance, that they can and do make a difference worth making, that the world is better for their existing, that they have worth even if those around them may not fully acknowledge it, and the like. Derivatively, such spiritual beliefs can and often do define fundamental lifestyles, courses of purposeful action, and patterns of social interaction for individuals within communities and throughout entire cultures.

This much, then, can be said for the value of spiritual beliefs in general. They have the power to profoundly influence and shape individual and collective life.

The Beliefs as Bases for Coping

More specifically, in considering respectful response to the dying and the bereaved, it must be stressed that concepts and beliefs constitute the principal means of their intellectual coping with reality. It is too easy to forget and underestimate the importance of the capacities of the mind and spirit to orient persons within reality and to support their discerning meanings in living within it. This may be especially so in a culture that is at least impatient with things intellectual, if not decidedly anti-intellectual. How persons think and believe decisively colors their experiences of themselves, others, and the world they share.

If persons also cope emotionally, behaviorally, and socially, it is worth noting that these other dimensions of coping are often decisively influenced by the manner of intellectual coping. That is, what persons believe has great impact upon what they feel, their evaluation of their feelings, and their choices about their appropriate expression, their choices of action and reaction, and their interactions with others. There is even a developing speculative literature that suggests profoundly important and too little understood mutual influences of beliefs and humans' organic or physical reactions to stress and crises such as those presented by dying and bereavement.[2]

To be sure, the dimension of intellectual and/or spiritual coping, that is, struggling to understand reality and to discern meanings within it, is inappropriately isolated from emotional, behavioral, and social coping. Persons cope as whole persons, in all dimensions of their lives at once. While there is an important purpose served in focusing on the dimension of intellectual/spiritual coping to clarify and to deepen understanding of its significance, it would be untrue to human reality to suppose that such coping is anything but intimately linked with each of the other dimensions.

One principal function of intellectual/spiritual coping is to help persons through concepts and beliefs to orient themselves to reality. Persons experience reality and their lives within it as presenting profoundly challenging questions of understanding. What is the true nature of reality? How is it organized? What are its fundamental dynamics, and what makes it change as it does? What is my place and that of my fellows within physical and spiritual reality? What kinds of creatures are we and what differences does that fundamental human condition make? How are we to understand the peculiar mix of physical and spiritual existence that we seem to enjoy? Are we free or determined? How am I and others affected by forces beyond our control and where, if anywhere, may we possibly have some influence? Are we alone in the universe? Is there divine influence on the course of events in reality and within our own lives? Does human life end in death or does all or part of us survive? What kind of life, if any, might follow? Many concepts and beliefs at the heart of traditional philosophies and religions enable persons to orient themselves within reality by providing answers to such questions.

A second principal function of intellectual/spiritual coping is to help persons through their concepts and beliefs to discern the meaning(s) of reality and of their lives within it. Questions of meaning have to do less with the shape and structure of reality and human life and more with the sense it makes that reality and life have such shape and structure. They are questions of value and purpose, of the potential for such things as satisfaction and fulfillment, the realization of value, experienced meaningfulness, salvation, and the like. "Why" questions of a distinct sort hold a prominent place in human wondering about meaning. Here the question is not one of the cause so much as the reason or purpose for that in question. In this spirit, persons have for nearly as long as language has been recorded wondered about such matters as : Why do we live? (What is (are) the purpose(s) of human life? What is (are) the purpose(s) of this individual human life?) Why is there suffering? (What is (are) the reason(s) for suffering? For this particular suffering?) Why is there death? Why this particular death, here and now?

In coping intellectually/spiritually with challenges to understanding the meaning(s) of life, persons are struggling with at least these four pivotal issues in an attempt to say "yes" to life: (a) Is small OK? That is, how is the supposed meaningfulness of human life compatible with our being so small and insignificant on a cosmic scale, that is, with our being so tiny in a vast universe and our lives lasting so little time in universal history? (b) Is change OK? That is, how is the supposed meaningfulness of human life compatible with there seemingly being nothing permanent and lasting either in reality or in our lives? (c) Is suffering OK? That is, how is the supposed meaningfulness of human life compatible with the prevalence of suffering as all beginnings have endings, all attachments are fleeting, and all commitments are impermanent? (d) Is uncertainty OK? That is, how is faith in the meaningfulness of living to be sustained when our grip on answers to questions such as these seems tenuous at best (if and when we have answers that are at all satisfying), when our attempts to discern answers to these most pressing questions seem so clouded with uncertainty?

Such questions of meaning take on added poignancy and urgency as persons encounter death and bereavement. Again, many concepts and beliefs at the heart of traditional philosophies and religions enable persons to discern the meaning(s) of reality and their lives within it by providing answers to questions such as these.

Edwin Shneidman (1980, pp. 183–193) in the last chapter of *Voices of Death* (and many others in other contexts), affirms that the firmness of conviction and not the content of conviction itself is the most significant factor when beliefs help persons to cope either with dying or with bereavement. The key factor is that the dying or bereaved be sustained by some means or other in the conviction that the life in question (be it their own or that of one for whom they care) has meaning. Caregivers dare not underestimate the power of spiritual concepts and beliefs in addressing fundamental questions of the nature of reality and its meaning as they serve this end. The human need here is palpable.

Respect Generally Conceived

Surely, part of respecting the spirituality of the dying and the bereaved involves cultivating a deep appreciation of the importance of the intellectual/spiritual coping in their lives. That is, respect for the spirituality of the dying and the bereaved requires understanding of how in part their thriving as the individuals they are derives from their being able to find their lives to be meaningful.

But there is more to the notion of respect than simply understanding how it is that persons thrive or flourish spiritually when they do. Caregivers must also develop understanding of the ways in which spiritual thriving can be inhibited, hindered, or undermined. In other words, human spiritual thriving is vulnerable, and caregivers must be acutely aware of that vulnerability.

Spiritual thriving can be adversely affected simply by the introduction of crisis events such as dying and bereavement into otherwise relatively untroubled living. With physical debilitation and enervation, disruption of daily routine, and interruption of normal patterns of interaction with others come stresses that test persons' capacities to maintain satisfying lifestyles, to remain engaged in meaningful activities and projects, to uphold fulfilling relationships, and to sustain faith and confidence that life is meaningful and worth living.

Moreover, the foregoing sections suggest that one of the major tasks confronting the dying and the bereaved is that of coming to terms with or making sense of both the event of death itself and of living in the shadow of the event, of thinking it through. If this is so, then the dying and bereaved are vulnerable to underappreciation of the significance of that task and to compromise of their motivation to address it.

But surely respecting persons (in their spirituality or otherwise) is not simply a matter of understanding or appreciating something about them, even something as important as how they can thrive and how that thriving can be undermined. Rather, respect involves acting in the light of such understanding, that is, translating such understanding into respectful response and behavior. The actions or omissions of caregivers themselves can affect significantly the spiritual thriving of those for whom they care. Minimally, respect requires that caregivers not interfere in the spiritual thriving of others, that they not exacerbate their vulnerability. A higher order of respect involves caregivers in finding ways to actively support, sustain, or facilitate spiritual thriving and to effectively and sensitively minimize that vulnerability.

The dying and the bereaved can experience considerable disorientation and confusion, and caregivers can cultivate abilities to support and promote their coming to understand the spiritual dimensions of their experiences and coping needs. They can learn means of helping them to sustain the motivation to meet the spiritual challenges. They can develop skills for supporting them in choosing alternative means of meeting these spiritual challenges and in acting on those choices. Finally, they can cultivate sensitivity to and abilities to respond flexibly to the spiritual individuality of those in their care.

Specific Dimensions of Respect

Intolerance and Proselytizing

The spiritual thriving of the dying and the bereaved may be hindered by intolerance or even proselytizing by caregivers. Where beliefs matter as much as spiritual beliefs do, and in particular beliefs about life, death, and suffering, and their meaning, it is quite possible that dogmatism and defensiveness will take root and flourish. Where they do flourish, tolerance for, much less appreciation of the sustaining power of, alternative beliefs is not likely. If deathbed conversions are exceedingly rare, especially where there is already firm conviction in place, and if firmness of conviction is crucial for spiritual thriving in such circumstances, then tolerance of alternative beliefs is essential if that thriving is not to be thwarted.

Caregivers, too, are struggling to come to terms with and to make sense of the deaths and suffering in the lives of those for whom they care. They are also affected by those deaths, albeit not in most cases as powerfully as immediate family and close friends. As with anyone confronting death, dying, and suffering, caregivers can find it quite disturbing to discover that they, too, are intellectually and spiritually challenged in the midst of circumstances where supposedly they have been prepared to function in a fully professional manner. They, too, rely upon concepts and beliefs to orient and sustain them. It can be especially challenging for them to resist the tendencies in themselves toward dogmatism and defensiveness, which derive from their own intellectual and spiritual needs and vulnerability. Recognizing that they may be tempted by such tendencies may well be a key to their avoiding the further temptations of intolerance or even proselytizing where they find their views to differ from those of the persons in their care.

Believing versus Knowing

There is an unfortunate tendency regarding beliefs about life, death, and suffering, and their meanings to confuse believing with knowing. While not underestimating the importance of beliefs in the lives of individual believers, one must be ever aware of the difference between conviction (however firm) and knowledge. Caregiver pretension to knowing here is especially dangerous. Humility is crucial as a firm base for the tolerance required.

In attending to the spiritual needs of the dying and the bereaved, respect would come easier if all involved could remember that in coming to terms with death we are interpreting mysteries and not simply solving problems. When confronting ultimate human limitation, it is salutary to remember the words of John Stuart Mill:

> Human existence is girt round with mystery: the narrow region of our existence is a small island in the midst of a boundless sea. To add to the mystery, the domain of our earthly existence is not only an island in infinite space, but also in infinite time. The past and the future are alike shrouded from us: we neither know the origin of anything which is, nor its final destination. (Mill)

The distinction between mysteries and problems is most useful here. Problems are by definition the kinds of challenges that cry for and often yield definitive solution. When confronted with problems, persons seek solutions that will transform the problematic reality, typically through decisive action. Mysteries, by contrast, do not yield. Rather, mysteries pervade the reality with which we must come to terms. The mysterious dimensions of reality transcend both our conceptual grasp and our control. Yet, they command our attention and compel us to respond. However, our responses are not comprised of reality-transforming actions. Rather, the mysteries remain as factors defining the human condition, and instead we transform ourselves as we come to terms with and attempt to make sense of them. In response we transform elements of our perspective, understanding, and life pattern.

Definitive answers to the most important questions of life and death and their meanings are beyond our grasp. Questions of the meanings of life, death, and suffering are questions about centrally important mysteries of life. Objective certainty is simply unattainable here. Acceptable answers to these mysteries are elusive and our hold upon them tentative at best. Yet many, if not most, are moved to continue the quest for answers to orient them within reality and sustain coping with such mysteries. Caregiver appreciation of this aspect of the human condition, that we are together challenged by life's fundamental mysteries, can promote the humility and tolerance required if the alternative perspectives and beliefs of those in their care are to be respected.

Surrogate Suffering Syndrome

In the intellectual/spiritual, as in the other dimensions of their experiences, the dying and bereaved are vulnerable to influences that encourage passivity and helplessness. Glenn Davidson (1980) has identified a pattern in caregiving that tends to have just such an effect, which he terms *the surrogate suffering syndrome*. This syndrome is a pervasive pattern in caregiving among professionals and nonprofessionals alike. It encompasses all attempts to shield persons subject to care from painful or otherwise difficult experiences. The idea is to bear the burden for the cared-for person, whether that person is a friend, a relative, or someone for whom one has professional responsibility. It is an attempt to run interference on pain. It is a very well-intentioned strategy for caregiving. Tragically, as with many well-intentioned modes of interaction, the intention is seldom realized. Indeed, there is room to doubt whether it could ever be realized. Can one person cry the tears of another? Can one person face the mortality of another? Can one person do the grief work for another?

Caregivers must realize that they can no more carry the burdens of intellectual or spiritual coping for those in their care than they can carry the physical, emotional, or social burdens. It is the dying and the bereaved themselves who face the challenges of coming to terms with and making sense of the events in their lives. At most, helping here can take the form of supporting persons in finding or sustaining confidence in answers and beliefs that they find functional.

A case study well illustrates this point. In a well-known film entitled "Death of the Wished-for Child," Professor Davidson focuses on the experiences of a young woman whose child dies within hours after birth. She is on the receiving end of every form of surrogate-suffering–style caregiving imaginable as caregivers attempt to spare her the difficult challenges. Little noticed is the repetition of the pattern in others' responses to her exploring questions of the meaning of the event in her life. At one point she recounts a scene in her hospital room. In the presence of her friend, a minister offers a "ten-minute sermon" on why she shouldn't be asking the "Why?" questions she is asking, because failing to find definitive answers will only be frustrating. When the minister leaves, her friend offers a counter-sermon on the importance of her continuing to question and urges acceptance of a particular answer having to do with the supposed connection of the inadequacy of her faith and that of her husband to the death of their child. The exchanges left her angry and frustrated, with her questions yet unanswered.

Clearly part of what is happening here is both the minister and her friend are attempting to spare her the difficulty of coping in her own way with the intellectual and spiritual challenges presented by the death. Also clear is the futility of any such attempts to spiritually cope for another. Each must find his or her own path, and any efforts by others can only be helpful if they encourage and support the first-person exploration of the issues by those they hope to help.

Hindrances and Inhibiting Factors

There may be inhibiting factors blocking the full and meaningful expression of spiritual values or exploration of spiritually pressing questions in medical and social contexts. In some circumstances access to spiritual leaders and counselors is limited or restricted. In others, access to spiritual community is compromised. In others, for example, in an Intensive Care Unit (ICU), space and privacy are limited. In others, medical procedures, including the use of drugs or apparatus, undermine lucidity or inhibit full expression. In still others, exploration of spiritual territory perceived to be too painful or stressful is discouraged by other persons such as family members. In all of these cases (and others like them) the respectful caregiver can at least minimize the hindrances and perhaps take positive steps to circumvent or overcome the obstacles to spiritual functioning, for example, by providing access to spiritual guides or community members, encouraging delays or relocation of ritual events to make participation possible, making space available, promoting at least temporary lucidity, compensating for reduced expressive functioning, encouraging exploration of difficult questions, and the like.

Underappreciation of Faith

In some instances full spiritual thriving is blocked by underappreciation of the value and power of the beliefs in question by the believers themselves. Persons often have firm convictions without fully comprehending the range of implications and applications of their beliefs. That is, they sometimes don't see how their beliefs speak to their current circumstances. Here it is likely vital that the dying or bereaved be placed in the hands of one who is skilled in helping them to see the connections so that they may derive from their beliefs the sustaining power within them. Priests, rabbis, ministers, chaplains, lay ministers, and the like should be among those most adept at doing at least this much even without extensive training in pastoral counseling.

I am confident that, when properly interpreted, all of the major religious traditions speak powerfully to the questions of the sustainability of confidence in the meaningfulness of life in spite of profound human limitation. The path to salvation that each defines marks the way to gentle but firm affirmation of meaningful life and the ultimate acceptability of our lives being small and insignificant and pervaded with change, suffering, vulnerability, and uncertainty.

Lack of Spirituality

It is possible for persons to come to experience dying or bereavement with no antecedently held firm convictions on spiritual matters. If Shneidman is correct, such a lack of conviction can be one of the most disturbing factors in such persons' experiences. What is a respectful response if one is concerned about the confusion and distress so often apparent or expressed? Again, imposition of the beliefs of the caregiver is just that: an imposition. Instead, encouraging and supporting exploration of spiritual issues of meaning in an effort to help the persons discover or develop for themselves sustaining convictions that are congruent with their values and life patterns is more respectful.

The convictions that matter most at the times in question are convictions concerning the meaningfulness of lives lived and now ending or ended and of lives that now must be lived following significant loss. The variety of beliefs that can be sustaining here should not be conceived too narrowly. For some, to be sure, the conviction will take root in traditional religious doctrine, be it theistic or nontheistic. For some, however, the conviction that life is meaningful may derive from less formal or creedal sources.

Victor Frankl (1984) in *Man's Search for Meaning* has suggested that persons can derive a conviction of the meaningfulness of life from (a) creative or productive activity that gives them a sense of contributing to others and the world around them, (b) experiences they find meaningful in themselves, including especially the experiences of loving and being loved, as well as such things as aesthetic and other pleasures and satisfactions, the experience of communing with nature, and encounters in reverence with the divine, and (c) experiences of penetrating their own suffering with meaning rather than being overwhelmed or defeated by it. All of these sources of meaning can be supported to some degree in the lives of both the dying and the bereaved.

Robert Lifton (1983) has urged in *The Broken Connection* that persons derive a sense of meaningfulness in their lives from beliefs that their lives are connected with something transcending. While some sources for such conviction are traditionally religious, some are not. Sources of such conviction can, according to Lifton, derive from perceived connectedness with a life to follow (literal immortality in various forms), or through such means to symbolic immortality as living on through one's works, in the memories of others, through the ongoing life of one's people, and the like.

Again, Edwin Shneidman (1980, p.5) in his *Voices of Death* prompts reflection on these matters through recounting the story of a young Russian woman, Marie Bashkirtseff, who died in nineteenth-century Paris and left the following remark in her diary:

> This is the thought that has always terrified me: to live, to be so filled with ambition, to suffer, to weep, to struggle, and, at the end, oblivion! as if I had never existed.

Clearly, Frankl in writing of making a contribution, Lifton in writing of symbolic immortality, and this young woman are all underscoring the potential of deriving a sense of meaningfulness in life from a belief that one's life has made a nontrivial difference, that the world is somehow a better place for one's having been here, or at least that all of the efforts and struggles do not come to nothing when death comes.

Such differences as one might make and take satisfaction in need not be earthshaking. Part of accepting the human condition and affirming life and its meaningfulness may entail accepting the idea that few if any make differences noticed by all. Rather, we all have opportunity to make differences where we are with what resources we have. Such differences can be known and appreciated by a few or even many, and faith in having made a difference can be sustained even if not all who have been touched by a life acknowledge such differences. It could well be that some can be quite content with having made a difference in the lives of family, friends, and peers and with a conviction that that difference will continue to matter to their survivors even after death.

Having said this much about the kinds of convictions persons might find sustaining, what kind of respectful response to the dying and bereaved might be in order? First, it should be remembered that not all will find traditional religious doctrine attractive, even where issues of the meaningfulness of their lives seem unaddressed. To be sure, it may be appropriate and effective to offer to bring the dying or the bereaved into contact with representatives of various religious orders.

However, should such offers be declined, there are other options yet available if distress about such spiritual matters persists. Life review is common among the dying and the bereaved. Reviewing lives to discern the presence of meaningful contributions, differences made, rewarding experiences, rewarding relationships with others, overcomings of tragedy, and the like can encourage and support a sense of meaningfulness. Assurances can be given that the dying will not be lost in oblivion, that the differences they have made will be remembered and appreciated after they have gone. Helping persons to renew, deepen, and maintain connections with others and to address unfinished business within relationships or in projects of significance to them can be very sustaining. Addressing issues of guilt and forgiveness (including self-forgiveness) may well be an important part of this process. Helping the bereaved to learn to sustain a loving relationship with those who have died can speak to this same spiritual need.[3]

Emotions as Obstacles

Spiritual thriving may also be blocked by the presence of dominating emotions, such as anger or guilt, which may in fact be deeply rooted in the beliefs of the dying or the bereaved. That is, the emotions may be so controlling in the situation that exploration of the underlying spiritual values and questions may be inhibited or stifled. For example, a person may be angry at God for what is believed to be an unfair or unjust death, or another might feel guilty based upon a belief in God as punishing for some unknown but presumably justified reason. In order to facilitate spiritual thriving in such cases, a skilled counselor must overcome the resistance that allows the emotions to dominate and gently but firmly invite, encourage, and support exploration of the validity of the beliefs, which are the basis of the emotions.

Dysfunctional Beliefs

Perhaps the circumstances within which it is most difficult to define a respectful response are those where the dying or the bereaved have firm convictions that are clearly dysfunctional. That is, it is quite possible that beliefs themselves may impoverish the lives of believers, compromise, or deaden their appreciation of the value and meaning of living, and ultimately undermine or inhibit their thriving as individuals and in their relations with others.

In such cases, respect requires extreme caution about judgment that the firmly held conviction is in fact dysfunctional. Such judgment is not to be confused with or supplanted by a judgment (a) that the belief "could not possibly be functional" simply because it is different from the belief of the caregiver, or (b) that the belief is serving a function that the caregiver finds undesirable, unpalatable, or the like.

Rather, the judgment that the belief is dysfunctional must be based on caregiver perception that the belief is in fact contributing to the disorientation of the person or clearly undermining the person's own sense of meaningfulness in the experience. For example, a person may believe that a sufficiently strong faith will reverse the inevitability of a loved one's death. Or, a person may be convinced that he or she is responsible for the death of another from cancer simply by virtue of a moral failing, and the person may be driven toward suicide by this guilt. In these cases unrealistic or meaning-destroying beliefs are dominant, human suffering is compounded, and such persons are headed for disaster.

Here it is good to remember that conviction, no matter how firm, neither changes the fundamental contours of reality and the human condition nor provides believers with immunity from suffering or death. At best it supplies means of coping with or living in the face of death and suffering. This was as much true for the founders of the great religions as it is for followers among the dying and bereaved today.

Where dysfunctional beliefs are present, respect for the believer requires recognition of the dysfunctional character of the belief and the courage to intervene caringly in the name of the person's own thriving. Again, imposition of alternative beliefs is inappropriate. Yet, encouragement of exploration of (a) alternative interpretations of the beliefs in question or (b) alternative beliefs compatible with the person's values and life patterns is appropriate and respectful. Here the caregiver might, for example, invite a religious believer to examine how the central figures in the great religions themselves found faith to be sustaining in their own encounters with death and suffering. A most compelling and powerful instance of this in interaction with Christians, for example, could be exploration of the story of the passion of Jesus where he confronted the prospect of dying, asked that his friends be close by, experienced and expressed fear, sorrow, and grief, and yet found his faith to be sustaining. The literatures of the great religions are filled with comparable and compelling accounts of central figures wrestling with issues of the compatibility of human limitation and finiteness and the meaningfulness of human life. Exploration of such texts and spiritual counseling can help the dying and the bereaved to consider how the meaningfulness of lives now ending or ended or yet to be lived by survivors is not nullified or cancelled by death.

Yet another fruitful approach might be to respectfully and sensitively explore and address the underlying emotions at the base of the believer's seemingly desperate attempt to control or manipulate reality with faith. Clearly, part of what seems so distressing in the typical case is the feeling of helplessness and powerlessness in the face of a reality or chain of events over which one has little or no influence. This helplessness and powerlessness, as well as feelings such as fear, anxiety, despair, extreme sadness, abandonment, guilt, and the like, may well be present. Inviting expression of such feelings can be a vital first step. Helping persons to find things to do and say, short of changing the realities of death and inevitable loss, may address the feelings and to some extent dissipate the felt need to magically manipulate the world through controlling belief.

These reflections on respect for the spirituality of the dying and the bereaved are neither exhaustive nor definitive. Rather, they provide a framework for understanding respect for spirituality in very general terms and beginning thoughts on specific ways of supporting and respecting the dying and the bereaved in their spiritual thriving and vulnerability in the shadow of death.

Notes

1. An earlier and far less detailed treatment of this theme was published as "Respect for the dying and the bereaved as believers" in the Newsletter of the Forum for Death Education and Counseling, 1983.
2. See, for example, the works of Bernie Siegel, Carl Simonton, Norman Cousins, and James Lynch.
3. On this subject see my earlier "Grief, Love and Separation." In C. Corr and R. Pacholski (Eds.), *Death: Completion and Discovery*. (pp. 139–147). Hartford, CT: Forum for Death Education and Counseling, 1987 .

References

Davidson, G. "Death of the Wished-for Child," a film produced and distributed by The Order of the Golden Rule, Springfield, IL, 1980.

Frankl, V. E. *Man's search for meaning*, 3rd. ed., New York: Simon & Schuster, 1984.

Lifton, R. J. *The broken connection: On death and the continuity of life*, New York: Basic Books, 1983.

Mill, J. S. *Three essays on religion*, New York: Greenwood Press, 1969.

Shneidman, E. *Voices of death*, New York: Harper & Row, 1980.

Nine

Spiritual Care of the Dying

Roderick Cosh

Roderick Cosh read physiology at London University and graduated in 1978. He then went to Oxford and trained for the Anglican priesthood and was ordained in 1981.

Rod served his first curacy in Swindon, Wiltshire, and during his five years there was part-time chaplain to the Seymour Clinic, the local acute psychiatric unit. During this time he taught ethics and spiritual care to student nurses. In 1986 he moved to The Royal Marsden Hospital, London, England, a leading international cancer center, where he was chaplain's assistant for a further five years. During this time he taught and lectured widely both nationally and internationally. In 1988 and 1990 he organized international symposia on spiritual and ethical issues in cancer care. Rod was a member of The International Work Group on Death, Dying, and Bereavement, The Ethics Advisory Committee of The Royal Marsden Hospital, and The Ethics Advisory Committee of The Royal College of Nursing. He has contributed to the three-volume work Oncology for Nurses and Health Care Professionals, edited by Tiffany.

He is at present vicar of St Augustine's, Whitton near Twickenham, London. He is looking at the spiritual care of the dying in the community with a view to setting up a parish-based day respite care centre for the chronically sick and terminally ill.

Rod is married to Pam and they have two children. Rod is an avid gardener in his spare time with a particular interest in alpine plants. He enjoys music both as a listener and player of the clarinet.

This seeing the sick endears them to us, us too it endears.
My tongue had taught thee comfort, touch had quenched thy tears,
Thy tears that touched my heart, child Felix, poor Felix Randal;[1]

Introduction

If we look back several centuries then the locus of care for the sick and
dying was to be found within organized religion. Within western culture,
this care resided with the Christian Church. However, concern was not
so much for the welfare of the dying but for the integrity of their mortal
souls.[2] With the rise of rationalism and its espoused scientific methodology, hope for the alleviation of suffering and the prolongation of life
brought a shift in faith towards that new citadel—medicine.

It is commonly suggested that we are now living in a post Judeo-
Christian society. Secularism is the order of the day, but this new
religion has brought with it as many problems as it has answered. For all
the alleviation that science has brought for the suffering of humankind,
it has not been able to address the ultimate questions that concern each
one of us. When the locus of care was with religion, dying was not so
much to be feared as death itself, and suffering was considered a normal
part of existence. With the challenge of science suffering is often minimized; death has ceased to be considered a normal part of the order of
things. Because science could not overcome the ultimate mystery of
death, death itself was by some seen as a failure and became a taboo
subject.[3]

However, a "wind of change" has arisen particularly in the last three
decades. It is becoming less acceptable, in health care, to treat only the
condition with which a patient presents. This is particularly the case
within nursing. Current nursing care models require that the whole
person should be cared for; body, mind, and spirit. Quite rightly, this has
been encouraged and has raised the standard of care because the emphasis now is on the unique individual who is affected by a disease and not
on the disease that generally affects groups of people. Now, the quality of
life for the individual and the quality of his or her care are becoming the
guiding factors in health care.[4,5]

Much of the influence for this change has come as the direct result of
the rise of the hospice movement, which has been a shining light in the
search for a balance between the physical, emotional, and spiritual care
of the terminally ill.

The American health care system was still operating under the Carte-
sian principle that assigned the noncorporeal, spiritual realm to the

church and the physical concerns to science. With this division suffer-ing was difficult to understand and alleviate.[6]

The word *holistic* has in recent years been much maligned, not least by those most threatened by it. This is a sadness for it is a useful word for an excellent concept, that is, an approach to care that takes into account the many facets represented within a human being. Holistic care does not treat the disease per se but the whole person.

This has led not only to a quantal leap in the ways the physical needs of patients are addressed, but also to an improvement in the psychologi-cal care given. Also, many health-care professionals are becoming aware that, in order to care for the whole person, the spiritual dimension has to be taken seriously. However, this is not always felt to be as easy to accomplish as other tasks.

The most common reason for a lack of confidence in looking at the spiritual needs of patients is the difficulty in defining exactly what is meant. Another reason is the feeling that the spiritual dimension is too personal for health-care professionals to pry into. Many health-care pro-viders feel that they are ill-equipped to deal with this area either because they themselves lack a personal faith or because their faith differs consid-erably from that of the person for whom they are caring. It is the intention of this author not only to try to allay some of the fears that health-care providers may have but also to try to offer some indicators that will give them the confidence to assist in spiritual care.

Religious Needs

When one speaks of spiritual care many health-care professionals insist on perceiving this as identical to religious care. This is not necessarily the case. Not all people would claim adherence to a formalised religion. A large proportion of the population may be described as comfortably agnostic. This, however, does not mean that they are not people of spiritual awareness, only that many do not seem to need to place their value systems within a codified or creedal belief system.[7]

Many think that when spiritual needs are raised all that is really being talked about are questions like, "What religion is the patient?", or "What denomination?", and "Is this important to him or her?". These are undoubtedly important questions. However, if one is to effect total care they do not reveal the total picture. The words *spiritual* and *reli-gious* are not necessarily synonymous. Religious needs are only a part of the greater whole-spiritual needs. Although within certain western societies only a minority adhere to specific religious beliefs, we should recognize that all people have spiritual needs.

Human Needs

Alastair Campbell, a sociologist, maintains that human needs fall into three basic categories:

1. The need for having,
2. The need for relating, and
3. The need for being.[8]

These needs are primarily existential and egocentric. Although, it has to be admitted, they do tell us something about the human condition, they are unable to describe it fully. What Campbell misses is the transcendent component of existence. We all need to be inspired, to attempt to ponder those things which are not only greater than ourselves but also those things which are beyond our control.

At the core of each of us there is a set of fundamental spiritual needs. For some these needs are fulfilled by adherence to a formalised religion; for others they remain distinct and unique.

> It is a fundamental human need to ponder the imponderable. From the dawn of time, human beings have desired to be able to put their own existence into some greater perspective and, from this, to attempt to make sense of those most puzzling of circumstances, such as birth, death and, above all, the meaning of life itself.[9]

Defining Spiritual Needs

There are many ways in which spiritual needs can be defined. One useful approach is that adopted by Highfield and Cason, who put them into the following categories:

1. The need for meaning and purpose,
2. The need to give love,
3. The need to receive love, and
4. The need for hope and creativity.[10]

Although these were described by Highfield and Cason in the early 1980s, these spiritual needs are by no means unique to them. Many of the spiritual giants of the past have variously described the spiritual needs of people in similar ways.

These are common to all humanity. However, they are most obvious at times of crisis in our lives. While life is good and "every thing in the garden is rosy" few of us see the need to address our spirituality; it is only when we are threatened or our lifestyle changes that our needs are put into sharper focus. A prime example of this is terminal illness. When we are faced with our own mortality or that of someone close to us, there is often a need to attempt to assess our spiritual needs. When someone has been given a diagnosis that is potentially life-threatening, then there are several things which they often wish to do.

Meaning and Purpose

First, a person in this situation will often want to look back over the life they have had and attempt to make sense of it, to try and find some meaning in it. This means that they will wish to affirm those things that have been successful and to acknowledge those that have not. This may include, but is not limited to, family, relationships, work, achievements, God. From this search for meaning in life, from acknowledgment of the successful and unsuccessful can rise purpose. Purpose to go on, to "fight the disease process."

Hope and Creativity

If meaning and purpose are retrospective, then hope and creativity are prospective. These issues are of the future. All human beings need hope and this is particularly true of people with cancer. Hope is a multilayered phenomenon, it may include such aspirations as, "I hope I get better", "I hope that my symptoms are controlled", "I hope I can be free of pain", "I hope I don't lose my dignity". It may include such things as a hope of the afterlife, or at least a hope that my belief system will be validated in death. Further, it may be hoped that that which has been of meaning and purpose to the individual may be affirmed by those who are important to him or her. From this hope can arise intense levels of creativity, not only in an artistic sense (some will take up writing, poetry, painting, or some other creative activity for the first time in their lives), but also in the ways in which relationships are addressed.

The Giving and Receiving of Love

Anthony Bloom, the Russian Orthodox Archbishop in London, maintains that we spend most of our lives either living in the past or planning for the future.[11] If one reflects on this for a moment, most of us would

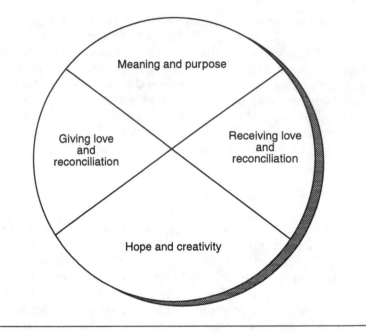

Figure 9.1   Spiritual needs

have to agree with him. We either look back on what has already taken place or we are looking forward to what may be. This is ultimately an act of self-deception. What has passed has passed and what is to be in the future we cannot directly affect. Bloom suggests that the most important time in our lives and the only one we have any power to shape is the here and now. For this reason, perhaps, our most important spiritual needs lie in the present—in our relationships. We all need to be reassured that we are loved and that others need our love.

Reconciliation

However, spiritual needs are not just about positive, affirmative, relationships. Spiritual needs are also about recognizing the "broken" in our lives. It is not only about love but also about the courage to be reconciled and to reconcile. This is particularly the case with anyone who is suffering from a life-threatening illness. Due to the disease process the patient can feel a rising sense of isolation. Sometimes cancer can be a real wilderness. The feeling of isolation is not something just experienced by people who are reverse barrier nursed. The disease process, the inability to be able to relate at the level one would wish to with family and friends, lack of human contact and, for those for whom it is important, a sense of isolation from their God, these are all important for us to be able to identify. This isolation can make a person feel different, certainly in degree if not in kind, from those who are significant to him or her. For all these reasons the reassurance of love, given and received, is essential.

This can be readily seen in one who experiences altered body image. A person who has a facial cancer may be rendered unrecognisable either due to the disease process or to the subsequent treatment. Nevertheless, he or she is still the same person inside and desperately needs to be affirmed as such. Such persons need the love that was theirs before and need the opportunity to reciprocate that love.

The need to give and receive love is not just about the positive aspects of relationships. It is also about reconciliation. Not all our relationships or actions in life are successful. There are failures and breakdowns, people do fall out of love, and relationships can be painful and negative. Often we see people who have been through a marital breakdown and out of the blue the ex-spouse will turn up at the bedside. This is seldom some romantic Hollywood-style reunion, but it is often a very profound experience. For by their sheer presence, acknowledgment of the failures of the past can be achieved and an acceptance of responsibility for those failures shown.

Living in the Present

The strengthening of relationships is also about a realisation of self-worth—a realisation that even though time may be a limited commodity, the dying are still living in the present. If we can sustain people in the present at the same time as being realistic for the future, then there is value and worth to be found in the here and now. A Sanskit proverb advises:

> Look to this day; it is life, for yesterday is already a dream and tomorrow is only a vision. But today, if well lived makes every yesterday a dream of happiness and every tomorrow a vision of hope.[12]

Of course, it is somewhat artificial for us to categorise spiritual needs into closed boxes. There is much overlap among the compartments of a person's spirituality. Spirituality for the individual is a whole and as such should be addressed. It is only when some part of spirituality is not fulfilled that we as carers should look at its component parts.

Isolation

One of the problems that has an impact upon the dying person is the rising sense of isolation he or she feels. Isolation may be experienced at many levels. Due to physical incapacity the dying person can no longer interact in the same way with family and friends. He or she is perceived and treated differently by those who are significant to him or her. This change is often appropriate for he or she may no longer be able to do the things that once gave pleasure or fulfilment. However, many things are assumed as the disease progresses. It seems strange that just because a person is terminally ill, his or her competence is brought into question. This sort of attitude, which is by no means uncommon, gives rise to situations in which the health-care provider can be compromised. "He must not know he's dying, it would kill him," was said in all seriousness not so long ago by the wife of a person with advanced carcinoma of the lung. What she was really saying was that if her husband was made aware of his prognosis she would have to accept it herself. But this attitude isolates the dying person, particularly if he is aware of his prognosis.

The closer that death draws, the greater the sense of isolation can be. Not only does the number of people the dying person interacts with grow smaller, but also there can be a sense of feeling different because he is about to experience death at first hand, something those significant to him are not. The danger, here, is that the dying person can be seen almost as different in kind from friends and family. The life of the dying person is not different in kind from those who are well and healthy, it is only different in degree. For us to perceive it otherwise may infer that we ourselves wish to deny that mortality is a natural and inevitable conclusion to life.

Caring for the Living

One term in common coinage within oncology is *care of the dying*. As much as this may be a useful shorthand for those who care for those with advanced or terminal cancer, its use can have unfortunate effects on our perceptions of care and who we care for. Perhaps what we should be keeping in mind is *care of the living* for then we have a chance of caring for the whole person. There are only two types of people, the living and the dead. If we talk about care of the dying, we consign people to a third and false category, to a waiting room. However, if we talk about *living people* at the same time as recognizing their limitations, then we can help them to begin to fulfil and maximise their quality of life. If spiritual needs can be addressed, patients can be drawn out of the isolation and affirmed as not only living but also of worth.

Spiritual Pain

For every health-care discipline involved in the multidisciplinary team there will be a different definition of pain. For the medic, pain is seen as neurophysiological response, the psychologist talks about psychological pain, the social worker will identify social distress. When spiritual needs are left unfulfilled, then it is appropriate to talk about spiritual pain. We must remember that however we as professionals define the pain we perceive in individuals, for the patient that pain is concrete. If we were to seek a universal definition of pain, we could do worse than to adopt the following: "Pain a direct response to dis-ease."[13] If we are not at ease with ourselves, we are likely to be distressed and in pain. If we are suffering from disease, we will also be in pain. This means that as advanced as symptom control is, it must become yet more subtle. We can no longer treat symptoms solely at a physiological level.

What we must acknowledge is that pain is not just a response to a physical problem, but may be caused by dis-ease at many different levels. If there is a lack of fulfilment in spiritual areas, then this ill-ease is likely to cause pain. Further anxiety and distress can exacerbate physical symptoms.

If we are to treat the whole person, then all facets must be addressed. As far as the spiritual component is concerned, if the spiritual, as well as the other, needs of the patient are fulfilled then the level of analgesia required will drop. As an hypothesis this perforce is speculative, however it does fit qualitatively.

The hypothesis may gain support from the gate theory of pain; it has been suggested that descending fibres from the higher centres may effect the opening of the gate, thus suppressing nociceptor activity.[14] If this is the case, then addressing spiritual needs may encourage firing in these descending fibres. Of course, this is a speculative statement and an exceedingly difficult effect to prove scientifically.

This does not mean that carers should address the spiritual distress within a person before giving them appropriate amounts of analgesia. If someone is referred for pain control, then the initial action must be to relieve the physiological symptoms. However, once the patient's medication has been titrated so that the pain is controlled, then if the spiritual needs are addressed effectively the frequency of break-through occurences of pain may drop.

What we are dealing with here is dis-ease at the very core of a person's being. In his book *Care of the Dying*, Richard Lamberton maintains that this sort of pain is "intractable":

> Physical pains we suffer alone; mental and social pains, particularly grief, affect the whole circle of our acquaintances. But the greatest pain

of all, a pain of the spirit is as great as mankind. It is the pain of the prodigal son. (Luke 15:11–32).[15]

However, this is not necessarily so. It may be true to say that greater sublety is required when addressing this sort of pain but I do not believe that it is a priori intractable. Even for the prodigal son there was reconciliation, reassurance that he was loved, and a relief of his distress.

Addressing Spiritual Needs and Pain

As already suggested, many health-care professionals lack the confidence to care for the spiritual needs of their patients. At this point it should be apparent that these needs are not peculiar to patients but common to us all. This fact should assist us in at least identifying the spiritual needs of others. To be able to identify these needs, however, requires us to attempt to do something about them if health care has anything to do with problem solving.

For this we need to develop skills. But, if we begin to over-professionalise this, to build up some sort of jargon for it, then it becomes something that only specialists can do. What we need to draw on are our human skills, for it is from this commonality that our best spiritual care arises. What are required are not the uses of specialist psychotherapeutic techniques nor passing the buck to a specialist minister, but the improvement of communication and above all listening skills. If spiritual needs are over-professionalised, then the care of them is put beyond the possibility of the patient, who is then further isolated.

As health-care professionals we need to develop skills that permit us to *be* with patients. Most of health care is about *doing* things for people, but if we are to affect any sort of spiritual care then we have to learn to be comfortable *being* with people. This demands the development of listening skills. The ability to listen with our eyes. In truth, "we have two eyes, two ears and one mouth and perhaps we should use them in that proportion."[16]

Many of the spiritual problems come from a deep-seated need to articulate potentially unanswerable questions and when these arise many feel impotent because of their inability to provide definite answers. Many will pose questions such as: "Why me?", "Why does God do this to me?", "Why doesn't He take it away?". It is dangerous to adopt the attitude that just because a question is posed it must be answered. There may be answers to the sorts of questions that arise commonly, at the same time there may not be. An important part of spiritual care is to allow people the time and space to pose the questions and to be comfortable in the knowledge that carers do not have to necessarily answer them. Rather than falling into the trap of trying to answer these questions, it is often better to be honest. Saying "I don't know" is sometimes not only honest but also reassures the patient that he or she is still human for having asked it. Explorations into doubtful theology or metaphysics can leave the patient even more isolated than before he or she dared to talk.

Further, it is unacceptable practice when these situations arise to rush off saying, "I'll just go and call the chaplain." Chaplains *are* an important part of the caring team, but the patient has chosen whom to talk to and in the first instance that carer should be comfortable in being with the patient before referring to someone else.

For us to be able to care for the spiritual needs of others we must, at times, be prepared to show our vulnerability. "Our ability to care is directly proportional to our vulnerability."[17] This is often seen as a weakness on the part of the carer, but if strength only comes when we can solve problems, then we have to accept that failure is a state we continually live with. Strength can come with a sense of vulnerability, for then we are most human.

Spiritual Health

So far the discussion has centered around the concepts of spiritual needs and spiritual pain, which in itself may not be totally helpful. The danger with consistently looking at the spiritual needs of the dying as problems to be addressed and solved is that we can deny the possibility of spiritual health.

An experienced senior hospice health-care professional one day called the chaplain to the unit to discuss a patient. It was felt by the person that Mrs. A had some difficulty coming to terms with her approaching death. The chaplain agreed to visit Mrs. A. At the end of a lengthy session with the patient, he was sure from what was articulated that Mrs. A had in fact come to terms with her own mortality. She felt that she had lived a fulfilled life, was loved by her relatives and friends, and that when the time came she would be content to be relieved of the suffering she was experiencing and "see, at last, the face of God." The chaplain relayed this to the referring person with his opinion that Mrs. A had come to terms with her own mortality and was reasonably happy about it. The referring person replied, "Yes, it's a worry isn't it?"

The assumptions here seem to be twofold: First, no one could come to terms with his or her own mortality readily. And second, no one could possibly come to terms with his or her own mortality without the intervention of a "specialist" health carer. Perhaps one reason for the response of the carers is that they have not come to terms with their mortality, but perhaps the other reason is an inability to accept situations on face value.

We most often care on the basis of problem solving. A patient experiences pain, this is a problem, analgesia is prescribed and administered, the problem is dealt with. Problem solving is a direct response to our need to *do* and, as already suggested, *doing* may not be the most appropriate approach to spiritual needs.

What is far more appropriate is to search for signs of spiritual health that can be built upon. If those areas in a person's spirituality that are of value can be affirmed by the carer, then not only is confidence built between carer and cared for, but also those areas of brokenness can be healed from a positive position of strength.

The Way Forward

> No man is an island, entire of it self.
> Everyman is a piece of the Continent, a part of the Main.[18]

So far in this chapter I have used the term *multidisciplinary* when talking about the teams who care for those with life-threatening illnesses. Perhaps we should be espousing a further development in this thinking and begin to talk about *interdisciplinary* rather than multidisciplinary. If we are to care for the whole person seriously then we can no longer work in loosely associated teams. Instead, our way forward is to obtain a balance of care by drawing together the differing ways in which we perceive a person. There are many overlaps in the way various professions address the needs of the patient and it is at these very boundaries that we can begin to cohese. Within the field of care of the dying, there is very little room for professional jealousy and protection. So often, life is, literally, just too short for this sort of pettiness. We must work together in an open and truly interdisciplinary way. It is only when we have achieved this that we can begin to affect total care for the body, mind, and spirit, the integrated human being—our patients and ourselves. As Donne wrote:

> Any man's death diminishes me,
> because I am involved in Mankind;
> And therefore never send to know for whom the bell tolls;
> It tolls for thee.[19]

References

1. Manley-Hopkins, G. (1948). *Felix Randal* in The Poems of Gerard Manley Hopkins, 3rd. ed., London: Cumberledge G. OUP.
2. Maddocks, M. (1981). *The Christian healing ministry*. London: SPCK.
3. Parker, J. (1984). *Cancer passage patterns of care—hospitals*. Proceedings of 3rd International Conference on Cancer Nursing. Melbourne, March, pp. 20–23.
4. Arcand, R. (1984). *Practice philosophies: The basis of a cancer nursing model*. Proceedings of 3rd International Conference on Cancer Nursing. Melbourne, March pp. 20–23.
5. Stoddard, S. (1979). *The hospice movement—a better way of caring for the dying*. London: Johnathan Cape.
6. Cassel, E. (1982). The nature of suffering and the goals of medicine. *New England Journal of Medicine*, 306, pp. 639–645.
7. Parker, J. *Op cit.*
8. Campbell, A. (1981). *The sense of well-being in America: Recent patterns and trends*. New York: McGraw-Hill.
9. Cosh, R. J. (1988). Spiritual issues in cancer care. In *Oncology for Health-Care Professionals*, Vol 2 Tiffany R. (Ed.), New York: Harper & Row.
10. Highfield, M. F., & Cason, C. (1983). Spiritual needs of patients: Are they recognised? *Cancer Nursing*, 6 June.
11. Bloom, A. (1988). verb cit. at The International Symposium on Spiritual Issues in Cancer Care.
12. Whitaker, A. (Ed.), (1984). *All in the end is harvest: An anthology for those who grieve*. London: Darta, Longman & Todd.
13. Cosh, R. J. *Op cit.*
14. Melzack, R., & Wall, P. (1988). *The challenge of pain*. 2nd ed. (pp.175-176). London: Pelican.
15. Lamberton, R. (1980). *Care of the dying*. (p. 61). London: Pelican.
16. Hull, H., Ellis, M., & Sargent, V. (1989). *Team work in palliative care*. (p.74). Oxford: Radcliffe Medical Press.
17. Prophit, P. (1984). Another chapter . . . nursing research unit at Edinburgh University. *Nursing Mirror* 159(20), 26–28.
18. Donne, J. (1982). Devotions on Emergent Themes. In Smith, A. J. (Ed.), *The Complete English Poems of John Donne*. London: Penguin.
19. Donne, J. *Op cit.*

Ten

Euthanasia— How to Die

Ulla Qvarnstrøm

Ulla Qvarnstrøm was in 1979 called upon to build an institute of nursing science at the University of Bergen, Norway. Since then a full academic program has been elaborated.

Professor Qvarnstrøm holds a degree in social science. She earned her doctoral degree (Fil dr) from the University of Stockholm, Sweden.

Professor Qvarnstrøm has published books in the fields of death and dying and nursing science in the Swedish language and published several articles on death issues and nursing in international scientific journals. She also serves on the editorial board of several international journals on death and nursing science.

In 1978 Professor Qvarnstrøm became a member of the International Work Group on Death, Dying, and Bereavement. She is a member of the Nordic organization "Care at the end of life," of the board of the Nightingale Society, and a member of the European Association for Palliative Care.

Introduction

The notion of euthanasia is probably as old as the biological fact of human death. Problems related to unbearable suffering, fatal disease, and euthanasia have always been a matter of paramount interest within the disciplines of nursing and medicine, and are continuously reflected in the ongoing discussions in the field of nursing ethics and ethics in medicine. The problem of euthanasia has been debated for centuries among the general public as well. In 1516 Thomas More recommended a system for euthanasia in which the dying person, suffering from unbearable pain, would be advised by a forum of priests and magistrates to shorten his life, either by committing suicide or by an action carried out by the authorities (Gruman, 1984).

As time went on, the ability of modern medicine, with all its advanced technology, to prolong life, even for those patients suffering from a fatal disease, has brought about a renewed debate among different

145

groups in society—theologians, ethicists, moral philosophers, lawyers, and health professionals. The general public is still involved in this discussion, through organizations such as the Voluntary Euthanasia Society, an international group in Great Britain, and the National Hemlock Society in the United States.

The literal meaning of the term *euthanasia* is "a good death," stemming from the two Greek words *eu* meaning good and *thanatos* meaning death. However, the issue of euthanasia is today too complex and diverse for this meaning to be adequate. Euthanasia and the dying process are closely related to the notion of the meaning of human life, and to the value of human life per se. That frame of reference is required for analysis and interpretation.

The Meaning of Life

The concepts of "the meaning of life" and "the value of life" have their roots in the philosophical conception of human life in general. Ancient Greek philosophers, Stoics, and scholastic philosophers have formulated standards for judging the value of human life. Modern philosophers have contributed their thinking about the meaning and value of human life. The French philosopher Rousseau, for example, maintained that the human being who has lived most intensely is not the one who has survived as many years as possible, but the human being who has most deeply perceived life.

The famous Austrian psychiatrist Viktor E. Frankl, who was a successor to the academic chair held by Freud at the University of Vienna, and who had spent several years in concentration camps, developed logotherapy, a therapy based on the fundamental assumption that there is *always* meaning in a human's life (Frankl, 1969). Frankl's existential philosophy is realistic in its essence and acknowledges that suffering, guilt, and death are phenomena that guide human existence. At the same time, the philosophy expresses how human suffering can bring about human growth and how despair can be transformed into human victory. It also comprises a foundation for basic tenets and assumptions, which together constitute three systems or triads. The systems form a chain of interconnected links.

The first triad consists of three basic assumptions: the freedom of will, the will of meaning, and the meaning of life. According to Frankl, the *freedom of will* is the free will of human nature, which is in some way determinative, since the will is that of a mortal creature. Man's freedom is not a freedom from conditions, but a freedom that makes it possible for the individual to choose between principles apart from those conditions the individual may confront. From this viewpoint the individual is free to create his or her own character, and is responsible for his or her own path of life. Frankl points out that it is important to keep in mind that it is not our traits of character, our drives or interests per se that play the role but how we approach these. The ability to make such decisions is what makes us human beings, equipped with an anthropological dimension of existence. This anthropological dimension means a transcendence beyond the biological and psychological dimension and opens a way to self-reflection and conscience. Frankl underlines that the conscience presupposes the human being's unique ability to grow beyond self, to value and judge his or her own actions on the basis of moral and ethical standards.

The concept *will of meaning* has its roots in the basic assumption that the human being lives intentionally, which means that he or she lives in order to reach a goal. The goal is to give life a meaning. Furthermore, the individual has an inborn drive to be creative and to realize values. The will of meaning is the human being's fundamental endeavor to find and to fulfill meanings and intentions of life. What then is "meaning"? According to Frankl's philosophy, meaning is a relative phenomenon because it is related to a specific person who in turn is involved in specific circumstances. From this point of view the experience of meaning differs from individual to individual and from day to day, and even from hour to hour. As a subjective relative phenomenon, meaning has a unique quality because it is closely related, not only to specific human experiences but also to human life as a whole. Conscience is the force that guides the human being in his or her search for meaning. As such, the will of meaning constitutes the second cornerstone of the first triad, basic assumptions of human existence.

The third basic assumption of this triad is the *meaning of life*. In the light of Frankl's existential philosophy it can be stated that life has a meaning, a meaning for which "Man" has always searched. Humans have the freedom to seek the fulfillment of this meaning. Frankl points out that humans can find meaning in life by creating a work or doing a deed; by experiencing goodness, truth, and beauty; by experiencing nature and culture; or by encountering another unique being in the very uniqueness of being human. The relationship among these three basic assumptions of the first triad and the tenets of the second and third triads is illustrated in Figure 10.1.

As mentioned, the concepts form a chain of interrelated links. The concept *meaning of life* in the first triad constitutes the second triad, which is made up of three concepts: (1) creative values, (2) experiential values, and (3) attitudinal values. These three types of values reflect the most important ways for the individual to find meaning in life.

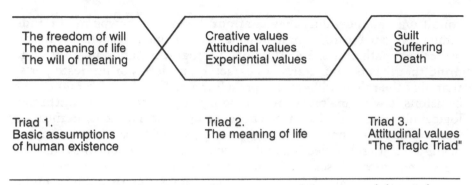

The freedom of will
The meaning of life
The will of meaning

Creative values
Attitudinal values
Experiential values

Guilt
Suffering
Death

Triad 1.
Basic assumptions
of human existence

Triad 2.
The meaning of life

Triad 3.
Attitudinal values
"The Tragic Triad"

Figure 10.1   Relationships among the concepts and the tenets of the triads

Creative values mean everything the human being gives to the world and *experiential values* mean everything the human being receives from the surrounding world. *Attitudinal values* imply the individual's attitude when confronting situations beyond his or her control. Because of these fundamental human conditions, life will always, in any situation whatsoever, have a meaning. According to Frankl, even those human beings who have lost both creative and experiential values will still be challenged by a meaning built into the true and dignified type of suffering. This attitude toward one's inevitable destiny, death, lays the foundation for the third triad, a meaningful attitude toward suffering, guilt, and death. The term *meaningful* in this sense means that the human being has the ability to transfer tragic and negative conditions into positive experiences with the help of transcendence of attitudes. As Frankl (1969, p. 63) so excellently expresses it: "Fate cannot be changed, otherwise it would not be fate. Man, on the other hand, can change. If not, he is not a human being. It is a privilege to be a human being and it is a part of the human existence to be able to shape and reshape itself." In spite of life's transcendence, the human being is responsible for taking advantage of all the opportunities that may come forth, using them in order to make real possibilities, or to realize values, whether creative, experiential, or attitudinal. From this viewpoint, the individual is responsible for what he or she is doing and how he or she copes with suffering.

As human beings we are all striving for happiness. By choosing the right path (with regard to values), we will be able to reach happiness even in hopeless situations. Within the framework of this existential philosophy, it is possible for every individual to find a meaning of life until the last breath at the moment of death.

However, many individuals experience emptiness and meaninglessness when confronted with circumstances like an incurable disease. In such a life situation, everything that has brought meaning to one's life seems to fall apart and be replaced by a feeling of existential vacuum. This type of existential experience Frankl names an "abysmal experience." He claims that such human experience has its roots in two very important facts. First, Man has no inborn drives or instincts to tell him what to do under such circumstances. Second, Mankind currently seems to have abandoned the conventions, traditions, and values that earlier in our history guided individuals in their efforts to find meaning in a hopeless life situation, to express their creativity, to make use of collected life experience, and to transcend attitudinal values into a higher dimension of the value of life. As a consequence, the individual becomes the victim of an existential vacuum. In such a life situation characterized by a complete lack of satisfaction with life, it is not difficult to understand a dying human being's request for euthanasia.

Satisfaction with Life

In his thorough analysis of the concept of happiness, the Polish philosopher Tatarkiewicz (1976) states that a satisfactory life consists of three cornerstones: the first factor is *life*, the second factor is *time*, and the third factor is *suffering*. These three elements and their specific interrelated meanings constitute the foundation for a satisfactory human life as a whole.

Tatarkiewicz defines the concept of life from three perspectives. First, life is a *biological* process, which occurs in the human organism between birth and death. This process makes no sense when we express our satisfaction with life. Second, life may be defined in terms of the *psychological* process that occurs in the human being's consciousness—the mass of perceptions, ideas, feelings, and so on, that pass through his or her consciousness between birth and death. This process does not meet the criterion for a satisfactory life.

The third definition of life is expressed in terms of "all events in which a man is involved and to which he reacts from birth to death... " (Tatarkiewicz, 1976, p. 20). Here life is an accumulation, not only of happenings within the psychological and physical self but also outside it. This applies even to events, in which involvement is passive. The boundary between one's own life and the life of others is not so distinctly defined in life as is a biological or psychological process. As Tatarkiewicz states: "My happiness is satisfaction with my life, but my life shares many of its elements with the lives of others" (1976, p. 13).

From this perspective, life means all the events the human being experiences and takes part in during his or her life cycle. Life can therefore be defined as a mixture of processes on different levels scattered in time and space. Only a few of those may take place within the organism of a given individual. From this point of view, Tatarkiewicz strongly argues that life itself has value regardless of situation.

The second cornerstone in satisfaction with life is the concept of time. Time is defined in a chronological order, the past, the present, and the future. *The past* implies not only pleasant or unpleasant experiences, it is also the foundation for a judgment of the present and the future. *The present* not only throws light on an uncertain future, but also influences past experiences. Tatarkiewicz states that a positive present experience will minimize past sufferings and strengthen pleasant experiences, while bad or negative present experiences tend to erase all the good ones the human being so far has sensed.

The future, which is not yet reached, may combine the past and the present. As Tatarkiewicz states: "In some cases they view the past and present in light of their dreams of the future, in others, anxiety about the future precludes all enjoyment of the present" (1976, p. 141).

From this point of view, time—the past, the present, and the future— is transcendental and in this transcendence the present plays a minor role as it quickly transfers to the past, whereas the future is of most importance for satisfaction with life here and now.

The third cornerstone for satisfaction with life is suffering. In his analysis of the concept of suffering Tatarkiewicz states: " ...there are as many kinds of pain as of pleasure and they can be similarly divided into two main groups: those derived from sensations and those derived from ideas" (1976, p. 79). When they get extraordinarily acute we name them *suffering*.

The German philosopher Schopenhauer expressed the suffering of humankind in the following well-known sentence: "Every individual has his proper measure of suffering allocated to him for all time by his nature and no man ever suffers less than his need." (Tatarkiewicz, 1976, p. 86). Suffering, which is a general term for all kinds of pain and discomfort, can be either physical or mental. While physical pain is a response to a stimulus and lasts as long as the stimulus lasts, mental suffering has its roots in ideas and has a cultural basis. Mental suffering is less connected to time than physical pain. According to an analysis of the concept of mental suffering, it has three specific characteristics:

1. Mental suffering is not governed by any organic process.
2. Mental suffering is painful, not only at the moment it actually happens or when we hear of it. It is also painful to recollect or to anticipate.
3. Mental suffering is closely related to time, the past, the present, the future.

The greatest mental sufferings are related to and caused by our imaginations of the future. This may be applicable to our fear of possible threats (e.g., death, injury, loss of liberty, separation); to our expectations of and uncertainty about the future; or to despair because of losses (e.g., loss of hope, loss of values).

Mental suffering has been described as having additional characteristics. The human being seems to have a suffering ceiling. Once suffering has gone beyond this ceiling, there seems to be a numbness to further blows so they can neither intensify nor deepen that suffering (Tatarkiewicz, 1976). One type of mental suffering tends to decrease the power of another type of suffering. Hence, there seems to be a neutralizing combination of forces among the kinds of mental suffering. The individual mobilizes compensation or an antidote to mental suffering. This can take the form of escaping into the future, blocking the thoughts with pleasant thoughts, daydreaming about things one may be denied, or thinking about suffering being shared with others who suffer in the same way. All these factors contribute to the decrease of the individual's mental suffering. However, the individual's despair, in this view, caused by loss of hope and an uncertain future are the absolute causes of the individual's dissatisfaction with life (Tatarkiewicz, 1976).

Confronting a life situation colored by all kinds of suffering and loss of love, the dying patient's request for euthanasia seems to be a rational thought.

The Concept of Euthanasia

As mentioned earlier in this chapter, the term *euthanasia* means a good death. One dictionary definition of euthanasia is a "gentle and easy death; bringing about of this, esp. in the case of incurable and painful disease" (Oxford,1976, p. 357). Usually, the concept refers both to the easing of the dying process and to the cause of death itself. Such general definitions of the concept are, however, too broad to have meaning for the dying or for health professionals in their care of the dying.

Today, the issue related to intentional and deliberate death and euthanasia moves our reflections on these questions beyond the traditional type of ethical-moral analysis. As Kenneth Vaux states in his article, "The Theologic Ethics of Euthanasia," we are no longer faced with the gruesome stipulates of an "ecological ethic" of weeding out the old and weak. Here we also move beyond the philosophic ethics that speak of "a right to die," professional ethics that affirm "a duty to preserve life," and legal ethics that prescribe acts of medical murder, even if the victim is a pleading patient and the perpetrator a compassionate physician (Vaux, 1989, p. 20).

From this multidimensional perspective a redefined ethic may be called upon in order to make the meaning of euthanasia and the right to die fully understood. It is time for an ethic, which partly stems from the dying patient's situation and which partly stems from the ultimate ground of human existence.

Types of Euthanasia

The literature describes different types of euthanasia: involuntary euthanasia, nonvoluntary euthanasia, voluntary active euthanasia, and passive euthanasia. All these types of euthanasia may be present in the care of the dying. These different types of euthanasia imply different justifications for killing another person (Vaux, 1989).

The definition of *involuntary euthanasia* is that it occurs whenever the decision to kill another person is implemented against the expressed wishes of the individual. From a moral point of view, involuntary euthanasia must always be considered a wrong action because such an action, regardless of all other reasons, deprives the individual of the value that stands above all others—life itself. *Nonvoluntary euthanasia* occurs whenever the decision to kill another person is made without the consent of the human being concerned, whatever the reason for the absence of such consent. Nonvoluntary euthanasia will take place in extreme circumstances, in which it might be reasonable to judge that the person would prefer death in comparison to the only alternative of existence at hand. *Voluntary active euthanasia* occurs when the decision to kill another person coincides with the individual's own wishes, and when he or she consciously approves of it, and of all aspects of its implementation. According to Vaux (1989), ethicists find voluntary active euthanasia, like suicide, morally justifiable, but as a human choice it may be ill advised. *Passive euthanasia* is commonly defined as a situation in which death occurs in the course of treating a terminally ill person by foregoing potentially life-prolonging measures. This definition of the concept has been explained in broader terms: "It is not considered obligatory to initiate CPR, antimicrobiological therapy, mechanical ventilation, or artificial nutrition and hydration when it is futile or only marginally helpful" (Vaux, 1989, p. 20). Furthermore, it is argued that patients are really not obliged to accept different kinds of treatment, such as surgery or organ transplantation, when crucial body organs fail (Vaux, 1989).

Other types of euthanasia have been labeled semiactive, semipassive, suicidal, and double-effect euthanasia (Lundberg, 1988). *Semiactive euthanasia* takes place when a physician disconnects a ventilator from a patient who is in a stable, vegetative state, as from a massive cerebral infraction, and who has no hope of regaining consciousness. *Semipassive euthanasia* occurs when medical treatment, nutrition or fluids, are withheld from a person in coma, for example, from postnecrotic cirrhosis or cerebral metastases. *Suicidal euthanasia* is exemplified by the patient who intentionally overdoses on narcotics, causing his or her own death. The drugs were prescribed for pain relief.

Another class of actions described in the literature has been designated *double-effect euthanasia*. From a moral point of view, it is acceptable that a terminally ill patient choose a treatment for relief of pain that may lead to death. Such pain remedy is regarded as ethically justified in that the administrator's primary intent is to relieve the dying patient's suffering, although it is possible to foresee the ensuing death. Such action must be based on the patient's or the family's consent. In such a situation, the patient's suffering is given first priority, even if the side effect is grievous. Many nurses have participated in such caring situations. The physician has ordered a dose of morphine, which the nurse realizes may contribute to hastening the patient's death. The nurse has no intention of killing the patient. Even so, the patient dies, and the nurse may, after the patient's death, feel guilt for causing death. This type of double-edged purpose and bivalent action in caring for the dying is certainly common and anxiety provoking for the staff. However, as Vaux has written, "Our moral tradition demands that we act courageously, even though our actions might result in double-effect euthanasia" Vaux, 1989, p. 20).

The Appleton Consensus

The increased debate on the subject of euthanasia has brought about two international conferences regarding nontreatment decisions in connection with incurable diseases. The conferences took place at Lawrence University, Appleton, Wisconsin, USA. In 1987, John H. Stanley, professor of ethics in medicine, science, and society, invited 30 guests representing Western Europe, Israel, and the United States to discuss the complicated issue of foregoing medical treatment with fatal disease. Subjects such as living wills, assessment of quality of life, the ethics of distribution of resources, the value of institutional ethical committees, and the role of the physician as decision maker were discussed. The most controversial issues that the group confronted were the attitudes towards euthanasia on request and the stopping of treatment when the patient is irreversibly unconscious.

At the second conference, the group reached consensus on several important issues in spite of their different cultural backgrounds and of their representing different professions such as medicine, philosophy, theology, judicial ethics, and economics. Out of this conference came the Appleton Consensus document, which is based on four commonly accepted moral values and principles, which summarize the norms for medical ethics within different cultural, religious, and political traditions. The four principles are autonomy, nonmaleficiens, beneficiens, and justice. The principle of *autonomy* demands respect for the choices the patient makes and which are in accordance with his or her own beliefs. It rests on the value that all human beings have a moral obligation to respect each other's autonomy as long as this respect does not infringe the right of others to decide over themselves. The principle of autonomy also includes respect for the individual's dignity and integrity, and for honesty and truth. Clearly, these values apply to patients and health-care providers alike.

Nonmaleficiens means that every human being has a moral obligation not to hurt another. In medicine the risk of an injury is morally justified only in the case that the injury is counterbalanced by the predicted good for the patient. The principle of *beneficiens* implies that every human being has a moral obligation to protect another, especially sick and suffering human beings. From a cultural and an individual point of view, this obligation may be interpreted differently, but in any case, people working in the health services have a special moral obligation to be useful to the patients they care for.

The *justice* principle implies that each person has a moral obligation to behave in a just and honest manner toward others with regard to the distribution of scarce resources and with regard to the respect for others' rights. The interpretation of these obligations depends on cultural and individual perspectives.

These four principles often conflict with one another and have to be balanced. They are given different importance in different cultures. The fact that they have been mutually accepted is, however, a most valuable cross-cultural foundation for analyses within medical ethics, discussion, and decision making.

The Appleton group could not reach consensus concerning dying patients' requests for intervention to terminate life (voluntary active euthanasia). The majority of the group stated that requests for voluntary euthanasia by competent patients suffering severely as a result of incurable disease may be understandable but are not morally justified. The group felt that statutory legalization of the intentional killing of patients by doctors is against basic morality and against the public interest as well. It was stated that physicians have an obligation to provide a peaceful, dignified, and human death with minimal suffering.

In exploring issues related to foregoing treatment of terminally ill patients, the group discussed these ethical decisions from three caring situations: (1) expression of an able patient's will is at hand and a written or oral will is at hand from a patient before he or she became unable to express his or her will; (2) patients who have been able to make decisions about their will, but no longer have such an ability and have not expressed their will, written or oral, before they lost their ability; and (3) patients that are not, and have never been, able to express their will.

With reference to the *first* type of decision, the group stated that if an able dying patient refused treatment that the physician finds to be in the patient's interest, the physician has to give the patient complete information and clarify any misunderstanding. If the patient still refuses treatment, this refusal has to be respected. In such a situation, the physician and the caring team are obligated to give palliative treatment and basic nursing care.

If an unable patient, while still able to express his or her will, has made it clear that he or she refuses a certain treatment, or the patient has chosen an attorney to make decisions, such principles or decisions shall be respected. The Appleton consensus group noted that, according to the orthodox Jewish tradition, the refusal of life-prolonging treatment is not morally accepted.

In the *second* type of decision, when any kind of expressed will is lacking, the physician in charge has to, as thoroughly as possible, make clear the patient's medical prognosis under various treatment conditions. He has also to take into consideration the likely preferences of the patient's "value history." The physician is obligated to inform the patient's family about the alternatives at hand.

If the physician is unable to predict the patient's wishes in such a situation, he or she has to collaborate with the caring team and the patient's relatives. The decision should be made on the basis of such concepts as: maintenance of the patient's identity and ability to cooperate with others, freedom from pain and suffering, and freedom from being a burden to other people. If the relatives and the caregivers agree, the caring plan should be implemented. It was noted that from an ethical point of view, it is not more problematic to terminate a certain treatment than to decide to refrain from starting that treatment.

The most controversial question in this part of the document was the statement on "persistent vegetative state," which means irreversible unconsciousness. Such a situation creates issues to be dealt with on a national basis with respect to each country's jurisdiction and traditions of decision making. However, the majority of the group formulated a statement concerning persistent vegetative state, which reads as follows: The patient who is reliably diagnosed as being in the persistent vegetative state (PVS) has no self-regarding interests. Unless the patient in the past has requested, or the family or the caregivers now can justify continuing life-sustaining medical treatments, there is no reason to use those treatments.

The minority opinion however, states that "While it may be true that the patient with PVS has no 'self-regarding interest,' it is not so obvious that no other moral interests are at stake, for example, the inherent value of life. Since patients with PVS clearly do not suffer from their state, their quality of life cannot be characterized as harmful to themselves. We therefore cannot accept a categorical statement which rules out life-sustaining treatments" (Stanley, 1989).

The *third* type of decision deals with situations when patients are unable to express their will or when they have never had such an ability. Under these circumstances, the group states that the adjustments to be made must in the first place be governed by the medical prognosis. Respect for the value of life does not mean an absolute duty, in any situation, at any price, to use life-sustaining treatment. Here, one is forced to trust "the third person's judgments" when evaluating the quality of life for these patients. The judgments have to be based on the principle of what is good and what is harmful to the specific patients. They may never contain judgments based on the idea of an individual's social value (Harris, 1985). The Appleton consensus document is of high value because it constitutes a starting point for discussions of principles regarding use of advanced medical technology and care of the dying and the complex issue of euthanasia.

Implications for Care

In the care of the dying, where the meaning of life is highly accentuated, the concept of euthanasia has been more and more in focus. In fact, so much in focus that in some parts of the world there is readiness to make active voluntary euthanasia legal, and thereby a part of the health services offered to patients. Having in mind the procedures put at work in the sixteenth century regarding care of the dying, legislation of active voluntary euthanasia is a frightening perspective. To proceed further in our history, the knowledge available to mankind about human life and death has to be incorporated in the care of the dying in a more systematic and active way than it has been up to this point.

In order to contribute to a meaningful existence at the end of life, health professionals ought to have systematic theoretical and clinical education in order to understand the meaning of the individual's need to anchor existence through his or her own life history and the traditions and values that have guided that life. In such a way, it may be possible for the staff to prevent the phenomenon of existential vacuum—the psychic state described above and which Frankl (1969) assumes to be of most importance as the cause of the dying person's hopelessness, despair, and loss of dignity.

It is very important that health-care personnel be familiar with and have a deep understanding of the nature of suffering—physical, mental, and spiritual suffering. In coping with a patient's suffering, the concept of time is of high value. In light of that fact, it is necessary for caregivers to have a knowledge of time, the structure of time, and its influence on present human experiences and future perspectives, especially regarding the prospect of different kinds of pain and the impact of pain on present and future life.

Caregivers who commit their working lives to dying patients and their families have to be educated and clinically trained in such a way that their behavior and professional competence creates a caring environment which, as a whole, never gives rise to thoughts of active voluntary euthanasia among dying patients. In such a caring environment, high moral standards can be preserved and the staff will never encounter the risk of becoming inhuman or losing respect for human life itself. The overall goal of care of the dying must therefore be to provide care that preserves human dignity, meaning of life, and happiness. In such care there is no room for development of procedures for carrying out the killing of human beings. Instead, it is care that has within its scope of caring philosophy an idea that human life has to end and, in light of that fact, the dying process has to meet death on its own premises. At a proper time, the dying leave this life because human beings are mortal.

References

Concise Oxford Dictionary, The, 6th ed. (1976). Oxford: Oxford University Press, 376.

Frankl, V. (1969). *The will to meaning.* Ohio: The World Publishing Co.

Gruman, G .J. (1984). Death and dying: Euthanasia and sustaining life. *Encyclopedia of Bioethics.* New York: Free Press.

Harris, J. (1985). *The value of life: An introduction to medical ethics.* London: Routledge & Kegan.

Lundberg, G. D. (1988). "It's over, Debbie" and the euthanasia debate. *JAMA,* 3259, (14.), 2143.

Stanley, J. M. (1989). The Appleton consensus: Suggested international guidelines for decisions to forego medical treatment. *Legeskr. Laeger 151,* 700–706.

Tatarkiewicz, V. (1976). *Analysis of happiness.* Melbourne International Series, Vol. 3. Warsaw: PWN/Polish Scientific Publications.

Vaux, K. (1989). The theologic ethics of euthanasia. *Hastings Center Report, 19* (1), 20. Special Supplement.

Eleven

Funerals: Life's Final Ceremony

Vanderlyn R. Pine

Dr. Vanderlyn R. Pine is a professor of sociology at the State University of New York, College at New Paltz. He is a former director of graduate studies for the M.A./M.S.W. Program in Sociology and a chair of the department. He holds bachelor's and master's degrees from Dartmouth College and a doctorate from New York University.

Dr. Pine is an internationally known lecturer on a broad array of topics including health care, adaptation to change, business planning and management, death education, and grief counseling. Among the groups and organizations to which he regularly speaks are state and federal emergency preparedness agencies, the American Red Cross, health-care facilities, and many local church, civic, volunteer, and community organizations. Dr. Pine serves on the editorial boards of several national journals. He has authored, coauthored, and/or edited eight books and more than 50 articles and essays.

He is a member of numerous professional associations and serves on professional advisory boards at New York Medical College, Columbia University, and the University of Minnesota. He is on the board of trustees of Northwood School, Lake Placid, New York. Currently, he is the president of the Association for Death Education and Counseling, an international professional association.

In addition to his university position, Dr. Pine operates a business and professional advisory consulting organization. He specializes in demographic trend analysis, market research, business management research, and business appraisals of closely held corporations and professional practices. He is a Certified Business Appraiser, an active member of the Institute of Business Appraisers, and is a contributor to the literature on statistical analysis and business appraisals.

The social importance of funerals has changed over time. Fifty thousand years ago, humans commemorated death with ceremony, and each death was of great importance because it represented a loss of collective strength to the clan or tribe. With the development of population growth, increased technology, and geographic mobility, the old style social order changed. For example, in ancient Egypt the importance of most individual deaths diminished, paralleled by the increase in importance of a few deaths, such as those of the pharaohs.

With the rise of western religions and an increased focus on the uniqueness of the individual, each member of the community was believed to have distinct societal value. This made individual funerals more important to the larger community as well as to the immediately bereaved. In this setting, funerals attained a distinctly social character.

In today's industrialized and generally impersonal society, the funeral is usually of major significance only to those close to the dead person. Some funerals may be of concern to a community, but only a few are of significance to society in general.

Theoretical Background

Throughout history, the funeral has addressed four major social functions. First, it serves to acknowledge and commemorate the person's death. Second, it provides a setting for the disposition of the dead body. Third, it assists in reorienting the bereaved to their ruptured lives. Fourth, it demonstrates reciprocal economic and social obligations between the bereaved and their social world.

Malinowski (1948, 53) notes how society is affected by death, observing that "(death)... threatens the very cohesion and solidarity of the group....(The funeral) counteracts the centrifugal forces of fear, demoralization, and provides the most powerful means of reintegration of the group's shaken solidarity and of reestablishment."

Malinowski goes on to explain that the despair, the funeral ceremonies, and the mourning behavior all serve to demonstrate the emotions of the bereaved and the loss experienced by the whole group. These aspects of death reinforce as well as reflect the natural feelings of the survivors. Moreover, death rites create a social event out of the biological event of death.

The funeral reinforces the bereaved person's role in society while affirming the social order itself. It also affirms family cohesiveness, and the extended family may convey a sense that it is part of a larger whole, that is society. In this way, a funeral demonstrates the "roots" of the individual, the family, and society.

VanGennep (1960) points out that certain ceremonies or "rites of passage" are observed in all societies for socially important events, such as a birth, a marriage, or a death. The funeral is simultaneously a rite of separation, a rite of transition, and a rite of incorporation.

As a rite of separation, the funeral separates the dead from the living. This is accomplished by disposing of the dead body through committal to such natural forces as the earth or fire.

As a rite of transition, the funeral assists in the transition in the status of the bereaved, for example, from wife to widow, by offering social support through condolences and by reinforcing reality. In this sense, even though the person is dead, the funeral aims to reintegrate the bereaved into society in spite of the death. Viewing the dead body, visiting the bereaved, and public mourning are examples of the rite of transition.

As a rite of incorporation, the funeral ceremonially incorporates the dead into "the other world," emphasizing that it is not sufficient merely to separate the living from the dead. In ancient Egypt, for instance, the newly dead were incorporated into the world of the "eternal dead." Similarly, through Christian sacraments, the dead are incorporated into a specific other worldly place, such as heaven, hell, or purgatory.

In analyzing funeral rites and mourning behavior, Durkheim (1965, 435) explains that funeral rites are ceremonies that designate a state of "uneasiness or sadness." The implication is that death produces personal anxieties that are addressed by the funeral ceremony. The funeral ceremony is indicative of a society's feelings and beliefs about death. Durkheim points out that funeral rites mirror a particular society's concepts about death. Furthermore, they provide a unique interpretation of life and death.

According to Durkheim, mourning behavior is neither a natural reaction nor a spontaneous release of emotions. He explains that many bereaved people are actors who feel obliged to "play out" their emotions through gestures that are sanctioned by society. In other words, if a bereaved person does not display his or her grief in an acceptable manner, the community will show its disapproval or impose some sort of sanction. Hence, Durkheim (1965, 443) states that:

> Mourning is not a natural movement of private feelings wounded by a cruel loss; it is a duty imposed by the group. One weeps, not simply because he is sad, but because he is forced to weep. It is a ritual attitude which he is forced to adopt out of respect for custom, but which is, in a large measure, independent of his affective state.

Although Durkheim considerably exaggerates the influence of society over the individual's actual emotional reactions, his point is well taken regarding the public functions of mourning for many people. Moreover, the person's affective state does fit into a general community attitude in which social expectations help facilitate the individual expression of grief (Kearl, 1989).

The social expression goes even further in that funerals involve some sort of material expenditure. This ranges from the payment for prayers and offerings to gifts of food, money, or jewelry, to the purchase of professional services and funeral merchandise. It is consistently found that by offering material payment for the funeral, the bereaved attempt to add a tangible expression to their public sentiments of grief, thus communicating to society the depth of their loss. These theoretical observations about the funeral provide a helpful background to assist in understanding particular customs and traditions. In light of the functions and benefits of mortuary activities, the specific practices in the United States (Pine, 1975; Habenstein and Lamers, 1960) can be seen to address these regardless of their modern relevance to scientific scrutiny.

Historical Background

Funeral behavior in eighteenth-century America generally included church funeral services followed by brief prayers at graveside ceremonies. Early Americans seemed to accept death as natural and inevitable and saw no reason to disguise it since death was so common and so often involved children. Funeral ceremonies were essentially simple, and the mourners actively participated by accompanying the coffin to the grave and filling the grave with dirt. As time passed, the mourning process took on an extensive social character, and rings, scarves, gloves, purses, and needlework were given to mourners as tributes to the dead.

American undertaking evolved by gradually adding specific funeral tasks previously carried out largely by other occupational groups or by the family. For instance, certain members of the community became expert at the "laying out" of the dead after a number of such experiences. By the end of the eighteenth century the laying out of the dead in larger cities had become somewhat of a specialty, and those willing to "undertake" that work came to be called undertakers.

During the nineteenth century the American undertaker became something other than a jack-of-all-trades. The functions that formerly were scattered among and performed by several trades were now fused into a single and unified occupation. An important reason for the rise to prominence was the church's unwillingness or inability to maintain authority over all aspects of the burial process. Furthermore, largely because of urbanization and changes in the social order, families were increasingly unlikely to do such things themselves.

Nineteenth-century American funerals were deliberately gloomy and distressing for the bereaved. As a result, there emerged a desire to provide a "beautiful" setting in which to experience loss, grief, and bereavement during the funeral. In cities, undertakers were called immediately upon someone's death. Generally, they came to the home and directed the funeral in the presence of and with the cooperation of the deceased's family. Embalming often was carried out in the home, and there were early attempts to "restore" the faces of the dead with liquid tints that had been developed by embalming chemical fluid companies.

One of the main reasons for the growth in popularity of embalming stemmed from the Civil War, when large numbers of soldiers died far from home. Because most families wanted their dead brought to their own burial grounds for final services, medical embalmers practiced their newly developed art on the battlefields of the Civil War.

The assassination of Abraham Lincoln brought about new public awareness of embalming. The funeral procession with Lincoln's body on display extended from Washington, DC, to Springfield, Illinois. As it progressed through many portions of the Northeast and Midwest, people along its path became aware that it was possible to view the dead for long periods of time. Although buried in 1865, Lincoln's body was so well embalmed that as late as 1899 it was viewed publicly and proclaimed to be in a perfect state of preservation. For such reasons, embalming became a more important aspect of the American way of death.

At the end of the nineteenth century states began to pass licensing legislation to regulate the practice of embalming. State boards of health began to be concerned about burial permits, and the filing of death certificates increasingly became required by state law. Thus, in addition to the technological, occupational, and social changes through which undertaking and embalming passed, the nineteenth century brought about legislative pressures that contributed to the growth of undertaking as an occupational specialty.

During this era, funeral services normally were conducted in the deceased's home. The undertaker would bring the supplies and paraphernalia and set them up in the parlor. A defined period of mourning placed restrictions on social activity for the bereaved surviving relatives. A basket of flowers was hung on the front door, replacing a crepe badge, which had been an earlier mark of mourning.

Religious services usually were held at the home or in the church. In either case, the funeral almost always concluded with a procession to the cemetery. A new aspect of the undertaker's job developed at this time. Someone had to remove all signs of the funeral from the home while it was vacant for the funeral procession. Thus, when the family returned home from the cemetery, there were no further funeral tasks to be done. The undertaker came to bear that burden.

Because of the need for funeral paraphernalia and other equipment, funeral establishments began to appear in urban areas. In small towns, undertakers began to use their stores' back room, their carriage building, or their living room to provide facilities for those families for whom the home no longer was appropriate for the laying out of the dead. Usually, undertakers used a specific room in which to lay out the dead and in which the bereaved could greet callers. This room replaced the parlor formerly used in the home of the deceased; thus, the undertaker's establishment came to be called a "funeral parlor." In this homelike setting, the undertaker supplied the casket, carriages, mourning materials, memorial cards, flowers, chairs, robes, pillows, and crucifixes, and generally was responsible for the direction of the funeral services.

The notion of the "funeral director" arose in the late nineteenth century, with several factors contributing to the development of this new occupation. Occupational mobility and the decline of the extended family led to the development of smaller houses and other living units. This change gave rise to a need for a building large enough to house big families gathered for mourning. Funeral parlors were built or existing houses modified to take into account the new needs of the bereaved and the caretakers of the dead.

As embalming became more sophisticated, the equipment to carry out this task became increasingly difficult to take into private homes. Embalming became a procedure in the laboratory or "preparation room" of the newly developed buildings housing the funeral director's equipment and supplies.

Transportation problems increased the difficulty of gathering the mourners for the funeral ceremonies at the church. Moreover, since the church did not encourage the development of a special room for the care of the dead, funeral directors found an additional reason to develop facilities to house such activities.

A combination of the need for a large parlor, a special laboratory, and a chapel-like facility evolved into what has become the present-day funeral home. This provided additional impetus for a specialist to carry out the new specialized tasks in such a setting (Pine, 1975). The funeral director came to look upon himself as being useful to society rather than as merely a provider of merchandise and equipment. This feeling led to the development of notions of administrative and managerial skills and the practices of funeral counseling as well as directing. It contributed to the occupational orientation as the provider of services, that is, as a professional personal service practitioner.

Funeral Customs Today

Until the past seventy years, death occurred at home in familiar surroundings in the presence of kin or close friends, and funerals were community events. Times have changed, however. Each year proportionately more people die in institutions instead of their own homes, and almost all of the dead are cared for by funeral directors in funeral homes. For present-day Americans, one of the common features of death is the employment of a funeral director.

The heterogeneity of the United States is reflected by differing funeral practices (Habenstein and Lamers, 1962). Funeral customs in the United States vary because of geographic region, ethnic background, religious affiliation, and economic and social class. Religious and ethnic groups tend to maintain unique traditional funeral practices.

Depending on where, how, and when death occurs, it is common to notify a physician or the police. Then, the cause of death is medically certified, either by a physician, a coroner, or a medical examiner. Finally, the family of the deceased chooses a funeral director. Generally, the choice is ethnically oriented, but at times may reflect social class, status, and geographic differences.

The dead body usually is removed from the place of death by the funeral director and taken to a funeral home. There, it is customary to embalm or otherwise sanitize through disinfection. Embalming includes dressing the body and "restoring it" (e.g., applying cosmetics) in an attempt to render the deceased lifelike and socially presentable for a public appearance.

The immediate family of the deceased generally makes the necessary arrangements for the funeral. For example, the place, time, and type of funeral service, the place of burial or cremation, and the type of casket, are a few of the choices that must be made. These and other elements of the funeral are interrelated and seem to be based on social class, ethnic, and religious attitudes.

Viewing the dead body is widespread in the United States and occurs at all social class levels. Usually, it is done during specified hours at the funeral home, but it may take place at the home of the deceased, or occasionally at the church where the service is to be held. During the viewing, friends and relatives spend time with the bereaved family. Religious and ethnic differences appear to be the bases for varying attitudes about the length of viewing and the attendant mourning customs. American viewing customs constitute a period of visitation for the immediate survivors, their kin, and their friends.

Most funerals in the United States include a religious service. At times there may be only a service by a fraternal or other organization, and occasionally there may be no service. The religious services are held either in the funeral home, the home of the deceased, or the church. With few exceptions, at the service there is little active participation in the funeral ceremony by the family or close friends. This is a uniquely American custom, and in many other parts of the world the family actually carries out these final ceremonial acts. In the United States, the activities of the ceremony are carried out by the funeral director, the clergy, and other professionals.

Generally, at the cemetery there are religious committal rites. Following the committal, it is common for the family to leave the cemetery with the casket still above ground. After the departure of the mourners, the funeral director supervises the lowering of the casket into the grave. As with other parts of the funeral, there is seldom active group participation at the cemetery except for the reciting of widely known prayers.

Earth burial is the most common means of final disposition, chosen for more than 80 percent of the annual deaths. Cremation is chosen for about 19 percent of the deaths annually. A small fraction of deaths are followed by body donation, and after the process of medical dissection the remains are either buried or cremated.

Funeral expenditure is divided among the funeral director, crematory or cemetery, clergy, and florist. The largest portion generally goes to the funeral director. Those charges usually include the professional services, the casket selected by the bereaved family, use of the necessary equipment and facilities, motor equipment, and other related items. This is unlike many societies in which funeral expenditure goes to other sources, such as religious or social groups or governmental agencies.

The level of funeral expenditure has caused criticism of American funeral practices. The most well-known critics have focused on contemporary funeral practices for their cost and lack of relevance in today's society. In addition to state departments of health, the Federal Trade Commission now regulates funeral directors in the conduct of their business. The underlying criticisms raise questions about the economic and social utility of funerals. Some of these criticisms are based on the belief that today's customs and practices were invented largely by today's funeral directors.

Clearly, some aspects of present-day practices are based on what funeral directors believed would meet community desires and keep pace with their competition. Even so, today's funeral customs reflect fairly widespread community values and beliefs. Funeral practices tend to follow ethnic, religious, and socioeconomic patterns. Moreover, American customs reflect a powerful multicultural mix.

Some of the recent criticisms reflect changes in public attitudes and behavior. Popular writing criticizing funeral customs has fostered some changes. Other changes have been promoted by organizations such as memorial societies that advocate inexpensive funerals and memorial services. Other changes have been brought about by increased education and geographic and social mobility, all of which may be accompanied by a tendency to try to handle death by rational and utilitarian rather than ceremonial or emotional actions. These attitudes make practices such as viewing the body and embalming seem unnecessary or unimportant.

Paradoxically, this tendency to avoid involvement with the dead body is occurring simultaneously with an increased awareness of the value of confronting death openly (Osterweis, 1984). Thus, even though some people believe that "remembering the person as he or she was" is less painful, a number of psychologists, psychiatrists, and other mental health professionals maintain that viewing the dead body helps reinforce reality by permitting the survivor to confront his or her loss directly. Similarly, direct disposition of the body with no public ceremony is an increasingly common alternative to the traditional funeral today, but it may deny the bereaved a social opportunity to cope with the loss.

The practice of cremation is growing in many parts of the United States, and it is increasingly accompanied by a tendency to avoid the cemetery. Traditionally, the cemetery has enabled society to express its basic values and to inform us about the sort of people buried there, of their place in history, and of their place in our lives. It is a further reflection of the paradoxical times that this reduced noting of family continuity is occurring simultaneously with an increased interest in our ancestral "roots."

Personal actions following death also have changed. No longer is death symbolically noted by mourning clothes or floral wreaths that publicly "announce" one's bereavement; rather, death in America today is increasingly a private concern (Fulton, 1976). However, because it is crucial to have social and psychological supports, the funeral is likely to be adapted to meet personal needs and help resolve grief.

The Six Facets of the Funeral

There are six facets of the funeral that are relatively universal and include social support, ceremonial ritual, sanitary disposition, visual confrontation, a funeral procession, and funeral expenditure (Pine, 1969).

Funerals are intended to offer social support. After a death, group support and the extension of sympathy and condolence is offered to the bereaved "to bring them comfort." The gathering of friends and relatives to pay their respects and offer condolence has been practiced commonly in every society. The point is that although funerals are for the dead, they benefit the living. From this perspective, funeral rites represent a *societal* effort to provide support for the bereaved. In addition, the *communal* effort of one's group is intended to help the bereaved gain emotional stability by letting them know that other members of the community care and that they recognize the impact of the loss. Thus, funeral customs have been perpetuated to benefit individual survivors within a framework acceptable to the society.

In this sense, funerals customarily utilize a ceremonial ritual. Often, funeral rituals are religious in nature, but they need not be. The ceremony provides a ritualized solution to the transitory problems created by death. For many people, a religious service validates choices made by individuals in pursuit of ends they regard as good. Different religious groups or other institutions practice different customs; in all cultures, however, there are always some aspects of the funeral that involve ceremonial rituals.

Incorporated into these rituals are practices for the sanitary disposal of the dead body that have been developed universally. Regardless of the religious practices involved, funerals most often provide a health function by the practice of sanitary disposal. Burial, entombment, and cremation all are attempts to eliminate the health menace of decomposing bodies.

Funerals generally call for some visual confrontation of the dead body. In their observations about funeral practices, anthropologists mention the common tendency of the survivors (or their agents) to render the dead body somehow different in appearance than does death itself. It is likely that this custom stems from the unhuman appearance of most bodies immediately after death. Additionally, it may be an effort to ease the farewell process by subsequent viewing of the dead in some culturally defined "proper" condition.

The culmination of these elements is usually some kind of funeral procession. The funeral procession can be thought of as a "family parade," which may include relatives, friends, and members of the community at large. In most societies, the procession is also viewed as "the final journey," which draws to a close the immediate post-death activities of the funeral ceremony. Naturally, there are various processional customs; however, the funeral procession allows a symbolic gathering of the clan as a climactic trip to the place of final disposition. Generally, the dead person's family and friends are aligned in a culturally specified order.

Funerals generally involve material expenditure. By offering material payment for the funeral, people add a tangible, measurable element to substantiate the intangible sentiments of loss that death elicits. Most cultures have clearly patterned and institutionalized customs of funeral expenditure. With these payment patterns, the bereaved are able to communicate their loss to society more easily. Funeral expenditure represents an effort toward social conformity and an attempt to express grief materially in the hope that it will be more socially acceptable.

The Social Meaning of the Funeral

It appears that these facets of the funeral operate in all societies, and that they aid bereaved people to cope with their feelings of loss and grief. Beginning with the initial psychological reactions to death, there are social forces that influence the bereaved and condition their responses to death. However, death does not involve the bereaved alone; it has an impact on others beyond them.

Blauner (1966, 378) points out that:

> Since mortality tends to disrupt the ongoing life of social groups and relationships, all societies must develop some form of containing the impact...(and) mortuary institutions are addressed to the specific problem of the disposal of the dead and the rituals of transition from life to death.

In this way the funeral serves as a ceremony that attempts to provide support, not just for the next-of-kin and friends of the dead person, but for the community as well. The purpose of the funeral goes beyond social support for the mourners. It also gives them an opportunity to understand their changing relationships with others because of the loss (Rando, 1991). In general, there are changes in one's social position vis-à-vis the group and society. Furthermore, these lead to social psychological changes which often alter one's perspective of death itself.

A funeral should enable a community to convey publicly its values and beliefs. These should include meaningful communications about the meaning of life and death and about the transition of the dead person from that society to a place "beyond" living. In this sense, then, the funeral should provide an opportunity for society to recognize death rather than to ignore it (Gorer, 1965).

Irion (1966) points out that there are three sociological norms for the funeral, and they grow out of the social–psychological effect of bereavement on individuals. First, for a funeral to be adequate it should make it clear that there is a shared loss and that the community supports the bereaved. As stated earlier, the ostensible object of the funeral is the dead body, but it primarily benefits the living because of its social nature.

Second, for a funeral to be adequate it should initiate the strengthening of relationships among the living. Thus, the funeral begins the reintegration of the bereaved into the group. It is as if the group says "We mourn with you, but you still are one of us, a part of our group."

Third, for a funeral to be adequate it should convey the element of finality of death. This should lead to the development of new interpersonal relations without violating the integrity of the previous relationship with the dead person. It is important that the element of finality should leave room for memories of the dead person. Thus, after death, even though no actual relationship exists, a funeral should recognize that there is a relationship at the level of memory.

Ideally, a funeral provides the bereaved with an opportunity to release their feelings (Pine, 1976). One of the beneficial aspects of funeral customs that call for a specific place for funerals to occur, for example, a church or a funeral home, is that socially uncharacteristic behavior such as publicly crying is appropriate. Ideally, the funeral takes place in a social climate in which people can express feelings such as sorrow, anger, depression, or relief with no fear or embarrassment.

Finally, for a funeral to be adequate it should provide the bereaved with a meaningful resource to help them understand and accept their loss. This may be accomplished in religious acceptance of the death, but it also can be accomplished through a philosophical view of what the death itself means in light of the nature of the universe and in light of one's personal view of mortality.

The potential for a funeral being adequate depends on the interdependent utilization of many dimensions. Just because a funeral may not fulfill a given dimension, it does not mean that the funeral is bad, but rather that it may be inappropriate. Thus, although some funeral practices may be seen as vestiges of the past, the funeral itself need not be.

Concluding Comments

The roots of funerals are connected both to survivor needs and the survival of the society (Feifel, 1977). Funerals provide a social mechanism for expressing sympathy and attempt to reintegrate the bereaved into society by giving them an opportunity to express their feelings of loss in a socially significant fashion. Furthermore, for the bereaved person who provides a funeral for a dead person, there may be the thought that someday he or she will be accorded a final tribute and that it might add a degree of meaning to his or her life.

Through the funeral ceremony, the bereaved are the center of attention, receiving social support and sympathy in a socially acceptable and comforting setting. Acceptance back into society is critical if the bereaved are to live meaningfully after the death of some significant person (Feifel, 1977). Most societies provide customs that give support through the period of bereavement. These customs are intended to help both bereaved people in particular and society in general. Moreover, funeral customs are oriented to helping accept loss through social–psychological empathy and the sharing of deeply felt emotional reactions.

References

Blauner, R. (1966). "Death and social structure." *Psychiatry, 29,* 378–394.

Doka, K. J., (Ed.), (1989). *Disenfranchised grief.* Lexington, MA: Lexington Books.

Durkheim, E. (1965). *The elementary forms of the religious life.* New York: The Free Press.

Feifel, H. (1977). *New meanings of death.* New York: McGraw-Hill.

Fulton, R. (Ed.), (1976). *Death and identity* (Revised Edition). Bowie, MD: The Charles Press.

Gorer, G. (1965). *Death, grief, and mourning.* Garden City, NY: Doubleday & Co.

Habenstein, R. W. & Lamers, W. M. (1960). *Funeral customs the world over.* Milwaukee, WI: Bulfin Printers.

Habenstein, R. W., & Lamers, W. M. (1962). *The history of American funeral directing* (Revised Edition). Milwaukee, WI: Bulfin Printers.

Irion, P. E. (1966). *The funeral: Vestige or value?* Nashville, TN: Abingdon Press.

Kearl, M. C. (1989). *Endings: A sociology of death and dying.* New York: Oxford University Press.

Malinowski, B. (1948). *Magic, science and religion.* New York: The Free Press.

Osterweis, M., Solomon, F., & Green, M. (Eds.), (1984). *Bereavement: Reactions, consequences, and care.* Washington, DC: National Academy Press.

Pine, V. R. (1969). Comparative funeral practices. *Practical Anthropology, 16*(2), 49–62.

Pine, V. R. (1975). *Caretaker of the dead: The American funeral director.* New York: Halsted Press.

Pine, V. R., et al. (Eds.), (1976). *Acute grief and the funeral.* Springfield, IL: Charles C. Thomas.

Rando, T. A. (1991). *How to go on living when someone you love dies.* New York: Bantam Books.

VanGennep, A. (1960). *The rites of passage.* Chicago, IL: The University of Chicago Press.

Twelve

Sibling Bereavement Research: State of the Art

Betty Davies

Betty Davies earned her B.Sc.N. from the University of Alberta, her M.S.N. from the University of Arizona, and her Ph.D. in nursing science from the University of Washington. Dr. Davies was postdoctoral fellow at the University of California, San Fransisco, being the first nurse awarded a postdoctoral fellowship from the American Cancer Society, California Division. Dr. Davies is a professor in the School of Nursing, University of British Columbia, Vancouver, Canada, and an investigator in the Research Division, British Columbia's Children's Hospital. Dr. Davies is the first nurse and the first psychosocial researcher to be awarded an investigatorship.

Dr. Davies has worked in the area of death, dying, and bereavement for more than twenty years. She has given numerous workshops related to coping with loss, particularly for families following the death of a child. Her seminal work pertaining to bereavement in siblings forms the basis for many presentations and publications. Dr. Davies has recently completed two collaborative research projects, which include exploring the experience of families caring for a terminally ill person and investigating the experience of nurses caring for chronically ill children during the terminal phase. Dr. Davies is a founding member of HUGS Children's Hospice Society, the driving force behind establishing Canuck Place, North America's first freestanding hospice for children. In recognition of her contributions to the field, Dr. Davies has been awarded the YWCA Woman of the Year Award in British Columbia, the Excellence in Nursing Research and the Award of Merit from the British Columbia Registered Nurses Association.

Much has been written about the process of mourning and bereavement in adults (Clayton, Desmarais, & Winokur, 1986; Engel, 1964; Glick, Weiss, & Parkes, 1974; Lindemann, 1944; Parkes, 1972; Parkes

The author wishes to acknowledge the valuable assistance of Brenda Eng, R.N., M.N., Research Assistant, Division of Nursing, British Columbia's Children's Hospital, in the preparation of this manuscript.

and Weiss, 1983; Rando, 1993; Raphael, 1983; Sanders, 1989); little attention however has been given to the phenomenon in children, and in particular, in siblings. When a child dies, investigations of the impact on those left behind has focused primarily on the parents. Much less has been written on the impact of such a loss on siblings, even though the child's response to major loss became a source of growing interest and considerable study in the 1960s and 1970s. There have been clinical and theoretical considerations of the younger child's capacity to mourn (Bowlby, 1963; Wolfenstein, 1966); epidemiological studies attempting to link adult depression to childhood loss (Birtchnell, 1970; Blinder, 1972; Brown, Harris, & Copeland, 1977; Hilgard, 1969); and descriptive studies of children's bereavement responses to the death of parents (Furman, 1974) and siblings (Cain, Fast, & Erickson, 1964; Kaplan, Grobstein & Smith,1976; Lewis, 1967; Payne, Goff, & Paulson, 1980; Stehbens & Lascari, 1974).

A bibliographic compilation by Fulton (1977) entitled *Death, Grief and Bereavement: A Bibliography 1845–1975*, contains a total of 309 citations classified under the general heading of "children." Of these, only 15 are listed under the subheading of "reactions to the death of siblings." Of these 15 references, only 5 were written during the period 1970–1975, the remaining 10 references were written before 1970 and of these, three were written in the 1940s. A novel written in German comprised one of the resources listed. Others focused on adults: three cited articles about the death of adult siblings and an additional four were about adult psychiatric problems associated with childhood experiences of sibling death. Only seven resources referred to bereavement experience by the child at the time of his or her sibling's death. Since the time of Fulton's compilation, descriptions of other work in the field have been added to the literature (Betz, 1987; Walker, 1993). Betz (1987) in her review of death, dying, and bereavement literature 1970–1985, noted that research in childhood bereavement primarily focuses on three areas of inquiry: long-term consequences of parental loss; the immediate and short-term effects of parental loss, and sibling death. A review of major studies conducted in the latter category of childhood bereavement is the focus of this chapter. Emphasis is given to research assumptions, methodologies, and implications that seem critical in the plan and design of further studies.

Sibling Relationship

> She was my everything. I learned a lot from her...There's...there's...a certain bond between...I should say there *was*, past tense...a certain bond between her and I[sic]: the loving, the friendship, the caring about every minute or wondering how they're doing or what they're doing

and...the searching, the...the understanding, the communicating, everything, there's such a deep bond.
    (*The 16-year-old sister of girl who had died 2 years earlier at age
    14*)

Although the primary emphasis in health care has traditionally been
placed on the parent-parent or parent-child dyad, there is a growing
recognition of the strong influence siblings have on one another. More
than 80 percent of children in the United States are siblings (Brownmiller
& Cantwell, 1976). The simple fact of numbers suggests that this is an
important area of research: in a family with a child with an illness or
handicapping condition or in a family experiencing the death of a child,
there may be one or more well children who deserve attention. Sibling
bonds are intense, complex, and of an infinite variety, and are especially
intense in childhood. Emotional relationships between siblings are dynamic, displaying varying degrees of loyalty, companionship, rivalry,
love, hate, jealousy, and envy (Walker, 1990). Sibling relationships are
obligatory relationships. For better or worse, children spend more time
together than any other family subsystem (Bank & Kahn, 1982; Siemon,
1984). Finally, a sibling relationship may span six or more decades;
individuals share greater portions of their lives with siblings than with
anyone else.

The important aspect of time span in the sibling relationship points
to the potentially powerful influence siblings exert on shaping each
other's identity, assuming varying roles with each other: mentor,
supporter, comforter, protector, and socializer. The sibling world has
been described as the testing ground "...where naked emotions, betrayal,
deceit, hate, jealousy and cruelty abound" (Siemon, 1984). Not to be
forgotten are the important "positive, sustaining aspects of respect, love,
and loyalty and a deep bond of both verbal and visceral communication"
(Carr-Gregg & White, 1987, p. 63). However, the common thread through
all sibling relationships is the ambivalence generated by sharing a common
environment as well as parental time, interest, and attention (Carr-Gregg
& White, 1987; Siemon, 1984).

During the 1980s, there was an upsurge of interest in the study of
siblings, focusing on a number of different but related themes. Primarily,
research focusing on siblings in special circumstances pertains to those
whose families are facing major stressors. The majority of research is
found in studies of children with disabled siblings and children whose
siblings face a life-threatening illness. Recent reviews of research on
siblings of handicapped children include those by Brody and Stoneman
(1983), Dunn (1988), Lobato (1983), McHale, Simeonsson, and Sloan
(1984); reviews pertaining to siblings of chronically ill children can be

found in Brett (1988), Drotar and Crawford (1985), McKeever (1983), and Van Dongen-Melman and Sanders-Woudstra (1986).

A narrow focus characterizes the methods and issues of existing research on atypical sibling pairs (Lobato, Faust, & Spirito, 1988). Literature on the family response to chronic childhood conditions has been described as fraught with methodological weaknesses within and definitional inconsistencies among studies (Birenbaum, 1987; Brett, 1988; Brett & Davies, 1988; Carr-Gregg & White, 1987; McKeever, 1983; Simeonsson & McHale, 1981; Spinetta, 1982;). Lobato et al. (1988) pointed out that the titles of many articles suggest that research has been conducted with families of disabled, ill, or dying children, but it has been a rare paper that looks beyond the reactions of mothers to fathers, no less to siblings. Given the emergence of family systems theory and the belief that adaptation and dysfunction are shared characteristics of family members, it is interesting to note that most of the current studies of "families" are dismembering; siblings are essentially excluded. Even in a comprehensive study, which stated that its focus was childhood cancer *and* the family, discussion of the sibling subsystem was markedly narrow and limited (Chesler & Barbarian, 1987). Much of the information on siblings remains founded on subjective and anecdotal forms of clinical investigation such as clinical interview and case report. Moreover, Carr-Gregg and White (1987) noted that it is often difficult to differentiate the effects of illness or handicaps on a sibling relationship from the intensity and ambivalence that is usually present. Some of the reactions that have been reported may not be unique to brothers or sisters but are, indeed, aspects of all sibling relationships exaggerated by extraordinary circumstances. Not surprising, the present research has been plagued with conflicting conclusions. Perhaps the most significant shortcoming has been that, with relatively few exceptions (such as Rollins, 1990), siblings have not been asked to speak for themselves (Carr-Gregg & White, 1987; Lobato et al., 1988). Descriptions of siblings' adjustment and response have relied heavily on anecdotal and descriptive observations of parents and/or health professionals. The resultant lack of understanding of the sibling relationship becomes especially problematic when health professionals attempt to deliver true family-centred care to families with a chronically ill or disabled child or to families following a child's death.

Behavioural Responses

Childhood bereavement in siblings primarily has been reported in the context of behavioural responses. Because children often work out their feelings through their behaviours and because behaviour represents a relatively easy way of assessing children's responses to critical events, it is logical that the focus of research in this area has been on behaviour. Many studies, however, define the behaviour changes seen in bereaved children as problematic if not even pathological, although positive responses have also been identified. Problems have included a range of behaviours, attitudes, emotions, symptoms, cognitions, and diagnoses. Reported research has produced contradictory findings on the frequency, severity, and persistence of problems resulting from a sibling's death. Until a more comprehensive description can be developed to encompass this complex concept, sibling response remains a proxy for sibling bereavement (Birenbaum, 1987).

Problem Responses

> My grades just kept getting worse...because of the death and stuff. I do remember I had a terrible time with not finishing things. I'd...I wouldn't even write my name on the sheet. I wouldn't take it home. It would lay in my locker and the next day when it was due, I'd say, "Well, I forgot it."
> (The 21-year-old brother of boy who had died 5 years before at age 11)

Three classic retrospective studies are frequently cited as evidence that siblings of a child who died are at significant risk of severe psychological problems (Cobb, 1956; Cain & Cain, 1964; Binger, Ablin, et al., 1969; Binger, 1973). Problems reported to be indicative of sibling maladaptation included school difficulties, somatic complaints, enuresis, nightmares, loneliness, depression, clinging, crying, confusion, antisocial behaviour, and jealousy. Similar problematic responses were reported in later studies (Payne et al., 1980; Tietz, McSherry, & Britt, 1977; Townes & Wold, 1977). A significant factor influencing the identification of problem behaviours is related to the manner in which the phenomenon is conceptualized. Given the psychopathology and disturbance perspective of early investigations, these behaviours are not remarkable. Until recently, sibling bereavement responses have been reported by parents and other health professionals *on behalf* of the siblings; their perspective has been problem-focused because of their concern for managing the children. While identification of these problems is important in describing responses, differentiating symptoms from diagnoses and identifying levels of severity are required if criteria for intervention are to be developed (Birenbaum, 1987).

The percentage of children reported to demonstrate problem behaviours varies widely, ranging for example from 9 to 87.5% in the samples reviewed by Davies (1983). In one of the most frequently cited studies on the impact on families of losing a child from leukemia, Binger et al. (1969) reported that in about half of the 20 families, one or more previously well-adjusted siblings had shown significant behaviour problems during the patient's illness and at least one member needed psychiatric help. Furthermore, maladaptive behavioural responses were reported to increase in severity after the child's death. Similarly, reports of more recent studies (Kaplan et al., 1976; Spinetta, Swarner, & Sheposh, 1981b) indicated that in approximately one-half of the families bereaved siblings showed behaviour and adjustment problems. By contrast, Stehbens and Lascari (1974) reported no consistent pattern of grief symptomatology following the death of a child from leukemia among surviving parents and siblings. Of the 20 siblings in the study, 70% were considered "back to normal" by their parents within a week. Decline in school performance, dysphoria, enuresis, abdominal pain, and restless sleep were reported but only as transient behaviours. Given the essential nature of an adequate grieving process, it would have been helpful to know how these children responded at a later time, and whether there were adverse repercussions of this rather abrupt return to normal. Martinson (1980) in a study of families whose child died at home, reported only 2% of the surviving 139 siblings had serious problems such as school failure, drug problems, and talk of suicide. Problems characterized as "mild" or "moderate" were experienced by 22% of the siblings; 76%, however, reported no problems. Particular caution must be employed in the interpretation of findings by Stebhens and Lascari (1974) and Martinson (1980) because a potential experimental bias exists—the focus of each study was on assessing the effectiveness of a treatment program but with no control or comparison group.

Deriving definite conclusions about bereavement behaviours in children is difficult; not only does considerable variation exist with regard to sample size, cause of death, ages of children, and time elapsed since the death, but also there is a lack of a consistent method of defining "behaviour problem." Bereavement literature indicates that complaints of bodily discomforts, sleep disorders, and loss of appetite are common to both children and adults. Under seemingly normal circumstances, the presence of such symptoms can be indications of stress in both adults and children. If however, these behaviours are considered to be components of normal grieving responses in children as they are in adults, then their presence in bereaved children is not cause for undue alarm. This raises the question of whether these "behaviour problems" in siblings are in fact indicators of maladjustment. As with adults, what would be significant is the intensity and duration of such behaviours, and the presence or absence of other behaviour problems.

In summary, studies of sibling bereavement indicate that a wide range of behaviour problems occur after the death of a child. Whether or not these behaviours are manifestations of normal grieving or are indications of maladaptive responses remains to be determined.

Positive Responses

> D. affected my life in many ways...her illness...being my sister...going through the chemotherapy process...her death made me what I am today...as far as religion...respect for other people: who they are and not just what they look like. And...the respect of living things. The respect of my body. I don't smoke, I don't take any drugs. Being able to talk about death. Life's too short not to be happy.
> *(The 17-year-old sister, 3 years after death of her 10-year-old sister)*

Experiencing a sibling's death results not only in problem behaviours; many surviving siblings experience positive outcomes as well. Recent research suggests that the experience, although painful, serves as an impetus for psychological growth. Surviving siblings perceive themselves as more mature than their peers, as being more sensitive and empathic to the situation of others, and as being better prepared to handle personal distress (Balk, 1983a, 1983b; Davies, 1987; Hogan, 1988; Hogan & Balk, 1990; Martinson, Davies, & McClowry, 1987).

Positive outcomes of sibling bereavement have also been noted in studies focusing on assessment of self-concept. Balk (1983a, 1983b) studied 33 bereaved adolescent siblings and found that the respondent scores on the Offer Self-Image Questionnaire were similar to Offer norm groups on all scales except for the Morals Scales; on the Morals Scale, the bereaved teenagers had scores significantly higher than the norm groups. In examining the long-term effects of sibling death on self-concept, Martinson et al. (1987) reported that the bereaved children had statistically higher self-concept scores on the Pier-Harris Self-Concept Scale than the Piers-Harris norm group. Twenty-nine siblings who participated in a home care program for the dying child (Martinson, 1980) formed the basis for analysis. Perhaps the circumstances of home care of terminally ill children fosters family cohesiveness in a manner supportive of self-concept. However, support for this deduction was not found in the interview with parents and siblings. In neither study was information presented about whether or not these children had a high self-concept before the death. In both studies, interview data provided additional information that the enhanced self-concepts derived from the siblings' perceptions of personal maturity and from the lessons learned about death and life.

Mediating Variables

Numerous studies have presented different variables as having predictive value in determining sibling adjustment and bereavement outcome. Attempts to isolate factors that affect the sibling relationship are com-

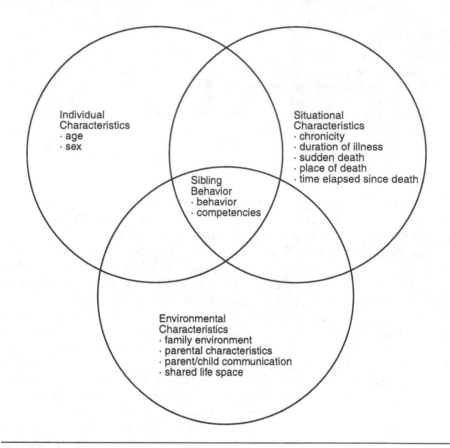

Figure 12.1   Conceptualization of the mediating variables that impact the phenomenon of sibling bereavement

plicated by the variety of variables investigated and the difficulty of establishing adequate control or reference groups. Findings are therefore not always consistent and few definitive conclusions can be drawn. Furthermore, systematic study of mediating variables has been limited. For the purpose of this discussion, mediating variables are categorized as individual characteristics, situational characteristics, and environmental characteristics. These variables interact with one another, coming together to impact upon the behaviour that is a manifestation of bereavement in siblings (see Figure 12.1).

Individual Characteristics

Individual characteristics refer to the age and sex of the surviving child. Blinder (1972, p. 173) suggested that the effect of sibling death on the surviving children is "influenced by the factors of age and sex which in a more general way influence the intensity of association, identification and competition generated."

Age. Until recently, no explicit examination of relationship between age differences in siblings and bereavement outcome has been included in studies of sibling bereavement. Studies that have included age as a variable report inconclusive results. Davies (1983) reported that behaviour was not significantly associated with the age of the bereaved children. In contrast, McCown (1982, 1987) found that younger children tended to demonstrate more problems. Boys and girls in the 6–11 year age group showed significantly more behaviour disturbance when compared to norms on a standardized test. This finding was not true of children in the 4–5 year or 12–16 year groups. Betz (1987) in a study of 32 children ranging in age from 2 to 19 years, also reported that significant differences in reactions were associated with age. Interview data obtained from parents and children following the death of a child indicated that school-age children most often reported withholding feelings, remembering the deceased, noncommunicativeness, and acknowledged spiritual presence. Adolescents reported avoidance behaviour and decline in school performance in comparison to other ages.

The effects of sibling death upon adolescents remain relatively sparsely investigated. Reports by Balk (1983a, 1983b); Hogan (1988), Hogan and Balk (1990), Grogan (1990), and Davies (1991) focus specifically on the bereavement responses of adolescent siblings. Balk (1983a, 1983b) investigated three overall categories of bereavement reactions among 33 adolescents whose siblings had died between 4 and 84 months prior to data collection. Statistically significant results emerged regarding effects on grades and study habits, perceptions of personal maturity, and increased importance of religious beliefs. Grief symptoms were reported to be consistent with typical adult bereavement responses (Lindemann, 1944; Parkes, 1972) although Balk (1983b) noted a lingering quality. Balk observed that one-third to one-half of the adolescents continued to demonstrate an acute emotional response to their sibling's death which did not diminish at the time of the interview. Furthermore, specific emotional responses were influenced by perceptions of family closeness and by perceptions of personal communication with family members. Within the adolescent group of bereaved siblings that were the subjects of Balk's study (1983a, 1983b) age differences were reported in relation to the expression of anger. Older adolescents (17–19 years of age) reported anger at the time the sibling's death happened and at the time of the interview; younger subjects (14–16 years of age at the time of the interview) did not.

Hogan (1988) examined the effects of time on the adolescent sibling bereavement process at two time periods: the first and second 18-month periods following the death. She noted a shift in the sense of assigning blame during the first 3 years following the death. Adolescents were more likely to assign blame to themselves during the first 18 months and then reassign it to God during the second 18 months. Tasks addressed over the period studied for the bereaved adolescents included: appraisal of blaming; survival guilt; culpability nightmares; concentration difficulties; sense of family incompleteness; sense of empathy and compassion for parents. Over time, mothers were identified as the principal person in the family that bereaved adolescents could talk to about their grief. By contrast, fathers were perceived as more distant and less available as time passed. More recently, however, Hogan and Balk (1990) reported that mothers held significantly different views of their teenagers' self-concept and grief than did fathers.

In examining the long-term effects of sibling bereavement, Davies (1991) put forth a theoretic scheme relating the experience of bereavement in early adolescence to the development of long-term responses. She suggested that the sense of personal growth and maturity arouses feelings of being different from peers, and may result in an intolerance of developmentally appropriate behaviours demonstrated by peers. Some siblings respond to these feelings by withdrawing from their peers at a time when peer relationships are critical to completing developmental tasks. For such siblings, feelings of sadness and loneliness become long-term.

Sex.   Contrary to general opinion, bereaved boys did not show more behaviour problems than girls although both boys and girls showed more behaviour problems in comparison to norms (Davies, 1983; McCown, 1982). Townes and Wold (1977) however, noted that withdrawal in girls and aggressiveness in boys were personality traits of children who manifested maladaptive adjustment to the prolonged illness and death of a sibling with leukemia. Balk (1983a) noted that literature on sex differences suggested that anger would be differentiated by sex. Contrary to expectations, he reported that anger was not associated with the sex of participants, but with age. These investigations have used a retrospective approach in the collection of data. Directions for future research examining the effect of age and sex on bereavement might investigate longitudinally the response of siblings to the death of a brother or sister in order to determine age-related changes in both boys and girls.

Situational Variables

The hardest part for me was when he was dying. Not right there that day he was on the couch, but about a couple of weeks before that. And even the year before that because everybody was going on the trains and driving to the city and I spent lots of time with grandmothers.
(The 19-year-old brother of a 10-year-old male patient)

Situational variables refer to characteristics of the disease and its subsequent trajectory that may impact upon sibling adjustment and bereavement. There is not yet sufficient research to determine empirically the relative importance of a child's disability or disease on sibling development, adjustment, and subsequent bereavement. At best, "the impact of childhood disease or disability on siblings may best be conceptualized as a risk or stress factor, the significance of which is mediated by other individual and family characteristics and resources" (Lobato, et al., 1988, p. 395).

Childhood Life-threatening Illness.   Chronicity, in and of itself, is a significant challenge to effective family and individual functioning. It is reasonable to assume that this challenge is made even more difficult when it is combined with the unpredictable and life-threatening aspects inherent in conditions such as childhood cancer (Adams & Deveau, 1987). The literature on siblings of children with cancer is at an early stage of conceptualization and methodology. Most of the literature has focused on the sibling of the dying child rather than on the sibling of the child with a life-threatening illness. Furthermore, literature has emphasized psychopathology and disturbance rather than coping and adaptation in siblings. Understandably, the majority of research in the area of childhood chronic life-threatening illness continues to focus on children with cancer as this remains the leading cause of death due to childhood chronic illness.

Several studies (Cairns, Clark, Smith, & Lansky, 1979; Lavigne & Ryan, 1979) reported that siblings confronted with a chronic life-threatening illness experience similar stress as their brother or sister who has cancer; in fact, siblings showed more distress than the patients in the areas of perceived social isolation, perception of the parents as overindulgent and overprotective of the sick child, fear of confronting family members with negative feelings, preoccupation with own health, and concern with failure (older siblings only) (Cairns et al., 1979). Similar findings were reported by Spinetta (1981, p. 139) in a three-year longitudinal study of families with a child with cancer that included 102 siblings. Spinetta summarized the findings by stating "if the patients' scores relative to the controls suggest a need for intervention, then siblings, when they score at the same level as the patients, have the same need for intervention. When the siblings score at significantly less adaptive levels than the patients, concern is raised regarding the fact that their needs are being met inadequately." Spinetta concluded that siblings live through the experience with the same intensity as the patient and will live the longest with disease-related memories and concerns. If such is the case, the nature of the illness before death potentially impacts the siblings' responses following the death.

No difference was reported in sibling bereavement outcome of children who died of leukemia or solid tumour (Davies, 1983). Stehbens and Lascari (1974) also reported no discernible relationship among type, number, or severity of anticipatory and after-death symptoms. Tietz et al. (1977), however, found high numbers of behaviour problems in the siblings in families where the ill child had died from a solid tumour. It was observed that these children suffered a great deal in their terminal stages with the development of paralysis and blindness. Davies (1983) surmised that the variables that need to be considered are not related to certain diagnoses per se, but rather the treatments involved, the extensiveness of the treatments, and the degree of suffering the child actually experienced.

Duration of Illness.   The concept of anticipatory mourning, a gradual relinquishing of hope as the illness progresses and death is expected, suggests that the longer the illness before the ill child's death, the less the disruption in the behaviour of the surviving children. Neither Davies (1983) nor McCown (1982) however found significant relationships between length of illness and behaviour problem scores. These findings are in contrast to those by Schwab, Chalmers, Conroy, Ferris, and Markush (1965) and Payne et al. (1980) who reported that grief reactions were related to duration of illness. Several explanations may account for these discrepant findings. One is that children between 6 and 16 years of age may not benefit from a period of anticipatory grief in the same way that it has been documented that adults do. A second is the way in which the variable was defined, most often as the number of months elapsed between the date of diagnosis and the actual death. This time period may not accurately reflect the time the surviving children had available to them to prepare for the death. A suggestion for further study then is to question the parents, or the children themselves, about when they became aware of their sibling's diagnosis and prognosis. When the loss of a sibling is preceded by an illness such as cancer, the pattern of relationships has already been disrupted by the illness itself, and so the disruption caused by the death is not as great as if a sudden death had occurred. It is possible that the greatest impact on children of having a sibling die from cancer is at the time of the diagnosis of the illness. It would be instructive to study children's behaviour at diagnosis, throughout the illness, and following the death.

Sudden Death.   An important mediating factor on sibling bereavement is related to the suddenness or expectedness of the death. Unlike illness that may have had some chronicity before entering a terminal phase, the results of acute or accidental trauma happen suddenly with no preparation. The impact of sudden trauma and impending death may throw the entire family into chaos, with no one able to coordinate necessary activities. It has been widely documented in the literature on adult bereavement that the cause of death is in itself a variable of importance in how survivors respond to a death. Bereavement following a sudden and unexpected death is more often characterized by greater stress (Carey, 1977; Fulton & Fulton, 1971; Parkes, 1972; Vachon, 1976). Parkes (1973) insists that time to prepare is particularly important for the relatively young. Parkes' comment refers to young adults, but the same stance applies to those even younger, to children. Whereas children who lose siblings through illness need a clear understanding of the cause of the disease and the changes through the course of illness, Stephenson (1986) observed that accidental or violent death may produce its own particular issues for the surviving sibling, because accidents often imply fault or preventability that may or may not be resolved within the family. Nixon and Pearn (1977) noted that 32% of siblings were significantly affected by the drowning death of their sibling. For these children, sleep disorders and feelings of guilt were common problems. Other authors (Rudestam, 1977; Stephenson, 1986;) suggested that children surviving the death of a sibling by suicide are at risk for subsequent disturbed grief reactions. Not only are the surviving children left to cope with their own grief as well as their possible feelings of rejection by the deceased child, there is the burden of coping with the negative and social stigma of being a suicide survivor. The family of a child who committed suicide often may focus on denying the reality of what has happened, even inventing a new version of the death and suppressing any further discussion of the event.

   Taylor, DeFrain, and Ernst (1986) identified unique factors exacerbating the grief of the families following the death of a child from sudden infant death syndrome (SIDS). Although the authors noted, based on their clinical experience, that subsequent children are at risk for the replacement child syndrome (Cain & Cain, 1964), few known published studies have examined sibling bereavement response following the death of a brother or sister from SIDS (Mandell, McClain, & Reece, 1988).

   In summary, there is a severe deficit of published literature pertaining to sibling bereavement responses when the cause of childhood death is other than cancer or cystic fibrosis.

Place of Death.   A reduced incidence of problems is suggested as a treatment effect in several recent studies using various supportive treatment approaches (Martinson, 1980; Mulhern, Lauer, & Hoffman, 1983; Stebhens & Lascari, 1974).

   In their evaluation of a home care program for terminally ill children, Mulhern et al. (1983) compared behaviour reactions of children whose siblings died at home with those whose siblings died in the hospital 3 to 29 months following the child's death. Using maternal reports on a standardized behavioural checklist, the investigators found that children from the home care program scored within normal limits, whereas those whose siblings died in the hospital had higher scores on fear and neurotic behaviour scales. However, caution must be employed in the interpretation of these findings: families who chose home care may have differed substantially from families who selected hospital care for the dying child. Lauer, Mulhern, Bohne, & Camitta (1985) subsequently examined children's perceptions and involvement during their siblings' terminal home care or hospital experience and correlated those factors to subsequent adjustment after their sibling's death. Nineteen children whose siblings participated in a home care program for dying children and 17 children whose siblings died in the hospital were interviewed one year after the death. Home care children described a significantly different experience from those whose sibling died in the hospital. The majority of the children who participated in the home care program reported that they were prepared for the impending death, received consistent information and support from their parents, were involved in most activities concerning the dying child, were present for the death, and viewed their own involvement as the most important aspect of the experience. By contrast, non-home care children generally described themselves as having been inadequately prepared for the death, isolated from the dying child and their parents, unable to use their parents for support or information, unclear as to the circumstances of the death, and useless in terms of their own involvement. Three major recurrent experiential differences noted by the children's self-report in these two groups were: preparation for the death, involvement in preterminal and terminal care, and parental accessibility for support. More recently, Lauer, Mulhern, Schell, and Camitta (1989) examined parental adjustment following a child's death at home or hospital 6–8 years earlier. Long-term data emerging from this study suggest that the early pattern of differential adjustment of home care and non-home care parents is generally a reliable predictor of long-term bereavement outcome. Parents who provided home care experienced a relatively efficient and enduring resolution of their grief. While this relationship requires further empirical testing among home care and non-home care sibling populations, these early findings provide more definitive support for the role of home care as a determinant of differential profiles of bereavement.

Time Elapsed.   Most studies of sibling bereavement, and in fact most bereavement studies, focus on the months immediately after the death or up to one or two years following the death. Consequently, the longer term effects of siblings' bereavement are relatively unknown. Several studies (Davies, 1987; Rosen, 1986; Spinetta et al., 1981b) indicate that symptoms persisted with siblings in the majority of families even two to three years after the death. Very few researchers have controlled for elapsed time since death. Among those who have are Payne et al. (1980). They found that a variety of problems subsequent to the loss of a brother or sister was evident in a larger percentage (36%) of those children whose sibling had died six months before than of those (22%) whose sibling had died two years before. Similarly, Hogan (1988) reported that adolescents demonstrated more problems during the first 3–18 months than during the 18–36 months interval after the death. Davies (1983) reported that internalizing behaviours were negatively correlated with time elapsed since the death; that is, over time (up to three years post-death) siblings became more withdrawn, anxious, and sad. The need for longitudinal studies is emphasized.

In reporting the secondary analysis of the data collected in Martinson's (1980) study, Davies (1987) indicates that at 7 to 9 years after the death, siblings reported that they continued to experience effects of the death. Several continued to dream about their deceased brother or sister; such dreams were not disturbing, but rather comforting in that they provided a feeling of closeness to the sibling. Feelings of loneliness and sadness persisted, not always in the forefront of their minds but still identifiable. Many of the siblings continued to think about their sibling frequently, many as often as once a day. Such thoughts were triggered by internal and external reminders, and were more prevalent at certain times, like when they themselves reached the age at which the sibling had died, or when they had children of their own. Similar results are emerging from an examination of adults who in their childhood lost a sibling (Davies, work in progress). Up to 10, 20, or 30 years after the death, siblings perceive that the death had a long-term impact on their lives, often as a constant reminder about the value of life. The long-term effects of sibling bereavement are not necessarily pathological even though periods of intense sadness may recur years later.

These data suggest two contradictions to common assumptions about the resolution of grief in siblings. First, the data indicate that the time required for the bereavement process in siblings is indeed longer than a year or two. Even many years after the death, the siblings were still experiencing pain and loss. Second, rather than saying things that suggested resolution, the siblings described something different. Instead of "letting go" of the loved one, the siblings and their parents detailed the continuing presence of an "empty space" (McClowry, et al., 1987).

> I can talk about my sister but it gets to me...she's always with me...I stop and think about her every once in a while. Especially if I see a girl that looks like her. That gets me wondering...What she'd look like now. I still miss her...she's still a piece of my life...a piece that's missing.
>   (An 18-year-old brother, 8 years following the death of his sister who died of cancer)

Environmental Factors

Environmental factors include those that contribute to the social-emotional atmosphere of the child's environment.

Family Environment.   The family provides for its members the necessary relationships, both in quality and intensity, out of which normal growth and development may occur. Because of these relationships, the system behaves not as a simple composition of independent elements, but coherently and inseparable as a whole (Watzlawick, Beavin, & Jackson, 1967). Following this perspective, illness or death of any family member is a potential assault on the family system. Consequently, when a child dies, the impact on the total family and each of its members must be considered.

Given the lifelong significance of sibling relationships, it seems unremarkable to posit that substantial changes in the health or functioning of a sibling will affect the other(s) and that these changes may correspond systematically to characteristics of the child, the family, and the disease or disability itself (Lobato et al., 1988). Sourkes (1980) noted that the total family's response and coping mechanisms affect the siblings' response, and stated that when dealing with a child with a life-threatening illness [or when a child dies], "the patient is the family."

A family may be distinguished according to its characteristic modes of perceiving and interacting with its social environment. Based on data from 111 families where a child had died of cancer from two months to nine years earlier, certain elements of family functioning were found to be characteristic of high- versus low-functioning families (Davies, Spinetta, et al., 1986). Findings suggest that each family responds as a unit to the death of a child and emphasize the need to study siblings in the context of their family.

Davies (1988b) described the environment in families where a child had died from cancer and examined its relationship to surviving sibling behaviour. She reported a significant relationship between cohesion and sibling behavioural response following the death of a brother or sister from cancer. The greater the degree of commitment, help, and support family members provide for one another, the fewer withdrawing and acting out behaviours reported for the bereaved children. Consistent findings were reported by Lauer et al. (1989) in an investigation of family cohesion and adjustment in relation to place of death. Davies (1988b) also indicated that families with a greater emphasis on social, cultural, recreational, and religious involvement tended to have children with fewer behavioural problems following a sibling's death. These findings suggest that further research is warranted into the role of social support for families following the loss of a child and that further examination of the impact of the family environment on sibling bereavement would contribute to a comprehensive approach to intervening with such families.

Parental Characteristics.   No reported studies have examined the relationship between parental characteristics and subsequent sibling bereavement response, even though parental grief is a critical factor in predicting subsequent sibling adjustment and bereavement (McCown & Pratt, 1985). Following the emotional contagion hypothesis, it would not be unreasonable to presume that the surviving children's adjustment is influenced by parental grief. Methodological limitations and challenges in the study of parental grief are similar to those found in the study of sibling grief. Rando (1983) indicated that parental grief response is influenced by such factors as sex of the parent, length of the child's illness, and time since the death. McCown and Pratt (1985) did not find any of these factors to be related to children's behaviour responses following a sibling's death. Rando (1983) also noted that self-reports of parental grief may not be valid because of the "stunned" response experienced following a significant loss. Spinetta et al. (1981b) reported that parents who were best adjusted after the death of their child were those who had a consistent philosophy of life during the course of the illness (which helped the family accept the diagnosis and cope with its consequences), who had a viable and ongoing support person to whom they could turn for help during the course of the illness, and who gave their child the information and emotional support the child needed during the course of the illness at a level consistent with their child's questions, age, and level of development. The impact of parental grief on sibling grief is an area in need of further empirical study.

Parent–Well Child Communication.   The importance of effective communication has been recognized as an essential element in facilitating individual and family coping with childhood chronic life-threatening illness. Adams-Greenly (1984, 1986) suggests that how a family communicates about the illness can be indicative of general communication patterns. In this regard, communication indicates not just telling of facts, but the creation of a climate that allows and encourages expression of feelings.

Parent–child communication about death and dying has been used as a predictor of coping in the ill child, the parents, and siblings. However, discrepant findings are reported that preclude definitive conclusions about the relationship between parent–child communication and sibling bereavement outcome. Townes and Wold (1977) reported in their study of 22 siblings of 8 leukemic patients that the siblings' evaluation of the patient's disease as life-threatening was related to increased parental communication about the implications of the disease and about the experience of living with the illness in the family. Early in the illness, poor adjustment was not associated with communication but rather with age and sex: boys and older children had more problems (Townes & Wold, 1977). The value of providing a similar "safe" forum for healthy siblings and the effects of such discussion on subsequent bereavement response has received little attention. However, available empirical research suggests that communication is a major factor influencing sibling adjustment or bereavement (McCown & Pratt, 1985). Factors influencing the extent and effectiveness of such communication among parents, dying children, and their siblings were investigated retrospectively with 77 mothers who were members of the Compassionate Friends Organization (Graham-Pole, et al., 1989). Mothers who talked more freely with dying children also did so with the siblings and that communication was more open with older than with younger children. The researchers concluded that this dialogue was very helpful for both the dying children and their siblings if the former were mostly at home immediately before death, if there was extensive and specific discussion about death and dying, when a parent was the major discussant (not significant for siblings), and if the family's religious faith was a significant source of support. However, following such discussions, the emotional state of the dying children and the siblings contrasted markedly. Mothers perceived the latter showing significantly more sadness, anger, denial, and fear. Not negating this finding, the authors questioned whether siblings need a different kind of communication that focuses specifically on their own loss and distress. Children's imaginations are highly developed, and dealing with the realities of death in the family may be both kinder and easier for them to cope with than the ordeal of experience by fantasy (Bluebond-Langner, 1978, 1989; Dominica, 1987). Despite several methodological limitations of this study, findings indicate appropriate communication is at least as important for survivors as it is for the dying child.

Birenbaum (1989a, 1989b) studied the relationship between parent–sibling communication and siblings' coping prior to and after the death of a child with cancer. Findings suggest a complex relationship between parent-sibling communication and sibling coping. Prior to death, parent–sibling communication was positively related to social competence (interpersonal, intrapersonal, and school functioning). This supports previous findings. However, this relationship was not found at any time after the death. Parent–sibling communication was inversely related to external behaviour problems following the ill child's death at each point in time but not before the death. Similarly, both Davies (1983) and McCown (1987) reported that expressiveness or openness of parent-well child communication was not significantly related to sibling behavioural response after a child's death.

Birenbaum (1989b) offers a hypothesis for these findings: parent–sibling communication is context-specific. Before death, talking about the illness and death is context-specific and thus has use for the sibling. Following the death, the situation changes. While open expression may pertain to many topics and areas of concern to family members, the discussion of the fear or sadness of death may be excluded. Similarly, the open expression of grief after the death may not be supported, even in the most expressive families. This observation puts into question earlier assumptions that parent–child communication during the illness positively affects both the coping strategies of the child during treatment and sibling bereavement outcome. Disease-related communication is not necessarily the same as communication surrounding death, dying, and grief.

Birenbaum (1989b) raises the question of whether health-care professionals have prepared families to believe that communication about the death and dying will increase siblings' coping following death. Further research should focus on the development of intervention studies to test possible causal relationships between increasing parent–sibling communication about the illness, the death, and bereavement response. The lack of relationship between parent–sibling communication and social competence after the death requires a reevaluation of our current clinical wisdom.

Shared Life Space. Shared life space has been suggested as an important predictor of behaviour outcome in siblings (Davies, 1988a; McClowry, et al., 1987). Life space as defined by Parkes (1972, p. 103) consists of "those parts of the environment with which the self interacts and in relationship to which behaviour is organized." Parkes proposed that the amount of stress that can be expected in bereavement seems to be related to how much of each other's life space the deceased person and the survivor have occupied. Following this perspective, the greater the shared life space, the greater the potential for intense disruption during bereavement. Findings by Davies (1983, 1985, 1988a) suggest that the siblings who were closest to the deceased child, experienced the most difficulty in that closer sibling relationships were associated with more internalizing behaviours in the surviving children. Davies (1987) also noted that the styles of grieving were related to the quality of the relationship. Siblings who described the deceased as being irreplaceable by anyone or anything experienced a continuing empty space. In contrast, others described the death as a loss but not with the same intensity as those whose death created an empty space. Further investigation of emotional closeness as a component of the concept of shared life space is warranted.

> There were light years between us.... S. had come at a time when she was a living doll to me, a live baby, and so it was fun to grow up with

her even though she was spoiled and got her own way most of the time. I can remember playing Barbie dolls and paper dolls and watching cartoons with her in the morning and sleeping with her...and every time I'd go out, I'd have to be home at such and such a time because S. was looking for me.

(Woman of 22 years whose sister, 9 years younger than she, had died at age 8)

Implications for Practice

An array of anecdotal and clinical literature provides guidelines for communicating with or helping healthy siblings cope with the dying and death of a brother or sister. Relatively few papers provide guidelines which derive from a research base; guidelines for oncology nurses based on research with bereaved siblings is one exception (Davies, 1993). Most of these guidelines are derived from clinical experience with children and serve as valuable and useful foundations for intervention (Gibbons, 1992). However, to date, few studies have documented the effectiveness of such interventions in preventing or alleviating problematic bereavement responses in siblings. Meanwhile, clinicians will continue to rely on what is currently known and what appears compassionate and appropriate. However, the importance of sound research on which to base interventions cannot be overemphasized. Moreover, the involvement of clinicians in research is critical if bereavement theory is to have clinical relevance. Rosen (1986), for example, presented a useful taxonomy for looking at sibling behaviours, which are categorized according to their function in helping the surviving siblings to cope with the loss of a brother or sister. Viewing a child's behaviour in terms of how it meets the child's needs to cope and adapt establishes a framework that serves as a first step toward greater clarity in interventions for bereaved siblings.

Future Research

This review of the literature points to the fact that there is no overriding theory related to the sibling relationship in sibling adjustment following the death of a brother or sister. An abundance of intriguing, related problems have been identified and have contributed to research efforts that are scattered and diverse. Because the concepts used were often not the same, observations of data were not commensurate. Studies and methods have not been replicated across disciplines; no clear cumulative structure has evolved and many fundamental contradictions remain.

Bereavement response in siblings is complex and requires further empirical testing.

The methodological limitations of reported research on siblings are similar to those in many fields of clinical inquiry. Larger samples with wider age spans and tighter controls are needed. Rigorous interdisciplinary research is necessary. Emphasis should be placed on theory construction derived from empirical data based on common, operationally defined concepts. Information is needed about how relationships between and among siblings change over time.

Important to note, the majority of investigations have used a retrospective approach in the collection of data. In some studies, observations of children's behaviours were based primarily on anecdotal accounts from third-party observers such as physicians and nurses. In several studies, interviews on children's behaviours were obtained from parents. Factors that warrant consideration in terms of eliciting interview data from parents include memory distortion, parental bias in reporting information, and limitations imposed by the pervasive mourning effects on the part of parents in identifying accurately their child's grief response. Few studies collected data from the children directly (Balk, 1983a, 1983b; Davies, 1987; Hogan, 1988). Factors that must be weighed in the interpretation of data from children's interviews are (1) "children are less likely to communicate honestly and openly with a researcher than is an adult; (2) children younger than school age have difficulty communicating their feelings accurately; and (3) children may feel inhibited in reporting feelings for fear of retribution and for need of maintaining status quo" (Betz, 1987, p. 47).

To reconcile diverse findings there is a need for research in which independent variables are systematically controlled and dependent variables are chosen which are sensitive to the influence of specific as well as globally defined factors (Simeonsson & McHale, 1981). Previous research has typically a one-sided view of the effect of the child's illness and death on the siblings, often with an orientation toward psychopathology. To clarify and extend previous research, efforts should be made not only to obtain information directly from the ill child and the siblings, but also when appropriate, to directly observe their interaction (methodological) and look at coping and adaptation as a process with a bidirectional nature of the relationship (content) with potential positive outcomes. As Sourkes (1980) emphasized, there are *mutual* feelings of anger and resentment as well as *mutual* feelings of protectiveness and caring. The reciprocal nature of the sibling relationship and its effect on bereavement outcome in the surviving sibling remains to be examined.

In review of research literature that focuses on children and their experience with chronically ill, terminally ill, and deceased siblings, the issue of timing becomes significant. One possible explanation for the discrepant findings may be the different time intervals between loss and the moment of investigation because the affective and behavioural effects of grief may vary in onset and duration (Lindemann, 1944). Although the expression of grief may alter with the lapse of time its intensity may not diminish, as was generally assumed. While there has been no dearth of studies that have examined the effects of childhood chronic illness on siblings at different points in time in the illness trajectory, similar attention and rigor in examining the effects of childhood bereavement on siblings have been severely limited. In only one known published study (Birenbaum, 1987) have sibling responses been investigated before, during, and following the death of a child with cancer. Given the lifelong significance of sibling bereavement, additional longitudinal studies of sibling responses to death of various causes at different points in time is warranted.

The critical importance of direct observation and interview with the siblings has been emphasized in studies of siblings of children with cancer (Brett & Davies, 1988; Iles, 1979; Kramer, 1981; Walker, 1988, 1990). Brett and Davies (1988) reported that well siblings showed more variety among themselves than did those of the parents in their appraisal. Several factors appeared to contribute to this variation: (1) cognitive maturation, (2) parental influence on the availability and interpretation of childhood cancer related information, and (3) heavy reliance on inferential reasoning in response to their immature cognitive abilities and to the limited family communication about the disease. That is, the children frequently created their own explanations based (to a large extent) upon inference from experience, nonverbal signals, and fantasy.

Low levels of agreement between parents' and well siblings' perceptions of coping with chronic childhood illness have been reported (Craft & Craft, 1989; Craft, 1986). Similarly, Hogan and Balk (1990) reported discrepant findings between mothers and bereaved adolescents regarding the adolescents' grieving responses. The discrepancy between parents' and children's perceptions of coping strategies point to the need for direct observation and interaction with healthy siblings. What children may view as helping them manage a situation may not be what parents perceive as helpful. As Kramer (1981, p. 169) noted, "regardless of how successfully well siblings appear to adapt to the illness experience, one must remember that a child's perception and interpretation of his world is very different from an adult's and reflects his level of cognitive development." Furthermore, the children may behave as the parents reported but they did not view these actions as managing their stress. Walker (1988) emphasized the need to assess each individual child for what he/she actually does—both what was helpful in leading to adaptation as well as what was not helpful or was maladaptive.

Creative investigative techniques may be necessary to help siblings "speak" about their experience. Differing levels of cognitive development and verbal ability in children necessitate the use of different methods of data collection apart from the more traditional methods of direct interview and observation. Projective techniques such as kinetic family drawings and other drawings have been used as a tool in the investigation of a number of family situations as well as children with health-care needs (Bossert & Martinson, 1990; Cornman, 1988; Eng & Davies, 1990; Rollins, 1990; Siegel & Kornfield, 1980; Spinetta, McLaren, Fox & Sparta, 1981a; Waechter, 1971; Walker, 1988; Wohl & Kaufman, 1985; Worden, 1985). A major assumption underlying projective tests is that the world is perceived uniquely from each person's perspective and therefore any representation given of it will reflect that person's attitude and understanding of the world (Hammer, 1981; Klepsch & Logie, 1982).

Grief involving the loss of a sibling does appear to diminish over time; however the real grief experience is individual and is affected by variables and the ways these are managed during and after the death. Children are active participants in all aspects of family life and interact with the environment with their own understanding of the events that occur. The death of a child is a traumatic event for siblings. The intensity of the immediate impact does seem to diminish over time, but the long-term effects, though not easily identified or measured, last a lifetime. The experience is influenced by a variety of mediating factors, some of which have been identified. To date, research has indicated that sibling grief is an individual journey that should not be expected to follow time limits and a specific path. With additional investigation, we shall continue to learn about the journey that begins for surviving siblings when a child dies or perhaps when it is first learned that an event with life-threatening potential is occurring.

> There were five kids in our family. I'm the oldest, and my sister who died was the youngest. We were alike, we were the good kids. The middle three were terrors. They've changed a bit over the years, but I still miss the special tie there was between M. and me. No one will ever take her place.
> *(The 33-year-old sister of child who had died 8 years earlier at age 15)*

References

Adams, D. W., & Deveau, E. J. (1987). How the cause of a child's death may affect a sibling's grief. In M.A. Morgan (Ed.), *Bereavement: Helping the survivors* (pp. 67–77). Proceedings of the 1987 King's College Conference. London, Ontario: King's College.

Adams-Greenly, M. (1984). Helping children communicate about serious illness and death. *Journal of Psychosocial Oncology, 2,* 61–72.

Adams-Greenly, M. (1986). Psychological staging of pediatric cancer patients and their families. *Cancer, 58*(2 Suppl.), 449–453.

Balk, D. (1983a). Adolescents' grief reactions and self-concept perceptions following sibling death: A study of 33 teenagers. *Journal of Youth and Adolescents, 12*(2), 137–161.

Balk, D. (1983b). Effects of sibling death on teenagers. *Journal of School Health, 1*(53), 14–18.

Bank, S., & Kahn, M. D. (1982). *The sibling bond.* New York: Basic Books.

Betz, C. L. (1987). Death, dying, and bereavement: A review of literature, 1970–1985. In T. Krulik, B. Holaday, & I. M. Martinson (Eds.), *The child and family facing life-threatening illness* (pp. 32–49). New York: J. B. Lippincott.

Binger, C., Ablin, A., Feuerstein, R., Kushner, J., Zoger, S., & Mikkelsen, C. (1969). Childhood leukemia: Emotional impact on patient and family. *New England Journal of Medicine, 280*(8), 414–418.

Binger, C. M. (1973). Childhood leukemia—emotional impact on siblings. In J. E. Anthony & C. Koupernik, *The child and his family: The impact of disease and death, Vol. 2.* New York: Wiley & Sons.

Birenbaum, L. K. (1987). *Effects of family nursing on sibling response to dying.* (Final Report: Grant Nos: 5RO1 NU00912 and 5RO1 NU00912-02S1. Portland, OR: Oregon Health Sciences University.

Birenbaum, L. K. (1989a). The relationship between parent-siblings' communication and siblings' coping with death experience. *Journal of the Association of Pediatric Oncology Nurses, 6*(2), 26–27.

Birenbaum, L. K. (1989b). The relationship between parent-sibling communication and coping of siblings with death experience. *Journal of Pediatric Oncology Nursing, 6*(3), 85–91.

Birtchnell, J. (1970). Depression in relation to early and recent parent death. *British Journal of Psychiatry, 116,* 299–306.

Blinder, B. (1972). Sibling death in childhood. *Child Psychiatry and Human Development, 2,* 169–175.

Bluebond-Langner, M. (1978). *The private worlds of dying children.* Princeton, NJ: Princeton University.

Bluebond-Langner, M. (1989). Worlds of dying children and their well siblings. *Death Studies, 13,* 1–16.

Bossert, E., & Martinson, I. M. (1990). Kinetic Family Drawings—revised: A method of determining the impact of cancer on the family as perceived by the child with cancer. *Journal of Pediatric Nursing, 5*(3), 204–213.

Bowlby, J. (1963). Pathological mourning and childhood mourning. *Journal of American Psychoanalytic Association, 11,* 500–541.

Brett, K. M. (1988). Sibling response to chronic childhood disorders: Research perspectives and practice implications. *Issues in Comprehensive Pediatric Nursing, 11,* 43–57.

Brett, K. M., & Davies, E. M. B. (1988). What does it mean? Sibling and parental appraisals of childhood leukemia. *Cancer Nursing, 11*, 329–338.

Brody, G. H., & Stoneman, Z. (1983). Children with atypical siblings. In B. Lahey, & A. Kazden (Eds.), *Advances in clinical child psychology, Vol. 6* (pp. 285–326). New York: Plenum.

Brown, G., Harris, T., & Copeland, J. (1977). Depression and loss. *British Journal of Psychiatry, 130*, 11.

Brownmiller, N., & Cantwell, D. (1976). Siblings as therapists: A behavioural approach. *American Journal of Psychiatry, 133*, 447–50.

Cain, A. C., Fast, I., & Erickson, M. E. (1964). Children's disturbed reactions to the death of a sibling. *American Journal of Orthopsychiatry, 34*, 741–752.

Cain, A. C., & Cain, B. C. (1964). On replacing a child. *Journal of the American Academy of Child and Adolescent Psychiatry, 3*, 443–456.

Cairns, N. U., Clark, G. M., Smith, S. D., & Lansky, S. B. (1979). Adaptation of siblings to childhood malignancy. *Journal of Pediatrics, 95*(3), 484–487.

Carey, R. G. (1977). The widowed: A year later. *Journal of Counselling Psychology, 24*, 125–131.

Carr-Gregg, M., & White, L. (1987). Siblings of pediatric cancer patients: A population at risk. *Medical and Pediatric Oncology, 15*, 62–68.

Chesler, M. A., & Barbarian, O. A. (1987). *Childhood cancer and the family: Meeting the challenge of stress and support.* New York: Brunner/Mazel.

Chesler, M. A., Paris, J., & Barbarian, O. A. (1986). "Telling" the child with cancer: Parental choices to share information with ill children. *Journal of Pediatric Psychology, 11*, 497–516.

Clayton, P., Desmarais, L., & Winokur, G. (1968). A study of normal bereavement. *American Journal of Psychiatry, 125*, 168–178.

Cobb, B. (1956). Psychological impact of long illness and death of a child on the family circle. *Journal of Pediatrics, 49*(6), 746–751.

Cornman, B. J. (1988). *Impact of childhood cancer on the family.* Unpublished doctoral dissertation. Seattle, WA: University of Washington.

Craft, M. (1986). Validation of responses reported by school-aged siblings of hospitalized children. *Children's Health Care, 15*(1), 6–13.

Craft, M. J., & Craft, J. L. (1989). Perceived changes in siblings on hospitalized children: A comparison of sibling and parent reports. *Children's Health Care, 18*(1), 42–48.

Davies, E. M. B. (1983). *Behavioural responses of children to a siblings's death.* Unpublished doctoral dissertation. Seattle, WA: University of Washington.

Davies, B. (1985). *Predictors of behaviour outcomes in bereaved siblings.* Paper presented at 10th National Research Conference: "Nursing Research: Science for Quality Care." April 9–11. Toronto, Ontario.

Davies, B. (1987). After a sibling dies. In M.A. Morgan, (Ed.), *Bereavement: Helping the survivors. Proceedings of the 1987 King's College Conference* (pp. 55–56). London, Ontario: King's College.

Davies, B. (1988a). Shared life space and sibling bereavement responses. *Cancer Nursing, 11*, 339–347.

Davies, B. (1988b). The family environment in bereaved families and its relationship to surviving sibling behaviour. *Children's Health Care, 17*(1), 22–30.

Davies, B. (1991). Long-term outcomes of adolescent sibling bereavement. *Journal of Adolescent Research, 6*(1), 83–96.

Davies, B. (1993). Sibling bereavement: Research-based guidelines for nurses. *Seminars in Oncology Nursing, 9*(2), 107–113.

Davies, B., Spinetta, J., Martinson, I., McClowry, S., & Kulenkamp, E. (1986). Manifestations of levels of functioning in grieving families. *Journal of Family Issues, 7*(3), 297–313.

Dominica, F. (1987). Reflections on death in childhood. *British Medical Journal, 294*, 108–110.

Drotar, D., & Crawford, P. (1985). Psychological adaptation of siblings of chronically ill children: Research and practice implications. *Developmental and Behavioural Pediatrics, 6*, 335–362.

Dunn, J. (1988). Annotation: Sibling influences on childhood development. *Journal of Child Psychology and Psychiatry, 29*(2), 119–127.

Eng, B., & Davies, B. (1990). *Effects of a summer camp experience on self-concept of children with cancer. Final Report.* Vancouver, BC: Canadian Cancer Society.

Engel, G. (1964). Grief and grieving. *American Journal of Nursing, 64*, 93–98.

Fulton, R. (1977). *Death, grief and bereavement: A bibliography 1845–1975.* New York: Arna Press.

Fulton, R., & Fulton, J. (1971). A psychosocial aspect of terminal care: Anticipatory grief. *Omega, 2*, 91–100.

Furman, E. (1974). *A child's parent dies: Studies in childhood bereavement.* New Haven: Yale University.

Gibbons, M. B. (1992). A child dies, a child survives: The impact of sibling loss. *Journal of Pediatric Health Care, 6*, 65–72.

Graham-Pole, J., Wass, H., Eyberg, S., Chu, L., & Olejnik, S. (1989). Communicating with dying children and their siblings: A retrospective analysis. *Death Studies, 13*, 465–483.

Grogan, L. B. (1990). Grief of an adolescent when a sibling dies. *Maternal Child Nursing, 15*, 21–24.

Glick, I., Weiss, R., & Parkes, C. (1974). *The first year of bereavement.* New York: Wiley & Sons.

Hammer, E. F. (1981). Protective drawings. In A. I. Rubin (Ed.), *Assessment with projective techniques: A concise introduction* (pp. 151–185). New York: Springer.

Hilgard, J. R. (1969). Depressive and psychotic states as anniversaries to sibling death in childhood. *International Psychiatry Clinics, 6*, 197–207.

Hogan, N. (1988). The effects of time on the adolescent sibling bereavement process. *Pediatric Nursing, 14*(4), 333–335.

Hogan, N., & Balk, D. (1990). Adolescent reactions to sibling death: Perceptions of mothers, fathers, and teenagers. *Nursing Research, 39*(2), 103–106.

Iles, J. P. (1979). Children with cancer: Healthy siblings' perceptions during the illness experience. *Cancer Nursing, 2*, 371–377.

Kaplan, D., Grobstein, R., & Smith, A. (1976). Predicting the impact of severe illness in families. *Health and Social Work, 1*, 71–82.

Klepsch, M., & Logie, L. (1982). *Children draw and tell.* New York: Brunner/ Mazel.

Kramer, R. F. (1981). Living with childhood cancer: Healthy siblings' perspective. *Issues in Comprehensive Nursing, 5*, 155–165.

Lauer, M. E., Mulhern, R. K., Bohne, J. B., & Camitta, B. M. (1985). Children's perceptions of their siblings' death at home or hospital: The precursors of differential adjustment. *Cancer Nursing, 8*, 21–27.

Lauer, M. E., Mulhern, R. K., Schell, M. J., & Camitta, B. M. (1989). Long-term follow-up of parental adjustment following a child's death at home or hospital. *Cancer, 63*(5), 988–994.

Lavigne, J. V., & Ryan, M. (1979). The psychosocial adjustment of siblings of children with chronic illness. *Pediatrics, 63*, 616–627.

Lewis, I. C. (1967). Leukemia in childhood: Its effects on the family. *Australian Paediatric Journal, 3*, 244–247.

Lindemann, E. (1944). Symptomatology and management of acute grief. *American Journal of Psychiatry, 101*, 141–148.

Lobato, D. (1983). Siblings of handicapped children: A review. *Journal of Autism and Developmental Disorders, 13*, 347–364.

Lobato, D., Faust, D., & Spirito, A. (1988). Examining the effects of chronic disease and disability on children's sibling relationships. *Journal of Pediatric Psychology, 13*(3), 389–407.

Mandell, F., McClain, M., & Reece, R. (1988). The Sudden Infant Death Syndrome: Siblings and their place in the family. *Annals of the New York Academy of Sciences, 533*, 129–131.

Martinson, I. M. (Principal Investigator). (1980). *Home care for the child with cancer* (Final Report: Grant CA19490). Washington, DC: National Cancer Institute.

Martinson, I. M., Davies, E. B., & McClowry, S. G. (1987). The long-term effects of sibling death on self-concept. *Journal of Pediatric Nursing, 2*(4), 227–235.

McClowry, S. G., Davies, E. B., Kulenkamp, M. E., & Martinson, I. M. (1987). The empty space phenomenon: The process of grief in the bereaved family. *Death Studies, 11*, 361–374.

McCown, D. E. (1982). *Selected factors related to children's adjustment following sibling death.* Unpublished doctoral dissertation. Portland, OR: Oregon State University.

McCown, D. E., & Pratt, C. (1985). Impact of sibling death on children's behaviour. *Death Studies, 9*, 323–335.

McHale, S., Simeonsson, R. J., & Sloan, J. L. (1984). Children with handicapped brothers and sisters. In E. Schopler & G. B. Mesibov (Eds.), *The effects of autism on the family* (pp. 327–342). New York: Plenum.

McKeever, P. (1983). Siblings of chronically ill children: A literature review with implications for research and practice. *American Journal of Orthopsychiatry, 53*(2), 209–218.

Mulhern, R. K., Lauer, M. E., & Hoffman, R. G. (1983). Death of a child at home or in the hospital: Subsequent psychological adjustment of the family. *Pediatrics, 71*(5), 743–747.

Nixon, J., & Pearn, J. (1977). Emotional sequelae of parents and sibs following the drowning or near-drowning of a child. *Australian and New Zealand Journal of Psychiatry, 11*, 265–268.

Parkes, C. M. (1972). *Bereavement: Studies of grief in adult life.* New York: International Universities Press.

Parkes, C. M. (1973). Anticipatory grief and widowhood. *British Journal of Psychiatry, 122*, 615–619.

Parkes, C. M., & Weiss, R. S. (1983). *Recovery from bereavement.* New York: Basic Books.

Payne, J. S., Goff, J. R., & Paulson, M. A. (1980). Psychosocial adjustment of families following the death of a child. In J. L. Schulman & M. J. Kupst (Eds.), *The child with cancer: Clinical approaches to psychosocial care— research in psychosocial aspects* (pp. 183–193). Springfield, IL: Charles C. Thomas.

Rando, T. A. (1983). An investigation of grief and adaptation in parents whose children have died from cancer. *Journal of Pediatric Psychology, 8*, 3–20.

Rando, T. A. (1993). *Treatment of complicated mourning.* Champaign, IL: Research Press.

Raphael, B. (1983). *The anatomy of bereavement.* New York: Basic Books.

Rollins, J. A. (1990). Childhood cancer: Siblings draw and tell. *Pediatric Nursing, 16*(1), 21–27.

Rosen, H. (1986). *Unspoken grief: Coping with childhood sibling loss.* Lexington, MA: D. C. Heath.

Rudestam, K. E. (1977). Physical and psychological response to suicide in the family. *Journal of Consulting and Clinical Psychology, 45*(2), 167–170.

Sanders, C. M. (1989). *Grief: The mourning after.* New York: Wiley & Sons.

Schwab, J. J., Chalmers, J. M., Conroy, S. J., Ferris, P. B., & Markush, R. E. (1965). Studies in grief: A preliminary report. In B. Schoenberg, L. Gerber, A. Wiener, A. H. Kutscher, D. Peretz, & A. Carr (Eds.), *Bereavement: Its psychosocial aspects.* New York: Columbia University.

Siegel, I. M., & Kornfeld, M S. (1980). Kinetic Family Drawing test for evaluating families having children with muscular dystrophy. *Physio-Therapist, 60*(3), 293–298.

Siemon, M. (1984). Siblings of the chronically ill or disabled child: Meeting their needs. *Nursing Clinics of North America, 19*(2), 295–307.

Simeonsson, R. J., & McHale, S. M. (1981). Review: Research on handicapped children: Sibling relationships. *Child Care, Health and Development, 7,* 153–171.

Sourkes, B. M. (1980). Siblings of the pediatric cancer patient. In J. Kellerman (Ed.), *Psychological aspects of childhood cancer* (pp. 47–69). Springfield IL: Charles C. Thomas.

Spinetta, J. J. (1981). The sibling of the child with cancer. In J. J. Spinetta, & P. Deasy-Spinetta (Eds.), *Living with childhood cancer* (pp. 133–142). St. Louis: C. V. Mosby.

Spinetta, J. J. (1982). Impact of cancer on the family. In J. M. Vaeth (Ed.), *Childhood cancer: Triumph over tragedy* (pp. 166–176). Frontiers of Radiation Therapy and Oncology, Vol. 16. Basel: Karger.

Spinetta, J. J., McLaren, H. H., Fox, R. W., & Sparta, S. N. (1981a). The Kinetic Family Drawing in childhood cancer: A revised application of an age-independent measure. In J. J. Spinetta & P. Deasy-Spinetta (Eds.), *Living with childhood cancer* (pp. 86–126). St. Louis: C. V. Mosby.

Spinetta, J., Swarner, J., & Sheposh, J. (1981b). Effective parental coping following the death of a child from cancer. *Journal of Pediatric Psychology, 6*(3), 251–263.

Stehbens, J. A., & Lascari, A. D. (1974). Psychological follow-up of families with childhood leukemia. *Journal of Clinical Psychology, 30,* 394–397.

Stephenson, J. (1986). Grief of siblings. In T. A. Rando (Ed.), *Parental loss of a child* (pp. 321–338). Champaign, IL: Research Press.

Taylor, J., DeFrain, J., & Ernst, L. (1986). Sudden infant death syndrome. In T. A. Rando (Ed.), *Parental loss of a child* (pp. 159–180). Champaign, IL: Research Press.

Tietz, W., McSherry, L., & Britt, B. (1977). Family sequelae after a child's death due to cancer. *American Journal of Psychotherapy, 31*(3), 417–425.

Townes, B., & Wold, D. (1977). Childhood leukemia. In E. Patterson (Ed.), *The experience of dying.* N.J.: Prentice-Hall.

Vachon, M. (1976). Stress reactions to bereavement. *Essence, 1,* 23.

Van Dongen-Melman, J. E. W. M., & Sanders-Woudstra, J. A. R. (1986). Psychosocial aspects of childhood cancer: A review of the literature. *Journal of Child Psychology and Psychiatry, 27*(2), 145–180.

Waechter, E. (1971). Children's awareness of fatal illness. *American Journal of Nursing, 71,* 1168–1171.

Walker, C. L. (1988). Stress and coping in siblings of childhood cancer patient. *Nursing Research, 37*(4), 202–212.

Walker, C. L. (1990). Siblings of children with cancer. *Oncology Nursing Forum, 17*(3), 355–360.

Walker, C. L. (1993). Sibling bereavement and grief responses. *Journal of Pediatric Nursing, 8*(5), 325–334.

Watzlawick, P., Beavin, J. H., & Jackson, D. D. (1967). *Pragmatics of human communication: A study of interactional patterns, pathologies and paradoxes.* New York: W. W. Norton.

Wohl, A., & Kaufman, B. (1985). *Silent screams and hidden cries.* New York: Brunner/Mazel.

Wolfenstein, M. (1966). How is mourning possible? *Psychoanalytic Study of the Child, 21,* 93.

Worden, M. (1985). A case study comparison of the draw-a-person and kinetic family drawing. *Journal of Personality Assessment, 49,* 427–433.

Thirteen

Helping Children during Bereavement

Elizabeth P. Lamers

Elizabeth Lamers holds a B.S. cum laude from the State University of New York at New Paltz and an M.A. in education (reading) from Sonoma (CA) State University. She is credentialled as both a classroom teacher and a reading specialist. She has worked with terminally ill and bereaved children for the last ten years. She has conducted workshops and lectured extensively on the dying child and return to the classroom, children and grief, children's literature and death. She is a member of Kappa Delta Pi (Honorary Education Society), the International Reading Association, the International Work Group on Death, Dying, and Bereavement, the Los Angeles County Bar Association Bioethics Committee, The Education and Prevention Task Force for the AIDS Regional Board for

the County of Los Angeles, chairs the AIDS Task Force for the American Red Cross, Santa Monica Chapter, and is a consultant for the Hospice of the Canyon in Calabasas and the Lamers Medical Group in Malibu, California.

Historical Background

Attitudes regarding children and death have undergone tremendous change in this century, particularly in the past twenty years. In order to be of assistance to children experiencing loss, it is necessary to understand some of the changes regarding children and death that have occurred during the last century.

The demographics of dying and death have changed greatly: at the turn of the century most deaths in any year occurred in children under 15 years old. Today most deaths in any year occur in persons older than 65 years. Dying once occurred almost exclusively at home after a short illness; it now occurs almost exclusively in some sort of health-care institution following a prolonged (and expensive) illness. Although the hospice movement has brought dying back into the home, the majority of elderly still die in some type of institution (nursing home or hospital).

As a result, children and even young adults today are separated from the reality of death (DeSpelder & Strickland, 1992).

The family has also changed. Children once grew up as part of a close "extended" family consisting of parents, grandparents, aunts, and uncles who lived in the same rural area. Today, so called "nuclear" families live in cities, often separated from relatives by hundreds of miles. Deaths of relatives once were occasions for family coherence; today deaths in families may pass unobserved. Many parents today have the attitude that children should be shielded from dying and the facts of death (E. Lamers, 1986a). It is common today for children not to attend funeral services (E. Lamers, 1986b).

Children in rural areas once were exposed to the dying and death in their families and among animals. They had repeated opportunities to be close to death, to ask questions about death, to participate in healing, religious and social bereavement ceremonies and rituals.

Children today are exposed to a different kind of death; the death of a "bad" person or a stranger on television. It has been estimated that children witness hundreds of such unreal, unrecognized, "unsanctioned" deaths by the time they enter high school. Children are exposed to death and violence regularly through TV and especially through the children's cartoons. Cartoons, however, only show death as reversible and death of the bad. As a model to learn about death, cartoons give children a constant and consistently distorted view (E. Lamers, 1986b).

Books about Death for Children

Children's books reflect some of the changes that have occurred in the larger society. The removal of death and dying from the child's sphere can be easily traced in their literature. *McGuffy's Eclectic Readers*, (1920) a series of textbooks used to teach children to read at the turn of the century, contained many selections and poems pertaining either to the death of a mother or of a child. These deaths were seen as a tragic, but natural part of life. Today school texts rarely, if ever, contain any references to death or dying. In *Little Women*, Alcott (1947, p. 464) told of Beth's death in a straightforward manner, adding in the next paragraph "Seldom, except in books, do the dying utter memorable words, see visions, or depart with beatified countenances;....", all common parts of a death scene in the literature of the mid-1800s.

Fairy tales have been sanitized; references to death have been removed or glossed over. For example, in the original *Little Red Riding Hood*, the wolf ate Grandma and Little Red, and there was no intervening hunter or woodcutter. The hunter/woodcutter was introduced as a way of rescuing Little Red and her grandmother, first by the hunter/woodcutter slicing open the wolf and letting them out. In later versions the hunter shoots the wolf before he eats either one. In other versions, even the wolf is spared to escape through an open window, or to become Little Red's pet.

Between 1940 and 1970 only a few children's books contained references to death. Two that have become classics are *The Dead Bird* by Margaret W. Brown (1965) and *Charlotte's Web* by E. B. White (1952). White's publisher initially refused to publish *Charlotte's Web*, unless the ending was modified to let Charlotte live. White refused. The book was criticized by reviewers who said that death was not an appropriate subject for children.

The separation of children from death has diminished somewhat in the last twenty years. Elisabeth Kübler-Ross' (1969) early work helped make death a subject that could be discussed and studied. Children's books in the late sixties began to discuss previously taboo subjects: divorce, sex, feelings, and eventually even death. During the 1970s and 1980s more than 200 fiction books were written for children with death as a major theme. Unfortunately very few measured up to the standard set by *Charlotte's Web*, *Little Women*, *The Yearling*, or *The Dead Bird*. During the same period some very good nonfiction books about death were written for children of various ages. (See resource list at end of chapter.)

This cornucopia of books on death has helped re-expose children to death. The hospice movement has also helped by reintroducing home care for the dying to many communities. Even so, many children are still insulated from death and often are discouraged from attending funerals. It is not unusual to find adults in their forties who have never attended a funeral (Newton, 1990).

Study of Childhood Loss

After World War II, behavioral scientists began for the first time to study the way children reacted to loss. The rise in delinquency following World War II focused attention on the loss experiences in early childhood of the adolescents involved. John Bowlby, a psychiatrist in England, published a three-volume study, *Attachment and Loss* (1980). His study of young children and their reaction to the loss of their mother-figure was prompted by his finding that most of the delinquents he was working with had lost one or both parent(s) before the age of five. Bowlby showed the relationship between the young child's responses to loss of the mother and adult grief. Bowlby divided the young child's response to the loss of a mother-figure into three phases: protest, despair, and detachment. Bowlby showed that even very young children do mourn.

Shoor and Speed (1963, p. 540) studied the relationship between early childhood loss of a parent or other close relative and delinquency. They pointed out that parental death could set the stage for at least four possible reactions in the child: (1) normal mourning with resolution of grief, (2) immediate pathological response, (3) delayed reaction leading to a psychiatric syndrome in later life, or (4) delinquent behavior.

Hilgard and others (1960, p. 369) studied anniversary reactions to a death. They showed that reactions to loss may present as depression (ranging from mild to psychotic level), as physical symptoms (ranging from hysterical conversion reactions to psychophysiological autonomic and visceral responses), or as organic illness (such as ulcerative colitis).

Needs of Grieving Children

There is no automatic grieving mechanism. We learn to survive grief through early loss experiences. We do not automatically handle grief in a successful manner. The tasks of grieving are multiple, and the process may be complicated by prior experiences with loss and grief, current physical health, the quality of the relationship with the deceased, the impact of the death, the age of the survivor, and a host of other variables. The following is a list of some of the things children need in order to begin to cope with grief. Lamers (1965) states that grieving children need:

1. to know they will be cared for.
2. to know they did not cause the death by their anger or shortcomings.
3. to know they will not necessarily die of the same condition or when they reach the same age as the deceased.
4. to know what is happening, if possible, before the death occurs.
5. factual knowledge about the cause of the death.
6. someone who will listen to them—to their questions, their fears, their fantasies; someone who will be consistent and reasonable; someone they can trust.
7. to establish a framework for conceptualizing death.
8. an opportunity, if possible, for honest interaction with the dying person, whether this is a grandparent, parent, or sibling.
9. opportunities for involvement and interaction after death occurs.
10. assistance in dealing with feelings that are too intense to be expressed.

Children and adults grieve in very similar ways. Both may cry, get angry, blame themselves for the death, have problems eating and sleeping. The greatest difference in the grief process of adults and children is that most adults can separate fact from fantasy. They know that in most cases they did not cause the death. Children often cannot tell fact from fantasy, and need to discuss their fears with an adult who can reassure them that they are in no way responsible for the death through their anger or shortcomings. This particular subject needs to be brought up by the adult even if the child doesn't mention it. Children may feel anxious, panicky, or guilty. Children may improperly associate something they did with or to the deceased with the death. Sometimes the connections children make can be farfetched, such as believing, as one boy did, that the glass of lemonade he made for his grandmother killed her. Children may deal with the fear that they caused the death through indirect questions, or they may hide the fear in silence. Children can also feel guilty that they were not "good enough" to prevent the death, such as one eight-year-old who explained to me that she felt that God was angry with her. When asked why she felt that way, she explained that she had prayed very hard over and over again that her Daddy would get well, and he didn't; he died. Therefore, her conclusion was that God must be angry with her.

How Children Respond to Loss

The spectrum of response to loss has many variables. To respond successfully to a death children must verify that a death actually occurred. This takes time and requires support. Death may cause children to feel vulnerable, especially when the death was violent or unexpected. The death of a sibling, classmate, or friend can lead to feelings of anger: anger at death for "taking" the person, at God for letting it happen, at the deceased for going away, and even at themselves for not being able to prevent the death. They may also feel anger at their parents for excluding them from information, or for not being available to talk about their feelings. Children may feel guilty for not having done enough for the person before death or for not being a good enough person. Children may feel death has cheated them of a long and satisfying relationship. They may feel that, in some way, they must be punished for their shortcomings and their angry feelings. They may assume mannerisms of the deceased or they may idealize the deceased person.

Those who work with grieving children must keep a basic premise in mind: all behavior has meaning (Lamers, 1965). A grieving child may withdraw or become aggressive or destructive. The child may strive to excel in school or may be unable to concentrate on studies. The child may determine to take up a career in medicine or nursing to help prevent death. Some children may develop thoughts of suicide. In brief, children do react to death, and at a much younger age than has been widely recognized.

Children may react to death with tears or, as one small child (aged 3 years) explained to me, "When I'm very, very sad, I laugh." Adults should not jump to the conclusion that a child is not sad or grieving just because the child is not crying. Children also have an ability to take breaks from their grieving and at times seem to forget the loss. Very small children may not realize the death has occurred, even though informed, until the time for the usual visit to the deceased person arrives. This is more apt to occur when the death occurs at a distance, when the child does not attend the funeral, and when there is a set pattern to the visits, such as a visit to grandparents every summer or every Christmas. The small child may be quite upset when the visit does not take place or when it does occur and the grandparent is missing. Only then may the reality of the death register with the child.

With proper support, children will ask the necessary questions, perhaps not all at once, but with increasing frequency as they become more trusting of the adult to whom they are addressing their questions. Parents need to know that they do not need to have the perfect answer to every question. Some questions have no answers even from experts, and children can accept this. Children's fears are not always voiced. Parents may be able to determine the existence of these fears by careful questioning. Parents and other adults should carefully address any possible fears during these discussions. For example, very few children will admit to the fear that they caused the death, and yet this type of magical thinking is common in children, particularly in very young children. The parent can address the fact that, in spite of our wishes, no one can cause a death through anger or prevent a death due to incurable illness or old age or an accident. To prevent this kind of magical thinking, fears need to be addressed whether or not the child openly expresses them. Adults also need to be aware that the child will take admonitions such as "pray for Daddy" very concretely and will feel responsible if the prayers are not successful. The eight-year-old mentioned earlier is an example of prayer taken concretely.

Adolescents and Bereavement

Adolescents have a much more difficult time expressing their emotions. They may show no immediate grief reaction or may display an exaggerated grief reaction. Adolescents, unlike younger children, often will not discuss their feelings about a death or impending death with their parents. They will instead seek out a trusted adult, called the *intimate stranger* (Fulton, 1985). This may be an aunt, an uncle, or some other relative, a teacher, coach, minister, or some other unrelated adult. They usually, are able to discuss their feelings more easily with this trusted person than with their mother or father. They need to know what can be expected during bereavement and a funeral. They need to know that feelings and behaviors that occur during bereavement, which might be considered abnormal at other times, are normal in a loss situation.

Variables Affecting Childhood Grief

Children will react differently to each death depending on: (1) the family reaction to that death and the particulars of the death; (2) who died; (3) how close they were to the deceased; (4) the circumstances of the death, sudden or over a long period of time; (5) whether or not the child had any unfinished business with the deceased; (6) the age of the deceased; the age of the child at the time of the death; (7) whether or not the living circumstances of the child will or have changed because of the death (W. Lamers, 1965). Each death will have a different impact on the child. Is it the father, whose death will change the economic circumstances of the family? Is it the mother, putting the care of the child in question? A sibling? A beloved pet, who was a constant companion? Was the person a public figure with whom the child identified, such as President Kennedy or Christa McAuliffe? With these latter two deaths it was possible to view the death over and over again on TV. One of Robert Kennedy's sons was found in his hotel room doing just that after his father was shot. How the death occurred will also influence the effect on a child or adult. If the death occurred after a lengthy illness, the child may have had time to adjust to the coming death, time to say goodbyes, and in some cases time to grieve before the loss. If some grieving has taken place before the actual death, there may not be the tears and other signs of grief that we expect at the time of a death. This does not mean that the child does not care or feels no grief at the time of death.

Suicide is particularly stressful on the family, children included. It often results in "unsanctioned grief." Whether or not it is an acknowledged suicide makes a difference to the child. If the family does not acknowledge that a suicide occurred, it can leave the child very confused. The fact that a death was a suicide should never be kept from the child. They eventually learn the truth, and the deception destroys the child's trust. The suicide of a peer can be very upsetting. The child may feel that he or she could have prevented it. The death of someone the same age makes death seem that much more real and possible.

Children base their beliefs and knowledge about death on what they have learned in their family. If parents feel comfortable with their own beliefs and knowledge about death, it is easier for them to talk to their child about death. If a child has grown up with animals that have lived and died, then that child will have a better understanding of death and grief than a child who has not experienced such a loss. A child who has experienced the death of someone close will likewise have a different perspective than a child who has experienced no losses or who has been shielded from losses by his family. If death has been a taboo subject, the child may have a very distorted view of death. Most children will at some point in their childhood ask questions about death. If these questions are answered in an open and honest way, it will prepare the child to seek the information and support needed when someone close does die. Children whose questions about death have been ignored or who have been told to talk about something more pleasant or, even worse, have been chastised for bringing up the "morbid" subject will go elsewhere for their information, most likely to a peer. Adults must keep in mind that children are very curious and have very active imaginations. If a question brings a reaction of horror from the adult questioned, a child may supply his or her own reason as to why this subject is too terrible to talk about. Quite frequently, a child's own answer is much more frightening than the simple truth. Very small children can become very confused by concepts such as heaven and an afterlife. Adults need to remember that small children are very concrete in their thinking.

Needs of Surviving Siblings

Surviving siblings may have special problems in dealing with a brother's or sister's death. The death of a sibling may be a double loss to the surviving siblings, because their parents may become so involved in their own grief that they withdraw from the surviving children. Survivors may feel that they cannot show their grief because it will make their parents more sad. The sadness may be replaced with acting-out to handle their own fears and anger. Unthinking adults may reinforce this thinking by making remarks such as: "You'll have to be extra good now because your parents have enough to think about with the death of your brother/sister." The sibling is also grieving and this statement does not acknowledge or allow the grief of the surviving sibling(s).

Parents can idealize the dead sibling to the point that the surviving sibling(s) can develop a dislike, if not hatred, of the deceased and/or the idealizing parent. Surviving siblings sometimes feel they are expected to follow in the footsteps of the deceased. They may distort their own personality to do this or they may rebel and strive to be the opposite. Parents may also try to replace the dead child by having another baby and will dote on the new baby more than the surviving sibling(s). Parents may also become overprotective of the surviving siblings.

The surviving sibling(s) need to know that they are as important to the parents as the child who died. Holidays that come soon after a death need to be celebrated as traditionally done in the family. If the holiday celebration is to be curtailed, it should be the whole family who decides, not just the parents. Small children can feel that they don't count if, for instance, a Christmas celebration is changed or greatly curtailed. I can still remember the feelings of worthlessness, of not counting when, the first Christmas after my brother's death was largely a nonexistent celebration "Because," my grandparents explained, "your parents don't feel much like celebrating since your brother's death." I wanted to scream, "What about me? Don't I count for anything?" I didn't, but it hurt. It also hurt when all my brother's toys and other possessions were disposed of without asking me if there was anything I wanted. It didn't occur to anyone that an eight-year-old sister might want something concrete with which to remember her ten-year-old brother. Surviving siblings should be asked if there is something belonging to the dead sibling that they would like to keep as a memento.

If the sibling identified with or idealized the dead sibling while alive, there may be problems such as intense anniversary reactions or the expectation of dying at the same age or in the same way. The expectation of dying at the same age and/or in the same way may also be part of the reaction to the death of a parent. This may not become evident until many years later.

Outcome of Childhood Loss

The outcome of a child's reaction to a death will depend on three major factors:

1. the psychological stability of the child,
2. the general stability of the family, and
3. the availability of opportunities to share feelings about the loss and to receive support from significant persons, especially from parents.

When one parent has died, the other parent may not be in a position to give the children the support they need. Children may seek another adult for support or they may delay their grieving until the surviving parent can support them in their grief.

Children need to know how the death occurred. They may need to ask questions like, "Did it hurt?" "Where is (the deceased) now?" "Can I die of the same thing?" "Will I die at the same age?" Children need to know whether a death was caused by an illness that is contagious or transmissible. In the absence of accurate information, the child may develop a host of needless fears about death and disease. For some questions there may be more than one answer. Or there may be answers on several levels. The answers from a parent will depend on the family belief system. It is important to ask the child what kind of information he or she is seeking. When the child asks, "Where is Grandma?", are they asking where is the physical body or are they really asking about heaven and an afterlife? Only by carefully listening to the child and asking questions can an adult be sure to have answered the real question the child was asking.

Children and Funerals

Children naturally ask questions about the funeral such as: What will happen at the funeral? What will happen to the body? The child should be encouraged to attend funerals, to say their goodbyes to a loved one or friend. This is another way a child can satisfy the need to determine that the death really occurred. In the time of turmoil following a death, they need to be included in the family ceremonies and grieving. One three-year-old in a family I worked with went to the rosary service for his father, but was deemed too young to attend the funeral. Later he had a very difficult time understanding that his father was buried in the grave.

Children are curious about the body, but almost always suppress their natural questions. When my father-in-law died, his eight-year-old great-granddaughter had no patience with her mother, who wished to visit with relatives and friends on her way through the rooms at the funeral home before saying her goodbyes to "Pa." Susan wanted to see Pa and kept tugging at her mother's hand to move on, until I took Susan in to see her Grandpa. She stopped walking and started looking at about two feet from the casket. Gradually she got closer and then the questions started. Could she touch him? Why was he cold? Why was his skin hard? Susan needed to confirm that he was really dead. Eventually I helped her place around Pa's neck the red carnation lei she had brought from Hawaii. Once Susan had her questions answered and the death confirmed, she could relax and visit with her aunts, uncles, and cousins. Children who do not get their questions answered will internalize them and worry needlessly.

Children's Understandings of Death

The stages at which a child understands death and the ages when these stages occur have been written about in the literature. Basically the stages are:

- Death is reversible and not permanent.
- Death is permanent, but only happens to the old, the bad, and strangers.
- Death is universal and happens to all things, and the realization that I could die, I might die, I will die.

The very young child (age 0 to 5 years) tends to believe death is reversible. The very young child who has had someone very close or a beloved pet die knows that death is not reversible; it is very permanent. It is difficult to assign ages to the other two stages of understanding death. Generally speaking, children between the ages of five and nine know that death is permanent and those older than nine years know that death is inevitable. Again, life experience can change the ages at which a child moves through the stages. Dying children of all ages reach a point where they realize that they will die, and that it is permanent (Bluebond-Langer, 1978). On the other hand, there are many adults who believe that only old persons and bad persons die, but deny that any one close to them will die. Life experience affects a child's understanding of death.

How to Help a Bereaved Child

For an adult to help a child when a death has occurred, the adult must first determine what the child knows and believes about death. If the lines of communication between the adult and child have always been open, this may be as easy as asking the child directly what he or she believes. Another way could be through reading one of the excellent books about death with the child. A book such as *The Tenth Good Thing about Barney*, by Viorst, or *Badger's Parting Gifts* by Varley, are two books that could be used with young children. (See references at the end of the chapter for more suggested books.) Adults must be sure when using books with children that the book is consistent with their own beliefs and ideas concerning death. Adults must always be truthful when discussing death with children. Grollman (1977) points out that to tell a child the deceased has gone on a long, long trip will not be consistent with what the child sees happening around him. If Grandpa has only gone on a trip, then why are people crying and being generally upset, and why didn't he say goodbye? When the child discovers the truth it is very hard to reestablish trust with the adult. The anecdotal literature has many stories from adults who were deceived about the death or impending death of a loved one (Galle, 1977). Most of the adults were angry and upset by the deception when they discovered the truth, in some cases many years later. I can remember when I was eight and my brother died.

My first reaction was the realization that I was the only one in the family who had expected him to survive to adulthood and that all those daydreams I had had about what it would be like to have an older brother as we grew up together really were pure fantasy. I felt very alone and left out.

When discussing death with children, it is best to raise the subject some time before the need arises to discuss a particular death. Death is a difficult subject and, like sex, should be discussed over a long period of time, in an age-appropriate manner. Unfortunately, this is not always possible. When a death occurs, explanations should be presented in a calm and careful manner by someone close to the child. It should be done without lurid, gruesome, or terrifying details. Words should be chosen carefully with attention to their possible meaning to the child. Children tend to be very literal; the younger the child, the more literal. Describing death as being like sleep or like going to sleep can be very frightening to children who may assume that they will die when they fall asleep.

Euphemisms should be avoided when discussing death with children. Words such as "lost" (why don't we find them again?), "passed on," "gone to his/her great reward," "no longer with us," "departed," have meanings other than death for children and can be needlessly confusing. Even adults can be confused or bothered by euphemisms. When I recently received a letter announcing that a colleague had "expired," I immediately had the urge to rush out and renew her for another month or two, at the very least.

The more discussions and opportunities children have to share their feelings, the less likely it is that there will be problems later from the death. If the adults feel unprepared to discuss death there are books such as Grollman's *Explaining Death to Children* or Gaffney's *The Seasons of Grief, Helping Your Child Grow through Loss*, which can help. These books may be available at the local library.

Professional Responsibilities

The professionals (i.e., nurses, social workers, clergy, funeral directors, etc.) in contact with a family in which there is an impending or recent death, should inquire about the children of the family. The professional's job is not to inform the children, but to gently help those close to the children to do this. Professionals should stress the importance of keeping the children informed and should explain how intuitive children are. Often children know something is happening without being told and their imaginations supply the unshared details. Professionals should be aware of resources for families, such as books, counseling centers, social workers, or psychologists. They can inform the family that children are able to handle death and funerals and that children do think about death even though they may not discuss it with the family members. Professionals might well point out to concerned parents that many references to death occur in children's games and jump-rope rhymes. References to death show up in children's writing, artwork, and poetry. A school assignment to write a poem for an English class will often result in one or two poems that refer to death or grief. When a pet dies, children will spontaneously arrange a funeral and burial.

Instinctively children know there should be some ritual for closure. If an adult is reluctant or even adamant about shielding the children, the professional should take the time to sit and talk with the adult about why he or she feels this way. Often it is discovered that the adult had an unfortunate and/or unpleasant experience with death during childhood and wants to protect the children from the same type of exposure. The adult may have memories such as being held up to the casket and being told to kiss the deceased good-by without any preparation. Through discussion about such childhood experience, it may be possible to show the adult that he or she has control and can make the death a positive experience for the children in the family.

Conclusion

Children are helped by seeing adults grieve. Grieving is not an inborn skill, something automatic; it is a learned skill. Children learn to grieve through coping with loss and watching the adults around them. Adults should realize that children will grieve in small increments and return to play or studies in between. The child's grief should not be minimized just because it doesn't show continuously. Parents and other adults should not underestimate the duration of the grieving process.

Children can and do survive grief. With adult support and guidance, children have the opportunity to grow though grief. Erikson (1975) pointed out that "Grief, successfully handled, can serve as the focus for new social and psychologic growth."

About the Resources

The resources listed at the end of this chapter are suggestions. Adults should read any book they are considering for use with a child. It is very important to determine whether or not the book fits the child and the particular situation before presenting the book to the child. I once gave several books to a colleague to use with her own children and did not mention she should read them first. She came back to me very upset. She had read one of the books to her children to help them understand the death of their great-grandmother. In this particular book the little boy dies of an allergic reaction to a bee sting. It was an unfortunate choice for her children because they were already afraid of bees, and now they were terrified. I had no way of knowing her children were afraid of bees. Had she read the book first, she would not have read it to her children. It is impossible for the professional to know every child in such detail, making it imperative that the adult using the books read them first.

References

Alcott, L. M. (1947). *Little women*. New York: Grosset & Dunlop. (originally pub. 1869)

Bluebond-Langner, M. (1978). *The private worlds of dying children*. Princeton, NJ: Princeton University Press.

Bowlby, J. (1961). Childhood mourning and its implications for psychiatry. *American Journal of Psychiatry, 118*(6), 481–489.

Bowlby, J. (1980). *Attachment and loss: Vols. I, II, III*. New York: Basic Books.

Brown, M. W. (1965). *The dead bird*. Reading, MA: Addison-Wesley.

Cain, A. C., Fast, I., & Erickson, M. E. (1964). Children's disturbed reactions to the death of a sibling. *American Journal of Orthopsychiatry, 34*, 741–752.

Carey, A. (1977). Helping the child and the family cope with death. *International Journal of Family Counseling, 5*, 58–63.

Cavenar, J. O., Nash, J. L., & Maltbie, A. A. (1978). Anniversary reactions presenting as physical complaints. *Journal of Clinical Psychiatry*, 369–374.

Crase, D., & Crase, D. (1983). Communication with children about death and dying. *Thanatos, 8*(1), 15–16.

DeSpelder, L. A., & Strickland, A. L. (1983). *The last dance: encountering death and dying*. Palo Alto: Mayfield.

Erikson, E. H. (1975). Personal communication.

Feinberg, D. (1970). Preventive therapy with siblings of a dying child. *Journal of American Academy of Child Psychiatry, 9*, 644–668.

Fredlund, D. (1978). The lemonade story. *Thanatos, 3*(3), 9–11.

Fulton, Robert. (1985). Personal communication.

Galle, J. E. (1977). The train that never came. *Thanatos, 2*(3).

Gogan, J. L., Koocher, G. P., Foster, D. J., & O'Malley, J. E. (1977). Impact of childhood cancer on siblings. *Health and Social Work, 2*(1), 41–57.

Grollman, E. (1977). Explaining death to children. *Journal of School Health, 47*, 336–339.

Harrison, S. I., Davenport, C. W., & McDermott, J. F. (1967). Children's reactions to bereavement: Adult confusions and misperceptions. *Archives of General Psychiatry, 17,* 593–597.

Hilgard, J. R., Newman, M. F, & Fisk, F. (1960). Strength of adult ego following childhood bereavement. *American Journal of Orthopsychiatry, 30*(4), 788–798.

Hilgard, J. R. (1969). Depressive and psychotic states as anniversaries to sibling death in childhood. *Int. Psychiatry Clinics IV,* 197–211.

Jackson, E. N. (1965). *Telling a child about death.* New York: Dutton.

Koocher, G. P. (1973). Childhood, death, and cognitive development. *Developmental Psychology, 9*(3) 369–375.

Kübler-Ross, E. (1969). *On death and dying.* New York: Macmillan.

Lamers, E. P. (1986a). Books, adolescents and death. In C. A. Corr & J. N. McNeil (Eds.), *Adolescents and death.* New York: Springer.

Lamers, E. P. (1986b). The dying child in the classroom. In G. H. Paterson (Ed.), *Children and death* (pp. 175–186). London: King's College.

Lamers, W. M. (1965). *Death, grief, mourning, the funeral and the child.* Milwaukee: Bulfin Press.

Lamers, W. M. (1986). Helping the child to grieve. In G.H. Paterson (Ed.), *Children and death* (pp. 105–119). London: King's College.

Lamers, W. M., & Lamers, E. P. (1987). *Children and their grief.* NFDA Caregivers Manual. Available from: National Funeral Directors Association, 11121 West Oklahoma Ave., Milwaukee, Wl 53227.

Lindcmann, E. (1944). Symptomatology and management of acute grief. *American Journal of Psychiatry, 101,* 141–148.

Lonetto, R. (1980). *Children's conceptions of death.* New York: Springer.

McGuffey's Eclectic Readers (Vols. 2–6) (1920). New York: Van Nostrand Reinhold.

McLendon, G. H. (1983, 1984). Be still prepared... A study of death and grief for teenagers. Part I, *Thanatos, 8*(2), 12–15. Part II, *Thanatos, 8*(3), 10–17. Part III, *Thanatos, 8*(4), 13-21. Part IV, *Thanatos, 9*(1), 14–20.

Newton, F. I. (1990). Children and the funeral ritual: Factors that affect their attendance and participation. Master's thesis, California State University, Chico.

Parnass, E. (1975). Effects of experiences with loss and death among preschool children. *Children Today, 4,* 2–7.

Rawlings, M. K. (1938). *The yearling.* New York: Scribner's.

Rando, T. A. (1988). *Grieving: How to go on living when someone you love dies.* Lexington, MA: Lexington Books.

Sahler, O. J. Z. (1978). *The child and death.* St. Louis, MO: C. V. Mosby.

Scott, F. (1981). When a student dies... *English Journal, 70,* 22–24.

Shoor, M., & Speed, M. H. (1963). Delinquency as a manifestation of the mourning process. *Psychiatric Quarterly, 37*(3), 540-558.

Siegel, B. S. (1986). Helping children cope with death. *Research Record, 3*(2), 53–63.

Wass, H., & Corr, C. A. (1984). *Childhood and death.* New York: Hemisphere.

Wass, H., & Corr, C. A. (1984). *Helping children cope with death: Guidelines and resources.* New York: Hemisphere.

Wass, H., & Shaak, J. (1976). Helping children understand death through literature. *Childhood Education, 53*(2), 80–85.

Wessel, M. A. (1975). A death in the family: The impact on the children. *Journal of the American Medical Association, 234*(8), 865–866.

White, E. B. (1952). *Charlotte's web.* New York: Harper & Row.

Williams, Y. (1988, March-April). Grief work is play: Dealing with children's grief. *The Forum Newsletter, 12*(2), 7–8.

Wolfelt, A. (1989). What bereaved children want adults to know about grief. *Bereavement, 3*(9), 34–45.

Resources

Children's Books about Death, Nonfiction

Bernstein, J. *Loss and how to cope with it.* New York: Houghton Mifflin, 1977.

Bernstein, J., & Gullo, S. J. *When people die.* New York: Dutton, 1977.

Corley, E. A. *Tell me about death. Tell me about funerals.* Santa Clara, CA: Grammatical Sciences, 1973.

Hodgson, J. *Hullo sun.* Liss, England: White Eagle Pub.

Le Shan, E. J. *Learning to say good-by: When a parent dies.* New York: Macmillan, 1976.

Langone, J. *Death is a noun.* Boston: Little, Brown, 1972.

Richter, E. *Losing someone you love. When a brother or sister dies.* New York: Putnam, 1986.

Rofes, E. E. & The Unit at Fayerweather Street School. *The kids' book about death and dying.* Boston: Little, Brown, 1985.

Segerberg, O., Jr. *Living with death.* New York: Dutton, 1976.

Stein, S. B. *About dying.* New York: Walker, 1974.

Children's Books about Death, Fiction

Alcott, L. M. *Little women.* New York: Grosset & Dunlop, 1947. (originally pub. 1869) (illness and death of sister)

Alexander, S. *Nadia the willful.* New York: Pantheon, 1983. (brother's accidental death)

Aliki. *Two of them*. New York: Greenwillow, 1979. (grandfather's old age and death)

Bartoli, J. *Nonna*. New York: Harvey House, 1975. (grandmother's natural death)

Blume, J. *Tiger eyes*. Scarsdale, NY: Bradbury, 1981. (father murdered in robbery)

Brown, M. W. *The dead bird*. Reading, MA: Addison-Wesley, 1965. (wild bird's natural death)

Bunting, E. *The empty window*. New York: Frederick Warne, 1980. (friend's illness and death)

Bunting, E. *The happy funeral*. New York: Harper & Row, 1982. (grandfather's funeral, Chinese-American customs)

Bunting, E. *A sudden silence*. New York: Harcourt Brace Jovanovich, 1988. (brother's accidental death)

Coutant, H. *First snow*. New York: Knopf, 1974. (grandmother's dying, Vietnamese Buddhist beliefs)

de Paola, T. *Nana upstairs and Nana downstairs*. New York: Putnam, 1973. (great-grandmother's and grandmother's natural deaths)

Deaver, J. R. *Say goodnight, Gracie*. New York: Harper & Row, 1988. (friend's accidental death)

Douglas, E. *Rachel and the upside down heart*. Los Angeles: Price, Stern, Sloan, 1990. (father's death, heart attack)

Gerstein, M. *The mountains of Tibet*. New York: Harper & Row, 1987. (reincarnation)

Hermes, P. *You shouldn't have to say good-bye*. New York: Harcourt, 1982. (mother's death, cancer)

Hickman, M. W. *Last week my brother Anthony died*. Nashville, TN: Abingdon, 1984. (infant brother dies of congenital heart condition)

Hoopes, L. L. *Nana*. New York: Harper & Row, 1981. (grandmother's natural death)

Kantrowitz, M. *When Violet died*. New York: Parent's Magazine Press, 1973. (pet bird's natural death)

Lee, V. *The magic moth*. New York: Scabury, 1972. (sister's illness and death, congenital heart condition)

Little, J. *Mama's going to buy you a mockingbird*. New York: Viking Kestrel, 1984. (father's death, cancer)

Mann, P. *There are two kinds of terrible*. New York: Doubleday, 1977. (mother's death, cancer)

Miles, M. *Annie and the old one*. Boston: Little, Brown, 1971. (grandmother's natural death, Navajo Indians)

Orgel, D. *Mulberry music*. New York: Harper & Row, 1971. (grandmother's death, illness)

Paterson, K. *Bridge to Terabithia*. New York: Crowell, 1977. (friend's accidental death)

Pfeffer, S. B. *About David*. New York: Delacorte, 1980. (friend's suicide)

Shreve, S. *Family secrets: Five very important stories*. New York: Knopf, 1979. (grandmother's death, illness; friend's suicide)

Smith, D. B. *A Taste of blackberries*. New York: Crowell, 1973. (friend's death, bee sting allergy)

Stevens, C. *Stories from a snowy meadow*. New York: Seabury, 1976. (personified animals, natural death)

Tobias, T. *Petey*. New York: Putman, 1978. (pet gerbil's death, illness)

Varley, S. *Badger's parting gifts*. New York: Lothrop, Lee & Shepard, 1984. (personified animals and remembering someone after death)

Viorst, J. *The tenth good thing about Barney*. New York: Atheneum, 1971. (pet cat's natural death)

Warburg, S. S. *Growing time*. Boston: Houghton Mifflin, 1969. (pet dog's natural death)

White, E. B. *Charlotte's web*. New York: Harper & Row, 1952. (death as a natural consequence of life)

Wilhelm, H. *I'll always love you*. New York: Crown, 1985. (pet dog's natural death)

Williams, M. *The velveteen rabbit*. New York: Holt, Rinehart & Winston, 1983 edition. (life and death, general)

Zolotow, C. *My grandson Lew*. New York: Harper & Row, 1974. (grandson remembering deceased grandfather)

Books for Adults

Fassler, J. *Helping children cope*. New York: The Free Press, 1978.

Furman, E. (Ed.). *A child's parent dies, studies in childhood bereavement*. New Haven, CT: Yale University Press, 1974.

Gaffney, D. A. *The seasons of grief, helping your children grow through loss*. New York: New American Library, 1988.

Grollman, E. (Ed.). *Explaining death to children*. Boston: Beacon, 1967.

Jackson, E. N. *Telling a child about death*. New York: Dutton, 1965.

Klagsbrun, F. *Too young to die: Youth and suicide*. Boston: Houghton Mifflin, 1976.

Rosen, H. *Unspoken grief: Coping with childhood sibling loss*. Lexington, MA: D. C. Heath (Lexington Books), 1984.

Rudolph, M. *Should the children know?* New York: Schocken Books, 1978.

Sternberg, F., & Sternberg, B. *If I die and when I do*. Englewood Cliffs, NJ: Prentice-Hall, 1980.

Fourteen

The Bereavement Process: Loss, Grief, Recovery

Joseph T. Mullan
Leonard I. Pearlin
Marilyn M. Skaff

Joseph T. Mullan was trained in the Program on Human Development at the University of Chicago where he took his Ph.D. in 1981. Currently, he is an assistant adjunct professor in the Human Development and Aging Program at the University of California, San Francisco. His research focuses on the development and maintenance of psychological well-being in adulthood, and particularly on the processes that determine whether life events and transitions affect psychological adaptation. Since 1988, he has been collaborating with Leonard I. Pearlin on studies of people providing care to impaired relatives or friends. He is looking at how caregivers' experiences, for example, feelings of loss, guilt, and mastery, affect how they adapt to the death of the impaired person.

Dr. Pearlin took his Ph.D. in sociology in 1956 from Columbia University. For the past 10 years he has been a professor of medical sociology in the Department of Psychiatry, University of California, San Francisco. Prior to that, he was a research scientist at the National Institutes of Mental Health. His writings and research have largely centered on chronic stress. He has been particularly interested in stresses that arise out of the structure of social life, such as in activities and relationships located within the occupational, economic, and family domains. The caregivers to the seriously ill and impaired, whom he is currently studying, exemplify people exposed to a host of enduring stresses. Dr. Pearlin's interest in bereavement is an outgrowth of the fact that caregivers are people who often live with the expectation of the deaths of loved ones and with the consequences of loss.

Support for this work was provided by the National Institute of Mental Health under grants #R37MH42122 and #MH44600. Authors are listed alphabetically.

Dr. Skaff received her Ph.D. in human development and aging in 1990 from the University of California, San Francisco. Prior to that she was a part-time lecturer in developmental psychology at San Francisco State University. During her doctoral studies she worked on the Alzheimer's caregiver study with Dr. Pearlin and Dr. Mullan and her dissertation was based on data from that study. The focus of most of her research has been the self-concept, particularly the role it plays in the stress process. Dr. Skaff's interest in bereavement grew out of an interest in loss, especially a sense of loss of self or identity that has been observed among spouses and adult children caring for their relative with Alzheimer's disease. She has been a research associate at the Center for Health Care Evaluation at the Veterans Administration, and recently returned to UCSF to work as a research psychologist with Dr. Mullan and Dr. Pearlin.

In this chapter we assume that death is embedded in a psychosocial process that has its beginnings in advance of the cessation of life and extends into the future for an indefinite period. It is a complex process, its complexity stemming in part from the fact that the death of an individual typically triggers emotional and material reverberations throughout the reaches of the deceased person's social network. Because the life-narratives of those constituting the network had been intertwined, the death of one may have far-reaching effects on the lives of others (Walsh & McGoldrick, 1991). Death is a biological event, but it is no less a psychosocial event, it can initiate or hasten a process entailing loss, grief, and recovery and their interrelationships, a process that often persists among survivors long after the death has occurred. This chapter is aimed at describing and explicating this process and its components.

Many of the views and observations presented here are based on two research projects we are conducting. One, underway now for several years, is a study of spouses and adult children caring for relatives with Alzheimer's disease. Because this is characteristically a disease of older people, the death of the impaired person is commonly experienced by caregivers. Sometimes death follows a brief period of caregiving and in other instances the caregiving may have gone on for many years. We have already had the opportunity to follow the survivors in these families from the time they were active caregivers to close to two years following the death of their relatives and we shall continue to follow them for an additional three years. The second study, less advanced than the first, is of friends, lovers, and family members caring for people with AIDS. Most of these caregivers are young and some of them share the same lifestyle (and occasionally similar health problems) as those for whom they are caring. For these people, survivorship may include not only the loss of another, but also a grim preview of their own life-course and its end.

Although there are some striking differences between these two groups of caregivers, there are equally striking similarities. Most notably, in each group the death of the loved one approaches gradually and is thus foreseen. In each group, too, caregivers witness a profound physical and/ or mental transformation taking place prior to death. The foreseeable nature of the deaths and the transformations that may precede death both contribute in these groups to the initiation of the bereavement process before the death occurs. Together, these two studies obviously embrace but a very small sample either of the circumstances under which people die or of circumstances that must be confronted by survivors; consequently, no claims can be made for the universal generalizability of our findings or speculations. Nevertheless, these two groups of caregivers enable us to observe with unusual clarity not only the acute phases of bereavement but also its early beginnings and late stages.

As we see it, there are three closely interrelated components making up the bereavement process: loss, grief, and, for some, recovery. We regard all three of these components as being subsumed by the overarching construct of *bereavement*. *Loss* refers to the separation from a part of one's life to which one was emotionally attached. *Grief* refers to the complex emotional, cognitive, and perceptual reactions that accompany loss. It may assume a variety of trajectories and expressions whose character may be shaped by the nature and intensity of the losses that are experienced. *Recovery* is the final component in surviving the death of a loved one. It may be true that time helps heal the wounds left by death. We believe, however, that what really counts in recovery is not only time itself but also the circumstances with which survivors must deal as time goes by: the nature of the losses they have experienced, the social and economic resources they can call upon, and their ability to restructure their lives. It may take time to deal properly with these kinds of tasks, but time alone does not guarantee the occurrence of recovery.

Although loss, grief, and recovery are conceptually discrete, they are not necessarily temporally discrete. Each may emerge very slowly and gradually and, perhaps, never completely displace the stage that preceded it. Particularly among those witnessing death after a lengthy physical or cognitive decline, for example, elements of loss may begin to surface long before death but continue to be freshly confronted after that death has occurred and grief is actively underway. Thus, in addition to those losses that might be experienced prior to or immediately after death, others may periodically come into focus following a considerable time interval. Similarly, we surmise both that grief may be coextensive with loss—including loss that occurs before death—and that it overlaps with steps toward recovery. People may have profoundly restructured their lives since caregiving and death and still feel flashes of pain (Wortman & Silver, 1990). Indeed, we assume that among those who have made a recovery that by any standard could be judged as a good adaptation, episodes of grief may nevertheless pepper the entirety of the survivor's life. This is particularly likely to be the case among survivors who stood in close relationship to the deceased person; that is, spouses, children, and lovers. Loss, grief, and recovery, then, may begin in advance of death and continue afterward. Moreover, they may overlap in time, thus having no clear or discrete experiential boundaries. For simplicity, however, our discussions of each will be separate.

Death, of course, is the key juncture in the bereavement process, surrounded by loss, grief, and recovery. These three constructs, however, are themselves rather global, each containing multiple dimensions around which there is considerable variability. Much of this chapter is aimed at identifying the dimensions of the constructs and their interconnections. In this way, we believe, we can illuminate the process underlying the survival of the death of a loved one.

Loss

We usually think of loss as entailing the involuntary separation of ourselves from something that had been a valued part of our lives. As we suggested earlier, death can accelerate loss but loss may have begun well before the death. We can assume that loss is most severe where it involves the death of a person who was an integral part of the survivors' lives. That is, where attachment to and identification with the deceased person were strong, where there was a functional and emotional intertwining of lives, where the relationship was of long duration and spanned a broad range of shared experience and history, death will leave the survivor feeling profoundly bereft. Yet, as important and disrupting as the sheer loss of a loved one is, there is more to loss than this alone. Especially in the case of our caregivers, the actual death may be only a single, albeit powerful, marker in the process of loss that antecedes death.

Let us first consider losses that impact directly on the dyadic relationship that the survivor had with the deceased. One of these is what we refer to as *the loss of persona*, something that is especially apparent in the experiences of our Alzheimer's and AIDS caregivers. Many of these caregivers are destined to observe dramatic and disheartening mental and physical transformations in those for whom they are caring. The progressive cognitive and functional deterioration in the person who is ill can leave caregivers feeling that the quintessential loved one no longer exists. Biological life goes on, but the person with whom attachments were forged in past times has largely disappeared. With the transformation of the impaired person, many of the elements of the caregiver's relationship with that person must also undergo transformation and disappearance. Our respondents, of course, are keenly sensitive to this loss of persona and the accompanying loss of relationship. As one widow put it:

> He couldn't speak anymore. Half the time I don't know if he even knew me. I think he knew I belonged to him, but he'd lost the relationship along the way.... The person that you found unique was gone.... He was gone two years before he finally passed away. As I say his mind went, he was incontinent, he was totally helpless. Everything that he had been: a witty, intelligent person and there was nothing left, just a shell.

These caregivers are certainly not representative of the entire population of people that experience the death of a loved one. But they do reveal a great deal about a type of loss experienced in relationships in which one of the parties is destructively altered by a chronic disease, an experience unfortunately widespread in our aging society and with our sophisticated life-sustaining medical technology.

Another form of loss, often occurring hand in hand with the loss of persona, is the *decline in expressive and affectional support* and exchange formerly provided by the impaired person. In the case of spouses and lovers, the loss of emotional and sexual intimacy may occur insidiously, but leave an emotional and physical gap (Parkes, 1972). The loss of affectionate exchange is of obvious importance in its own right. Additionally, to the extent that the transformed or deceased person was a source of esteem and self-validation, death may leave the life of the survivor in an expressive vacuum.

The *loss of the companionship* that was habitually shared with the relative or friend is also likely to be felt strongly. One widow reported missing the "daily chitchat" that she had shared with her husband around dinnertime. An adult daughter mourned the loss of her mother's companionship on shopping trips they had loved to share. The collapse of deeply ingrained daily routines can leave caregivers with large empty spaces in their lives.

Another aspect of the survivor-deceased relationship around which loss is experienced concerns *instrumental support*. Like affection and companionship, this involves the loss of something that had been built into everyday life. It may appear mundane, but it is a loss capable of imposing considerable hardship. In long-standing relationships, death can destroy an intricate division of labor that was established: one might have become expert at doing laundry and the other at repairing the washing machine. The point is that with the decline of the patient's vitality, or the occurrence of death, the caregiving partner is frequently left without the skills, time, or energy to compensate for the instrumental activities that the deceased person had brought to the relationship.

Still looking at the dyadic relationship, there is a somewhat different kind of loss that can occur with the demise of the patient. This is *the loss of mattering*. Mattering refers to the gratification one feels as a result of being needed, being important to another person, being able to do something for that person (Rosenberg & McCullaugh, 1981). It is the other side of social support. One of the motivations for caregiving is the fulfilling experience of making a difference in another's life. To the extent that caregiving had become a central element in the lives of caregivers, the death of the patient may deprive the survivor of a role from which to extract a sense of purpose (Wortman & Silver, 1990). In no longer having a person to whom they matter, the lives of caregivers can be stripped of meaning and mission.

The transformation of a loved one, and the disappearance of affectionate exchange, emotional and instrumental support, and mattering have in common the fact that they each involve losses rooted in the structure of the dyadic relationship between the caregiver and the impaired or deceased person. Other losses are broader in scope and involve activities, roles, and relationships other than those centering on the dyadic relationship. Collectively, they may be thought of as losses of previously established lifestyle. One of these entails the survivor's *loss of status* in the community. In instances where the survivor's status depended on the occupation or activities of the deceased individual, the survivor may experience a fall from status after the death. The signs that a loss of status has occurred may be diverse: the survivor no longer receives invitations from those who earlier extended them to the pair, or subtle signs of homage are no longer accorded. In general, if the friends and associates affiliated with the deceased were of higher status than those primarily allied with the survivor, then the survivor may experience a loss of status. Particularly in a generation where wives' social status was often achieved through their husbands, the loss of status may be keenly and bitterly felt.

Of course, an attenuation of social ties can occur for reasons other than the loss of status conferral. A "couple identity" and the social network in which it is embedded often has a structuring effect on social life. Thus, it is common for widows and widowers to report a gradual *loss of contact with former social ties* made up of couples (Lopata, 1979a). Such constriction frequently occurs before death among our Alzheimer's caregivers, who report a loss of contact with other people as the dementia of their relatives progresses. Friends may simply no longer feel comfortable being around the impaired person, or the behavior or physical condition of the patient may preclude involvement in social activities. In the case of the caregivers whose partners are placed in a care facility, the caregiver may experience the "social widowhood" of a person without a partner, yet still feel the ties of marriage. Even adult children may find that contact with the larger family system is diminished. This is particularly likely to be the case where the impaired or deceased parent, usually the mother, served as the "kinkeeper" for the family, the person who actively maintains family ties and rituals (Troll, 1990).

Somewhat related to status and affiliative losses that the survivor may experience is a *loss of material resources*. If death results in diminished finances or reduced income, the survivor might find that the material footing on which he or she earlier stood is no longer there. We know from previous studies that when the loss of a loved one is accompanied by the loss of income, the impact of the death is more severe than in instances where these resources are left intact (Pearlin & Lieberman, 1979; Umberson, Wortman, & Kessler, 1989).

Thus far we have discussed losses involving the decline or disappearance of elements of the dyadic relationship to which the survivor had been habituated and broader losses, involving status, resources, and network. A third genre of loss entails the *loss of past and future*. With regard to loss of the past, there is some indication from our studies that the disruption of certain relationships by death, especially parent-child relationships, can leave survivors feeling cut off from their own biography. Parents are the chroniclers of their children's distant past; when parents are lost, so too is the recounting of that portion of the survivor's life. No one is left to fill in the blank spots. The death of the last parent may leave a surviving adult forever separated from that part of his or her own childhood that was known only to their parents.

As distinct from *personal* history, the death may similarly entail the loss of *family* history. This history is more than a genealogy; it is a journal of past relationships that help make sense out of the present. With the demise of the oldest generation, skeletons (or genies) are unlikely to be let out of the closet and the hidden flaws and follies of family members will probably forever remain hidden. For adult children the opportunity may be lost to learn more about their parents as people and about that small subculture that was unique to the family.

With regard to a *loss of future*, briefly, we find that debility and death often disrupt the visions of the future that survivors had shared with their loved ones. A variety of plans and expectations may be shattered: for travel, for retirement, for love and companionship, for the pursuit of deferred goals and interests, and, in general, for the enjoyment of the hard-earned fruits of years of labor and waiting. The loss of a cherished future, often nurtured by long-standing dreams and hopes, can understandably be a bitter pill.

Finally, we come to a *loss of self* or of identity, often noted in the literature (Lopata, 1979a; Marris, 1974; Moss & Moss, 1989; Parkes, 1972; Peretz, 1970; Stroebe & Stroebe , 1987). To a large extent, the loss of self is inseparable from the losses we have discussed above. Thus, the loss of relationship, of community standing, and of the continuity of one's own life-course are all likely to have an impact on one's understanding of oneself. To the extent that what has been lost was central to the organization of the thoughts, activities, and emotions of the caregiver, the self that survives death will not be the same as the self that had existed before death and disability. It is this altered self that leads people to grieve not only for their departed loved ones but also for their departed selves (Marris, 1974).

The self, in many instances, is not merely changed from its previous composition but is diminished. People can feel that they have become lesser beings. This is a result of two conditions. One exists where the deceased or disabled person was a major source of positive feedback to the survivor, reaffirming and reinforcing the elements of self that the survivor prized. In the absence of this feedback, these prized elements may wither and recede. Second, caregiving can expand to the point that it drives out other activities and commitments of the survivor. By the time of death, consequently, the survivors report that they "have lost a sense of who they are" or "an important part of themselves." We refer to this phenomenon as *role engulfment*, a situation that leaves little of a person's identity that is not tied directly to the incapacitated or deceased person (Skaff & Pearlin, 1992).

What we wish to emphasize in this discussion is that loss is not an undifferentiated experience. On the contrary, it is possible to identify a wide array of losses: the loss of affective exchange, of instrumental and emotional support, of mattering to another person, of companionship and the activities it entailed, of network and social affiliation and status and economic resources, of life-course continuity, and of self and identity. Among people who have experienced the death of a person with whom they had stood in a close relationship, therefore, there is likely to be considerable variation in the substance and intensity of the losses that they encounter. Moreover, we should not assume that loss is synonymous with death, for some losses begin to emerge prior to death.

Much of the discussion that follows will stress that both grief and recovery are somewhat dependent on the nature of the losses. The recognition and assessment of the multiple dimensions of loss, therefore, is an essential step toward understanding the process that influences how survivors ultimately fare after the death of a closely related person. If we are able to identify the dimensions of loss and their scope, we submit, some of the mystery surrounding survivors' adjustments to death will be dissipated.

Grief

We define *grief* as the complicated set of emotional and cognitive responses that accompany loss. As we have explained, loss is not a uniform experience; as a result, grief varies in form, intensity, and duration. No consensus exists in the literature on the variety of emotions that grief includes. However, it is clear that the principal emotion associated with grief is depression. It may be a low-grade dysphoria in people who continue to function in their usual social roles but who live their lives in an emotional valley. Or it may be more severe, immobilizing the survivor psychologically.

It is important, we believe, to distinguish grief from mourning. We define mourning as a more ritualized response to death, involving activities, often religiously prescribed, such as attending a wake or funeral, sitting *shiva*, wearing certain clothes, visiting the grave, or saying prayers for the dead. Little is known of how mourning, as we define it, contributes to adjustment to death.

Beyond the emotional components of grief and mourning rituals, there are also more ideational or cognitive components of grief. It is these that we shall emphasize here. We label them cognitive not to imply that they lack any emotional aura; far from it. They involve thoughts and echoes from the past, changing images of the deceased, and efforts to maintain ties and to separate oneself from the deceased. These manifestations of grief are likely to come and go as the survivor alternately forgets and then joltingly realizes that a loved one has died. We shall outline several of these manifestations of grief. While not everyone experiences all of them, nor with the same intensity, probably some are experienced by most people following the death of someone close.

Often, thoughts and memories of the deceased person occupy the bereaved. These memories and images may come unbidden; they may intrude into consciousness even when the survivor is making a concerted effort to concentrate on something else. People often talk of finding themselves thinking about the person or remembering things they had not thought about in years. For some, these thoughts and memories may persist and constitute a stable backdrop to ordinary consciousness. It is as though reviewing the deceased person's actions, mannerisms, and moods helps to consolidate images in a form in which they can comfortably endure in memory. Perhaps this is a way of holding onto the person, or an idealized composite of him or her, even while confronting the reality of the loss.

Perceptual illusions—seeing, hearing, or sensing things that are not there—can also occur, sometimes causing people to worry about the state of their own mental health. But these fleeting moments are often understood for what they are, a misinterpretation of a sound or sight. At times, these illusions may be part of the normal perceptual process that one employs to fill in the blanks in the world, sustaining the habits and perceiving the continuity that had been there until the death. Or, as attachment theorists suggest, these perceptual illusions are understandable as part of a normal search in which the survivor is *trying* to find the deceased by picking up some sign of him or her (Parkes, 1972). These illusions may signal an underlying tension between the need to recognize the reality of death and a desire to hold onto the past, a tension sustained by the longing for the deceased person that accompanies bereavement. This wish to be reunited with the deceased is often spoken of as an intense yearning that comes suddenly and initially causes pain, for it inevitably is accompanied by the aching knowledge that the wish will be unfulfilled.

Particularly in the acute phase of grief, people often report a kind of dissociation from the normal flow of events in the world and from their characteristic sense of connectedness to it. As they struggle between grasping a new reality and clinging to an old bond, they feel numb internally. They may also feel that their sense of time is disrupted and that they are watching things from a distance. This unsettling mix of feelings and dissociations seems to be the internal counterpart of the external discontinuity brought on by death.

These common grief reactions seem understandable enough as people grapple with the tension between facing and accepting the reality of death and trying to preserve some continuity in their world. At times, this "conservative impulse" to hold onto the past, as Marris (1974) calls it, may involve brushing the reality of death aside. In any case, the intellectual recognition of death is accompanied by a deeper emotional sense of the loss.

The grief experienced by survivors, we should note, will be influenced by the kind and quality of the relationship the survivor had with the deceased (Futterman, Gallagher, Thompson, & Lovett, 1990; Wortman & Silver, 1990). Was the relationship marked by distance or closeness, by affection or hostility? On an intuitive basis, it would seem that these kinds of attributes of the relationship should make a difference to the intensity and duration of bereavement. However, they may not make the kind of difference we expect. For example, one might suppose that a stormy relationship ended by death would produce but limited grief. We have learned, however, that such a relationship can also leave the survivor bearing an unpleasant reservoir of guilt. In turn, guilt can intensify and prolong bereavement. As loss takes place within the context of a relationship, grief will inevitably be affected by the history of the relationship. This history includes not only the closeness between the survivor and the deceased and the amount of conflict they experienced, but also any "unfinished business" left by the death (Lopata, 1979a).

It is therefore not surprising that some of the bereaved caregivers whom we have studied feel regrets and guilt about how they acted toward the deceased person. They feel a sense of having broken a standard, of having treated a weaker, dependent person less kindly than they should have. If anything, it is surprising that more caregivers do not feel these regrets, for the caregiver role is a setting in which guilt may easily arise. It is a difficult and enduring set of demands that often cannot be met; patient behavior may seem bewildering especially as cognitive decline continues; and even if the past relationship was generally positive, the demands of the role can give rise to frustration and anger, and the guilty wish for relief.

Fundamental to the distinction we make between loss and grief is the difference between the objective loss of an important element in life and the recognition and realization of the loss. While the loss and the realization of loss may coincide at death, this neat simultaneity rarely exists in our experience. That is, as we discussed earlier, caregivers facing the transformation of a cognitively impaired relative often develop a strong sense of having lost the person and important elements in their relationship, such as companionship, expressive support, and intimacy, well before their relative's biological death. Conversely, survivors may not recognize immediately all that has been lost with the death of their impaired relative. It may take some time for them to realize just how much they depended on the person's presence to structure their days, and more than this, how much they depended on the person's needs to provide meaning and purpose to their lives.

We mention this disjunction between objective loss and sense of loss because both may affect the form and duration of grief, before and after death occurs. For example, when a husband becomes progressively impaired, a wife must begin to make adjustments in her life to compensate for his impairments. These adjustments may begin to take their toll on her energy and well-being before she has recognized exactly what has happened. Because many dementing illnesses, in particular, are insidious in their onset and progress rather slowly, caregivers may not immediately recognize declines in functioning and the consequent losses with which they are dealing.

If recognition is the first step in the development of a sense of loss, realization is the second. It is the subtle process whereby people move from the simple ability to recognize a deficit to the deeper realization that something is irrecoverably missing from their lives. At the simplest level, the first psychological task is to recognize the losses one is facing. Immediately after the death, this basic understanding may come and go; as survivors engage in familiar plans and activities, they may temporarily forget that the person is no longer alive. But typical patterns of thoughts, feelings, and behavior elicited by familiar circumstances no longer fit the new situation. This lack of a fit is one sign that change is needed, and it engenders in survivors a sense that things are out of kilter. The common patterns of responding assume that the world has remained constant and continuous, that one's typical ways of reacting to things will be appropriate. Death is a breach in this continuity that throws into question the meanings sustained by these experiences.

For many caregivers, the immediate impact of death is dramatic. However much they may have realized the losses they were experiencing, and may even have grieved to some extent for them, death is immediately related to intense grief. Our impression is that intense grief is associated with the realization of some losses more than others: losses involving the relationship with the deceased appear to affect grief more immediately than those involving the less personal aspects of the deceased, such as social status or network relationships.

Over time, these intense feelings, particularly depression, illusory experiences, and the sense of unreality, diminish. Many survivors, however, continue to review images and memories of the person, but these images are less and less associated with pain. Initially, the review of their relationship with the deceased may increase their sense of loss, for this is the time in which they uncover the many things they have lost with the illness and death. The bouts of grief noted by others (Bowlby, 1980) may be related to these successive discoveries. But as this grief process continues, what remains, particularly for those whose sense of self has not been undermined by the losses encountered, may contain many positive elements. Survivors may recognize their accomplishments as caregivers; they may take satisfaction in having performed a difficult job in a loving way; and they may realize their own strengths in relationships, as friend, lover, partner, or companion. And these realizations may represent the first steps toward recovery, to which we now turn our attention.

Recovery

In the vast literature dealing with adaptation to death, attention is often limited to the diminution of distress over time, particularly decreases in the level of depressive affect. Time *qua* time is usually considered to be the dominant condition that somehow explains the easing of distress. Thus, people who study bereavement are usually interested in knowing whether depression begins to taper off at 3 months, 6 months, or a year and whether, should distress continue beyond some normative span, this is indicative of some deep-seated pathology. What is lacking in this exclusive reliance on time itself as an explanatory factor in the easing of distress is that it ignores what survivors are doing or not doing as time passes (Osterweis, Solomon, & Green, 1984). It may very well be that time alone does tend to ease the anguish of bereavement. But in our view, to assume that time is capable of explaining change also assumes that survivors are passive, merely waiting to be healed by the passing of time. However, there is reason to believe that people are often active participants in their own recovery.

What do people do that hastens their movement through bereavement and into recovery? There is no simple answer to this question, largely because the range of functional behavior in which people can conceivably engage is enormously varied. Further, just what comprises recovery is not clear. Because some symptoms of grief can recur for many years, recovery does not mean merely an end to symptoms (Osterweis et al., 1984). Nor does it necessarily mean a return to a previous level of functioning (Wortman & Silver, 1990). For some it may mean an opportunity for positive growth, a new lifestyle, or a sense of mastery and competence (Mullan, 1992). Despite these kinds of unanswered questions and unresolved issues, some focus to the matter of recovery can be achieved. We begin by pointing out that the behavior functional for the course of recovery probably depends, at least to some extent, on the nature of the losses one has experienced. More specifically, it depends on whether losses are *reversible* or *substitutable*.

By reversible losses we refer to those that can be turned around or retrieved. It may appear fanciful to talk of reversible losses in the case of the death of a closely related person. After all, the person is gone, never again to have the presence he or she once had. However, although the loss of the person that occurs with death is irreversible, there are other losses attendant upon death that may be reversible or partially reversible (Marris, 1974). This assertion can be understood by referring back to our catalogue of losses. Let us suppose, for example, that the survivor has experienced a loss of status or of financial resources following the death. Although there is no assurance that these kinds of losses will be reversed, there is nothing intrinsic to them that would prevent them from being turned around. Similarly, any constriction in the range of the survivor's social network that might have occurred prior to or following death is reversible. One begins to make new friends, reactivate old friendships, become engaged in leisure-time pursuits, join clubs and organizations, and so on. Essentially, then, there is a genre of loss that can be reversed through social reintegration and, we believe, the more quickly and completely such reversals occur, the faster will be the psychological recovery from bereavement.

We should point out that it is difficult to substantiate these assertions empirically. It is simple enough to determine whether decreases in the duration of psychological distress are correlated with the reversal of social losses. What is not clear is whether reintegration frees one from distress, if relief from distress enables one to seek reintegration, or if their influence is mutual. To discern the directions of effect, it is obvious that longitudinal observations are needed.

Some losses that are not reversible are substitutable, what Moos and Schaefer (1986) refer to as alternative rewards. For example, the deceased person can no longer be a realistic source of affection or of support, although survivors may imagine they are carrying on comforting dialogues with their deceased loved ones. However, other people with whom the survivor interacts may begin to compensate for these kinds of losses. Indeed, it is not unusual for survivors to bond quickly to others with the hope that the love and understanding they had before will be theirs again to enjoy in their new relationships. Indeed, both among spousal caregivers to Alzheimer's patients, especially husbands caring for wives, and lovers caring for AIDS patients, it occasionally happens that new intimate relationships are established before the death of the loved one. We assume that these new relationships substitute for those that can no longer be sources of affection. In the instances where this has occurred, the caregiver remains committed to providing care to the impaired person.

When we think about the loss of exchange, we usually consider only the loss of affection and support one might have earlier received from the deceased person. As we described earlier, however, there is another side to this loss; it is the loss of mattering. There is some indication that one of the forces that drives caregiving is the desire to matter to another person, to be important to that person's welfare. The adage that it is better to give than to receive may have some psychological truth. At any rate, recovery may involve not only finding others from whom one can receive support and affection but also others to whom one can again matter by giving support and affection. Among informal AIDS caregivers, for example, it is not unusual following the death for the survivor to assume caregiving activities with another friend. Although these activities may be directed by a sense of mission as well as by personal attachment, these survivors may be substituting one individual with another in order to retrieve a sense of mattering.

Finding replacements for those roles that have been lost is another part of the recovery process that may involve substitution of new roles (Stroebe & Stroebe, 1987). This may be more difficult for older spouses who may have fewer roles to move into, but younger spouses, lovers, and adult children, may substitute work or family roles for the caregiver role.

Recovery, then, can be charted by the survivor's efforts to reverse losses and, where they are irreversible, to find substitutes or compensations for what cannot be retrieved. We believe that recovery can also be discerned on a different and somewhat more subtle level. Among our samples of caregivers, death typically does not occur after a short period of caregiving but, rather, follows a lengthy, difficult, and lacerating burden. There is nothing graceful in the dying of either Alzheimer's patients or people with AIDS. In many instances, caregivers are left to deal not simply with the fact of death but, even more difficult, with the mode of dying. They witness loved ones stripped of autonomy and dignity. Like most of us, caregivers who search for distributive justice in life are also likely to look for it in death. Most assuredly, such people will find their search frustrated and their sense of fairness assaulted. There is basically little or no redeeming justice to be found in this kind of dying. If one of the tasks of recovery is to find meaning in death (Wortman & Silver, 1989), then a major task of recovery is to overcome the outrage at a death that has assaulted the dignity and personhood of the deceased.

We believe there may be a tendency for caregivers to generalize from the specific horrors and injustices of the dying they witness to the nature of the world about them. This world may now be seen as a less secure place, a place where distributive justice cannot be expected, an indifferent and uncaring place, and, above all, it may be viewed as a place from which the surviving caregiver may feel profoundly alienated and alone. These are issues that we are just beginning to explore empirically and we could at this point easily be overly assertive about these darkened worldviews. Wortman and Silver (1990) have suggested that a worldview already in place before the death may predict how successful a person will be in coping with death. This worldview may be a philosophical orientation or religious belief, but, they suggest, persons who can immediately incorporate their loss into an undamaged worldview will cope successfully. There is the possibility, of course, that on the heels of a slow and transforming death, even a strongly positive worldview will be clouded. One adult daughter told us:

> There was one other problem when I lost my dad; I lost my religious faith for about a year and I felt so empty. There had always been those absolutes in my life: my faith and my dad.... I had a lot of anger over his suffering. I always expected that since he lived such a good life his death would be commensurate.

We do not yet know how widespread these changed worldviews may be or whether there is a softening or tempering of them that is associated with recovery. In the case of AIDS, where death is untimely and where grief may be tied not only to the death of an individual but also to the threat to an entire community, we expect to find negative worldviews both more pronounced and slower to dissipate.

Earlier we discussed the multiple aspects of loss of self or identity that may occur both preceding and as a result of the death of someone who was an integral part of one's life. When we talk about recovery in relation to the self it is important to keep in mind that the death may bring not only loss but also the potential for positive growth and enrichment of self (Moss & Moss, 1989; Wortman & Silver, 1990). For widows and widowers, the recovery process may involve establishing a new identity as a single person (Lopata, 1979a). Although this may be painful and slow, it carries the potential for a new and more positive sense of self (Lopata, 1979b; Parkes, 1972). As one widow put it, "I'm more self-reliant. Doing my own thinking, not looking to see if he (her husband) approves of what I'm doing." Some of the tasks include finding new roles to replace those lost, establishing a new social life as a single person, and revising one's view of oneself in terms of future hopes and plans. The meaning of these tasks will most likely vary by life stage (Wortman & Silver, 1990) and gender (Umberson et al., 1989).

Adult children may experience rather paradoxical feelings at the death of a parent. On the one hand, they keenly feel the losses that we have described; on the other hand, however, they often feel a sense of personal growth or enrichment (Moss & Moss, 1989). Thus, although they may lose a lifelong source of positive feedback about the self that had been provided by the parent, they frequently gain a new sense of "coming into one's own" (Kowalski, 1986). The death of a parent may also remind them of their own mortality and the time left to accomplish their own goals. Adult children who lived with the parent before death and who may have forfeited significant portions of their own lives may find the restructuring of their own separate identities to be particularly difficult.

For spouses and adult children who cared for their relative for an extended period of time, the death of that relative is even more likely to have both positive and negative effects on the sense of self. The loss of self that some of our Alzheimer's caregivers experienced prior to the death of their relative may be lifted as they are relieved from the role that had so engulfed them. The recovery of a former sense of self or rebuilding a new sense of self will, we believe, depend on how well they are able to find new sources of self-evaluation by establishing new roles or by reengaging in old ones.

For anyone who experiences the illness and death of someone close to them, there is the potential for that experience to lead to a new sense of self-confidence, competence, and mastery (Calhoun & Tedeschi, 1989–1990; Moos & Schaefer, 1986). Being relieved of the burden of caregiving but also knowing that one was able to deal with a very difficult situation appears to have a positive effect on sense of self. Preliminary analyses of data on our Alzheimer's caregivers reveal that there is an increase in a sense of mastery among those recently bereaved (Mullan, 1992). Further examination of the effects of bereavement on sense of self are currently underway.

It should be evident that we are only at the beginning of our quest to understand recovery. Yet we are confident that it represents more than the simple wearing away of grief with time. As important as time may be as a healer, recovery depends on the active efforts and cognitive realignments of the survivors. It also depends on the situational contexts in which loss and bereavement occur. In this regard, we want to learn if employment in an absorbing occupation hastens recovery, independently of the other conditions. There is some indication that it does (Marris, 1974). In our own work we know that having outside employment can protect those who are still caregiving from a loss of self (Skaff & Pearlin, 1992). We also suspect that such characteristics as one's age and ethnicity may make a difference. A life-course perspective would be particularly useful in both predicting and understanding some of the elements of loss and the potential paths to recovery (Wortman & Silver, 1990). While it is obvious that much remains to be learned about recovery, it is clear that it ultimately rests on both the reconstruction of a social life and the reconstruction of self.

Discussion

Death and dying are inevitably unique experiences for survivors. There is a multitude of ways in which the surrounding conditions may combine to make each person's confrontation with the death of a loved one different from that of others. Yet, certain threads can be detected that seem to cut across the unique aspects of survivorship. Together, these threads enable us to describe not only how individuals and groups may differ in their survivorship but also how at some level they may be seen as sharing certain things in common.

These things are loss, grief, and recovery, constructs very familiar to students of death and dying. What we have sought in this chapter is, first, to give some elaboration to these constructs. Although they are familiar, their substance and dimensions are not yet satisfactorily specified. Second, we have attempted to identify some of the linkages among the three constructs. This attempt is guided by the assumption that the eventual adaptations to the death of a loved one are best understood within the framework of a process encompassing loss, grief, and recovery. We do not assume that these are three discrete stages in the process, such that one begins only as another ends. But we do believe that they constitute the foundations for describing the experiential trajectories of survivors and for identifying the conditions that help to explain variations in these trajectories.

Our perspectives on bereavement and the processes that we believe give it meaning and direction are admittedly colored by the two groups of former caregivers we are studying, one having cared for relatives with Alzheimer's disease and the other for people with AIDS. It is the very striking differences between these groups that helps to highlight their common experiences. In the one group, the deceased are generally at the older end of the age spectrum and the other in the center of young adulthood. The normative expectations of the "acceptable" age of death are obviously disparate for the two.

On average, the Alzheimer's group will have been active caregivers for a longer time than the AIDS group. Yet, in each case, circumstances have forced a recasting of relationships that had drawn their strength from the exchange of love and intimacy to those that were largely based on one person giving and the other receiving. This recasting itself may produce a swirl of emotions and conflicts that must be dealt with along the entire course of the survival process.

Although among the children of parents with Alzheimer's disease there is some fear of heritability, it is the AIDS caregivers, particularly close friends and lovers, who may read into death a scenario of their own fates. To some extent, then, recovery depends on the participants in both groups reconciling not only the losses created by illness and death but also the threats they may feel to their own lives. This task, by and large, is much greater among AIDS caregivers. It is these caregivers, too, who often experience loss as a more encompassing phenomenon than that involving the demise of an individual. Where the caregiver and person with AIDS are part of a larger community with which they closely identify, as is often the case, then the death of the individual can also be interpreted as a gradual chipping away of the entire collectivity. In a real sense, there is the loss of community by attrition and, while the survivor might recover eventually from the death of a loved one, he may never recover from the loss of community.

In thinking about surviving the death of a loved one as a process, it seems to us that loss and its many dimensions are the key to much of what follows. The sheer range of losses that are experienced and the intensity of the losses would be major factors regulating the cognitive substance, emotional sensitivity, and length of active grieving. As we have discussed, we similarly regard recovery as closely dependent on loss. Although we can offer no empirical evidence in support of this assumption at the present time, it seems reasonable to suppose that to a substantial extent recovery occurs as people are able to reverse losses that are reversible and to find substitutes for those that are not.

A major perspective we hope to convey with this chapter is that survivorship and the process it entails are highly complex and variable. At this time the information that will answer the many questions surrounding survivorship is largely absent. That is less of a concern to us than knowing how to raise the kinds of questions that will guide the gathering of productive information. This chapter, we feel, succeeds more in bringing together questions worth asking than in providing answers that eventually need to be sought.

References

Bowlby, J. (1980). *Loss (Attachment and loss, Vol. III)*. New York: Basic Books.

Calhoun, L. G., & Tedeschi, R. G. (1989–1990). Positive aspects of critical life problems: Recollections of grief. *Omega, 20* (4), 265–272.

Futterman, A., Gallagher, D., Thompson, L. W., & Lovett, S. (1990). Retrospective assessment of marital adjustment and depression during the first 2 years of spousal bereavement. *Psychology and Aging 5*(2), 277–283.

Kowalski, N. C. (1986). Anticipating the death of an elderly parent. In T. A. Rando (Ed.), *Loss and anticipatory grief* (pp. 187–199). Lexington, MA: D.C. Heath.

Lopata, H. (1979a). Grief work and identity reconstruction. In I. Gerber, A. Wiener, A. H. Kutscher, D. Battin, A. Arkin, & I. K. Goldberg (Eds.), *Perspectives on bereavement* (pp. 12–25). New York: Arno.

Lopata, H. (1979b). *Women as widows: Support systems*. New York: Elsevier.

Marris, P. (1974). *Loss and change*. New York: Pantheon.

Moos, R. H., & Schaefer, J. A. (1986). Life transitions and crises: A conceptual overview. In R. H. Moos (Ed.), *Coping with life crises: An integrated approach* (pp. 3–28). New York: Plenum.

Moss, M. S., & Moss, S. Z. (1989). The death of a parent. In R. A. Kalish (Ed.), *Midlife loss: Coping strategies* (pp. 89–114). Newbury Park, CA: Sage.

Mullan, J. T. (1992). The bereaved caregiver: A prospective study of changes in well-being. *The Gerontologist, 32*(5), 673–683.

Osterweis, M., Solomon, F., & Green, M. (Eds.) (1984). *Bereavement: Reactions consequences, and care*. Washington, DC: National Academy.

Parkes, C. M. (1972). *Bereavement: Studies of grief in adult life*. New York: International University.

Pearlin, L. I., & Lieberman, M. A. (1979). Social sources of emotional distress. In R. Simmons (Ed.), *Research in community and mental health* (pp. 217–248). Greenwich, CT: JAI Press.

Peretz, D. (1970). Development, object-relations, and loss. In B. Schoenberg, A. C. Carr, D. Peretz, & A. H. Kutscher (Eds.), *Loss and grief: Psychological management in medical practice*. New York: Colombia University.

Rosenberg, M., & McCullaugh, B. C. (1981). Mattering: Inferred significance and mental health. In R. Simmons (Ed.), *Research in community and mental health*. Greenwich, CT: JAI Press.

Skaff, M. M., & Pearlin, L. I. (1992). Caregiving: Role engulfment and the loss of self. *The Gerontologist, 32*(5), 656–664.

Stroebe, W., & Stroebe, M. S. (1987). *Bereavement and health: The psychological and physical consequences of partner loss.* Cambridge, MA: Cambridge University.

Troll, L. (1990). Death of the oldest generation. Paper presented at the Annual Meeting of the Gerontological Society of America, Boston, MA.

Umberson, D., Wortman, C. B., & Kessler, R. C. (1989). Widowhood and depression: Explaining gender differences in vulnerability. Paper presented at the Annual Meeting of the American Sociological Association, San Francisco, CA.

Walsh, F., & McGoldrick, M. (1991). Loss and the family: A systemic perspective. In F. Walsh & M. McGoldrick (Eds.), *Living beyond loss: Death in the family* (pp. 1–29). New York: Norton.

Wortman, C. B., & Silver, R. C. (1989). The myths of coping with loss. *Journal of Consulting and Clinical Psychology, 57,* 349-357.

Wortman, C. B., & Silver, R. C. (1990). Successful mastery of bereavement and widowhood: A life course perspective. In P. B. Baltes & M. M. Baltes (Eds.), *Successful aging: Perspectives from the behavioral sciences.* New York: Cambridge University.

Fifteen

Helping the Bereaved through Social Support and Mutual Help

Phyllis R. Silverman

Phyllis R. Silverman, Ph.D., LIC. S. W., is Co-Principal Investigator of the Child Bereavement Study, a longitudinal prospective study of the impact of the death of a parent on school-age children. She is also a professor at the MGH Institute of Health Professions and an associate in social welfare in the Department of Psychiatry at Massachusetts General Hospital and Harvard Medical School. She developed the concept of the widow-to-widow program and directed the research project that demonstrated its effectiveness. She has served as consultant to several task forces on bereavement and primary prevention convened by the National Institutes of Mental Health; and has consulted with hospices, hospitals, and social agencies across the United States and abroad on issues of bereavement, mutual help, and prevention. She is the recipient of the 1991 presidential medal from Brooklyn College, City University of New York, for her outstanding contributions to the fields of bereavement and social welfare. She spent the 1993–1994 academic year at Haifa University on a Senior Fulbright Research Fellowship. The National Center for Death Education recognized her as a pioneer in the field of thanatology with its 1994 award. In addition to her social work degree from Smith College School for Social Work, she holds an Sc.M. in Hygiene from Harvard School of Public Health and a Ph.D. from the Florence Heller School for Advanced Studies in Social Welfare at Brandeis University. She has published extensively in professional journals and has written several books on widowhood and mutual help groups.

The Nature of Social Support

Lois Murphy observed in studying development in children that most practitioners and researchers focus primarily on the achievement of autonomy as the goal of development. Competent children, she observed, not only know when they need help but know how to solicit such help be it for approval and love or for concrete assistance (Murphy, 1974). Murphy's observation points to the fact that we are social creatures and the need for others is essential to human life. To deal with the various vicissitudes and stresses of living we must acknowledge the importance of relationships and the interdependencies among people that make a viable life possible. This is true not only in the young but throughout the life cycle. The literature on the new psychology of women has made these truths even clearer (Gilligan, 1982; Miller, 1986). These researchers are talking about the centrality to human life of connection and care between people, and that only in relationships do we grow, develop, and adapt.

These observations from Murphy's research into the effect of stress and from studies of the psychology of women are in some ways joined as we turn to recent research on social support (Belle, 1988; Barnett, Biener, & Baruch, 1987). This research, focusing primarily on periods of stress, documents the value of social support as a mediator of this stress (Garmezy,1987). The availability of support, which means the availability of others, seems to be correlated with adaptive behavior that involves coping effectively with the stress so that it is possible to carry on with life, as opposed to maladaptive behavior that can be dysfunctional given the nature of the stress (Belle,1989; Gottlieb, 1981). Cobb (1976), one of the earliest researchers to study the phenomenon, defined social support as information leading to the subject believing: that he is cared for and loved; that he is esteemed and valued; that he belongs to a network of communication and mutual obligation. Caplan (1976) defined support in terms of the functioning of a support system that is a continuing social aggregate that provides individuals with opportunities for feedback about themselves and for validation of their expectations about others, which may offset deficiencies in these communications within the larger community context. In such relations, Caplan continues, the individual is dealt with in a personalized way—people speak his or her language, guide him or her in what to do, offer feedback about what he or she is doing, and can provide extra supplies of money, materials, and skills. Eckenrode and Gore (1981) noted that it is not possible to understand the value of support without looking at the context in which it occurs and the responses of the recipients. They suggested looking at the social network in which the stress and available support are embedded. A focus on the social network brings to the fore those who are actors in the network, how they interact, and what help they provide (Gottlieb, 1981; Vachon, 1988). Vachon (1988), in her review of the growing literature on social support, defines support as a transactional process requiring a fit between the donor, the recipient, and the particular circumstances. Gottlieb (1990) reinforces this point by reminding us that support is a process and that to understand the nature of support and its effectiveness it is essential to understand the interaction between those involved, how it gets expressed, and to what it leads.

Belle and her colleagues (1982) found that depressed low-income women often had dense potential helping networks, that is, there were many people with whom they were in contact and from whom help might be expected. Nonetheless these women often felt isolated, and unsupported. Belle found that potential helpers in the network were more interested in taking than in giving in spite of the clear need in others. We are talking about an interactive, reciprocal process that cannot be understood outside of the psychological and social context of those involved. There is a need, then, to not only identify the actors in the situation, but their resources, attitudes towards help from others, and ability to respond to their own needs and the needs of others.

Another factor to consider in both the provision and the receipt of support is the gender of those involved. Differences may emerge between how men and women define their needs, what they define as appropriate help, as well as the kind of help they themselves can provide (Barnett, et al., 1987). Gilligan (1982) and Miller (1986) have suggested that we will learn more about care and connection from studying women's experience. Lyons (1989) in a study of how adolescent girls develop, points to the growing concern of these young women to learn to care for others and to respect the reality of others. These adolescents were not striving for individuation and separation, which are typically considered the primary developmental issues of adolescence. Instead these girls aspire to be interdependent, that is to be in relationship with others in a new way.

Using men's experience (Levinson, 1978) as the norm has led to a focus on individuation and autonomy as the goal of development. The consequence of this focus became clear in my studies of the widowed (Silverman, 1987). Widowers, for example, talk of needing to learn to reach out to others and take responsbility for their social life, which was usually a role their wives had played in their marriage. They have no trouble making decisions and their sense of integrity and self remain intact. Widows report needing to learn to make decisions, to speak out for themselves, and to develop a new sense of self. They usually report knowing themselves in terms of their relationship to others, i.e, as wife or mother (Silverman, 1987). Men seem to have difficulty reaching out for help of any kind, they seem to think they should be able to manage by themselves (Cook, 1988; Silverman, 1987). Some men found it easier to join a poker group than to come together to talk about feelings (Campbell & Silverman, 1987).

In a study of widows and widowers caring for dependent children (Silverman & Worden, 1992) found that the vast majority of both men and women reached out to women for assistance and support. Women have been the providers of support in our society. They are accustomed to this role and accept themselves in this role. Women talk of needing to be needed. Widowers talked of learning to care as one of the lessons the few who joined together with other widowed people, learned. It was a new experience to be helpful, to exchange feelings with others, and to see the value of this kind of personal involvement. For many men it was a new experience to have a male friend with whom they shared (Silverman, 1987; Campbell & Silverman, 1987).

In looking at stressful situations we often consider them static, as if the actors and the stress remained constant over time and unrelated to the context in which they are acting. A stress is rarely a single event or activity. For example if we assume that a widowed person is simply reacting to the death of the spouse, and that is the single event to which he or she is responding, we are overlooking a large part of the stress the widowed person is experiencing.

Stress, for the widowed, may come from the exhaustion and perhaps relief after having watched a spouse suffer a long illness which the death ended; from young children who must now grow up in a single-parent household and who make new demands on their sole parent; or from the fact that they are themselves old and not well and for the first time find themselves living alone. Stress also occurs for some families who have never faced death, and have no way of seeing it as an expected part of the life cycle. Stress may also emanate from others in the network who cannot tolerate the pain associated with bereavement and that is so much a part of the reality of the newly widowed. These others may withdraw or pressure the widowed to be "over" their loss in a very short period of time (Silverman, 1981,1986). Stress then emanates not only from the sadness and sense of loss, but from the changes in the social context in which the survivors must live the rest of their lives. With the passing of time, the bereaved's needs will change, as will their circumstances. These changes will not occur in a vacuum but as a result of interaction among the actors at work in this system, some as helpers, some as beneficiaries, some as both. Help, or support, then cannot remain the same but has to respond to the new conditions and new problems (Silverman, 1966, 1986; Vachon, 1988; Gottlieb, 1990). When we talk then of support we are talking about the very fundamental nature of relationships and of care that is only possible in the context of these relationships and that makes for special bonds between people. We need to understand how this care is expressed in any given community and whether the community values the need for such care not only in response to a given problem but as part of the essence of the human condition.

This paper focuses on the needs of the bereaved. Death of a loved one is something that all of us will experience. While we may see many

deaths as untimely and out of turn in the life cycle, death itself ultimately cannot be avoided. It is the price that we all pay for being alive
and we will all be bereaved if we are involved in relationships. We are
looking then, at a universal stressor to which we all need to learn to
respond. When we talk about the availability of social support in a
community at the time of a death, we are talking about the very basic
quality of life in that community.

This quality is related to how people understand bereavement. Do
they see it as an illness that needs to be expunged like a germ or as a
legitimate human expression of pain and sadness that brings with it a
need for change? Quality of life in a community is also related to what
help is available and how people utilize it. If we agree that the help
should be responsive to the need, these two considerations are really
very much related. The remainder of the paper will focus on the needs of
the bereaved and how they are met by the available helping networks in
their communities and the support these networks can provide with
particular emphasis on mutual help.

The Nature of the Bereavement Process

The understanding we have of bereavement is reflected in the vocabu-
lary available for describing the widowed person's grief. We talk of a
"time of healing,"of "getting over it," and of "working it through." We
say "You will recover." The images associated with these phrases imply
that grief is an illness from which one recovers with appropriate treatment. The expectation of such treatment is that it will at the least
relieve the mourner's pain and at the most remove it entirely. Implicit
too is that grief ends and that people will pick up their lives and carry on
as before. The affective and psychological aspects of grief are emphasized
in this approach; so that the crying, sadness, pining, feeling alone, and
feeling cheated by the loss come into focus as the primary issues to be
attended to. This approach can result in major deception of the bereaved
as they try to conform to the expectations of their social network. With
the diminution of these feelings, they expect that their grief will be
"resolved." When they are unable to achieve this goal they can feel
defective and stigmatized as if something must be wrong with them.
Their grief is long and pervades most aspects of their lives, which are
irrevocably changed and cannot be reconstituted as before (Silverman,
1981; Lopata, 1988). The death of a spouse, or of any other person who
was very much a part of the survivor's life, leads to major disruptions in
the way the mourner's world is constructed, the way they see themselves in relationship to that world, and in the very habits of daily living
(Silverman, 1986; Klass; 1988; Shamgar-Handleman, 1986).

In reality pain may be tempered by time but time does not heal. The widowed don't recover; rather they make an accommodation to their new situation. This involves both dealing with the inner sense of loss, accepting the pain as part of living, and learning to remember the deceased with ease and satisfaction. Ultimately finding a new sense of self is involved that requires finding a new place for themselves in the world as a formerly married, now single person. Help for the widowed must be responsive to their need to legitimate their feelings and to learn to live in a new way in the world (Silverman, 1966, 1969, 1976).

Helping Networks

As we look at the nature of help that is available in any community, we begin with the central unit of the family and move beyond that to the neighborhood, to the community, and then to the professional helping system. The primary unit of social support is the family. Caplan (1976) identified how the family functions as a provider: of care, of approbation, of material needs, of feedback. The family anchors the individual in a social network and in the larger society. Gottlieb (1981) looks at the helping networks in any given community and considers the social distance between them. He considers the access to the system and whether or not people working in the system receive remuneration for this work. Gottlieb finds that the further away from the nuclear family unit the helping system is the less personal are the services provided. The family maintains a system of mutual obligation to its members who are connected by marriage, birth,or adoption. Providers of service in the professional community offer care and services because they have a societal mandate to do so and there is a fee for this service. Payment for services is the primary obligation of the client or patient; the other obligation may be to comply with the advice of the professional (Hughes, 1971). There is no expectation of reciprocity. Help is more specialized and division of labor is clear. In the family, in the neighborhood, and in friendship help is offered as a matter of personal obligation and there is a sense of mutuality and reciprocity. The helpers' expertise in this informal system comes from their knowledge of the recipient and from their experience and their own value system (Gottlieb, 1981).

As we look at the impact of the death of a spouse we return to the social impact of this loss. In their roles as husbands and wives, men and women find a way of framing and focusing their daily lives and of providing each other with appropriate support. This unit is irreparably disrupted when one of the spouses dies. This source of support is gone. The nature of this support can vary. The widowed individual can lose, for example, a companion with whom to share ideas, the primary financial provider in the family, or the primary nurturer of the family. Exactly what is lost depends on the way these individuals constructed their marriage as well as the dictates of the community that provides a major frame for defining the meaning of marriage (Silverman, 1986). The widowed individual has to turn for assistance to family members, friends, neighbors, and beyond.

What happens when these helpers are not able to respond to the bereaved in a way that is helpful? Often the mourner is referred to professionals for assistance (Osterweis, et al., 1984). These professionals could be clergy, physicians, or mental-health therapists. Clergy, unless they have a psychological orientation, may rely on prayer and concrete advice. Physicians usually prescribe medication to relieve what is designated as symptoms of grief. The mental-health professional generally focuses on the psychological aspects of the process. Whatever the help may be, the message to the bereaved is that there is something wrong and with the correct professional help he or she will get over the grief. This can further stigmatize an individual who already is feeling disoriented in the face of a disrupted sense of self (Silverman, 1981). On the other hand, this type of assistance may be very useful to people and should not be discounted outright. When such a profound and complex disruption has occurred, however, no one kind of assistance is usually sufficient. Dakoff and Taylor (1990) have documented that different help is expected from different helpers in a helping network and therefore the helpfulness of any given act is in part related to its source. For example, in this study esteem and emotional support were valued from family members and not from physicians. When physicians provided specific information they were seen as very helpful to people with cancer.

The bereaved, and there is rarely a single mourner even in the death of a spouse, need each other and their families to share their feelings about the deceased, to remember together, and to support each other as they acknowledge their pain and loss. They need friends to help with the concrete tasks of living and managing their family from the time before the funeral to afterwards as they try to establish a lifestyle appropriate to their new situation. They need the funeral director and the clergy to help with burial and mourning rituals. In the long run, religion can be very important in trying to find a way of living with the fact that people die. We begin to see how a helping network is composed (Silverman, 1986).

There is still another dimension of support, which may not be available from anyone who has not had a personal experience with widowhood. The widowed need to know that most widowed people have similar experiences and they need to find role models for how they can build their lives anew. We talk a good deal about peer influence on adolescents but we need to consider that this may be a need throughout the life cycle. At each new stage or phase we seek others who have gone before us to learn from them what Goffman has called "the tricks of the trade" (Goffman, 1963). If the widowed do not have people in their network who have been widowed, they may seek others outside this network. The growth of mutual help organizations has made us increasingly aware of this need for others who have had a similar experience. Hamburg and Adams (1967) pointed out that learning is made easier when the helper is one step ahead of the person in need and has experience with the problem to use as a guide. These organizations are based on the premise that in times of stress people need others, as role models and teachers who have had a similar experience (Silverman, 1966, 1969, 1978, 1980, 1986; Gartner & Reissman, 1977; Leiberman, Borman, et al., 1979; Powell, 1987).

Gottlieb (1981), looking at the continuum of help available in the community, talks about intentional communities. These are places that people establish or seek to meet needs that cannot be met in their existing networks. These are in contrast to what is called the *informal helping network* consisting of family and friends or formal professional networks. Some researchers have talked about these intentional communities as natural helping efforts (Pancoast, Parker, & Froland, 1983). Intentional seems a more accurate term because such initiatives are consciously designed and carried forward. They are not based on professional knowledge, which is used in the more formal system but on experiential knowledge (Borkman, 1978), mutual reciprocity, and peer relationships. People join together as members of the organization not as clients, and the members control the resources and determine what help the organization will provide and by whom it will be provided. These organizations have a formal structure resembling a club or other type of voluntary association (Silverman, 1978, 1982).

Mutal Help and the Bereaved

Historically the bereaved have probably been helping each other since people have been living in communities and mourners needed solace. Habits of the past often fall into disuse. As society became more specialized, especially in this century, we have witnessed the professionalization of services once performed by citizens for each other. People became self-conscious about their lack of credentials to help in times of stress and no longer recognized as legitimate the experience they may have amassed from living. Informally people helped each other and sometimes without much fanfare set up programs to help each other in churches and community centers (Silverman et al., 1975). Not only did people in general not legitimize this type of help but those responsible for planning community services did not recognize this mutual assistance as important or relevant.

Over the past three decades this has been turning around as more and more professionals have recognized the limitations of their efforts. This has been accompanied by a growing recognition of the fact that in most communities there are people who are known for their helping qualities. They were identified as natural helpers and some professionals aligned themselves with them in helping programs (Pancoast et al.,1983). The New Careers for the Poor Program in New York (Pearl & Reissman, 1965) recognized that residents of a given community were more successful than the professionals in engaging disadvantaged families from that community, in helping programs. People with problems were not waiting for the professionals to help them. They never really abdicated this responsibility. Alcoholics Anonymous had already established their efficacy as a resource for alcoholics with much greater success than any professional initiative. Katz (1970) had documented the early efforts of parents of retarded children and children with mental illness to take the initiative in developing services for their children through mutual help organizations. Consciousness of the positive impact of these efforts of people with common problems to develop intentional communities through which they could help themselves and each other was growing among professionals (Gartner & Reissman, 1977). This awareness was enhanced by the U.S. President's Commission on Mental Health (1978), which recommended that there be clearinghouses in every community to make information available about mutual help groups in that community. There are now a number of clearinghouses throughout North America and in many parts of Europe (Madera, 1990).

In the late 1960s there were two parallel initiatives that led to lasting mutual help programs for the widowed and for bereaved parents and that changed the nature of services available today for the bereaved in any given community. Compassionate Friends is an organization for bereaved parents that was developed by the chaplain in an English hospital in response to his growing awareness of the sense of aloneness and isolation from others experienced by parents whose children died in that hospital (Stephens, 1972). This program was imported to the United States in the 1970s and has grown to a national organization with chapters in many parts of this country (Klass, 1988). While professionals are consultants to this organization, bereaved parents provide the leadership and are the primary helpers.

The Widow-to-Widow program was a demonstration-research project at Harvard Medical School (Silverman, 1966, 1986; Silverman, et al., 1975). It was based on the finding that the only people who seemed to be helpful to the newly widowed were other widowed people (Maddison &

Walker, 1967). The goal of the original program was to develop an early intervention program for the newly widowed that might prevent them from subsequent emotional problems. A target community was designated and five widows reached out to every newly widowed woman under the age of 65 in that community. The program demonstrated the value of early outreach, that is, that an unsolicited call from another widow was appreciated by the newly widowed. The widowed helper was able to use her own experience in helping the newly bereaved acknowledge and deal with her grief and then learning to find new direction in her life. This program became the model for grassroot efforts in many communities in the United States and abroad (Silverman, 1986). It also served as the model for the Widowed Persons Service sponsored by the American Association of Retired Persons (1988). In England it served as the model for the National Widows Service.

Vachon and her colleagues in Canada demonstrated the effectiveness of the Widow-to-Widow approach in a replication of the original program. They, however, had a controlled population of newly widowed women who were not invited to participate in the intervention. They identified a high distress group and a sample of these women were assigned to the intervention program. At 6, 12, and 24 months, the women in the intervention group reported better physical health, less anticipation of further difficulty in adjusting to their loss, less contact with old friends and more investment in new relationships than did control subjects. Lieberman and Videka-Sherman (1986) found that participation in mutual help groups had specific positive mental health effects as compared to a control group who did not have this experience.

Tracy and Toro (1989) compared natural or mutual help and professional helping processes. While different types of helpers were found to react differently to clients, all clients felt helped by a sequence in which helpers provided some direction in response to the client emotionally examining what was happening. Successful mutual help leaders were more likely to use self-disclosure as a helping technique. The most important part of Tracy and Toro's findings is that each of these types of helpers seem to be training the client in a unique manner of behavior and responses. Other studies have looked at the value of mutual help groups as compared to, for example, brief psychotherapy (Marmar et al., 1988; Lund, 1989). They juxtapose these two helping modalities as if they are mutually exclusive. They also look at the mutual help experience as if help that is provided is mainly in a group experience similar to what is offered in group therapy with the main difference being in the preparation and experience of the leader. No differences were found in outcome as far as who was leading the group (Lund, 1989). It may be that being in a group is a helpful experience to the newly bereaved as Yalom et al., (1988) observed. However, the help offered in one setting should not compete with help in another setting. They are not mutually exclusive, nor are they the same type of help.

What is ignored in these studies is that mutual help involves more than a group experience and that the context in which the help is provided may also impact on its success. In a mutual help organization, members are peers who make their own decisions about what happens and who can move from the role of recipient of help to that of helper (Silverman, 1976). Help is offered in many ways: through one-to-one outreach, telephone hotlines, social activities, newsletters, educational meetings, group discussions, legislation and advocacy activities, and through becoming leaders and helpers in turn. In a professionally led support group, members are screened by the agency and are in the subordinate role of client. They have no ongoing relationship to the agency and are not responsible for the continuing life of this helping experience. Help is primarily through psychological or educational counselling in group or in individual sessions (Lieberman & Borman, 1979; Silverman, 1976, 1980; Yalom et al., 1988).

Help in a mutual help setting has its own dynamic. Help is effective because people (1) find others so that they feel less alone and less unique, (2) have their feelings legitimized, (3) get specific information about their problems and a sense that there is something they could do about them, (4) have role models who could provide alternative ways of solving problems and with whom they could identify, (5) can and do assume responsibility for the ongoing life of the organization, and (6) find the ability to help others. As they move away from the death event, meaningful help also involves extended social activity. Their affiliations provide the opportunity to "repeople their lives" (Silverman, 1970).

The remainder of this chapter presents data on how this helping process is expressed in a mutual help experience. Data will focus on several aspects of the helping process: finding others like themselves, getting new perspectives on their widowhood, and becoming helpers in turn. Data is from a questionnaire that was mailed to members of several mutual help organizations for the widowed (Silverman, 1988a, 1988b, 1988c). Most of the members received unsolicited invitations to participate in the organization.

The Value of Finding Other Widowed People

Most people are surprised at their reaction to first meeting another widowed person. They did not expect such responsiveness:

> The people really understood what I was going through. I could bare my
> soul and no one turned a deaf ear.
> When I said Sunday was so long—it was nice to have someone else
> agree with me.

Most of these widows and widowers were involved with family and friends but meeting others "in the same boat" had a special meaning:

> I have tried, but meeting other widows in To Live Again are the only ones who understand; my closest friends who still have their husbands, I can feel—they almost think you can do whatever you please and they can't hear me when I try to let them know, so I have stopped trying.

Not only were there others to listen, to say "I felt the same way," but the others were there for as long as they were needed:

> Since we take time to listen to each other I got it out of my system by telling it over and over again about his last days, the conversations we had, the finding him dead, the doctor coming, seeing his body go out of the house.
> I often wondered how I would have survived. The first year all we did was share our feelings and emotions every step of the way.

Feelings were legitimaized and the widowed no longer felt so alone:

> I realized for the first time that I am not the only person who lost a spouse.
> I realized that the things I was experiencing and feeling were normal.
> It helped me get involved in new friendships. It kept me connected to others. My friends had disappeared and every other group I went to were couples.

People talked of developing a sense of optimism and hope as a result of this sharing. They also found role models:

> I began to see from others who had coped, who looked happy and had made it, that I had something to look forward to.

Information they received was as helpful as being listened to:

> The lectures were helpful and the grief workshops were very good. Widowed people need perspective on what is happening to them.

Learning from Others Like Themselves

The widowed began to see alternatives to how they defined themselves and how they lived their lives:

> You have to let widowed people know that there are no quick fixes, no easy answers, that through the hurts and upsets of a big adjustment one evolved into something that surprises even yourself, that each of us is loaded with gifts and untapped talents.

Several widows reflected on how their participation helped them change:

> The most important thing a widow must learn is to like herself and believe in herself and her own abilities. She has to learn to choose her own priorities in life. To Live Again taught me that.
> They never used the word "never," "just do it!" Tell yourself "I can do this" and it worked.

Some, especially the men, began talking about developing empathic qualities:

> I became much less selfish with my time for others. I became much more understanding of the problems of the newly widowed. It got me out with a lot more friends.

Women, in contrast, talked about new confidence they were developing, as well as their growing independence, and how the groups helped them achieve this:

> It (the organization) gave me permission to be a different person. It made me feel and understand that there is no written creed that says you have to be married to be happy.
> Not only did Widowed Persons Service occupy my time and my mind. I began to feel that I can do things on my own.
> They gave me suggestions, not rules. It became clear that I was going to have to make a new life for myself.

Helping Others

Both widows and widowers reported new ways of being connected to others through membership in these organizations. This was not simply because of the help they received but because of the new opportunities for mutuality that they found, not only in their social lives but in their ability to help others. These people had rediscovered Reissman's (1965) observation that helping others is a very effective way of helping oneself.

> Working with WPS has given me a purpose in life. It keeps me busy and allows me to give service to widowed persons, especially the newly bereaved. I need to be needed and I am.

For many women this role was a continuation of the one they had filled in their family. But now they found a new way of expressing themselves in the caretaking role:

> I can understand the newly widowed because I could not forget such a lost soul feeling as I had. I am better because in turn I am helping someone else.

The men, however, talked of helping themselves through helping others as a brand new experience:

> It's the secret—by helping others you help yourself. Other than my children, TLA and the work I do with it is the most important thing in my life. I feel I am really doing something worthwhile and it makes me feel a sense of real accomplishment.

Most people mentioned that the feeling of being needed gave them purpose in life. In the role of helper, people found a valuable and meaningful way of being connected to others and to themselves: "In helping others I help myself." This is the real meaning of mutual help—the exchange and mutuality that takes place between people as they cope with common problems.

Conclusions

The importance of connection to others and being involved in caring relationships cannot be underestimated, especially at times of stress in people's lives. Not only does care need to be offered but people also need to accept it as appropriate. It is not only the province of professionals mandated by society to provide this attention to people in need. It is beholden on each of us to be involved in helping and caring networks. These networks make the human condition viable and meaningful. Mutual help efforts are one such caring enterprise, and are particularly helpful when a death occurs.

References

American Association for Retired Persons. (1988). *Widowed persons service: Directory of services for the widowed in the United States and Canada.* Washington, DC: American Association for Retired Persons.

Barnett, R. C., Biener, L., & Baruch, G. K. (1987). *Gender & stress.* New York: Free Press.

Belle, D. (1982). *Lives in stress: Women and depression.* Beverly Hills: Sage.

Belle, D. (1987). Gender differences in the social moderators of stress. In R. C. Barnett, L. Beiner, & G. K. Baruch (Eds.), *Gender & stress* (pp. 257–277). New York: Free Press.

Belle, D. (1989). (Ed.). *Children's social networks and social supports.* New York: Wiley.

Borkman, T. (1978). Experiential knowledge: A new concept for the analysis of self-help. *Social Service Review*, 445–456.

Campbell, S., & Silverman, P. R. (1987). *Widower: When men are left alone.* New York: Prentice Hall.

Caplan, G. (1976). Family as a support system. In G. Caplan & M. Killilea (Eds.). *Support systems and mutual help.* New York: Grune & Stratton.

Cobb, S. (1976). Social support as a moderator of life stress. *Psychosomatic Medicine, 38*(5), 300–314.

Cook, J. A. (1988). Dad's double binds: Rethinking father's bereavement from a men's studies perspective. *Journal of Contemporary Ethnography, 17*(3), 285–308.

Dakoff, G. A., & Taylor, S. E. (1990). Victims, perceptions of social support: What is helpful for them? *Journal of Perspectives in Social Psychology, 58*(1), 80–90.

Eckenrode, J., & Gore, S. (1981). Stressful events and social supports: The significance of context. In B. H. Gottlieb (Ed.), *Social networks and social support* (pp. 43–68). Beverly Hills: Sage.

Garmezy, N. (1987). Stress, competence, and development: continuities in the study of schizophrenic adults, children vulnerable to psychopathology, and the search for stress-resistant children. *American Journal of Orthopsychiatry, 57*, 159–185.

Gartner, A., & Riessman, F. (1977). *Self-help in the human services.* San Francisco: Jossey–Bass.

Gilligan, C. (1982). *In a different voice.* Cambridge, MA: Harvard University.

Gottlieb, B. H. (Ed.) (1981) Social networks and social support. Beverly Hills: Sage.

Gottlieb, B. H. (1990, August). *Quandaries in translating support concepts to interviewers.* Paper presented at the Annual American Psychological Association Convention, Boston, MA.

Goffman, E. (1963). *Stigma: Notes on the management of spoiled identities.* Englewood Cliffs, NJ: Prentice-Hill.

Hamburg, D. A., & Adams, J. E. (1967). A perspective on coping: Seeking and utilizing information in major transitions. *Archives of General Psychiatry, 17,* 277–284.

Hughes, E. C. (1971). *The sociological eye.* Chicago: Aldine-Atherton.

Katz, A. H. (1970). Self-help organizations and volunteer participation in social welfare. *Social Work, 15*(1) 51–60.

Klass, D. (1988). *Parental grief: Solace and resolution.* New York: Springer.

Levinson, D. J. (1978). *The seasons of man's life.* New York: Knopf.

Lieberman, M. A., Borman, L. D., & Associates. (1979). *Self-help groups for coping with crisis.* San Francisco: Jossey-Bass.

Lieberman, M. A., and Videka-Sherman, L. (1986). The impact of self-help groups on the mental health of widows and widowers. *American Journal of Orthopsychiatry, 56,* 435–439.

Lopata, H. Z. (1988). Support systems of American urban widowhood. *Journal of Social Issues, 44*(3), 113–128.

Lund, D. A. (Ed.). (1989). *Older bereaved spouses: Research with practical applications.* New York: Hemisphere.

Lyons, N. P. (1989). Listening to voices we have not heard. In C. Gilligan, N. P. Lyons, & T. J. Hammer (Eds.), *Making connections: The relational worlds of adolescent girls at Emma Willard School* (pp. 30–72). Troy, NY: Emma Willard School.

Madera, E. J., & Meese, A. (1990). *The self-help sourcebook.* NJ: St. Clares-Riverside Medical Center.

Maddison, D., & Walker, W. L. (1967). Factors affecting the outcome of conjugal bereavement. *British Journal of Psychiatry, 113,* 1057–1067.

Marmar, C. R., Horowitz, M. J., Weiss, D. S., Wilner, N. R., & Katreider, N. B. (1988). A controlled trial of brief psychotherapy and mutual-help group treatment of conjugal bereavement. *American Journal of Psychiatry, 145*(2), 203–209.

Miller, J. B. (1986). *Toward a new psychology of women* (2nd ed.). Boston: Beacon Press.

Murphy, L. B. (1974). Coping, vulnerability, and resilience in childhood. In G. V. Coelb, D. A. Hamburg, & J. E. Adams (Eds.), *Coping and adaptation.* New York: Basic Books.

Osterweis, M., Solomon, F., & Greene, M. (1984). Bereavement intervention programs. In Osterweis, Solomon, & Green (Eds.), *Bereavement: Reactions, consequences, & care.* Washington, DC: National Academy.

Pancoast, D. L., Parker, P., & Froland, C. (Eds.). (1983). *Rediscovering self-help: Its role in social care.* Beverly Hills: Sage.

Pearl, A., & Riessman, F. (1965). *New careers for the poor.* New York: Free Press.

Powell, T. (1987). *Self-help organizations and professional practice.* Washington, DC: National Association of Social Workers.

The President's Commission on Mental Health. (1978). *A report to the president from the president's commission on mental health* (Vol. 1). Washington, DC: U.S. Government Printing Office.

Riessman, F. (1965). The "helper-therapy" principle. *Social Work, 10,* 27–32.

Shamgar-Handleman, L. (1986). *Israeli war widows: Beyond the glory of heroism.* Massachusetts: Bergin & Garvey.

Silverman, P. R. (1966). Services for the widowed during the period of bereavement. *Social work practice.* New York: Columbia University.

Silverman, P. R. (1969). *Study of spoiled helping: Clients who drop out of psychiatric treatment.* Unpublished doctoral dissertation, Brandeis University, Waltham, MA.

Silverman, P. R. (1970). A re-examination of the intake procedure. *Social Case Work, 51*, 625–634.

Silverman, P. R. (1976). The widow as caregiver in a program of preventive intervention with other widows. In G. D. Caplan & M. Killilea (Eds.), *Support systems and mutual help* (pp. 233–244). New York: Grune & Stratton.

Silverman, P. R. (1978). *Mutual help groups and the role of the mental health professional,* Washington, DC: U. S. Government Printing Office, NIMH, DHEW Publication No. (ADM) 78–646, Reprinted 1980.

Silverman, P. R. (1980). *Mutual help: Organization and development.* Beverly Hills: Sage.

Silverman, P. R. (1981). *Helping women cope with grief.* Beverly Hills: Sage.

Silverman, P. R. (1982). The mental health consultant as a linking agent. In D. E. Biegel & A. J. Naparstek (Eds.), *Community support systems and mental health* (pp. 238–249). New York: Springer.

Silverman. P. R. (1986). *Widow to widow.* New York: Springer.

Silverman, P. R. (1987). The impact of parental death on college-age women. *Psychiatric Clinics of North America, 10,* 387–404.

Silverman, P. R. (1988a). Research as process: Exploring the meaning of widowhood. In S. Reinharz & G. Rowles (Eds.), *Qualitative gerontology* (pp. 217–240). New York: Springer.

Silverman, P. R. (1988b). In search of selves: Accommodating to widowhood. In L. A. Bond (Ed.), *Families in transition: Primary prevention programs that work* (pp. 200–220). Beverly Hills: Sage.

Silverman, P. R. (1988c). Widowhood as the next stage in the life cycle. In H. Z. Lopata (Ed.), *Widows* (pp. 170–189). Durham, NC: Duke University.

Silverman, P. R., Mackenzie, D., Pettipas, M., & Wilson, E. (Eds.). (1975). *Helping each other in widowhood.* New York: Health Sciences.

Silverman, P. R., & Worden, J. W. (1992). Children's reactions to the death of a parent in the early months after the death. *American Journal of Orthopsychiatry, 62*(1), 93–104.

Stephens, S. (1972). *Death comes home.* (1st American Ed.), New York: Morehouse-Barlow.

Tracey, T. J., & Toro, P. A. (1989). Natural and professional help: A process analysis. *American Journal of Community Psychology, 17*(4), 443–458.

Vachon, M. L. S., & Stylianos, S. K. (1988). The role of social support in bereavement. *Journal of Social Issues, 44*(3), 175–190.

Yalom, I. D., Vinogradov, S., Stone, W. N., & Maclennan, B. W. (1988). Bereavement groups: Techniques and themes. *International Journal of Group Psychotherapy, 38*(4), 419–446.

Sixteen

Loss of a Pet

Morris A. Wessel

Morris A. Wessel, M.D., received his B.A. from Johns Hopkins in 1939 and his M.D. from Yale in 1943. He continued graduate training at Babies Hospital, New York, and at the Mayo Foundation in Rochester, Minnesota. In 1948 he joined Yale Rooming-In Project, a clinical program serving mothers, fathers, and infants during the lying-in period. Dr. Wessel entered pediatric practice in 1951 and retired recently after 42 years of serving parents and children in the New Haven, Connecticut area. A study that Dr. Wessel and colleagues titled "Paroxysmal Fussiness in Infancy Sometimes Called Colic" published in 1954 is regarded as a classic in the field.

In 1969 Dr. Wessel joined Dean Emeritus Florence Wald of the School of Nursing, the Reverend Edward Dobihal, Chaplain of Yale New Haven Hospital, and Dr. Ira Goldenberg, Professor of Surgery at Yale Medical School in a study of patients experiencing a terminal illness.

This group concluded in 1971 that there was need for a separate facility for terminally ill patients in the New Haven community. This decision led the members of this group to work intensively planning and eventually establishing what is now the Connecticut Hospice in Branford, Connecticut.

Dr. Wessel became particularly interested in bereavement in children and adolescents. In 1993 he received the American Academy of Pediatrics Practitioner Research Award. In the citation Dr. Howard Pearson, President of the American Academy of Pediatrics noted:

"Through his office research, Dr. Wessel has influenced a generation of pediatricians, family practitioners, and child psychiatrists.... As a renaissance physician and scholar, Dr. Wessel has been a master of the office-based observational study. In his life-long pursuit of new knowledge about common issues in pediatrics, he serves as an outstanding model of a practitioner researcher.... With more than 200 publications and presentations, Dr. Wessel has written about such diverse topics as colic, feeding techniques, thyroid dysfunction in pregnancy, adoption, corporal punishment, and death and dying.... More recently, he has provided much insight and understanding to the process and impact of death and dying in children and their families."

A Bit of History

Twenty five years ago I was invited by Florence Wald, formerly Dean of the Yale University School of Nursing, to participate in a study concerned with the care of terminally ill patients at the Yale New Haven Hospital. The observations and deliberations of this group over a period of several years led to the conclusion that there was definite need for a specific program and institution to provide home care and in-patient care for terminally ill patients. This led to the planning 20 years ago for what is now the Connecticut Hospice in Branford, Connecticut.

Participation in these discussions alerted me to consider the bereavement process as family members experienced the loss of a beloved individual. I became aware of how little attention I focused on the needs of children at these tragic moments. I wondered how I as a primary pediatrician might support and enhance the capacity of parents and children to deal with significant losses. My interest in this sphere soon was recognized by parents and children in my practice and by my colleagues. I am pleased that as I reflect on the past 20 years I can report that discussions of tragic losses became accepted in my role as a primary pediatrician. Many parents found it as appropriate to seek my advice when a death occurred as it was when a child presented symptoms of an upper respiratory infection!

I assumed that my experiences in handling tragic losses in families I served would enable me to adapt with equanimity when my dog Dobisch suffered inoperable cancer of the jaw. After much deliberation and soul searching, her increasing weakness, apathy, and poor appetite motivated me to take her to the veterinarian to be "put to sleep." I was unprepared for the intensity of my grieving over the death of my companion of 14 years. The preparation and publication (*New Haven Register*, June 29, 1990) of this article eased considerably my mourning process.

An Unexpected Grief

Dobisch, our 14-year old Siberian Husky-German Shepherd died a few weeks ago. This loss is far more painful than I ever imagined.

I miss our walks, which she demanded at 10:15 each evening.

I now become restless at this hour; I try to read the newspaper, or a novel, or watch television, but to no avail. Nothing relieves the empty feelings that well up as I realize that the evening jaunts of many years duration are no longer possible.

What is it about my relationship with Dobisch that produced joy, comfort, and relaxation for the fourteen years she was a member of our family?

For me, owning a dog meant the anticipation upon entering my home of having Dobisch rise from her slumbers, wander to the front door, and greet me warmly—jumping up, barking, and wagging her tail.

I took great comfort in knowing that she always would be there to offer this royal greeting.

I continue now as I open the door to call her name, still hoping she might appear from somewhere.

Brisk walks or meandering strolls in the evening were more than valuable healthful exercises. Our nightly excursions possessed a deeper meaning.

One satisfaction was the lack of demands in the relationship. True, when Dobisch wanted to go for a walk she would bark and even rub against my body, until I roused myself from the television or the newspaper.

But once out the door, we could walk in utter silence, or I could talk aloud and she would look up at me with an approving expression. I have organized many speeches and articles by talking aloud to Dobisch as we wandered through the neighborhood.

On other occasions, when things weren't going well, I bitterly cursed the world shouting in anguish or in anger. I have cried aloud during these jaunts.

Dobisch would look up, rub against my legs, communicating that she cared and wished to comfort me during these stressful moments. She demanded little in return. A pat on the head and a kind word were all she sought to let her know that I appreciated her efforts.

As a pediatrician, my days are full of demands. Each encounter with a child, parent, or colleague, important and satisfying as it may be, does drain one's energy. The limited demands of a dog, who gives much and expects little, provides a welcome relief from an exhausting day filled with intense interpersonal experiences.

On our evening strolls, we met an astonishing number of neighbors and over the years I developed great respect for my neighborhood.

On any evening I have met a virologist, neurologist, surgeon, psychologist, teacher, my own rabbi and cantor, a Protestant minister at one of the churches on the Green, and a Nobel Prize economist, to mention only a few friends who also took evening jaunts with their dogs.

Conversations, which usually began with talk of the dog's health, what veterinarian they used, or what food they gave their pets, soon led into discussions of the daily events in the medical and university community, city, national, and international politics. I would rarely meet these friends if not for our dogs.

Those evening walks with Dobisch were rejuvenating and relaxing moments offering time for soul-searching, friendly conversations, introspection, and an opportunity to put the tensions of daily living aside. I miss those nightly jaunts a great deal.

Part Two

Issues for Caregivers

Seventeen

What Do I Say?

Gail Egan Sansivero

Gail Egan Sansivero, R.N., M.S., OC.N. is currently the Clinical Nurse Specialist in Oncology-Hematology at the Albany Medical Center in Albany, New York. In addition to her experience in medical oncology, Ms. Sansivero has practiced in surgical oncology and hospice home care.

Ms. Sansivero's areas of clinical interest include symptom management, vascular access, and methods of drug administration. Her research interests focus on clinical decision making for both health professionals and people coping with cancer. Ms. Sansivero speaks frequently on clinical oncology nursing topics, and is active in the Oncology Nursing Society. She is the mother of two freckle-faced redheads, Brendan and Meghan.

Perhaps the most frequent question posed by students and neophyte health-care practitioners working with dying patients is, "What do I say"? This request for "scripting" of practitioner and patient–family interactions reflects a variety of emotions and uncertainties. And although shared most often by caregivers with limited life or professional experience, all of us sometimes wonder just what to say.

Wondering what to say implies an assumption that communication will occur or that there is something to say. Whether verbal or nonverbal, effective and clear or not, messages are exchanged. These messages may reflect mood or information and sometimes are emotionally charged. It is at the emotional times that the novice may ask, "How do I maintain my professional demeanor and still communicate intimately with my patients? What should I say?"

Feeling at a loss for words can increase anxiety and contribute to feelings of professional inadequacy. For many health professionals, especially those in acute care settings, the imminent death of a patient in itself heightens tension. Concerns for psychological comfort of the family, psychological and physical comfort of the patient, and other concerns of the moment (other patients, administrative responsibilities) combine to place multiple demands on the individual at once.

In addition, one must remember that, despite their knowledge base, caregivers are the products of their society and thus share anxieties and uncertainties about cancer and other life-threatening illnesses. These illnesses, particularly cancer, are often dreaded, and considered hopeless and incurable despite data that suggest otherwise. In fact, in a study of registered nurses on general medical-surgical units, nurses identified cancer patients as terminally ill significantly more often than patients ill from other chronic illnesses (Groszek, 1981). Particularly for those in acute inpatient tertiary care settings, it may seem that almost everyone with cancer has unusual, advanced, or (at least potentially) incurable disease. The more than five million cancer survivors in the United States alone may be viewed as individual and "miraculous" success stories, isolated from what is the norm in the professional's daily work experience.

This acute care system is ill equipped, in many cases, to handle the needs of the dying patient and family and to support effective caring (versus curing) interventions. Often focused on limiting costs, minimizing complications and length of stay, acute care hospitals are task-focused operations. High acuity and caregiver shortages may mean long, sometimes frantic, shifts. Kudos go to the nurse manager who is at or under budget, the physician whose patients enter and leave the system quickly and without complications, and to the social worker who finds caregiving resources in the community at a moment's notice. Caregivers sitting at the patient's bedside are routinely interrupted with requests for assistance with other patients or for information, prefaced by the classic line, "Are you doing anything right now?" The message to both caregivers and patient is clear—physical activity demonstrates the provision of care. Talking, touching for comfort, and supportive presence have become, in the view of some, expendable in the hospital of the nineties.

Several forces have combined to place this type of pressure on patients, caregivers (both professional and significant others), and health-care institutions. Occurring within a few short years of each other were the worsening of the health-care provider shortage and the implementation of the prospective payment system. Staffing shortages have been attributed to a decline in the number of college-age students, a perception of decreased desirability of health care as a career, and expanding career options particularly among women (who traditionally chose caring professions).

These shortages have been exacerbated by increasing acuity in both ambulatory and inpatient settings. Technological advances have allowed us to shorten recovery periods in acutely monitored situations, and also to intervene in specific disorders previously thought to be difficult or impossible to have a significant impact on. But these advances have been costly, and overall health-care costs in the United States have risen to account for larger and larger proportions of the gross national product. Legislative and consumer pressure to limit these costs resulted in prospective payment systems, which reimburse at a given level for a given diagnosis. Opportunities to enhance reimbursement for a particular patient are purposefully limited by health-care reimbursement systems to the most costly of exceptional cases.

Although these economic and labor forces have had a major impact on the health-care system, the expectations of consumers for compassionate and supportive care have not necessarily lessened. In fact, at a time when fear and apprehension about survival, treatment options, and quality of life may be of primary concern, the patient may expect particularly helpful and supportive communication from health professionals.

The Beginning Health-Care Provider

Many factors contribute to a beginning practitioner's discomfort in dealing with dying patients. She or he is likely to have very limited, if any, direct personal experience with death and dying. Because most Americans die in hospitals, the average individual's first experience with dying is likely to occur here. The opportunity to experience death in the home among supportive family and community members is rare. In addition, family participation in preparation of the body is routinely delegated to professional funeral home directors. So the health-care practitioner finds him or herself in a clinical situation with a dying patient without really knowing what to expect. The health-care practitioner may have seen a dead body before, but not an actual death. These can be very different experiences.

She or he probably has questions about what the death will be like, questions that may be asked by the patient's family (e.g.; "Will he bleed to death?", "Will he choke?"). The beginning practitioner's knowledge base of specific disease processes may make it difficult to anticipate and respond appropriately to the patient's physical needs. Managing epidural catheters, dealing with patient-controlled analgesia devices, and implementing creative strategies to decrease dyspnea are skills that are usually developed during years of practice. In addition, interventions unlikely to impact on the patient's status or comfort may be ordered by medical practitioners expert in acute care but poorly versed in palliative care.

Despite the growth of the hospice movement in the United States, many patients/families are faced with care dilemmas and limited options. Adequate home care (hospice or otherwise) is still difficult or impossible to obtain in many communities across the country. Physicians may feel pressured by institutions' utilization management departments or by third-party payors to justify patient stays by ordering diagnostic tests or interventions whose results and implementation do nothing to change the ultimate outcome or to increase comfort, and that may, in fact, contribute to discomfort.

This reliance on the known "tools of the trade" has an effect on the dying process in several ways. First, it may decrease anxiety for health-care professionals who are accustomed to a "cure" orientation. The performance and scrutiny of these tasks allow the nurse and physician to focus on the physiological—on numbers and films and documents rather than on the patient, the individual. These data are familiar, understandable, and give practitioners something concrete to do. Of course, for many terminal patients, this type of intervention, particularly extensive diagnostic workups, makes no difference in either the quantity or quality of their life. The performance of routinized tasks, however, is often familiar and comforting to families, who have visible evidence that something is being done and can focus on numbers ("What's his blood pressure?", "Oh, his temperature is better"). This focus is manageable in scope and may introduce a dialogue, or topic of conversation, between professionals and family. These procedures may also serve to divert attention from more emotional and stressful issues or problems in the patient's family.

Because fewer deaths occur at home (NCHS, 1988), the beginning health-care practitioner (as well as the public) may have unrealistic expectations about death and dying. If one's experience is limited to depictions of death in the mass media, one would think that death is generally rapid and relatively painless—with perhaps a few short words of closing verbalized by the dying person to a loved one, then closed eyes, a droop of the head and death—all rather neat and tidy except for a bit of blood here and there. The reality of prolonged dying with wasting (cachexia), emotional distress, and sometimes severe physical distress is, at the least, disconcerting. Air hunger, pain, diarrhea, anorexia, and tumor pressure can be symptoms difficult to control even in experienced hands. Many patients die slowly, over weeks and months. During this time, everyone (professionals and family alike) may experience physical and emotional exhaustion from the continuing demands of the situation and the caregivers' needs for support.

Fear in working with dying patients is common. Fear may be related to the elements already discussed (e.g., limited knowledge, lack of experience) or an aversion to dying patients. It would be naive to think that health-care practitioners learn to easily accept patients' deaths and become "used" to them. Although many professionals do learn to handle these situations effectively and in fact seek them out because of their importance, others become involved only when necessary and avoid working with dying patients. This "cure versus care" dichotomy applies to many health-care professions. Health-care providers select specialties that bring them more or less close to dying and death.

The Experienced Health-Care Provider

Compared with a neophyte colleague, the experienced health-care provider is much more likely to possess expertise in the clinical area and to know how to work effectively within the organization in which he or she is employed. Clinical situations are managed effectively, and the individual is able to predict patient needs and anticipate deterioration (Benner, 1984). The experienced health-care practitioner has worked with the realities of clinical practice—the resuscitation attempts, complex symptom management, desperate patients and families. Opportunities to accumulate a repertoire of important knowledge and skills have occurred over time. The ability to integrate these experiences, to enhance professional and personal skills, sets apart the experienced health-care practitioner.

He or she is able to use and respond to "gut" instincts (which actually may be a subconscious, rapid and comprehensive assessment) in dealing with imminent problems. The experienced health-care practitioner can care for patients and families without becoming entangled in complex family situations. He or she celebrates the individuality of those for whom she cares, and makes life after death a reality by making the best of her patients a part of herself. This seasoned caregiver is able to say good-bye, to grieve, and then to go on. He or she is continually challenged in professional practice, yet is able to respond quickly and precisely, analyzing seemingly isolated complaints and responding in the context of the whole situation.

Ongoing Problems

The organizational system, although familiar, may be a continuing source of stress if it does not support the health-care practitioner's ability to practice in a manner consistent with his or her values. Health-care systems frequently have an impact on clinical practice in a variety of ways such as setting quotas for number of patients seen or procedures performed, or by placing extensive bureaucratic demands on clinical staff (removing the most expert from the bedside). The frustration experienced can result in a commitment to change the system from within, to accept the system's limits and its influence on care, or to resign.

For the experienced and inexperienced practitioners in almost any speciality, identification with the patient/family is a reality of clinical practice. Some practitioners find it difficult to work with parents with young children and many choose not to work with children with cancer. Others may find that working with older adults is too much of a reminder of an ill parent or grandparent. Recognizing our own vulnerabilities is a healthy component of self-assessment. It is up to each individual to determine whether these emotional "Achilles' heels" serve to heighten empathy and ability to care, or cripple objectivity.

Whatever the conclusion, one cannot care effectively for others while ignoring one's own needs. The volume of caring energy each of us has to give must be replenished through relationships, laughter, physical activity, creative expression, or other sources of joy and meaning. As C. W. Metcalf (1987) notes, "You can't give away what you don't have." Any of these activities helps us place perspective on the personal and professional elements of our lives.

Patients and Families

For patients and families, a variety of factors have an impact on communication with each other and other members of the health-care team. Both stress and fear can inhibit verbal inquiry and conversation. The stressors can be associated with concerns about a disease, its symptoms or prognosis, the health-care environment, family dynamics, and social mores. For example, a patient may be reluctant to ask questions for fear that his inquiry will be interpreted as meddling in the health professional's business. Another patient may feel inadequate with the language of medicine, and feel embarrassed in posing questions to the health-care team. All these people share, to one degree or another, dependence on the health-care professions for information, symptom management, advice, and direct care. The patient may be uncertain about treatment choices, if offered, and the relative value of various interventions. For dying patients and their caregivers, more so than ever, benefits of possible therapies are weighed against economic, psychologic, and physical risks. Solutions to clinical problems in the patient's past (e.g., treatment of minor infections or gallstones) may seem simple in comparison to the profoundly complex decisions of living and dying.

For some patients, the symptoms associated with their disease or its treatment make conversation difficult. For the patient with a laryngectomy or tracheostomy, nonverbal methods of communication exist but may require a significant investment of energy. Other patients experience gastrointestinal distress, tumor pressure, weakness, malaise, and pain, all of which have an impact on an individual's desire and ability to communicate. Symptom-management strategies may also affect communications as they alter consciousness, create fatigue, or disturb cognition.

The health-care environment itself, with high-tech equipment and a perception of depersonalization, can contribute to difficulty in communicating. Health-care practitioners, typically in groups, make "rounds" to visit patients, outnumbering the patient sometimes by as much as 10:1. Physicians, nurses, and others may stand in white coats (sometimes identified by hospital identification tags) far above the patient and talk in numbers and professional jargon. They are likely to stay only a few moments. In this intimidating setting, patients frequently forget to ask their questions and almost certainly decide against broaching more sensitive topics such as sexuality. In contrast, for some patients the hospital may be identified as a very safe place: a place where caregivers are not shocked by intimate questions and needs, a place where someone who knows what to do will respond in the event urgent care is needed. In this case, both patients and family may abdicate responsibility for the provision of direct care while accepting the strictures imposed by the institution.

The patient's home provides an entirely different venue for interaction. Here it is more often the patient or family who is in control, with the health professional as a guest. Statements about values and preferences abound in the form of decorating style, family portraits, and choice of home activities. It is much easier for most patients to be themselves in this setting, especially with consistent caregivers with whom they are comfortable.

Talking with Dying Patients

In thinking about talking with dying patients and their families, a few guidelines may be helpful. Perhaps most important is to convey caring for the patient. This can be done in a variety of ways (verbal and nonverbal) that are as unique as the individual. Simple presence during quiet moments, technical procedures, and happy times—these moments of closeness are important. A soothing touch during a dressing change or bath, a hug, or even eye contact communicates investment in the patient. The words chosen are not as important as the feeling of caring—this will come through in the most inarticulate of interactions. There are always creative ways to communicate with patients who do not speak English or patients who cannot speak at all. These same methods are used to a lesser extent in more usual, verbal interactions and enhance (or contradict) our verbal messages. These communication skills, and the ability to detect nonverbal clues, are important in establishing rapport.

A basic yet sometimes overlooked aspect of dialogue with patients is the establishment of who the person is—the person beneath the high-tech gadgets, the individual in institutional garb. Many patients are delighted when interest is expressed in their personal lives, and willingly share stories about family, careers, and experiences. Families and friends may be willing to share stories if the patient is unable to verbalize.

These stories, this history, can be kept alive in the institutional setting by placing posters, photos, and cards in the patient's room. Even in critical care units, a photo or two can be placed in clear plastic and taped to the bed rail so the patient can view it. Tape players (with earphones if necessary) can provide familiar, soothing, and happy music, for distraction during procedures and comfort at night. Personal objects and hobbies should be accommodated when at all possible. Although this attention to personalizing the hospital environment may crowd already limited space, each object can provide us clues about the individual entrusted to our care. How much more fulfilling for health-care professionals to care for someone they can get to know as an individual, rather than someone to whom they cannot relate.

Patients frequently describe as very important "the little things" that health-care professionals do. They include closing doors for private conversations, equalizing heights to promote eye contact and dialogue, introducing oneself by name and role, and touching. These aspects of communication can quickly become overlooked by professionals in a work environment that has become, to them, very familiar and comfortable. Patients, however, notice this attention to detail, and, in my experience, appreciate the concern it demonstrates.

Establishing a trusting, caring relationship with patients can be done by expressing an interest in the patient and family as unique individuals, by communicating caring and sensitivity, and by presenting oneself as an "askable" professional. The "askable" professional is knowledgeable in the clinical area in general and in the patient's case in particular, and is approachable to questions, rather than aloof or defensive. This "askable" practitioner invites the patient and family to participate in decision making and problem solving while remaining available for expert advice.

Having Fun Is Okay

Sometimes staff and families behave around dying patients as though they are in a library or church. Movements and conversation become muted and limited. Lights may be dimmed, and extraneous noise eliminated. Although such an environment may be peaceful and relaxing, lack of any activity may promote "death-watch" situations in the patient's room. In these situations, the family surrounds the bed, but does little talking or touching. Each visitor is monitored. The patient's movements and needs are paramount but are anticipated with anxiety. It becomes quite stressful for everyone involved to maintain this level of attention in so narrow a focus.

It is often helpful to encourage a more normal pattern of activity. Simulating the patient's home environment and making a hospital room an expression of the patient's personality can be a lot of fun. Decorations such as posters, photos, handmade blankets, recreation equipment, music, and other individual expressions, all tell us something about the person: one woman who continued to wear her own clothes (not pajamas) and kept a small spinning wheel in her room; another young woman (manager of a college hockey team) kept sports photos and hockey sticks in her room, and wore only the team uniform. These familiar items not only made statements about their interests and joys, but also made the hospital a more comfortable place for them. Caregivers enjoy visiting these patients, because they feel they are able to make personal connections quickly.

One can use these situations to learn more about a particular patient, even one who is unable to respond. Questions such as "Tell me about Jane and what she is like" or "What does this teddy bear mean to Joe?" invite the family to share memories and provide us the opportunity to personalize interactions. Favorite tapes can be played when the family must leave, or stories can be retold during physical care.

For many patients it is comforting to know that life continues, that their family continues its usual pattern. Encouraging families to participate in normal activities (card playing, needlework, etc.) and conversation at the bedside helps many patients relax. Even if unable to participate in the interaction, the patient can simply enjoy listening to familiar voices and sounds.

Humor is a coping strategy utilized by many health-care practitioners and patients in dealing with stressful environments. Although little research exists regarding the specific benefits of humor and laughter, the data available suggest that patients utilizing humor may cope effectively with stress and have higher perceived morale (Simon, 1988).

Humor may serve several functions in the clinical setting, from reducing tension to communicating messages among friends and professionals in an indirect manner (Simon, 1989). The value of a creative and open sense of humor can be incorporated into daily clinical practice, not only through jokes and the sharing of ancedotes, but also through funny movies, photos, and skits. These and other enjoyable activities may assist in developing relationships between health-care practitioners and patients by creating a shared closeness, one in which alternative methods of thinking can be explored (Bellert, 1988).

Questions from Patients

In the hospital setting there are some fairly routine questions—questions we ourselves might ask were the circumstances similar.

"Am I Dying?"

This question may be asked to confirm an earlier message, to clarify information, to seek a prognosis, or rhetorically. It tests the trust and values of the professional-patient relationship. Fortunately in the 1990s, truth in information exchange between physicians and patients is the norm (as compared with the early years of cancer therapy when many patients were told neither their diagnosis nor prognosis).

It is important to assess the situation or context in which this question is asked. Specific physical symptoms, events, or professional behaviors may have precipitated this inquiry. (Simple admission to a cancer unit may be enough for some patients to ask this!) For some patients, a yes/no answer is not what is sought despite the apparent direct nature of the question. Asking the patient, "Why do you ask?" or "What makes you ask?" may assist the practitioner in getting at the patient's underlying concerns. As with the child who asks, "Where did I come from?" (seeking information on geographic location versus biological development), the patient may be communicating uncertainty and anxiety more than the request for a simple answer. Frequently the patient is most acutely concerned with a recent clinical change (i.e., onset of dyspnea, increased pain, etc.), which has been interpreted as an ominous or uncertain sign.

If a direct answer is really what is requested, a simple "yes" (without explanation) is too harsh a response, in my opinion. (Gentle truth is always better). Better would be a description or summary of the patient's current status with a realistic outlook for the immediate future. An estimate of longevity is not necessarily called for, though it should be given in terms of a range of time if specifically asked for.

A follow-up can be, "What about dying concerns you?" Concerns about pain and being alone are common, and often outweigh fears about dying itself. By asking such an open-ended question, the health-care practitioner communicates to the patient a willingness to discuss dying and what it means to that individual.

"What Would You Do if You Were Me?"

This is an uncomfortable question that can really put caregivers in an awkward position. No one knows for sure what he or she would do in the same circumstances, which is an honest and direct answer that can be used. In addition, it is important to make sure that the individual has enough information to make treatment and care choices, and to feel comfortable with those decisions.

Assisting families to come to consensus in these areas may also ease stress for patients, who may be trying to please loved ones with their choices. Interventions that reduce situational anxiety may also help patients process information, weigh choices, and make decisions (Scott, 1983; Welch-McCaffrey, 1985). An intimate knowledge of the patient and family will make it easier for the health-care practitioner to guide them in clarifying options and choosing one consistent with moral beliefs and cultural values.

"How Will I Cope with the Pain?"

Unfortunately, the myth of intractable cancer pain still exists in the United States. Fear of pain and of being unable to "stand it" is common. The reality is that many patients with cancer experience pain. Various studies estimate the incidence of pain in patients with advanced cancer at 50–80 percent (Portenoy, 1989). Of those who experience pain, creative pharmacologic and nonpharmacologic techniques exist that can effectively manage pain while maintaining quality of life. Patient/family education about pain etiology and pain therapy can alleviate many concerns, and free the patient to concentrate on other activities. Of course, all efforts should be made to control pain with limited treatment related side effects (e.g., somnolence, constipation, etc.)

Other Fears. Other fears expressed by dying patients include the loss of control—of one's self, of one's life, of one's body, of one's identity (Pattison, 1977). The many dimensions of loss of control and dignity are complex and may be intertwined. A basic message health-care practitioners can give to patients for reassurance is that no matter what happens, the patient is still an individual with personal preferences; that changes in body image or loss of functions do not the person make. In a trusting relationship, the patient may be able to ask for support to calm these fears. A recent patient who was quite meticulous in her personal grooming was able to ask her nurse, "When I am unable to put my make-up on for myself, will anyone care enough to do it for me?" Encouragement and support from health-care practitioners who assist the patient in identifying those activities over which the patient does have influence may help. Assurances can also be given regarding the presence of staff nearby to respond to needs and concerns, and plans can be made to involve significant others in staying with and assisting the patient.

"What Should I Tell My Family?"

Concerns about how and what to tell loved ones about dying and prognosis sometimes prompt patients to ask for guidance. It is optimal that the patient be told diagnostic and prognostic information with his or her significant other, so that a support system is immediately available. The patient and family are then hearing the same information, and can assist one another in interpreting it later on. Involving loved ones in this process also communicates the health-care team's acknowledgment of the importance of a family focus of care.

So many times patients are worried that either they or their families will "fall apart" when discussing dying. A typical conversation between the wife of a dying man (WDM) and a health-care provider (HCP) might be:

WDM: I can't talk to my husband about this, but he knows he's dying.

HCP: What is it about talking with your husband about dying that worries you?

WDM: I don't know—I just can't. I'll cry.

HCP: You'll cry.

WDM: I'll cry and I won't be able to stop, and then he will cry.

HCP: You would both be crying.

WDM: Yes.

HCP: And then what would happen?

WDM: We would both cry...and then, I don't know.

HCP: What's the worst that you think might happen if you talked to him and you would both cry?

WDM: That we would cry, and I can't stop.

This typifies the "double-bind conspiracy," when a wife cries for 20 minutes outside her husband's room, then quickly dabs her eyes and enters his room and attempts to act as though nothing is wrong. Does her husband really not see this? He may, but may also want to protect her, or protect her need to protect him, etc. When asked if it would be all right for their spouses to cry in front of them, most people in my practice say it is. Yet in the interests of control and protection, and perhaps because of fear and uncertainty about how to proceed, a conspiracy of silence often exists.

Fortunately, people are not like Humpty Dumpty—"falling apart" does not mean that one cannot be put back together again—that control, perspective, and calm cannot be regained. Holding in tears and sorrow takes a tremendous amount of emotional energy and is difficult to maintain for long periods in stressful situations. Sharing sorrow allows family members to grieve together, and to support one another, share information, plan together, and begin to mobilize resources.

Allowing patients the freedom and support to speak from the heart to their families may be all that is needed. It may be helpful to tell families that their loved one wishes to speak to them about dying, so that they are prepared and ready. In some cases it is helpful for the health-care practitioner to offer to facilitate these family discussions or simply to be present to answer questions. By fostering an environment conducive to this type of sharing, the health-care practitioner demonstrates caring for personal needs of the patient and family.

"Is There Hope?"

Hope is a broad concept, with individual meaning. Hope speaks not only (and not always) about longevity, but perhaps most important, about meaning and values. Scanlon (1989) describes the hoping person as one who expects to attain some good in the future that is personally meaningful. Brown (1989) says hope is not a single act, but is a process of feeling, thought, and action that may change with time but is characterized by coping behaviors that focus on achieving a realistic goal.

Asking the patient, "What do you hope for?" may elicit unexpected responses. Hope does not necessarily imply that the patient is unrealistic or uninformed about the future. Where one might think that the patient would say he wanted to live many more years, many patients cite an upcoming event (birth, marriage, graduation) as a goal or describe an interaction or quality of life wished for ("I hope I see my grandson again", "I want to be able to be pain free for a few days"). Often these goals can be approached, if not necessarily attained. These goals often have a short-term focus and health-care practitioners can support the patient's hopefulness through interventions to enhance the patient's self-esteem and self-confidence. Reviewing past accomplishments and current strengths assist the patient to identify skills and mobilize resources toward goal attainment. The health-care practitioner can also become a partner with the patient in realistic goal setting and achievement, by providing appropriate clinical information and education, and instituting therapeutic interventions that support optimal function.

Behavior of Dying Patients

In addition to what they say, dying persons tell us much about how they feel by their behavior. Doors may be closed, curtains drawn, the patient unwilling to get out of bed, or the patient may act as if no illness or alteration in lifestyle has occurred. The patient may lash out in anger at everyone who enters his or her space. The patient may be inappropriately jovial. The variations in nonverbal expression are as individual and unique as is each patient. Interpreting these behaviors takes energy, persistence, and a willingness to risk becoming involved with a patient who may be asking for help.

Communicating acceptance of an individual's unwillingness to speak, especially in depressed patients, may come through touch and consistent assignment of caregivers. The caregiver who has regularly cared for a particular patient is more likely to be able to interpret nonverbal behavior simply because of experience with that patient. The informal knowledge of a patient's preference or routine is rarely documented in the patient's chart in a useful manner for other caregivers. Rather, this information is catalogued in the mind of the professional who cares most often for the patient and is used to influence the pattern of daily activities in the patient/health-care practitioner partnership. In this way, the interaction of the two individuals can become more individualized and intimate over time as each gains experience and sensitivity to the other.

Using quiet moments and touch with patients, though perhaps easiest to do in situations where a patient–professional partnership is established, are effective ways to communicate. Sharing silence, a hug, soothing massages, or simply holding a patient's hand can be personal statements of support, condolence, empathy, and caring. These "good touches" represent a very obvious form of reaching out. So often in inpatient environments, physical touching is done largely in the performance of technical and sometimes uncomfortable procedures.

The health-care practitioner can also provide the patient with acceptable outlets for emotions that are difficult to verbalize. The angry patient may be given a pillow to punch or exercise equipment to "work it out." The patient who is despairing can be given a hug, a box of tissues, and the presence of a caring professional. Music, art therapy, diversional recreational activities, and support groups are options for patients who may respond to creative interventions in expressing themselves.

Consistent interaction and a continual acceptance of the patients for themselves (no matter how difficult their behavior) gives the patients permission to express themselves without worry of alienation. Mood swings and changes in coping style are expected and should be accepted. Teaching the patient and family that frequent variations in mood are normal occurrences often relieves anxiety for the patient wondering about his or her own mental stability, or even neurologic disease.

Behavioral manifestations are as individual as each patient, and should be evaluated for meaning on an individual basis. Families may be helpful in interpreting behavior ("He always does that when he's worried") and suggesting helpful interventions.

Although the patient may be unwilling or unable to discuss a given behavior, thought, or feeling at the time, the health-care practitioner can note an observation of the patient's distress to let the patient know that the health-care practitioner is sensitive to the patient's cues. Commitment to assisting the patient to meet these needs must then follow.

Caring for Oneself and Others

Caring for dying patients can be emotionally draining and difficult. For a truly involved and committed health-care practitioner, much personal energy is utilized in clinical situations that demand an attentive, active listener who is capable of utilizing all his or her professional resources. So that this energy can be recycled continually into patient interactions, the health-care practitioner must initiate strategies to replenish this energy reserve.

A very basic way one can care for oneself is to make a commitment to practice in a manner consistent with one's own professional and personal values. The realities of the everyday demands in a busy institution may sometimes make doing so difficult, but the peace that results from a job well done is key to professional satisfaction and a clear conscience.

Coupled with a clear notion of one's professional values is an ever-expanding knowledge base. Acquiring appropriate theories and interventions (pharmacologic, communication skills, etc.) allows the practitioner to impact positively in a variety of clinical situations, to respond to a variety of needs. The curiosity, which drives the development of this scientific basis for practice, is stimulated with each new unusual clinical presentation or problem, so that knowledge is continually growing. This professional curiosity or thirst for intellectual stimulation should be supported in one's own career, and fostered in the mentorship of colleagues.

Peer- and self-review or critique is yet another method through which health-care practitioners can evaluate their strengths and weaknesses, and examine specific aspects of role performance. These reviews can be stimulating opportunities to validate skills, identify areas for further growth, and review accomplishments. Oftentimes, an honest, evaluative look at one's practice is helpful in maintaining a sense of perspective, preventing one from becoming inconsolable over a difficult professional issue or situation, and in restoring balance.

Maintaining an open posture to learning from patients and families is a wonderful way to contribute to one's personal and professional growth. For many practitioners, the gifts of wisdom and perspective gained from patient–family interactions are enduring reminders of positive partnerships in health care. Although we have but one opportunity to live our lives, our patients' lessons in courage and coping serve in some ways as rehearsals for those who learn from them. These lessons can be integrated into our own lives if we allow ourselves the sensitivity to hear and see them, and the humility to accept them.

Although bringing closure to relationships, particularly if intense or long-term, can be initially difficult, the ability, and need, to finish one's business is important in processing one's work. Saying good-bye requires an acknowledgment of the uniqueness of an individual, of what has transpired in a relationship. It is the beginning of processing all that has occurred, and of integrating these experience into ourselves. Bringing closure may occur when ending a relationship with a patient, when bidding a dying patient farewell, even at memorial services. The ability to articulate the process of closure serves as a component of the grieving process for special relationships, and allows us to complete one encounter so that energy may be mobilized for the next one.

For professional relationships to be mutually satisfying, opportunities must be made to give and receive peer support. Being able to support one another within and among health-care teams is another way to maintain morale and camaraderie in a stressful work setting. As with the open posture one takes with patients and families, an openness to the energy levels and concerns of our peers allows us to learn from another's perspective and to provide caring when needed. This ability to foster a safe and nurturing professional environment provides a strong base for the practitioner who is then free to move on to the more unpredictable world of bedside practice.

Summary

Working with dying patients can be a very rewarding and enriching experience. The opportunity to share significant life experiences with a patient and family is life affirming in many ways. Each patient can help each practitioner become a better person—to teach us about coping with adversity, about strength and love, and about what is really important in this world. The greatest tribute we can give them is that a part of them lives on in us and others whose lives they have touched. This may be the true meaning of life after death.

Case Studies

Celebrating Life Is a Part of Dying

Mary was a 66-year-old woman with metastatic small-cell lung cancer who lived in her home with her boyfriend of many years. Her three grown daughters lived nearby. I was privileged to be the hospice home-care nurse for Mary. Mary was bedbound most of the time because of metastatic disease and overall weakness. I visited her on a regular basis for symptom control and family support. One day Mary and I were sitting talking, she in her bed and I sitting beside her. I noticed the many rings she had on her hands. I asked her to tell me the story of each one of those rings, what its history was, what they meant to her, how she had come to have and wear them. And as we talked about each one, she came to the wedding band that she had on her right hand. She told me that this was a wedding band that she had bought for herself one day in the local "five and dime." At the time of her purchase, she was a clerk at the same store and had been teased by many of her coworkers for buying a wedding ring for herself. Mary and her boyfriend, Fred, had been in their relationship for almost 30 years. I asked, "Mary, why is it that you and Fred never got married?" She proceeded to tell me how her first husband left her when they were both very young and had three young children at home. She had never divorced him for a variety of reasons. A short time later, she met Fred and they lived together happily and raised the children in a typical family style. Legally, she was not free to marry Fred because she was never divorced. It turned out that her first husband had just recently died, however, so she was now really free to marry Fred. I'm not really sure why this occurred to me, but I said, "Mary, do you want to get married"? and she said, "Well, I'd love to marry Fred." It was obvious that they were very much in love with each other and very supportive of each other, having had a good relationship over all these years. So I said no more about it, and concluded my visit shortly thereafter.

On my way out, I stopped to talk with Fred (who had not been present during my conversation with Mary). I said, "Fred, would you like to get married?" And he looked at me and laughed a little bit as if I were joking. And I said, "No, Fred, would you like to marry Mary?" He started to cry because he had really wanted to marry Mary for the entire 30 years that they were together but had not been able to. He was as much in love with her that day as he had ever been. So I told him about the conversation I had had with Mary about her rings and that she had expressed an interest in getting married. I said, "If you want to get married, why don't you go talk to her about it?" I waited out near the front door and Fred went to Mary's bedside and got down on his knees and proposed to his companion of 30 years. At that point, I think everyone was crying. Needless to say, Mary said *yes*.

What is important to know is that, at this time, Mary was very, very sick. We anticipated that she would die within a week or so. She was very short of breath and had oxygen at all times. But Mary and Fred told me that they would like to get married right now! My job became that of coordinator to make this wedding become possible. In the next 48 hours, I and my coworkers at the hospice home-care program obtained a waiver on Mary's and Fred's blood tests, got a marriage license, arranged flowers and food, and so forth. Her three daughters were involved in all the planning, arranged for a minister, and planned a reception in the house. Two days later, Mary and Fred were married in their home. We helped Mary put on a wedding dress, although she was unable to get out of bed; she looked just lovely. Her family, physicians, and nurses were all in attendance at a beautiful event—one that we will never forget.

That night Mary and Fred stayed together in the house without any caregivers. My advice to them was to put all the side rails up on her hospital bed so neither one would fall out! Mary died three days later. Her wedding flowers were placed on her grave. It was a very memorable experience for Mary and Fred and their family and for all of us who had the privilege of working with Mary and Fred.

This Is My Experience

Jenny was a 56-year-old single woman with metastatic inflammatory breast cancer. She lived alone in a mobile home by the banks of a river with her two cats about whom she cared very deeply. She had numerous friends who lived in the area and who were very supportive and assisted her with activities of daily living. I saw Jenny on a regular basis; as her hospice home-care nurse, I provided support and assisted her at least once a day with dressing changes for very difficult management of inflammatory breast cancer lesions, which extended over her abdomen and onto her back. These dressings changes were very painful to Jenny and her method of coping with the stress and the pain was to "curse" during the procedure as a way of verbalizing what the whole experience meant to her.

This became a routine for us. Each day as I started to take her dressing off, Jenny would swear and curse and talk about how difficult this was for her and how angry she felt about it. Because we were very close, sometimes I joined in, validating for her how difficult it must be. One day after a month or so of doing this, I was the one to verbalize about this difficult experience. Jenny stopped me and looked at me and said, "It's not your breast!" I looked at her and said, "You're right!" Despite how much I had shared with Jenny of this difficult experience over quite a length of time, at that point I had overstepped my bounds and she had let me know it. She was the one who was experiencing the pain of dying with a cancer that was very difficult to manage and with such significant impact on her quality of life. Jenny and I maintained our relationship until she died, and she was a pleasure to work with. I will not forget her for teaching me about the difference between what a patient experiences and what a nurse experiences, and how not to overstep one's bounds and intrude on another's territory.

Sometimes I Don't Want To Talk about It

Nancy was a 33-year-old woman with widespread ovarian cancer. She was happily married to a very supportive man, and the mother of a four-year-old daughter. Nancy's disease and symptoms necessitated frequent inpatient stays, and over a three-year period, her condition steadily deteriorated despite aggressive therapy. Many staff nurses became very close to Nancy and her husband over the years, and for many, it was difficult to accept that Nancy's time was very limited.

I as the clinical nurse specialist, tried to visit Nancy at least every other day when she was in, and occasionally spoke to her on an out-patient basis. On one of her last admissions, I visited Nancy alone. She had at that point, two ostomies, a nasogastric tube, and had completed all therapy. We began talking about what was on her mind that day. One of her comments to me was noteworthy. She said, "You know, everyone comes in here and expects me to be crying. They think if I'm not looking sad or crying that I don't know I'm dying. I can't do that all the time. I know I'm dying, but I've got to live, too. I have to do my normal family things. I wish people would just come in and talk about usual stuff—jokes and things."

I shared her comments with the staff. They were relieved to know that Nancy understood the seriousness of her condition and agreed to "lighten up" their interactions with her. This exchange promoted a tone of interaction that was very helpful to Nancy and her family. She was able to tell us where she was emotionally, and allow herself and the staff to function in usual patterns as much as possible.

Nancy went home with multiple appliances, tubes, and IV pumps. She made arrangements for her daughter's kindergarten registration and was back within two months, when she died on the unit. Her husband visited the unit several times in the two years after Nancy's death to share memories and obtain support. Nancy's lesson to us, on *living* in the face of approaching death, is an important one. It is a lesson we would do well to remember.

References

Bellert, J. L. (1989). Humor: A therapeutic approach in oncology nursing. *Cancer Nursing, 12*(2): 65–70.

Benner, P. (1984). *From novice to expert.* Menlo Park, CA: Addison-Wesley.

Blanchard, C. O., LaBrecque, M. S., Ruckdeschel, J. C., & Blanchard, E. B. (1990). Physician behaviors, patient perceptions, and patient characteristics as predictors of satisfaction of hospitalzied adult cancer patients. *Cancer, 65(1):* 186–192.

Brown, P. (1989). The concept of hope: implications for care of the critically ill. *Oncology Nursing Forum, 9*(5): 97–105.

Dyck, S., & Wright, K. (1985). Family perceptions: The role of the nurse throughout an adult's cancer experience. *Oncology Nursing Forum, 12*(5): 53–56.

Groszek, D. (1981). Nurses' identification of patients as terminally ill. *Oncology Nursing Forum, 8*(4): 33–37.

Metcalf, C. W. (1987). Humor, life and death. *Oncology Nursing Forum, 14*(4): 19–21.

Morris, T. (1986). Coping with cancer: The positive approach. In Watson, M., & Greer, S. (Eds.); *Psychosocial issues in malignant disease.* (pp. 79–85) Oxford: Pergamon Press.

National Center for Health Statistics, U.S. Department of Health and Human Services, 1988.

Pattison, E. M. (1977). *The experience of dying.* Englewood Cliffs, NJ: Prentice-Hall.

Portenoy, R. K. (1989). Cancer pain. *Cancer, 63:* 2298–2307.

Scanlon, C. (1989). Creating a vision of hope: The challenge of palliative care. *Oncology Nursing Forum* 16(4): 491–496.

Scott, D. W. (1983). Anxiety, critical thinking and information processing during and after breast biopsy. *Nursing Research, 32*(1): 24–28.

Simon, J. M. (1988). Humor and its relationship to perceived health, life satisfaction, and morale in older adults. Dissertation, University of Texas at Austin.

Simon, J. M. (1989). Humor techniques for oncology nurses. *Oncology Nursing Forum, 16*(5) 667–670.

Spross, J. A., McGuire, D. B., & Schmitt, R. M. (1990). Oncology nursing society position paper on cancer pain, Part I. *Oncology Nursing Forum, 17*(4): 595–605.

Thorne, S. E. (1988). Helpful and unhelpful communications in cancer care: The patient perspective. *Oncology Nursing Forum, 15*(2) 167–172.

Welch-McCaffery, D. (1985). Cancer, anxiety, and quality of life. *Cancer Nursing, 8*(3): 151–158.

Yasko, J. M., & Fleck, A. (1984). Prospective payment (DRGs): What will be the impact on cancer care? *Oncology Nursing Forum, 11*(3): 63–72.

Eighteen

Satisfactions and Stresses for the Social Worker

Zelda Foster

Kay Davidson

Zelda Foster is chief social worker at the Department of Veterans Affairs, Brooklyn Medical Center. She has written on psychosocial issues in a wide range of areas including discharge planning, work with people with AIDS, and employee assistance programs.

Her investment in developing new services is demonstrated by her leadership in bringing to the Brooklyn VAMC a major center for treatment of homeless veterans, hospital-based home care, employee assistance, and adult day health-care programs.

Throughout her professional career, Ms. Foster continues to carry an enduring commitment to impacting the lives of dying patients and their families. She published a pioneering article in 1965 titled "Social Work Management of Fatal Illness," and served as first president and cofounder of the New York State Hospice Association. Although currently an educator and an administrator, her roots as an oncology social worker remain a guiding force in her personal and professional life.

Kay W. Davidson, D.S.W., is an associate professor at Hunter College School of Social Work in New York City. She brings to her current teaching position many years of experience in England and the United States as a practitioner and administrator in social work in health and mental-health care. Dr. Davidson has published articles and chapters on social work practice with families, social work in health care, and social work education. She has coedited, with Sylvia Clarke, Social Work in Health Care: A Handbook for Practice, *a two-volume compendium used by hospital social work administrators, practitioners, and teachers.*

Dr. Davidson has conducted research on support groups for social workers working with cancer patients and on hospital social work roles and functions, both in the United States and Britain. She is an active member of both the Society of Administrators Social Work in Health Care and the National Association of Social Workers and is on the editorial board of Social Work in Health Care *and a consulting editor for the* Journal of Teaching in Social Work.

*A*uthors' *Note.* This paper represents the practice wisdom of two social workers who have worked with the dying for the past thirty years. It is presented from the social work viewpoint, but the ideas, the stresses, and the satisfactions are not carried by social workers alone. It is in the nature of their particular responsibility to patient and family to see many of these needs earlier and at times more clearly than other caregivers. It is also a part of their responsibility to communicate to other professional helpers their thoughts, recommendations, and questions. Although written by social workers, this chapter is for all helpers of dying patients.

Almost 30 years ago on a hospital ward for veterans with Hodgkin's disease and leukemia, a young social worker felt alone and awed by what was taking place around her. She was participating in a ward culture where life-and-death events were unspoken and unshared, and young men were dying lonely and isolated. No one told them they were dying. Yet beneath the silence was turmoil and chaos; the terror of nightmares. This milieu conflicted with her feelings and her understanding of human need. This was the "conspiracy of silence" that prevailed until the 1960s. Patients and health-care providers were becoming less able to repress the, terror and pain of separateness the silence tried to cover (Foster, 1965).

Across the country, health professionals were becoming attuned to what dying patients were experiencing alone, and what they as helpers were also experiencing. Their recognition grew, and they faced their own feelings. The conspiring silence and expectations of professional distance were challenged and overturned. Leaders in this revolution in dealing with dying were Dame Cicely Saunders, in England, and Elisabeth Kübler-Ross, in the United States; treating, speaking, and writing. The influence of these charismatic women and the tenor of the times reshaped professional roles, fostered patients' rights, and placed value on emotional openness.

The 1970s "war" on cancer and the belief that a cure was on the horizon made ever-expanding resources available for massive scientific efforts on behalf of cancer patients. This investment has had a divisive impact on our societal view of care. The expectations of physicians and scientists support our wish and dream for lasting health. Until that cure is found, however, another set of values needs to be underwritten by financial and professional commitment. That commitment is to those whose lives are now caught on the chronic, downward course of incurable illness. They, in contrast to the "survivors" who have responded to intervention, symbolize the failure of curative treatment. As long as treatment fails for some, we have the responsibility to care for those who are dying of the disease and for the relatives, friends, or others affected by that death. While medicine continues to seek to cure, social workers and other care providers must pay attention to the quality of life remaining for those who face the ineffectiveness of cure-oriented procedures.

When a patient questions whether treatment will succeed, the social worker must be ready to bear with that person in the time of uncertainty. The patient may be concerned with "what if" matters, such as the making of a will that has been neglected, and planning for the care of dependent relatives. This kind of work can go on concurrently with medical treatment and offers a sense of relief and accomplishment to those who seek to prepare for the possibility of dying soon. The social worker, like other caregivers, must be able to assess when clients are unable to take such steps, leaving "unfinished business," because they cling to the hope of cure.

The Contemporary Role of Social Work: Where Do We Find Social Work for the Dying?

At the beginning of the 1990s the changing roles of patients and health-care providers are more complex than they seemed when a freer and more expressive society was unfolding. Social workers continue to provide services in all the settings in which patients die: hospitals, hospice programs, and at home. The specific setting influences the nature of the service, but does not change the basic responsibility and mission. The commitment to dying patients and their families is based on knowledge and skills in helping them cope with uncertain and often dreadful futures. Valuable services are provided when people are guided or accompanied through their inevitably lonely journey.

What are the current constraints on the health-care professional? Professionals must be socialized to their roles as helpers within complex institutions. The cultures of institutional settings may press heavily on them and may cause value conflicts. Fiscal restraints, regulations, narrowly defined roles and functions, and unrelenting workloads have impact on the capacity of hospital social workers to deliver meaningful service to dying patients. Entering the intimate lives of patients, communicating, and recognizing their pain is less feasible when professionals know they cannot find ways to provide humane and caring responses from dwindling resources. Within these realities, how does social work define its role? In what ways do material constraints influence the social worker's capacity for meeting psychosocial needs? There are social workers who try to exclude the institution when they define their helping activities, viewing the social work role as professionally contained. Institutional limits frustrate and demean their sense of professional expertise. More frequently, hospital social workers struggle to reduce impediments in the hospital just as they work to eliminate other obstacles to clients' lives in the rest of the world. These social workers see as a core responsibility helping both patient and family cope with the illness in the context of the institution in which care is being given.

To disengage from the institution would jeopardize the social work voice in advocating for changes. The social workers' professional skills prepare them to influence social policy within or outside the institution, or to realistically face up to unmet need. Clinical work with clients and organizational influence cannot be separated within the health-care institution.

Carving, Enlarging, and Holding the Social Work Role

Social workers can help to engage the institution in efforts related to human needs. If social workers fail to pay attention to the survival needs of the institution, the price paid is high. Others will define social work from a narrow and limited viewpoint of what they see as within the province of social work (Lister, 1980; Olsen & Olsen, 1967). Patient needs, well known to social workers, will often be disregarded, along with the social work capacities to meet them. When roles are reshaped by others, the social work voice in advocating for unmet needs and changes in social policy will be diminished. Social work staff and social work management need to be on the watch for what will interest those who do not know clients so intimately. Social workers will observe patient needs that are beyond their capacity to handle, but as a force within the institution, they can call attention to those needs and offer proposals to meet them. If no voice is raised, social work's influence and professional contribution to the way institutional choices are designed will be diminished.

Social workers intervene with systems, agencies, and resources, empowering clients and providing opportunities for mutual aid in groups (Germain & Gitterman, 1980; Schwartz, 1976). They represent patients' interests inside and outside the health-care setting, often doing work in which their professional colleagues would take great pride if the work were more visible to them. Social workers play pivotal roles with a wide range of services. These include supportive counseling based on "tuning in," listening, using educational skills and therapeutic interventions in complex interpersonal conflicts, family upheavals, situations of stress, and role changes. Some patient needs are created by the illness while many are precipitated by the course of the illness and the treatment imperative.

Applying Skill to Changing Needs

Some social workers are developing an important place in pain and symptom control for dying patients. They may provide direct treatment of symptoms through hypnosis or imagery techniques. Others are integral members of interdisciplinary pain control teams. There is a significant body of knowledge about pain and its emotional and social contexts (Saunders & Baines, 1989). Social workers contribute to the treatment team's effectiveness by assessing the psychosocial aspects of pain and helping to plan individualized interventions (Loscalzo & Amendola, 1990). Social workers often find their major role in activities that educate and change attitudes of health-care professionals. Institutions have many biases and barriers to appropriate pain management for patients with advanced cancer (Melzack, 1990). As advocates, social workers can bring their influence to bear at the case, unit, and overall institutional levels. This requires both line workers and social-work managers to acquire and use technical knowledge and interdisciplinary leadership skills related to pain management. One reason for social workers' involvement in this work is their knowledge and respect for the hospice form of treatment. Some social workers joined other health professionals and clergy to promote the hospice approach to care early in its development (Foster, 1979). By 1985, there were more than 1400 hospice programs across the United States (Hach & Wilson, 1986). Hospice programs, modeled on Saunders' work, focus on providing opportunity for dignity, freedom from physical pain, and support in emotional pain, to provide compassionate care (Milner, 1980).

Setting Priorities

Many traditional social work functions are subject to reconsideration or are in actual jeopardy in current hospital practice. Patients may be admitted to general medical and surgical units for short stays, in a climate where discharge planning is the core of the institutional view of social work's domain. Pressure for early discharge requires the social worker to make a short-term care plan. The patient and family, however, are dealing with a long-term problem and need longer follow-up care and service. This is an item that has slipped from the institutional agenda. Continuity of care during the downward cycle and terminal phase of illness is not a priority for acute care institutions. The worker on a medical service, following institutional priority, is unable to follow dying patients or to offer the continuity of care needed during terminal illness. How can such incomplete and fragmented care be rationalized?

With the advent of DRG's and other cost-containment policies, social work's contribution may be valued in some institutions only for its cost-saving discharge planning effort. Social workers in these settings are faced with the need to resist, to prevent and overcome policies and role assignments that dehumanize care and threaten professional values. In a "bottom-line" versus humanistic climate, specific populations are considered burdensome to the institution. The elderly cancer patient in need of chronic care is often seen as a costly drain on resources. A mixed institutional viewpoint, seeking both quality and economy, pushes the social worker between the needs of patient and institution. This presents both stress and challenge. In setting priorities, the worker may feel pushed to attend more closely to obstacles to discharge, and may be losing sight of stressful family relationships and impaired coping in the face of loss and life transitions. The discharge planning process, with its exploration of feelings, assessment of needs, review of options and resolution through counseling, advocacy, and teamwork, is as essential to hospital personnel as to the patient and the family.

The profession's commitment to systemic change and mediation, to assure organizational responsiveness to individual needs is diminished without constant attention to basic principles. Social work practice must always set clear priorities and remain invested in underserved populations. Humanizing the care of the dying and bereaved is essential to sound social work and will assure the long-range alliance of the profession to values held by enlightened, humane public opinion.

In the 1980s our system's characteristic fragmentation of services continued as special interest groups vied for diminishing resources. Those groups able to capture public attention and funding are empowered, while less dramatic work is underfunded. At this time, social workers in AIDS programs, hospice programs, and oncology services have opportunities to undertake more extensive counselling than those in other parts of the health-care system. The social worker assigned to a medical or surgical service must also work with dying patients but may have limited professional support for such work, and consequently limited satisfaction (Davidson, 1985). The demands are heavy, but service is classified as acute rather than "death and dying," so that the worker is in jeopardy for lack of recognition of the emotional stress of the work.

Social workers need the support of colleagues who understand the commonality of the work and the disparity of support.

Hospice as Model

The work of social workers in hospice is more clear. They carry out functions that deepen the connections between patients and their families, enabling sharing and opening up relationships between patients and staff. Such health-care professionals encourage intimacy, meaningful communication, problem solving, and resolution. Closeness to the emotional pain of patients and families and continuous exposure to death and loss are consequences of this work. Rusnack, Schaefer and Moxley, (1988, p. 18) define the generic foundation of social work there as ecological, enabling "social workers to coordinate the transaction of the terminally ill patient with his or her family and with the hospice staff as well as to coordinate transactions between the hospice and its service network."

Satisfactions and Problems in the Social Work Role

From their earliest days in health care, social workers have known it was important to focus on feelings experienced by patients about their illness. Nevertheless, emphasis has often gone to other aspects of meeting biopsychosocial needs (Johnson, et al., 1990; Davidson & Clarke, 1990). More time and effort may be invested in locating resources, advocacy, and interdisciplinary activities than in direct, one-to-one supportive counseling with sick patients or their emotionally stressed family members. Social workers experience strain between the needs of patients for help with their reactions to their illness, especially in life-threatening situations, and the needs of the caring institution and its staff. The advent of AIDS and the complexity of its psychosocial considerations have dramatically restored and affirmed the value of comprehensive clinical services (Foster, 1989). With respect to current research AIDS is in a prestigious position with a client population successfully articulate and able regarding the needs confronting it. The social worker assigned to an AIDS or oncology program can develop a population approach attuned to meeting a range of needs because the psychosocial component of care is more broadly understood by clients, families, hospital administrators, and government agencies (Clarke, 1983). The work of a social worker on a medical service may actually involve extensive counseling with patients and families, who are facing impending death, but this work may go largely unrecognized by the broader public (Davidson, 1983).

Pressures Affect Priorities

In most hospitals, the time available to provide services to patients being transferred home or to other facilities is short. Social workers and other professional staff feel a conflict between agency demands and the needs of patients. How is this handled? In some situations, workers use the time pressures, along with finding the painful situations of their clients hard to bear, to rationalize cutting time spent with patients (Davidson, 1983). Desperate pressures of time and heavy caseloads contribute to the gaps in social work services to dying patients.

Staff other than social workers experience the stress of patients who die. Lohmann (1977) noted that strong personal relationships between long-term patients and their caregivers may leave staff subject to loss and grief when patients die. Recognition of personal mortality is inevitable for social workers and others involved with dying patients and their families (Dunkel & Hatfield, 1986). How can it be handled better? Avoidance or withdrawal have been common practices. Reid (1977) describes the worker caught between the two powerful forces of professional commitment to the client and very human personal reactions. Literature on death and dying and the establishment of organizations devoted to the care and study of the dying, focus attention on the needs of health professionals as well as patients for support and encouragement in their efforts (Harper, 1977; Koocher, 1979; Taylor-Brown, et al., 1981). Workshops and publications on dying and bereavement have proliferated, and there is a reduction of taboos about discussing death as evident in the publication of such journals as Loss, Grief and Care, The Hospice Journal, and The Journal of Psychosocial Oncology.

Practice wisdom suggests that helping patients to put their affairs in order, to grieve, and to face separation from their loved ones and their unfulfilled hopes can bring workers satisfaction (Pilsecker, 1979; Macks, 1988). The profession is moving in that direction, but it is difficult work. Workers know they have time pressures, but is that the basis of reluctance to become involved in this painful work? The social worker's reflections on how helping efforts may have failed the person who has died often become clear and painful, causing discomfort and doubts about competence. All too often, the worker has to live with uncertainty about the efficacy and value of work with a client who dies (Pilsecker, 1987; Dunkel & Hatfield, 1986; Macks, 1988).

Role Blurring

The overlapping roles and functions of doctors, nurses, chaplains, and social workers require dialogue and development of agreement within our own profession and among other disciplines about social work's role and function (Davidson, 1990). Energy, imagination, and effort can overcome the barriers to communication resulting from differences in the socialization of various disciplines (Mizrahi, 1986).

Kulys and Davis (1987) have noted that social work's longstanding difficulty in reaching concensus with other health-care professionals about their domain has made it possible for nurses equally to claim the psychosocial realm of care as their own. Nurses' claim to the psychosocial area has been strengthened by lack of clarity on the part of patients and families about social work's role. Often the social worker is seen only as important in the provision of concrete services (Kulys & Davis, 1987). We need to look at the need to make our role more visible in the context of time shortages and institutional pressures that distort the image projected by the work that we do. This varies in different institutions, but clarity about scope of responsibility is important if we are to maintain a visible sense of direction for the profession (Davidson, 1990).

Value Conflict

Social workers on oncology units have various stresses related to particular characteristics of the setting. They are on an interdisciplinary team and are working with dying patients. However, their domain with respect to direct service to patients and families varies. They may find themselves in turf battles with nurses. They may have conflict with the values of the treatment unit and their own viewpoint on the value of aggressive treatment. Often there is little attention to dying patients who are no longer candidates for treatment. On the other hand, some patients will be treated beyond the point where their quality of life is preserved or bettered. The social worker's highlighting of the disparity between the doctor's recommendation for aggressive treatment and the patient's wish to die may sometimes alienate the worker from medical colleagues and from distressed families. The social worker's emphasis on the patient's quality of life, death with dignity, and respect for the patient's own wishes may be in conflict with the viewpoint of professionals committed to a primarily biological approach. Social workers have to be mindful that they too can be influenced by the powerful impact of institutional philosophy. The development of living wills, advanced directives, and health-care proxies will support the efforts of health-care professionals and encourage patient participation in decision making.

Healing the Hurt of Work with the Dying

Early in the development of hospice, the term *staff pain* was used to refer to the impact of work with dying patients on health-care providers.

Davidson (1985) reports social workers' concerns with identification, fear, and feelings of loss. The stresses of their work carry over from professional to personal lives, and they feel vulnerable and intensely aware of the preciousness of time. Workers report on the difficulty of watching the patient's deterioration and death and they are troubled by sharp awareness of their identification with their clients (Davidson, 1983). More has been written about identifying stress than about how to cope with it. It is important to know that stress from this cause gives workers a sense of their contribution. Being open to pain and grief also opens the worker to healing, through the satisfaction of caring, helping, and sharing.

This is more vivid in hospice work, but the principles operate everywhere. A similar complex set of reactions is observed in social work with AIDS patients. Such work offers prestige, resources, and opportunities to undertake research and to teach. This is a partial compensation for the anguish and turmoil of exposure to painful death in young people. In work with AIDS patients, social workers experience many stressors but there is gratification from their contribution and use of creative skills. The balance of pain and healing these workers experience is similar to that of St. Christopher's Hospice where one-third of the social worker's time is deliberately devoted to teaching activities (Earnshaw-Smith, 1989). They may play a vital role in the life of patient, family, and loved ones as they help the patient plan for the remaining part of life and for childcare and other vital affairs after death. With the AIDS population, social workers face the cruelty of young people dying, the grief of relationships torn apart by debilitation, impending death, and sometimes stigma, guilt, and terror. The intensity and intimacy of relationships with patients and their significant others makes the impact of loss and pain severe. Staying with this challenge, which it seems one cannot do, suspends defenses and gives the helper creative access to unknown, or at least unused, clinical skills. The capacity to help is thus deepened (Benner & Wrubel, 1989).

Recently a change has occurred in the work with AIDS patients. The clarity of the issue of death and dying has been lessened by the development of high-technological treatment that causes AIDS to be viewed and treated as a long-term chronic disease. Once again, social workers welcome progress in physical treatment, but the problems faced by patients with a disease both chronic and fatal is complicated. The social worker is offering help with living under difficult, uncertain conditions in the constant shadow of approaching death. This kind of participation in fighting the disease is a new stress to AIDS social workers.

Helping Colleagues

As a colleague, and often a friend of those offering physical treatment, the social worker understands and respects their determination to treat. Their ethic is to do all that they know how to do as long as life lasts. However, the social worker also understands and is responsible for helping the patient who knows that life will soon be over and wants to consider, with help, having aggressive treatment stopped. To know and understand this conflict is to live with a painful and unavoidable dilemma. How can the worker deal with this conflict? First, comes honest acceptance of the dilemma. As part of the treating institution, the social worker is responsible for helping the patient with needs, other than medical, that exist because of the disease and its treatment. Second comes interdisciplinary work, calling on other professionals to meet the patient's needs. Third is the recognition that if cure and care are not a dichotomy, while the effort to cure goes on, social well-being must also be preserved. What does the patient want, and how can the social worker help? When the patient wants above all else to go home to die, a difficult conflict can arise. When the patient wants to attend to legal and financial matters in preparation for death, and the social worker helps with this, interdisciplinary peers may disapprove. Administratively, the social work department has a responsibility to help its workers with these issues of empathy, mortality, and the concurrent collaboration with disciplines with whom there may be honest conflict.

To try to find ways of communicating the patient's and the social worker's viewpoint is a heavy responsibility. Concern about these matters without ability to influence administrative and medical decisions is difficult to handle. Being seen by team members as valuable because one helps patients and families, which is part of the total team approach, is of value so far as it goes. It does not offset the sadness deriving from differences in power, perceptions, and values when the nature of service for final days of life for the patient is the issue at hand. Teamwork has elements of both support and frustration.

The worker's role as a provider of support for other staff varies. This exemplifies how the lack of a clearly defined role as helper, both to clients and staff, increases stress. When social workers take on the task of support to other team members who find it hard to cope with dying patients, it is helpful if that role can be recognized and valued. The form may be a structured support group, or it may be informal availability to staff to talk about the feelings and experiences they have had with patients. There are rewards whether this work is formal or informal, but because education and a sense of helpfulness are known to lessen stress, institutionalizing this role can help social workers gain gratification from being recognized as knowledgeable as well as helpful. Otherwise, despite the gratification of offering support to others, there is isolation for the social worker who wonders, "Who is there for me to talk to?" One worker asks, "Where do I go? We give a depressed doctor a chance to talk, but the social worker is left without help. Consultation and supervision are not used that way" (Davidson, 1983). Our knowledge of ways to offset stress needs to be brought to bear on and influence our own planning structures.

Programs That Enhance Worker Satisfaction

In work with dying patients, teamwork and exchange of skills take on special meaning as staff members are touched by loss, by seeing pain, suffering, and disruption of lives. They must tackle their own feelings of fear, frustration, and helplessness in the face of it all. They must resolve the conflict between impulses to avoid what is distressing and a sense of responsibility to meet the needs of clients and colleagues. Social workers need to identify whether their own needs are being met and find ways to experience greater satisfaction. Supervisory and peer support programs help social workers recognize and cope with their own reactions to life-threatening illness, death, and bereavement so that patient care remains a priority and the work is more satisfying (Nelsen, 1980; Mor & Laliberte, 1984).

> As we seek to understand the effects of human loss and to unearth resources to triumph over it, we are continually made aware of our own unresolved and still painful feelings of past losses and traumas. It is in acknowledging these together that we create that sharing, supporting community which can continue to be alongside our patients and families in sickness and anxiety, in despair and hope, and through bereavement. (Earnshaw-Smith, 1988, p.12).

Programs to provide support and guidance require that social-work managers advocate for and establish peer support groups and look for ways to develop multidisciplinary mutual aid groups. Social workers need to be placed on teams to reduce isolation and provide opportunities for professional development. In hospice programs, staff meet with visiting professionals and teach informally as well as in formal classes and seminars. The sense of achievement, competence, and practical expertise that is fostered by teaching about their work is a valuable source of support to staff. Administrators in many social work departments who encourage invitations for staff to speak at conferences and to write for books and journals endorse significant educational activities that are very supportive to the workers. It is also important to have time protected for vacations, and days away from practice, while engaged in other professional contacts.

Another example of a staff support program is the formation of a peer group that emphasizes mutual aid, exchange of information, and coping skills (Davidson, 1983). A one time-limited group, which met for nine sessions, was made up of M.S.W. social workers in a large, urban hospital, all of whom worked with cancer patients as part of their assignment. The leader was not a member of the department but an expert in the field of social work with cancer patients. Each session lasted for an hour and a half, with a high level of attendance and punctuality. Members volunteered to participate because they found their work with patients stressful. Within the group, workers identified their common problems, and used daily experiences to help others deal with issues differently. They provided social reinforcement, proposed methods of coping, developed ideas for change, demystified problems, and offered information to each other. Comparing experiences and feelings reduced the sense of isolation. They were empowered by the common theme of sustaining the ability to be helpful to patients, families, and colleagues from other health disciplines.

As a result of the program, members reported that they were able to use the group to modify problematic aspects of their work. They reported that the group had helped them feel their difficulties were common to other workers and that they were better able to cope as a result of the support received. Some noted that their self-awareness had been heightened, enabling them to modify attitudes that had adversely affected their work. Others reported learning alternative ways to cope from other group members. One worker spoke of developing more realistic expectations of what could be accomplished and developing greater awareness of how much interventions with clients helped. An increase in assertive behavior, which enabled them to communicate better with other health-care team members, was reported by several members.

Favorite parts of the program were sharing, support, and acceptance by others of feelings and ideas, including concerns and fears about their work. Intrusion of the meetings into working schedules and pressures to complete assignments were least liked (Davidson, 1983).

Managers, besieged by survival issues of workers and survival issues of institutions, need to view these as related and of comparable importance. Attention to the needs, struggles, and growth of workers is the lifeline of providing critical services to those in need, both patients and families.

Summary

We have experienced both pain and commensurate growth during the past thirty years as we have worked with the dying and their loved ones, as we have taught students and workers, as we have tried to communicate courage and joy to those who want to learn about this work. The window that opens into the inner life of the client facing death offers a way to help them but it also opens the social worker to mourning, grief, the reawakening of past losses, and unresolved conflicts. To protect ourselves from empathy with the dying is to hide ourselves from a part of life that concerns us all, and that offers healing along with pain.

References

Benner, P., & Wruble, J. (1989). *The primacy of caring: Stress and coping in health and illness.* Reading, MA: Addison-Wesley.

Clarke, S. (1983). Hyman J. Weiner's use of systems and population approaches; Their relevance to social work practice in health care today. *Social Work in Health Care 9*(2): 5–14.

Davidson, K. (1983). Development of a support program for social workers serving cancer patients. Unpublished D.S.W. dissertation. City University of New York, New York.

Davidson, K. (1985). Social work with cancer patients: Stresses and coping patterns. *Social work in Health Care 10*(4): 73–82.

Davidson, K. (1990). Role blurring and the hospital social worker's search for a clear domain. *Health and Social Work 15*(3): 228–234.

Davidson, K., & Clarke, S. (1990). Social work in health care: A handbook for practice. Binghamton, NY: Haworth.

Dunkel, J., & Hatfield, S. (1986). Countertransference issues in working with persons with AIDS. *Social Work 31*(2): 114–117.

Earnshaw-Smith, E. (1987–1988). *Annual report and yearbook.* St. Christopher's Hospice, London, England.

Earnshaw-Smith, E. (August, 1989). Director of social work at St. Christopher's Hospice, London, England. Personal interview with K. Davidson.

Foster, Z. (1965). How social work can influence hospital management of fatal illness. *Social Work 10*(4): 30–35.

Foster, Z. (1979). Standards for hospice care: Assumptions and principles. *Health and Social Work 4*(1): 118–127.

Foster, Z. (1989). The treatment of people with AIDS: Psychosocial considerations. In I. Corless and M. Pittman-Lindeman (Eds.), *AIDS: Principles, practices and politics.* (pp. 33–35). New York, NY: Hemisphere.

Germain, C., & Gitterman, A. (1980). *The life model of social work practice.* New York: Columbia University.

Hach, J., & Wilson, S. (1987) Women and hospice care. In S. Stellman (Ed.), *Women and cancer.* pp. 155–163, New York, NY: Harrington Park.

Harper, B. (1977). *Death: The coping mechanisms of the health professional.* Greenville, SC: Southeastern University.

Johnson, H., Atkins, S., Battle, S., Hernandez-Arata, L., Hesselbrock, M., Libassi, M., & Parish, M. (1990). Strengthening the "Bio" in the biopsychosocial paradigm. *Journal of Social Work Education* 26(2): 109–123.

Koocher, G. (1979). Adjustment and coping strategies among the caretakers of cancer patients. *Social Work in Health Care* 5(2): 145–150.

Kulys, R., & Davis, M. (1987). Nurses and social workers: Rivals in the provision of social services? *Health and Social Work* 12(2): 101–112.

Lister, L. (1980). Expectations of social workers and other health professionals. *Health and Social Work* 5(2): 41–49.

Lohmann, R. (1977). Dying and the social responsibility of institutions. *Social Casework* 58(9): 538–545.

Loscalzo, M., & Amendola, J. (1990). Psychosocial and behavioral management of cancer pain: The social work contribution to comprehensive care. In K. Foley (Ed.), *Advances in pain research and therapy,* (pp. 429–442), New York, NY: Raven.

Macks, J. (1988). Women and AIDS: Countertransference issues. *Social Casework* 69(6): 340–347.

Melzack, R. (1990). The tragedy of needless pain. *Scientific American* 26(2): 27–33.

Milner, C. (1980). Compassionate care for the dying person. *Health and Social Work* 5(2): 5–10.

Mizrahi, T. (1986). *Getting rid of patients: Contradictions in socialization of physicians.* New Brunswick, NJ: Rutgers University.

Mor, V., & Laliberte, L. (1984). Burnout among hospice staff. *Health and Social Work* 9(4): 274–283.

Nelsen, J. (1980). Support: A necessary condition for change. *Social Work* 25(5): 388–392.

Olsen, K., & Olsen, M. (1967). Role expectations and perceptions for social workers in medical settings. *Social Work* 12(3): 70–78.

Pilsecker, C. (1979). Terminal cancer: A challenge for social work. *Social Work in Health Care* 4(1): 369–379.

Pilsecker, C. (1987). A patient dies—a social worker reviews his work. *Social Work in Health Care* 13(2): 35–45.

Reid, K. (1977). Nonrational dynamics of the client-worker interaction. *Social Casework* 58(10): 600–606.

Rusnack, B., Schaefer, S., & Moxley, D. (1988). "Safe passage": Social work roles and functions in hospice care. *Social Work in Health Care* 13(3): 3–19.

Saunders, C., & Baines, M. (1989). Living with dying: The management of terminal disease (2d. Ed.). New York: Oxford University.

Schwartz, W. (1976). Between client and system: The mediating function. In R. Roberts & H. Northen (Eds.) (pp. 171–197). *Theories of social work with groups*. New York: Columbia University.

Taylor-Brown, S., Johnson, K., Hunter, K., & Rockwitz, R. (1981). Stress identification for social workers in health care: A preventive approach to burn-out. *Social Work in Health Care* 7(2): 91–100.

Nineteen

Physiotherapy in Terminal Care

Betty O'Gorman

Betty O'Gorman was born and brought up in London. She trained as a physiotherapist at King's College Hospital, London, from 1957–1960. She remained on the staff there until 1965, becoming Deputy Superintendent of the Outpatients Department. From 1966 to 1971 she worked in a busy outpatients department of a large suburban hospital. She joined St. Christopher's Hospice in 1973 and became Superintendent Physiotherapist in 1979.

She is coauthor of a chapter on MND (ALS) in Cash's Textbook of Neurological Conditions for Physiotherapists, *author of a chapter on pain management in terminal care in* Pain Management Control in Physiotherapy, *coauthor of a chapter on MND in* Hospice and Palliative Care: An Interdisciplinary Approach, *and a contributor to the symptom control chapter in* The Management of Terminal Malignant Disease, Third Edition.

Betty O'Gorman was a founding member in 1989 of the Association of Chartered Physiotherapists in Oncology and Palliative Care (ACPOPC), of which she is currently chairperson. She represents ACPOPC on the Professional Committee of the National Council for Hospice and Specialist Palliative Care Services and is a member of the Committee's Working Party on Ethics. She has lectured on physiotherapy and rehabilitation in palliative care in Canada, the United States, Hong Kong, and China.

Betty O'Gorman is married and has three sons. Her interests include travel, good food, and wine.

Physiotherapy for the terminally ill is an essential part of the multidisciplinary approach. It is as much the right of the terminally ill patient as any other to receive the best appropriate treatment. Sadly this is not always so. Many patients have been labelled *terminal* and have therefore missed the opportunity to receive appropriate physiotherapy. Because of this, independence can be lost, leading in turn to immobility, lack of self-esteem and self-worth, and a downward spiral in the patient's expectations. Mary McAteer (1990) says, "other factors must be taken into account to ensure that there is no gap between caring and curing."

However, with positive input from the physiotherapist much can be achieved, enabling the patient and family to reach their goals, even if these be short-term and necessarily changeable. The physiotherapist is involved in many areas of the patient's physical management, but the two most common are maintaining or restoring mobility and the overall management of the patient's comfort.

The physiotherapist's role in the treatment of the terminally ill patient is unique. No other discipline has the hands-on skill so appropriate in this context. "The core of physiotherapy is our hands, for we are a profession which uses hands and handling to assess" (Williams, 1986).

There may be a reluctance or lack of knowledge by the caring professionals of what can be achieved, or overprotection by a well-meaning family. Even more disastrous for the patient are uncontrolled symptoms, because not only will they cause distress but they will be a certain barrier to effective physiotherapy, should it be offered.

Multidisciplinary Team Approach

No physiotherapist, whether in a hospice, hospital, oncological unit, or home situation, can work in isolation. The work and stresses involved are much too demanding. In the multidisciplinary team there are grey areas with one discipline overlapping another, especially among closely aligned professions such as physiotherapy and occupational therapy and, to some extent, medicine and nursing. As a good team member, the physiotherapist should not mind if another member of the team suggests something that should have been thought of by the physiotherapist.

In order for the multidisciplinary team to function well, it must communicate on all levels by means of

- informal verbal discussion and passing of information,
- accurate notekeeping,
- weekly team meetings, and
- family meetings.

These meetings not only make the team work effectively, they act as a means of staff support, especially when the going is not smooth.

The physiotherapist has a responsibility to the team to make an initial physical assessment of the patient's condition and capabilities: to assess whether pain is present and what exacerbates it; to assess, where appropriate, specific areas of muscle power; and then to plan a treatment régime and inform the team of this. This plan needs constant reviewing and updating as the patient's condition alters.

Meetings with the patient and family and appropriate team members (not always the whole team) are needed to impart information to everyone at the same time and to make ongoing plans for treatment, management, and short-term goals such as trips home.

Besides the multidisciplinary team, there is the physiotherapy team itself. It will probably consist of several physiotherapists and physiotherapy aides, volunteers, and students. The same rules apply to this "team within a team" as to the interdisciplinary team, and obviously it has an important role to play in mutual support because the physiotherapists usually relate easily to each other.

Counselling

Physiotherapists are not natural counsellors, having been taught and versed in the question-and-answer regimen necessary to discover the patient's needs and to decide on an appropriate treatment. It is therefore necessary for the physiotherapist to understand—and perhaps also to have undertaken a counselling course—in order to know when to switch roles from active physiotherapy to active listening and possibly to counselling during a treatment session, because this is often the time the patient chooses to confide his or her fears. In this way the physiotherapist can listen and then contact the appropriate team member. The physiotherapist must ensure that not only the family and patient receive the relevant information, but the rest of the team as well.

McAteer (1989) says, "Physiotherapists can, and must be prepared to, step out of their more traditional role as purely physical therapists and be available to offer their patients, not only physical treatment, but a counselling relationship as well."

Grief and Loss

In order to work efficiently in this field the physiotherapist needs to understand the reactions to terminal illness and that of grief and loss. Not only the ultimate grief and sense of loss for a life coming to an end, but for ongoing grief and losses along the way. The loss of function of a limb, to coordinate one's body, to be independently mobile, and maybe the role in a family, will all be met by grief and loss. At times the physiotherapist will be the team member dealing with this problem, and knowledge of grief and loss processes and the range of individual responses is important.

McAteer (1989) says, "The physiotherapist who is committed to a holistic model of health care will be concerned to give attention to the nonphysical needs of the patient." Baines (1985) adds, "Symptom control in terminal illness is not just a technique of using drugs correctly. It involves attention to the whole personality of the patient, his hopes, his fears, his family, his philosophy of life. Unless these are taken into account the likelihood of good symptom control is small."

Physiotherapist and Patient

In any physiotherapist/patient situation, a relationship develops. Most treatments are undertaken on a one-to-one basis. Sometimes this relationship is naturally closer. Physiotherapists working in the field of terminal care cannot insulate themselves from becoming involved because in so doing they will not give their best efforts. However, accepting this and the support available, both inside a hospice setting and in the "outside world," will help. The majority of patients who receive physiotherapy will die, leading to a sense of loss to the physiotherapist.

This loss to the physiotherapist will be helped by taking pride and satisfaction in the patient's achievements, however small these may be.

It must also be realised that treatment régimes must be flexible, sometimes moving backwards and forwards as the patient's condition, goals, and needs fluctuate. Similarly, physiotherapy is not necessarily of paramount importance to the patient every day—they may wish to save their energies for an outing, the hairdresser, or a special visitor.

It is important to offer these choices to the patient so that, despite many areas of loss, they are able to retain some control.

Physical Management

It is only because of good symptom control that physiotherapy can be practised in terminal care. Primary pain control is not due in the main to physiotherapy but to medication. However, physiotherapy does have a contribution to make. Total cooperation among the medical, nursing, and physiotherapy staffs must not be undermined by inefficient physiotherapy that could cause pain. There are no pain barriers to push through in this field.

Efficient physiotherapy is sensitive to the patient's needs and is planned to maximise each individual's potential. Patient's goals are often simple—the desire to mobilise independently to the bathroom, to walk in a garden with family, or to sit out of bed regularly.

The physiotherapist also needs to understand the disease process, not just the diagnosis, and to have a working knowledge of the usage and dosage of the drugs used so that an appropriate contribution can be made to the overall management of the patient.

General Principles of Physiotherapy

In all treatments the following essential guidelines should apply:

1. Commence treatment as soon as possible on a daily basis.
2. Consider the patient totally.
3. Consider the safety of the patient.
4. Do not make false promises.
5. Take care at all times. Inappropriate, vigorous physiotherapy could cause distress, an increase in pain, and even a pathological fracture.
6. Listen to the patient's observations of his or her symptoms; they could indicate a pathological fracture or an incipient paraplegia because pain-relieving drugs may mask a new pain.
7. Do not make a patient's deterioration obvious by his or her physiotherapy. Do not take the patient off treatment while he or she is aware. Scale the treatment down to the patient's capabilities.
8. Be prepared to counsel the patient.
9. Consider the relatives, involve them in the patient's treatment and goals, and share their achievements.

Rehabilitation programs cannot be set, but treatment must be given on a day-to-day basis and short-term goals set and achieved.

Physiotherapeutic Measures to Alleviate Pain

Exercise

Many patients suffer from multipathology. This can be a mixture of malignant and nonmalignant conditions that may well have predated the malignancy or may consist of multipathology entirely from malignancy. Patients with a variety of conditions can be assisted with exercise. To maximise mobility and maintain independence, appropriate exercise is required of patients with the following conditions: amyotrophic lateral sclerosis, ALS (Motor Neurone Disease, MND in England); brain tumours (primary or secondary) leading to hemiplegia, hemiparesis, or ataxia depending on the site of the tumour; spinal tumours (primary or secondary) that lead to possible paraplegia or paraparesis; lung tumours and tumours of the bronchi; sarcomas and bony metastases that may have sustained a pathological fracture needing operative repair.

Regular exercise, either active, active-assisted, self-assisted, or passive, is needed to prevent joint and muscle stiffness possibly leading to contractures. All paralysed or partially paralysed limbs must be exercised and instruction given to the patient, nursing staff, and relatives on how to perform the exercises. Deformities must be prevented because they lead to unnecessary discomfort and distress, making even simple nursing procedures difficult.

Similarly appropriate exercise is needed for any nonmalignant condition that the patient has, for example osteoarthritic joints or spine, rheumatoid arthritis, neurological conditions such as multiple sclerosis or previous polio, amputations, and so on, or if the patient has sustained a pathological fracture with or without operative repair.

Mobilisation of Stiff Joints

Regular exercises are needed to attempt to mobilise stiff joints. Occasionally radiant heat pads, ice, or (if there are no metastases present) ultrasound may be used on the affected joint plus appropriate manual therapy techniques, for example, the gentler "mobilisation" procedures. In the case of ALS patients, particular attention must be given to the shoulder joints.

General Mobilisation of the Patient

Patients lose their ability to be mobile as a result of various factors. Uncontrolled symptoms, pain, loss of appetite, nausea, vomiting, diarrhea or constipation can lead to immobility and therefore weakness. The physiotherapist is not necessarily treating the condition from which the patient is suffering, merely the consequence. If the patient is allowed to remain inactive, he is quite likely to suffer general aches and pain, and the risk of pressure sores increases.

Almost inevitably the patient will have weakened legs, so an active scheme of leg exercises should be taught. These are kept simple and the patient is encouraged to repeat them 2–3 times in the day. They often need to be written, due to a poor short-term memory and also to involve the relatives. When the quadriceps will contract against gravity, standing with assistance (if necessary) will be attempted, followed by walking. When the patient is mobile, attention can be paid to any other weak areas and they can then be exercised accordingly. Rollator walking frames are particularly useful for the generally weak patient or those with pathology in the arms, thorax, or upper spine, because they allow the normal walking pattern to continue without the need to lift a walking frame. Those patients who remain only just mobile need encouragement from a physiotherapist, sometimes a scheme of active leg exercises, and possibly assessment for a walking aid. If generalised weakness or dyspnea remain a problem, then an electric wheelchair will afford a degree of independence and mobility.

Positioning

The physiotherapist needs to advise the nursing team on the positioning of patients in bed, reclining armchairs, and wheelchairs. The use of small pillows and cushions, often custom-made, are far more effective than large conventional pillows for supporting limbs and head. Bed cradles are necessary to relieve the pressure on the legs and also allow the patient some freedom of movement.

Limbs that are paralysed, grossly oedematous, fractured, affected by osteoarthritis or rheumatoid arthritis, and so on, need maximum support in a good anatomical position. Particular attention needs to be paid to keeping the ankle joint at a right angle and abducting the arm away from the trunk at approximately a 15° to 20° angle.

When there are primary or secondary lesions in the spine, collars and/or spinal supports may be needed. The position of the trunk and head in relation to gravity needs to be considered. A mattress variator or electric bed (see section on ADL) will help positioning.

To minimise the effect of gravity on the body, the patient should be inclined back from the vertical. By doing this, either in bed or in a reclining armchair or wheelchair, the line of gravity will pass in front of the head and neck through the thorax. A further advantage to the patient of being placed in the semireclining position is the relief of pressure of the thorax on the abdomen. This allows the diaphragm to work more efficiently and so aid breathing. This is relevant when the spine is collapsing due to pathological changes. In ALS patients, with severely weakened abdominal and trunk muscles, and in the severely dyspneic patient, special mattresses and cushions such as Spenco, Roho, and low airloss beds will aid comfort by minimising pressure on the body and the pain that comes from constant pressure. T.E.N.S., radiant heat pads, or icepacks can be used for the relief of breakthrough pain or pain associated with attempting to mobilise.

Aids to Daily Living

Splints and Supports

Aids to daily living are needed quickly, as are constant updates on their efficiency and any necessary alterations. Lively or rigid splints and lightweight orthoses may be needed, but with careful, continual assessment of their value so the patient is not inconvenienced by them more than can be helped.

A sling, especially a gutter sling, is useful for supporting a fractured or oedematous arm. Soft collars from sheet foam, or lightweight rigid ones, sometimes help pain in the cervical region, although positioning, plus the use of small neck pillows as mentioned before, are often of more help. The position of a mattress variator or bed with an electric facility to alter the back and foot position will give patients independence over their position and also aid their comfort.

General Relaxation

The teaching of general relaxation is particularly valuable to the patient suffering emotional pain, anxiety, or dyspnea. If relaxation is taught in conjunction with a tape recording, the patient can practise alone and, when proficient, use the tape during times of acute anxiety, dyspnea, or attacks of pain. Occasionally several patients will benefit from relaxation therapy in a group.

Lymphoedema

Unfortunately the patient with the lymphoedematous limb secondary to a cancer is often told "nothing can be done." This is not so, and the limb (arm or leg) can be treated effectively with a daily regime of massage, compression bandaging, and exercise for a two-week period. Following a reduction in the size of the limb, an elastic compression garment will need to be worn constantly to contain the size of the limb. In the case of a terminal care patient, it may be that treatment oscillates between bandaging, compression garment, and possibly a combination of both at times, if not to improve the swelling, at least to contain it.

The regime of treatment is complex and referral to Lymphoedema Advice on Treatment (Regnard, Badger, & Mortimer 1988), Management of Limb Oedema in Patients with Advanced Cancer (Gray, 1987) or Management of Lymphoedema-Guidelines (Badger & Twycross, 1988) are recommended for the complete details.

Massage

This can play a part in the treatment of acute stiff necks and low back pain in conjunction with gentle mobilisation of the affected area. Sometimes massage is used when a patient has local pain but also needs a one-to-one contact treatment, and particularly in the very anxious tense patient.

Chest Conditions—Breathing Exercises

Pain in the chest is not necessarily relieved by physiotherapy, but discomfort can be helped by the use of breathing exercises, light clapping and shaking or expiration, and the teaching of efficient coughing. Similarly, correct positioning and support of the patient in conjunction with teaching local relaxation of the head, neck, shoulder girdle, and thorax will all help patients with chest pain and discomfort.

Some patients are going to die from a chest condition. Primary or secondary lesions may be present in the lungs or bronchus with possibly a superimposed infection. It is quite inappropriate to attempt to clear secretions from the chest of a dying patient with postural drainage.

When patients with chest pathology or an infection are referred for treatment, physiotherapists need to know whether the treatment is to be active or palliative; otherwise they will question their own efficiency. If it is to be an active treatment, the patient will be on an antibiotic, possibly a mucolytic, and with light clapping and shaking and efficient coughing an attempt will be made to clear the chest of secretions. If the treatment is to be palliative, there will certainly be no antibiotic and if the patient is sleeping it is not so important to disturb them for treatment. Sometimes what begins as an active treatment changes to a palliative one if the patient does not improve.

Physiotherapy continues as long as the patient is being helped. If secretions in the upper areas of the lung fields become a problem, causing distress and noisy respiration, then the appropriate medication will be given. An opiate such as diamorphine 2.5 mg–5 mg and hysoscine 0.4mg–6 mg will reduce the secretions and act as a sedative and amnesic. The dyspneic patient is often anxious; to be short of breath for any length of time is frightening. General relaxation, if taught and practised with the aid of a tape, often helps. The patient needs to be taught efficient use of their chest by practising breathing exercises and how to improve their exercise tolerance. They should be instructed to undertake one activity at a time—not to walk and talk, to stop and rest before they become very breathless, to speak in shorter sentences with rests in between. An electric wheelchair may assist the dyspneic patient to have a degree of freedom.

If secretions are present, helping to clear them will aid air entry, and again this may be achieved with light clapping and shaking and teaching efficient coughing.

Pain Control and Its Assessment

It is the physiotherapist who must assess whether a patient is pain controlled or not. Many patients are judged, quite accurately, to have no pain at rest. This may not be so, however, on mobilisation. It is here that the physiotherapist must use skills of assessment and report to the team. The use of transelectrical nerve stimulation is often of benefit in the control of chronic pain. (See Frampton, 1988).

Conclusion

Very few terminally ill patients decline physiotherapy. However ill and weak most patients are, they welcome the fact that a noninvasive positive treatment is offered and surprisingly, more for them than the physiotherapist, they achieve much more than their expectations would allow them to believe possible.

Acknowledgments

The author wishes to thank Jenny Chambers for her enduring patience in typing this chapter.

References

Badger, C., & Twycross, R. (1988). *Management of lymphoedema: guidelines.* Oxford, England: Sir Michael Sobell House, Churchill Hospital.

Baines, M. (1985). *Introduction to symptom control.* London, England: St. Christopher's Hospice, Sydenham.

Frampton, V. (1988). *Pain management and control in physiotherapy,* London, England: Heinemann Physiotherapy.

Gray, R. (1987). The management of Limb Oedema in patients with advanced cancer. *Physiotherapy—Journal of the Society of Chartered Physiotherapy,* 73, 10, 504–506.

McAteer, M. (1989). Some aspects of grief in physiotherapy, *Physiotherapy—Journal of the Society of Physiotherapy,* 75, 1, 55–58.

McAteer, M. (1990). Reactions to terminal illness, *Physiotherapy—Journal of the Society of Physiotherapy,* 76, 1, 9–12.

Regnard, C., Badger, C., & Mortimer, P. (1988). *Lymphoedema advice on treatment.* Beaconsfield, Bucks, England: Beaconsfield Publishers.

Williams, J. (1986). Physiotherapy is handling. *Physiotherapy—Journal of the Society of Physiotherapy,* 72, 2, 66–70.

Part Three

The Future of
Thanatology

Twenty

Regulatory Issues

Judi Lund Person

Judi Lund Person gradutated with honors with a BSW from the University of North Carolina at Greensboro and a masters degree in public health from the University of North Carolina at Chapel Hill. She has been Executive Director of Hospice for the Carolinas (HFC)—formerly Hospice of North Carolina—since 1980. Hospice for the Carolinas is the state hospice organization, serving North Carolina since 1977 and North and South Carolina since 1993. The organization provides technical assistance, legislative and regulatory advocacy, and educational services to the 100 hospice programs in the two states.

Lund Person served for six years on the board of directors of the National Hospice Organization (NHO). She has both chaired and served on numerous national committees including the legislative task force and the AIDS resource committee. A winner of the prestigious Peter Keese Award for the advancement of hospice care in North Carolina, she has led Hospice for the Carolinas to four national awards, including the 1993 NHO President's Award for Excellence in Educational Programming.

A recognized national leader in the field of hospice care, Lund Person consults across the country with state hospice organizations and local hospice providers, specifically relating to statewide data collection and legislative and regulatory advocacy.

Lund Person has served on the boards of several statewide nonprofit health and volunteer organizations. She is a founding member, and also served as president, of the recently created North Carolina Center for Nonprofits.

Introduction

In the past few years, the complications of increased medical technology and the emphasis of the medical community on "treating at all costs" has created a growing awareness of the legal and regulatory issues that face health-care providers who care for terminally ill patients.

This chapter will provide an overview of the key legal and regulatory issues that are part of the field of death and dying. While not intended to be a detailed analysis, and limited by issues pertinent to the United States, the concepts will help to focus this discussion and give the reader additional resources to pursue.

Patients' Rights

The concept of patient rights is not new. As early as 1901, the New York courts ruled that "every human being of adult years and sound mind has a right to determine what shall be done with his own body" (Kelly, 1981). Continued concentration on the topic over the last two decades has brought it to the attention of the health-care community and the courts as well as the public.

In 1973, the American Hospital Association approved a "Patient's Bill of Rights," which included the competent adult patient's right of informed consent and the right to refuse treatment (Siner, 1989). In that same year, the judicial council of the American Medical Association recognized the "reciprocal rights and duties of physicians and terminally ill patients. It was recognized that physicians had a moral obligation to share the burden of responsibility with their competent, terminal patients as to what life-prolonging measures might be used" (Siner, 1989). Along with the right to refuse medical care are the rights of patients to make choices regarding the type of treatment, the right to decide to terminate treatment, the right to all comfort measures available, and the right to the truth (Musgrave, 1987).

The case of Karen Ann Quinlan in 1976 was a milestone, because it was the first case involving the withdrawal of life-sustaining medical care from a permanently incompetent adult. "Karen Quinlan was a 21-year-old who ceased breathing for two 15-minute periods. Her friends attempted resuscitation. In the emergency room, she was resuscitated and placed on a respirator. One year later, she was in a chronic persistent vegetative state, ventilator dependent and receiving nutrition through a nasogastric tube" (Emanuel, 1988). The family's decision that the respirator be discontinued conflicted with the attending physician's opinion that discontinuation of the respirator was a violation of medical ethics. The case went to the New Jersey Supreme Court, which established the following framework (Emanuel, 1988) for reviewing this and future cases:

1. Is there a right to terminate medical care?
2. What types of care can be terminated?
3. From what types of patients can care be terminated?
4. Who should act as the decision maker?
5. What are appropriate criteria for justifying the termination of medical care?

In their decision, the N.J. Supreme Court decided that an individual's constitutional right to privacy included a right to refuse medical care, and recognized this right for incompetent patients (Siner, 1989). Since the Quinlan case, many state courts have ruled that the individual's right to refuse medical care is permissible.

As a result of the attention given to the Quinlan case, and increasing questions and pressures from the medical community and the public, the President's Commission on the Study of Ethical Problems in Medicine and Biomedical and Behavioral Research (1983) issued its final report, "Deciding to Forego Life-Sustaining Treatment." The report clearly recognized patient autonomy in issues concerning terminal care and pointed out the need for an appropriate surrogate to act in accordance with the patient's wishes (Siner, 1989). One of the guidelines with far-reaching implications recommended by the President's Commission was the document "Physician's Responsibility toward Hopelessly Ill Patients," which included the withdrawal of artificial feeding (Wanzer, Adelstein, Cranford, et al., 1985).

The most recent court test of patient rights was the decision by the U.S. Supreme court in June, 1990, in the case Cruzan v. Director, Missouri Health Department. The Cruzan case will be explored in depth later in the chapter.

Advance Directives

Advance directives is the name given to the two types of directives to medical personnel by which patients maintain control over the care they receive, in the event they lack the capacity to do so at the time treatment decisions need to be made. The advance directive is based on the assumption that health-care providers prefer to make decisions for patients in a way that reflects as closely as possible the patient's own views. The two types of advance directive are the living will and the durable power of attorney.

Living Wills

The living will was originally proposed in 1967 by Louis Kutner as a way for "a patient with a terminal illness to document and specify the nature of future medical care in the event of incapacitation" (Siner, 1989). The legal principle of the living will is the right of a competent adult to refuse treatment. California enacted the first Natural Death Act in January, 1977, specifying that the living will would be used in the case of a terminal condition. Living will statutes were originally adopted by states to allow patients to make decisions about their care before they become hospitalized or incompetent. As of this writing, 47 states and the District of Columbia have enacted living will statutes, also known as Natural Death Acts, Medical Treatment Decisions Acts, as well as by other names. The states that do NOT have a living will statute include Massachusetts, Michigan, and New York. (Choices in Dying, June 1993). See Table 20.1 for more information.

As living will legislation has been implemented by various states, experts have identified the following problems with the living will statutes:

1. The term *terminally ill* is defined differently in each state, according to Fenella Rouse, executive director of the Society for the Right to Die, New York City (Hudson, 1989). Many states' living will statutes limit the application to "terminal and incurable" conditions. Not all living will statutes include brain death and persistent vegetative state as part of the legal definition of death.
2. Only 9 percent of adults in the United States have drafted living wills (Hudson, 1989).
3. In some states where the statute does not specifically allow family members to make health-care decisions for an incompetent relative, decisions about withholding life support are more difficult and leave family and health-care providers dissatisfied with the process (Hudson, 1989).
4. Physicians are never sure that the living will represents the continued choice of the patient; and also say that the living will does not cover the "exhaustive mix of conditions that interact on a critically ill patient" (Hudson, 1989).
5. There is confusion about the definition and interpretation of *extraordinary/ordinary care.* This wording refers to the language in some living wills that specifies "no extraordinary means will be used to prolong my life should I become terminally or incurably ill." The definition of *extraordinary* is subjective at best, and is confusing in some instances when applied in a medical treatment setting.

Durable Power of Attorney

Some states have provided a durable power of attorney (DPA) statute, which authorizes a person designated by the patient to make medical decisions for the patient, in the event of the patient's inability to make that decision for him- or herself. The DPA may also allow the person holding the durable power of attorney to authorize the withdrawal or withholding of life support, although that right is not automatically granted to the designated person.

As one example, Ohio has adopted a durable power of attorney for health care (DPA/HC) statute, which restricts who may be appointed as the decision maker or "agent," restricts who may serve as a witness, and most significant, restricts what decisions can be made by the agent (Carlson, 1990).

As spelled out in Ohio law and described by Carlson (1990), the durable power of attorney statute stipulates that:

1. the document must specifically authorize the agent to make decisions when the patient has lost capacity;
2. it must be signed and dated by the maker;
3. any competent adult may be the agent except the following: the treating physician, the physician's agent or employee, or any employee or agent of the health-care facility;
4. the DPA/HC must be either witnessed or notarized. If witnessed, there must be two eligible witnesses who personally know the maker. Those ineligible to be witnesses are: any person related to the patient by blood, marriage, or adoption; any person entitled to benefit in any way from the death of the principal; any person designated as the agent in the document; and any physician or any employee or agent of a physician or of a health-care facility.
5. the DPA/HC is valid for only up to seven years; however, if the maker is incompetent when it would expire, the DPA/HC continues.

It is important to note that the DPA/HC in Ohio is not a living will and it is not a set of treatment orders. Rather, it is the election of an agent to make those decisions when they become necessary. However, the durable power of attorney statutes differ in other states. In North Carolina, as in some other states with durable power of attorney statutes, the statute contains a clause authorizing the proxy (agent) to consent to medical treatment, but does not specifically mention refusal to consent or authority to instruct cessation of life-sustaining treatment. As a result of the Cruzan decision, (which will be explicated later in this chapter), clarifying work on this topic is beginning in state legislatures in many states.

As shown in Table 20.1, every state has either a living will or a durable power of attorney statute for health care. Alabama and Alaska have only a living will statute; Massachusetts, Michigan, and New York have only a durable power of attorney for health care (Choices in Dying, June 1993).

In addition to the living will and durable power of attorney statutes, some states have adopted very specific laws affecting the withdrawal of hydration and nutrition. As an example, Connecticut has adopted a Removal of Life-Support Systems Act. In Florida, the state constitution was amended to recognize a right to privacy in medical treatment decisions (Blum, 1990).

Table 20.1   States with no living will or durable power of attorney statutes

State	No Living Will Statute	No Durable Power of Attorney Statute
Alabama		x
Alaska		x
Massachusetts	x	
Michigan	x	
New York	x	

Patient Self-determination Act

On November 5, 1990, President Bush signed into law the Omnibus Budget Reconciliation Act of 1990. Sections 4206 and 4751, referred to as the "Patient Self-determination Act," require providers of services under the Medicare and Medicaid programs to inform patients of their right to appoint a proxy and draw up written instructions for the desired limits to medical care to be activated if they become incapacitated. Hospitals and other health-care providers were required to set up systems by December 1, 1991, to comply with the new law. Senator John Danforth calls the bill "the Miranda law for patients" (Hudson, 1991). The law is also designed to require those states without any advance directive statute to enact such legislation, as shown in Table 20.1.

Under the provisions of the law, any health-care provider receiving Medicare or Medicaid dollars is required to ask admitted patients whether they have advance directives, either a living will or a durable power of attorney. If the patient does, the health-care provider must document that fact in the patient's medical chart. The law requires that the agency maintain written policies:

1. to provide written information to each individual concerning (i) his or her rights under state law (whether statutory or as recognized by the courts) to make decisions concerning medical care, including the right to accept or refuse medical or surgical treatment and the right to formulate advance directives; and (ii) the written policies of the provider or organization as to the implementation of such rights;
2. to document in the individual's medical record whether or not the individual has executed an advance directive;
3. not to condition the provision of care or otherwise discriminate against an individual based on whether or not the individual has executed an advance directive;

4. to ensure compliance with the requirements of state law respecting advance directives at facilities of the provider or organization; and
5. to provide (individually or with others) education of staff and the community on issues concerning advance directives.

Several problems exist with the new law, which neither requires that a copy of an advance directive be attached to the medical chart nor that the location of such a document be specified. According to Anne Murphy, a health-care attorney with Coffield Ungaretti Harris & Slavin, Chicago, "it is possible that a patient could become comatose and [no copy of the document would be in the medical chart and] the document couldn't be located" (Hudson, 1991). Regulations for the law have been published by the Health Care Financing Administration and states have produced materials about the Patient Self-Determination Act to distribute to health-care organizations. To assist hospitals in complying with the new law, the American Hospital Association produced a free guide on how to comply with the act (Hudson, 1991).

Since the Cruzan decision and the Patient Self-determination Act, nursing homes have begun addressing the need for advance directives for nursing-home residents, and are offering brochures on the living will and the durable power of attorney, lectures and meetings for residents, and periodic checks to update the residents' wishes (Eubanks, 1990). Another outcome of the Patient Self-determination Act is the establishment of ethics committees in nursing homes, which aid the implementation of advance directives and the protection of residents' rights. To assist nursing homes in establishing ethics committees, the American Association of Homes for the Aging and the American Association of Retired Persons have created a video and booklet on how to establish a nursing-home ethics committee (Eubanks, 1990).

Do Not Resucscitate

The do-not-resuscitate (DNR) treatment decision has been the subject of intense interest, focused especially on the terminally ill patient. The President's Commission for the Study of Ethical Problems in Medicine and Biomedical and Behavioral Research, as discussed by Enck, Longa, Warren, and McCann (1988), raises three critical points regarding DNR:

1. resuscitation is a very painful and intrusive procedure;
2. efforts to resuscitate a dying patient are only successful in approximately one in three attempts, and of those patients who survive, only one-third are eventually discharged; and
3. the success of resuscitation efforts is generally difficult to assess without the availability of a full range of resuscitation procedures.

The commission made three chief recommendations to hospitals for the development of DNR policies: (1) hospitals should develop explicit policies, "on the practice of writing and implementing DNR orders," (2) hospital policies should recognize the need for balanced protection of patients, and respect the right of a competent patient to make an informed choice, and (3) hospital policies should provide a means for appropriate resolution of conflicts, and also mandate internal review (President's, 1983). Since 1988, all hospitals are required to have formal DNR procedures for accreditation (Emanuel, 1989).

In 1988, the Emergency Medical Services Committee of the American College of Emergency Physicians adopted a position statement for the use of do-not-resuscitate orders in the prehospital setting. The development of such a policy was necessitated by the increasing numbers of terminally ill patients who are provided care in the outpatient or home setting, and whose wishes for resuscitation are unclear, especially to the emergency medical personnel. The American College of Emergency Physicians (ACEP) provided guidelines for state and county Emergency Medical Service (EMS) agencies to withhold CPR from patients known to be terminally ill. In their recommendations, the ACEP guidelines state:

1. medical treatments limited by a "do-not-resuscitate" order should be clearly defined, and in the event of cardiopulmonary arrest, cardiac resuscitation would not be initiated. This would not imply that other medical therapies, such as IV fluids in the dehydrated patient, should be withheld from patients for whom they are medically indicated.
2. a legally valid, widely recognized form should be available for presentation to prehospital personnel when they are called to the scene of a "do-not-resuscitate" patient.
3. there should be an option not to execute a "do-not-resuscitate" order by the responding personnel if:
   a. the patient is able to express a wish to be resuscitated prior to cardiopulmonary arrest;
   b. family members or the patient's designee express a wish to initiate resuscitation;
   c. the patient's responsible physician requests that resuscitation efforts be undertaken; or
   d. the prehospital personnel have any doubts about carrying out the "do-not-resuscitate" order.

The position statement has encouraged some states to develop do-not-resuscitate protocols for emergency medical personnel for use in the prehospital setting. Using a multidisciplinary group of physicians, ethicists, attorneys, and representatives from hospitals, nursing homes, hospices, and home-health agencies, a uniform method for alerting EMS personnel of the presence of a DNR order can be developed. Such systems are in use (at this writing) in twenty-four states (Choices in Dying, June 1994).

The Nancy Cruzan Case

On June 25, 1990, the United States Supreme Court issued an opinion in the case of Cruzan v. Director, Missouri Department of Health, the first right-to-die case to be heard by the U.S. Supreme Court. Nancy Cruzan, 26, was in a car accident in 1983. When paramedics arrived at the scene they could not detect any respiratory or cardiac function. With cardiopulmonary resuscitation, her breathing was restored, but permanent brain damage was sustained. From 1983 until her death, she existed in a persistent vegetative state, where she was oblivious to her surroundings and without voluntary movements. She had reflex actions and could breathe on her own, but was unable to receive adequate nutrition without a feeding tube. A gastrostomy tube was surgically implanted four weeks after the accident.

In 1987, when there was no longer any hope for her recovery, Nancy Cruzan's parents requested that the gastrostomy tube be removed. Cruzan did not have a signed living will, but had verbally expressed to a roommate her desire not to live "like a vegetable." When the hospital staff would not allow the removal of the tube unless there were a court order, Nancy's parents sued. In the Missouri trial courts, the judge concluded that Cruzan had a fundamental right to liberty, both in the federal and state constitutions, to be free from further treatment. He ordered the tube removed.

An appeal by state officials to the Missouri Supreme Court overruled the trial judge, stating that "there was no state or federal constitutional right retained by an incompetent person to override the state's 'unqualified' interest in life." The Missouri living will law allowed for the removal of life-sustaining treatment only when death is inevitable 'within a short time;' it does not allow the removal of artificial feeding tubes (Kamen, 1989).

The U.S. Supreme Court, in its opinion, focused on a limited portion of the case—whether Missouri could require a clear and convincing standard of proof to allow the withdrawal of a life-sustaining treatment from an incompetent patient. The U.S. Constitution permits a state to require the provision of life-sustaining treatment to an incompetent patient unless there is "clear and convincing" evidence that the patient while still competent authorized the withholding of treatment. The decision was based on the due process clause of the Fourteenth Amendment, (no State shall deprive any person of life, liberty or property without due process of law), different from the lower courts, which based their decisions on the patient's right to privacy. Of note in the Supreme-Court decision is the assumption made by the Court that artificial nutrition and hydration are considered medical treatment. Justice O'Connor wrote a concurring opinion, which expressed her support for appointed proxies to make health-care decisions as a safeguard against failing to honor a patient's wishes (Pearlman, 1991).

The Supreme-Court decision is limited in scope and gives guidance only to Missouri in this case. No other state is required by this decision to change state law or ethical standards that allow the withdrawal of life-sustaining treatments. It continues to underscore the importance of written, advance directives, and the communication that should occur between patient and physician while the patient is competent and able to make health-care decisions. At the same time, a significant education process will be required if the use of written advance directives is to be widely accepted, since at this writing only 9 percent of adults in the United States have living wills. States will continue to have difficult choices for patients with no advance directives and no proxy decision makers.

Hospices and the Regulatory Process

In 1994, there were more than 2100 hospices throughout the United States. As providers of health care to terminally ill persons and their families, hospices are confronted on a daily basis with the issues raised in this chapter. In addition, hospices must meet the federal requirements for Medicare reimbursement as a hospice, the various state requirements for Medicaid reimbursement, as well as other state requirements for hospice programs. The Joint Commission on the Accreditation of Healthcare Organizations provided an accreditation process for hospice programs from 1981 through 1990, and discontinued the process in 1990, due to the small number of hospices that had opted for the voluntary process. As of January 1995, the Joint Commission will include standards for hospice care, which are included in the JCAHO *Accreditation Manual for Home Care*. The National Hospice Organization (NHO) published the *Standards of a Hospice Program of Care* in 1993 and added a *Self-Assessment Tool* in 1994 to assist hospices in meeting standards. The National League for Nursing is using the NHO Standards as the basis for an expanded accreditation process for hospice programs through the Community Health Accreditation Program (CHAP). The accreditation process will be available in early 1995.

Thirty states have state licensure laws for hospice programs, which regulate the use of the name *hospice* and specify the minimum standards that each hospice must meet. Hospice licensure laws have been more difficult to enact in recent years for a number of reasons. These include the fact that states are no longer regulating programs to the degree done previously, the lack of new licensure programs, and the budget difficulty being experienced in many states with the accompanying personnel cuts. Medicare certification is often viewed by hospices as a substitute for state licensure, and is effective for those programs that are Medicare certified. As of July 1, 1993, the Health Care Financing Administration announced that 1395 hospices were Medicare certified.

A Certificate of Need (CON) law, which regulates the number of hospices that may provide care in a service area, is also in place for some states with licensing laws. In states where CON exists, a Certificate of Need application must be filed and approved before a hospice can begin providing care. The approval process considers how many hospice patients are already being served in the area, and whether the area needs another hospice program. Certificate of Need laws are in a constant state of flux by state legislators, as they consider how much regulation should be provided to hospice programs and other providers of health care. Some states have now abandoned their Certificate of Need laws for hospices and home health-care agencies, and consequently, the number of hospice programs in a given area is increasing, resulting in competition for patients.

The late 1980s and early 1990s saw the development of rules for hospice inpatient units and hospice residences. Hospice inpatient units provide acute and subacute care for hospice patients who need a short-term inpatient stay. The unit may be located at a hospital or nursing home, or could be a freestanding hospice inpatient unit not connected with another provider. Hospice residences are designed for those patients without adequate caregivers, with frail caregivers, or who need supervised residential care. The hospice community believes that the need for hospice residences will increase dramatically as the population ages, as more elderly widows and widowers living alone need hospice care, and as families are living greater distances from each other and cannot directly provide care for elderly parents. The hospice residence is an important option for those patients.

The hospice movement has matured since its beginnings in the 1970s and will continue to provide leadership in the care of terminally ill patients and their families. Hospice programs and their administrators will be challenged by the regulations that affect the care of the terminally ill, as well as those that affect hospice specifically.

The Future of Regulatory Issues

Regulatory and legal issues concerning death and dying will continue to increase in complexity, as health-care technology increases in intensity and offers further challenges to decision makers. The Cruzan ruling is a reflection of the legal impact on patient care and ethical decision making. As technology advances, new regulations will be drawn and new ethical decisions will need to be made. The area of regulation is fluid and will change as new situations present themselves. It can be hoped that the foundation has been laid for future decision making with the cases and issues presented in this chapter.

References

Blum, J. D. (1990). The legal dilemma of stopping artificial feeding. *The American Journal of Hospice & Palliative Care, 7*, 42–48.

Carlson, R. A. (1990). Ohio's new law: What the durable power statute can do... and what it can't. *OHIO Medicine, 86*(6), 435–440.

Choices in Dying. (June 1993). State statutes governing living wills and appointment of health care agents. Author, 200 Varick Street, New York, NY 10014-4810.

Choices in Dying. (June 1994). Statutes authorizing do-not-resuscitate orders. Author, 200 Varick Street, New York, NY 10014-4810.

Emanuel, E. J. (1988). A review of the ethical and legal aspects of terminating medical care. *The American Journal of Medicine, 84*, 291–301.

Emanuel, L. L. (1989). Does the DNR order need life-sustaining intervention? Time for comprehensive advance directives. *The American Journal of Medicine, 86*, 87–90.

Enck, R. E., Longa, D. R., Warren, M., & McCann, B. A. (1988, November/December). DNR policies in healthcare organizations with emphasis on hospice. *The American Journal of Hospice Care, 5*, 39–42.

Eubanks, P. (1990, November 20). Nursing homes seek advance directives. *Hospitals, 64*(22), 52–54.

Guidelines for 'Do Not Resuscitate' orders in the prehospital setting. (1988). *Annals of Emergency Medicine, 17*, 1106–1108.

Hudson, T. (1989, November 20). Right-to-die: An executive report. *Hospitals, 64*(22), 33–40.

Hudson, T. (1991, February 5). Hospitals work to provide advance directives information. *Hospitals, 65*(3), 26–32.

Joint Commision on the Accreditation of Healthcare Organizations. (1994). Accreditation manual for home care.

Kamen, A. (1989, August 8). Missouri case may become ultimate test of 'right to die.' *Washington Post*, p. A1.

Kelly, L. Y. (1981). Legal aspects of patients' rights and unethical practice. In Thompson, J. B., & Thompson, H. O. *Ethics in Nursing,* New York: Macmillan.

Musgrave, C. F. (1987). The ethical and legal implications of hospice care. *Cancer Nursing, 10,* 183–189.

National Hospice Organization. (1993). Standards of a hospice program of care. Author, 1901 North Moore Street, Suite 901, Arlington, VA.

National Hospice Organization. (1994). Self-assessment tool, standards of a hospice program of care. Author, 1901 North Moore Street, Suite 901, Arlington, VA.

Pearlman, R. A. (1991). Clinical fallout from the Supreme Court decision on Nancy Cruzan: Chernobyl or Three Mile Island? *Journal of the American Geriatrics Society, 39,* 92–97.

President's Commission on the Study of Ethical Problems in Medicine and Biomedical and Behavioral Research. (1983). *Deciding to forego life-sustaining treatment.* Washington, DC: US Government Printing Office.

Siner, D. A. (1989). Advance directives in emergency medicine: Medical, legal and ethical implications. *Annals of Emergency Medicine, 18,* 1364–1369.

Wanzer, S. H., Adelstein, S. J., Cranford, R. E., et al. (1984). The physician's responsibility to hopelessly ill patients. *New England Journal of Medicine, 310,* 955–959.

Twenty-one

The Struggle to End
My Father's Life

Zelda Foster

*Zelda Foster is chief social worker at the De-
partment of Veterans Affairs, Brooklyn, Medical
Center. She has written on psychosocial issues in a
wide range of areas including discharge planning,
work with people with AIDS, and employee assistance programs.*

*Her investment in developing new services is
demonstrated by her leadership in bringing to the
Brooklyn VAMC a major center for the treatment of
homeless veterans, hospital-based home care, employee assistance, and adult day health-care programs.*

*Throughout her professional career, Ms. Foster
continues to have an enduring commitment to influence the lives of dying patients and their families.
She published a pioneering article on the subject in 1965 titled "Social Work Management of Fatal Illness," and served as first president and cofounder of the New York
State Hospice Association. Currently an educator and administrator, her roots as an
oncology social worker remain a guiding force in her personal and professional life.*

This couldn't be happening to me. All the paths taken in my adult life
led me toward a different direction. It was so clear and all of it had fallen
in place up until now. I clutched my father's health-care proxy in my
hand as I stood in a city hospital emergency room beseeching the hospital administrator to allow the withdrawal of my father's life supports.
The events of the weekend grew more unreal with each passing obstacle
and dehumanization. I, a cofounder of the New York State Hospice
Association, the chair of a hospital task force on the withholding and
withdrawal of life-sustaining treatment, and proponent of more rational
decisions regarding medical futility, stood there helpless and trapped in a
bureaucratic maze of indifference.

It began on Friday night, November 5th, when my 90-year-old mother
phoned for us to drive right over. My father wasn't right. I dressed
quickly. As we drove on rain-slicked streets further hampered by a car

accident ahead creating delays, I felt dread. My father was 93. I knew that one day a phone call would signal his death. As my husband and I raced into the house, we found my mother sobbing bent over him. My first thought was what a good death this was. He hadn't really been ill, only somewhat symptomatic for two weeks. What an easy death in his bed alongside his beloved wife of 67 years. I felt his face. He was so warm, so alive. The words crept out, words I'll always regret: "Call an ambulance." They came and they did what they were trained to do. They resuscitated him for more than one hour after he stopped breathing and then took him to the closest city hospital. As the four men and one woman worked over him, as the two policemen stood by, I wondered how I was going to stop what had been placed in motion.

My sister and her husband arrived. My daughter came to stay with my mother. We raced to the emergency room, and waited interminably in a room, demanding over and over that we be permitted to see my father and to speak to a physician. Finally, my sister and I were allowed in, but not the sons-in-law who had each loved my father for more than 30 years. My sister and I saw my father attached to machines and were told by the nurse that there was minimal brain function. We told her we had a health-care proxy. We asked to see a physician. The physician who had examined him was no longer there. When the staff heard that we wanted to sign a Do Not Resuscitate (DNR) order, a physician was called. This would mean that if my father's heart stopped beating again, resuscitation would not take place. The physician came after another delay, barely spoke to us, and gave us the paper to sign. We were pushed out of the emergency room after only several moments with our father, with no opportunities for us or our husbands to begin saying our goodbyes to him. How could we, his daughters, be unable to protect and safeguard him as his mind and spirit had left his vacant, devoid-of-personhood body. What disrespect to force that body to breathe!

Almost imperceptibly at first, then, incrementally more apparent to our parents, we had become their caregivers. These proud, immigrant parents who had devoted their lives and hopes to us became less able with time. They struggled to remain independent and in fact as grandparents and great-grandparents, they succeeded in maintaining a caring, giving role. How he would have despised this indignity, this mindless invasion.

The emergency room administrator on duty officiously told us that treatment could not be withdrawn once started. I wanted to scream out, "Haven't you heard of the New York State Health Care Proxy Law or the Federal Self-determination Act?" I knew there would be no way of convincing him that there was no distinction between withholding and withdrawing treatment, or that my father's health-care proxy allowed us to decide on his behalf. We left at 3 A.M., deciding to return Saturday morning to see the daytime administrator. We were certain that if reason did not prevail, at least the law would. How could a New York City hospital in 1993 not obey the law? Could our father's and our rights to protect his wishes be abrogated? We learned that yes, yes, yes—they could be abrogated. Obstacle after obstacle was placed in our way. The daytime emergency room administrator sent us to the day hospital administrator. She told us that since my mother was listed as the first proxy and the daughters as the second, we needed to prove that she was unable or unwilling to serve in that role. This felt manageable. We contacted her two geriatricians, each located at major teaching hospitals in New York City. Both called the hospital and then were told they needed to put their statements regarding my mother's incapacity in writing and mail it. How absurd when one imagines the number of days that would take. Instead, I went to Manhattan to pick up one letter and brought it to a now evening administrator. Further obstacles were presented. An attending physician was required and none were available until Monday. This led to further endeavors on Sunday morning but we were told by the daytime administrator after her consultation with the hospital CEO that the proxy allowed the withdrawal of only nutrition and hydration, not other life-sustaining treatment. Our explanation—that New York State law requires a separate statement regarding nutrition and hydration and that statement was only an added proviso not a provision standing alone—fell on deaf ears. No explanation helped. We were dealing with not only ignorance, but also an impenetrable bureaucratic wall.

My mother only understood that my father was dead. She saw him die. There was no way she could comprehend that a machine was forcing breath. She kept asking when was the funeral, expecting it immediately in keeping with Jewish tradition.

By Sunday afternoon, we felt desperate and began enlisting legal help. We contacted several of my daughter's law professors. I prepared a letter outlining each obstacle we had encountered. On Monday morning at the hospital where I work, colleagues armed phones and a fax machine. We faxed my letter to Brooklyn Legal Services where an attorney was waiting to receive it.

Brooklyn, New York
11:00PM, Sunday, November 7, 1993

Ms. Lauren Shapiro, Esq.
Ms. Cynthia Schneider, Esq.
Brooklyn Legal Services
105 Court Street
Brooklyn, N.Y. 11201

Dear Ms. Schneider and Ms. Shapiro:

This letter is written to provide clear evidence of a grievous abridgement of the Federal Patient Self-determination Act and to express anguish created by this injurious disregard of our rights.

At this time, my father, who is 93 years old, continues to be maintained at _____ Hospital on a respirator despite my continued and clear demand, acting under a proxy in his behalf according to his wishes, that he be disconnected. _____ Hospital's latest refusal, in a continuing series of changing reasons for denial, is the negation of our New York State proxy, which was executed by an attorney and indicated agreement by my father to the cessation of life support as well as nutrition and hydration in the event that he was incapacitated. _____ Hospital's insistence that there is only agreement stated in the proxy to withdrawal of hydration and nutrition not life-sustaining treatment thwarts my father's wishes and is patently ignorant of New York State law regarding this proxy. The attached proxy refers to nutrition and hydration only as an explicit added proviso as per state law. _____ Hospital's demand that I seek a court order is a total abrogation of the intent of a health-care proxy, which has as its purpose the avoidance of the need for a court order and the protection of patient rights.

This information and hospital decision was imparted to me November 7, 1993, at about 8 AM by the weekend hospital administrator, a Ms. T, who presumably was advised by the hospital CEO. The above decision was the last made by _____ Hospital in what has been a series of evolving obstacles and objections raised since Friday night, November 5, 1993, when my father was taken by EMS ambulance to the Emergency Room at approximately 11:30 PM.

This is the sequence of events that has transpired until now, along with the names of hospital personnel and their decisions:

1. My father experienced a cardiac arrest in his home, late Friday evening, November 5, 1993. EMS was called and was able to resuscitate him using CPR. He was then taken by ambulance to _____ Hospital.

2. The family, me, my sister, my husband, and my sister's husband—were not allowed to see my father and no one was available to talk to us for around an hour. After many demands, we were able to view him and talk to the nurse caring for him. When she explained that he was not conscious or responsive, we asked to speak with the doctor who had initially seen him, to execute a DNR and have my father removed from the respirator. We had left the proxy home in haste and were willing to get it.

We were told that this initial doctor was unavailable and we never got to speak to him. A new physician was paged. After that doctor arrived, the ER Administrator, who was then present, told us officiously that one can withhold life-sustaining treatment, but not withdraw it. The doctor said that was not so, but the administrator was disbelieving. We agreed to return the next morning with my father's health-care proxy.

3. We returned the next morning, Saturday, November 6, 1993, at about 8AM. An ER coordinator, although pleasant, had no sense of patient rights proxy procedures and process. She advised us to speak to Ms. T.

4. We contacted Ms. T. a short time later by phone from home. Ms. T. advised us that since my mother's name, she is 90-years-old, was listed first and mine second on the proxy, we had to prove that my mother was not competent to act on this proxy and that a physician would have to state this to Ms. T. by phone.

5. With great difficulty two physicians, Dr. F from NYU Medical Center and Dr. L from Long Island Jewish Hospital, who had treated my mother were located early that afternoon. Both called Ms. T stating that my mother was not able to act on the proxy. Ms. T then advised them that they would have to put this in writing

and mail it. Dr. F of NYU's geriatric practice wrote a letter, which my husband drove from Brooklyn to NYU to pick up in the late afternoon and then brought to _____ Hospital about 7:00 PM Saturday night.

6. On arriving, we contacted Mr. A, the evening administrator, who, upon receipt of this letter, advised me, my sister, and my husband that only an attending MD could disconnect the respirator and no attending was available. We demanded that an attending be contacted and brought in to meet our right to not have life-prolonging treatment and to allow our father to die with dignity. He agreed to do the best he could to meet our request.

7. At about 8 AM on Sunday morning, November 7, 1993, I phoned Ms. T to ask if an attending was contacted. It was then that she told me that she had been advised by the Hospital CEO that our proxy was not satisfactory despite the fact that it was drawn up and executed by a lawyer and met the terms of New York State law. She advised that the CEO insisted that we seek a court order.

The Hospital has created one obstacle after another to challenge our rightful request that our father be allowed to die with dignity. It has in doing so caused an abridgement of our rights to carry out our father's wishes and has cost us such considerable pain and anguish that we seek immediate relief and additionally the censure of the Hospital.

Sincerely,

ZELDA FOSTER

Attachments: Proxy
              Dr. F's letter

We simultaneously contacted Choices for Dying, where we had an attorney who was ready to receive our letter. I called the State Department of Health's local office, only to be told by their complaint division that one cannot withdraw treatment with a heath-care proxy. I called the Albany office and had corroborated that this of course was erroneous. A physician friend sat with me, waiting to see what further impediments might be thrown in our path. Finally, a call came from the hospital's patient representative. The calls from our lawyers and the New York State Department of Health had pressed the right buttons. I was asked how physicians in New York City could state that my mother was unable to act as proxy as she was in a nursing home in Florida. What total negligence! No one had said that my mother was in Florida. In fact if she were, would this have indeed made her unable to act as a proxy? Finally, he (the patient representative) decided to call my mother and ask her if she was unwilling to act as a proxy. How does a person judged by two physicians to be unable to act as proxy be placed in a position to receive a phone call she could not possibly comprehend? We allowed him to call, knowing that my aunt would receive the call and respond by stating that he was to deal with the daughters.

A call came soon after from a physician asking if I would like to be present when the life supports were removed. My daughter, a friend, and I drove to the hospital. In the gentle care of two physicians who extended much warmth to us, my father within moments slipped into death.

I will always associate his death with these events. The days we needed to grieve were taken from us as we struggled with an indifferent and incompetent system. The nightmare of helplessness and dehumanization stays with me. Certainly, my knowledge and power did eventually result in a response, but how hard it was to effect it. I will think of others less knowledgeable, not well-connected, and know that they would have no guidance and advocate. Because of this, I wrote many letters, including official complaints to appropriate State and City departments, to the Task Force on Life and the Law, and to the Health Care Financing Administration. It seems certain agencies bear no responsibility, politely offer tokens of apology, perhaps excuses, or agree to respond at a later date. So far, there has been only recognition that the hospital's weekend procedures needed improvement. Apparently its Ethics Committee made recommendations. How I would have liked to be at that meeting, but after all I'm only the person whose rights and whose grievous loss was unacknowledged. No one addressed the emergency room procedures that allowed indifference, inhumanity, and plain crude displays of incivility.

As we consider the gravity of the Federal Patient Self-determination Act and State proxy laws with respect to patient rights, we must be more vigilant. Rights are not assured in the absence of humane, responsive environments. Procedures have value but the essential value is in the connection between people in a helping system of care. Unembraced by respect and concern, I said my first goodbyes to my father among strangers.

Perhaps this experience will serve us well in the future. If it happened to me, it could certainly happen to any of us. This tells me that the direction I have taken almost all of my adult life with regard to death with dignity has total meaning and value. As a social work leader, I have helped instill this in others. Only I know now in the most personal way that we must press on. The struggle and our firm determination must and will continue.

Twenty-two

Death Education
for Children

Hannelore Wass

Dr. Hannelore Wass is a professor of educational psychology at the University of Florida. She is the founding editor of Death Studies, *one of the leading journals in the field, which she edited for fourteen years and which has been instrumental in defining the field of death, dying, and bereavement and its application in education, counseling, and care. She has published more than seventy research papers and chapters, and authored or edited eleven books. Her research has focused primarily on the development of children's understanding of death, effects of destructive themes in the media on children's perceptions, attitudes, and behavior, and on ways homes and schools can help children cope with death-related experiences and concerns. Dr. Wass is consulting editor for a book series on* Death Education, Aging, and Health Care, *in which thirty volumes have appeared, and ten others are in production. Dr. Wass teaches two graduate courses on death at the University of Florida and has lectured widely in the United States and abroad. She is a charter member of the Association for Death Education and Counseling and has served on its board of directors. She also serves on the board of directors of the International Work Group on Death, Dying, and Bereavement. Currently she is working on the third edition of the highly regarded textbook* Dying: Facing the Facts.

Introduction

Education has been a major thrust of the death movement from the outset. Pioneers pointed at a societal condition, denial and avoidance of death, that needed to be changed. They called for scientific study of human responses to death, envisioning the establishment of a *Wissenschaft,* a field of inquiry (Feifel, 1959), the knowledge and insights from which would then be applied in practice and policy. None of these purposes can be accomplished without education. Such education needs to be directed at all levels, for lay persons and professionals, at all

335

ages. It can be provided in various forms through a variety of social agencies such as educational institutions and the family, and presented in various ways both formally and informally.

Education in general is, of course, a major vehicle for communicating information, ideas, and understanding. Knowledge is concerned with developing and changing attitudes and values. Education also directly influences attitudes and values. It helps to define, clarify, and strengthen them. It also addresses the range of feelings experienced in the learning and educational processes and helps to manage them. The ultimate concern of education is constructive behavior.

The aims of death education in this broadest sense are the same as the fundamental aims of the death movement and of the field that has been evolving from it, as well as the agencies and organizations that are concerned with application in practice and clinical intervention. These aims lie, ultimately, in promoting the quality of life and living for ourselves and others and in helping to create and maintain the conditions that bring it about. The aims of death education are of special significance today and to achieve them has a special urgency. Rapidly advancing technologies have led to more and more specialization and fragmentation in matters of people's welfare such as health care, child care, social services, and education, depersonalizing important aspects of these functions.

Medical advances have raised new questions and created uncertainties and controversies about such fundamental aspects of existence as when life begins and ends, what constitutes medical treatment, what are individuals' rights as opposed to the obligations of the state in determining the manner of their dying or the timing of it, and whether health care for the elderly should be rationed or withheld to reduce health-care costs.

There is also much suffering and hardship and untimely death experienced by many people in many nations and within our own society. The spread of AIDS, substance abuse, and destructive behaviors against self and others are among the most troubling aspects of our time. They threaten not only the quality of life, but life itself.

We need informed, thoughtful people who are emotionally healthy, who care for themselves, and who are caring of others, to help work out solutions to these problems. Education is a major vehicle for producing such people. Children represent society's potential. They are the link to future generations. Survival and betterment are inevitably bound up with them. Any education about death, dying, and bereavement needs to be concerned with children.

Culture as Death Educator

Whether we know it or not, agree or disagree, children are recipients of death education by our action as well as inaction. Children grow up in society, learn from it, absorb its wisdom, myths, practices, its ambivalence, and its anxieties. Children adopt many values and beliefs from significant adults in their world such as parents, teachers, public figures, sports heroes, and famous entertainers. They also learn from their physical and symbolic environments. Thus, inevitably, children learn fundamental lessons and develop basic attitudes about death when they visit a cemetery, take part in a memorial service, observe adults discussing the subject among themselves. Children learn from myriads of nonverbal behaviors that accompany speech, such as the tone of voice, an expression on the face, the tightening of a facial muscle, a gesture, an abrupt silence when adults become aware of the child's presence. Children learn by watching the evening news, a television war movie, a crime series, a slasher film, when playing with their toys and games, and by observing dead animals in their backyards or on the way to the school bus.

This kind of death education is informal, mostly unintended, but powerful nonetheless. It is an ongoing process, part of the child's enculturation or socialization. It takes place at various times, in a variety of circumstances, and with varying degrees of emotional intensity. This learning prepares the child for his or her functioning and interaction as an adult.

Unfortunately, for a number of children in our society the question is not one of death education, unintended or intended, but of keeping these children alive and safe. An alarming increase of violence in the home, on the street, in the neighborhood, and on the playground, affects substantial numbers of school-aged children and youth, particularly in inner-city ghettos. Violent crimes have increased steadily throughout the 1980s (Uniform Crime Reports, 1991) and continue to increase in the 1990s. After accidents, violence is now the primary cause of death of young people. Deaths by homicide have increased by 300 percent in the age group 15–24 years (Lore & Schultz, 1993). Many young people live with the trauma of having been a witness to deadly violence. Even larger numbers are victims of violence because they live in constant fear for their lives. Across the country thousands of children and adolescents carry guns and other weapons to school. At a recent convention, the National Education Association announced that it would seek a special federal grant to help more schools buy metal detectors and hire security guards (Naylor, 1993). In such a context the concepts of death education as they have evolved in the field of thanatology seem irrelevant at best. Installing metal detectors in schools and increasing security patrols in school corridors and cafeterias may be helpful measures in the short term. But only broad-based, long-term prevention such as fighting poverty and substance abuse, creating job and career opportunities, and cleaning up the inner cities—all known risk conditions for violent behavior—can alleviate the problem.

Whether an encounter with death is the loss of a family member or peer through violence or illness, or the more remote experience of daily deaths on the evening news, the child experiences deaths as much as adults do, although not necessarily with the same meanings. If these experiences are troubling to adults, they are also troubling to the child. How the child is helped to understand and make sense of such experiences and how he or she is comforted in the face of them, are important questions for a society to answer.

Because today's average life expectancy is higher than in previous eras, because in the social structure of our society young adults form their own families and do not typically live with their elders, and because most people die away from home, many children do not experience the death of a family member. Often grandparents or other relatives who die in distant geographic regions were not emotionally close to children. Ironically in the same society, at a time of personal remoteness from death, children are continuously bombarded with it through the mass media. The type of death in the media is primarily violent. Not only is there much violent death reported daily on the news, but violent death is also a preferred theme in the popular culture. One need only casually peruse the listings of the feature films playing in the movie houses, or of the home videos that are popular as sales items or rentals, and sample the television fare for any given week, to be impressed by the preponderance of death, especially the spectacular, violent type. Death brings in millions of dollars for the entertainment industry and for advertisers. Although this kind of death experience is indirect and the full power of its long-term impact yet to be determined, many health professionals, pediatric specialists, and now also government officials, as well as many others, are deeply concerned about the profoundly adverse effects that experiences may have, such as distorted views of reality, fears, apathy, numbness, and destructive behavior.

There is good reason for this concern. Children spend many hours watching television. The National Coalition on Television Violence has estimated that in the course of their school years children will have watched nearly 40,000 episodes depicting violent deaths on television alone (Naylor, 1993). Such depiction occurs despite compelling evidence, gathered over several decades, of the negative effects of televised violence on children, (Surgeon General's Scientific Advisory Committee, 1972; Pearl, Bouthilet, & Lazar, 1982). Violence on television programs has continued to increase throughout the 1980s and since then. Only the threat of legislative action by the U.S. Congress (Hefner & Karlak, 1993) has brought promises from leaders of the television industry to lower the levels of violence in prime-time programming. Children are also major consumers of films and active participants in the home video market, which remains entirely unrated. Moreover, because of the nature of the medium, the typical death scenarios presented visually tend to be dramatic spectacles that often are of graphic detail but are superficial, seldom permitting viewers to become involved and to develop empathy for the victims. The pain of death or the grief of survivors are seldom shown in any depth. Frequent exposure to such presentations, along with other adverse circumstances at home or in school, contribute to the alarming increase in destructive youthful behavior (Bender, et al., 1992; Gentry & Eron, 1993) and to the special callousness increasingly found in acts of violence reported in the national press.

Parents as Death Educators

As the primary social unit, the family teaches the child the basic facts and values about himself or herself, the world, life, and death. Through their cognitive mediation, reassurance, and nurturance, parents have a fundamental role in helping the child to understand, evaluate, and manage his or her death experiences. Many parents are uncomfortable discussing death with their children and tend to avoid it There is still a tendency among parents and in the general public to believe that children are incurious, unaware, and unaffected by death and that, therefore, adults best leave that topic for later years.

We have known for some time, however, that children, even at very young ages, are curious, thoughtful, and concerned about death. They observe and gather data, interpret and misinterpret them, assimilate or accommodate them, and store what they have learned. They are as interested in death as they are in almost everything. They ask fundamental questions, to which philosophers and theologians have sought answers through the ages. For example, they ask, "Why did the hamster die?" "Where was I before I was born?" They also ask seemingly trivial questions, some of them disturbing to adults. For example, they ask questions related to the processes of death and decomposition. "How long does it take for a body to rot to the bones?" "Why do people die with their eyes open?" "What is rigor mortis?" "Why do people get buried alive?" "Does hair still grow after you die?" (Wass, 1984b). The nature of the questions reflects the child's level of cognitive development. Studies suggest that the child's understanding of death advances in discernible patterns from immature to more mature, from ego-centered to ego-decentered, and from concrete to abstract. We know, for instance, that the preschool child's understanding of death is guided by reasoning processes that are qualitatively different from those of the adult or even older child. The child uses magical, animistic, or other immature reasoning. Thus he or she understands death as a state of immobility or sleep, a temporary condition that can be reversed. It is important for parents and others to know this and to avoid reinforcing such thinking by their own explanations. Knowing the young child's thinking pattern is particularly important when a parent or sibling dies and parents and others are trying to help the child comprehend what has happened and reassure the child that his or her own life, care, and well-being are not threatened (Wass, 1984b).

Children also develop different kinds of fears and concerns depending on their developmental stage, life circumstances, and experience. Children fear the dark, monsters, vampires, werewolves, the devil. They fear being dropped, abandoned, buried alive. They fear losing parents, grandparents, and their own lives through individual violence, war, environmental destruction, nuclear destruction, or disease. To manage some of their death-related fears, it appears that children also develop mechanisms and behavior patterns of their own, such as magic practices and superstitions, humor, and denial (Wass & Cason, 1984). But parents can do a great deal to put the child's fears in perspective, and to reassure and comfort the child.

The first priority is, of course, that we provide a physically safe environment. In addition, the child needs a social environment that is psychologically nonthreatening. In an atmosphere of love, trust, and openness in which joyful and distressing events and all kinds of thoughts and feelings are shared, children are more likely to express fears they may have about death, to share disturbing thoughts, and to ask questions about the subject. Parents can encourage such expression, serve as sounding boards, comforters, and guides.

While many of the child's questions about death may be triggered by events and experiences that occur outside the home, parents can also "create occasions" to provide experiences that teach basic lessons about life and death. For instance, keeping a pet, especially one with a short life expectancy, enables the child to learn first-hand about the life cycle. It provides the child a natural opportunity to tend, love, and grieve for another creature, all with the caring guidance of parents.

Parents can be important resource persons guiding their children toward vicarious experiences with death through literature. Many excellent books on the market, written by sensitive writers for children of all ages, deal with the death of pet cats, dogs, birds, the death of grandparents, friends, siblings, parents. Psychologists have long noted the striking power such experiences can have for changing children's attitudes as well as informing, comforting, and entertaining the child (Wass, 1984c).

Parents are needed as monitors and mediators of the violence, real and fictional. Today such mediation is more important than ever. Commentary is needed to help children put violent behavior in perspective, to let children know violence is not inevitable, and to teach them that tolerance, caring, cooperation, and collaboration are better alternatives for people living together. Parents can also be role models for the child to develop healthy habits, constructive recreational activities and play, and to develop empathy and cooperative attitudes toward others, all antidotes to the violence and destructiveness prevalent in the popular culture, and increasing in the real world (Wass & Stillion; 1988; Gentry & Eron, 1993).

As more parents become informed about their children's intellectual capacities, interests, fears, and needs with respect to death, as they become more comfortable with the subject and more aware of the important function they can serve, they will be more likely to understand and interact in helpful ways with their children. There are a number of guidelines and suggestions and a variety of resources to assist parents with such efforts (e.g., Grollman, 1990; Wass & Corr, 1984).

Formal Death Education

The pioneers in the death movement recognized the need for education about death, dying, and bereavement for all levels and age groups as part of our cultural education. They also proposed more structured and systematic approaches of the kind provided in educational institutions. In this sense, formal death education can be viewed as the planned efforts undertaken or experiences provided involving death, dying, and bereavement.

The first and most prominent death educator was Dan Leviton. A health educator, he drew analogies to sex education in the taboo aspects of death-related topics, pointing at resistance from parents and the community to such education. He considered the ultimate goal of death education to be self-improvement, happiness, and health, and believed health educators to be an ideal group for leading such efforts in the schools (Leviton, 1969). Numerous articles and several books were published in the 1970s and early 1980s offering guidelines, activities, curricula, and resources for formal death education at various levels and in a variety of subject areas, most prominently in health education (e.g.,

Gordon & Klass 1979; Wass et al., 1980, 1985; Crase & Crase, 1984; Wass & Corr, 1984; Leviton, 1991).

We can only guess how much death education occurred in the schools without adequate empirical study, but judging from the considerable volume of publications in the 1970s and 1980s there were encouraging developments, especially in health education at the high school level. But by the mid 1980s progress seemed to have slowed, and programs eroded (Pine, 1986). A national survey confirmed this assessment. In that study it was found that less than one fifth of the schools carry out any systematic death education at the middle and high school levels and less than one tenth do so in the lower grades. Moreover, teachers said they do not lead discussions about death when students bring up the subject, and half of the teachers said such occasions rarely happen (Wass, Miller, & Thornton, 1990a).

There are probably a number of reasons for this lack of death education today. In recent years schools have come under severe criticism and pressure to produce more scientists and engineers. In our era of knowledge explosion it has become increasingly more difficult to decide what should be included in the schools' curricula. In the race of competing subjects and content the basic skills of reading, writing, and arithmetic and the sciences have traditionally won and seem to be winning now over the arts, humanities, and the developmental and social needs of the students.

In addition, few teachers have had any professional preparation in the area of death and dying. Currently there is little if anything about death in the curricula or even the textbooks for education majors. In fact, the knowledge that has been generated in the past 40 years or so has not yet been incorporated into the mainstream disciplines and fields in the other helping professions (Wass, 1992). For instance, there are few texts in general medicine, nursing, psychology, social work, human development, or counseling that include any but the most superficial treatment of death. And there are no licensing and board examinations in these professions that include items about dying, death, and grief, not to mention integration of death-related content into the professional curricula in these fields. Mainstreaming death-related knowledge is a high priority to accomplish appropriate education and support for children.

However, there have also been encouraging developments indicating that schools are becoming responsive to children's needs.

Crisis Intervention

We know today that children's responses to the loss of a loved one are not unlike those of adults except for those specifically related to their cognitive-developmental level. The kinds of things that help adults with their grief also help children. Because bereaved children are in school for most of the day, it helps when teachers, counselors, and other staff, and classmates as well, are supportive, understanding, and caring. When a child's parent or sibling has died, parents who normally nurture the child, are often so devastated by the loss that they are unable to provide any kind of comfort or care for the bereaved child. It is therefore especially important that the school assist the child during the crisis period.

Sometimes a classmate or other member of the school community dies. In 1986 nearly 40,000 children and young adults died in the United States, three-fourths of the deaths resulting from accidents or violence (Wass, 1991). A child is likely to lose a schoolmate through death *sometime* during the school years. The school can help the child grieve these deaths also. A schoolmate's death, especially when it is sudden and violent, affects surviving children deeply. Often this is the first personal encounter with a human death. The death of a young person, especially a peer, makes the child aware of his or her own vulnerability. That may be extremely threatening. The child may react with a host of feelings from rage to agitation, from denial to despair, and with a host of extreme behaviors, from aggression to withdrawal. In such situations crisis intervention and other counseling are essential for helping children to manage their reactions. Such help is indeed available to some extent. The study by Wass, Miller, and Thornton cited earlier showed that nearly 20 percent of U.S. public schools have some sort of grief counseling and support program for individual students, and to a lesser extent, for groups, or else recommend outside counseling.

Studies of child and adolescent suicide (e.g., Curran, 1987) have given us more insights and understanding of this problem. We are better able to describe behavioral symptoms of depression and suicide and know more about events and experiences in the child's life that may trigger suicidal episodes (Stillion, McDowell, & May, 1989).

Perhaps shaken out of complacency by high suicide rates in recent years, and by extremely high estimates of the incidence of suicide attempts and suicidal ideation in the young, health officials, health professionals, and educational leaders have urged schools to participate actively in preventive and interventive efforts. Many state departments of education have established mandates for the schools to provide such programs. A number of excellent programs have already been developed (e.g., Leenaars & Wenckstern, 1991) and are in fact offered. We found that a fourth of the nation's public schools provide some sort of suicide intervention and that such a program addresses at least *some* of the needs identified in recent research (Wass, Miller, & Thornton, 1990a).

Grief support and suicide intervention are primarily special programs designed to go into operation when a crisis occurs. They are not part of the regular curriculum. Nonetheless, they are planned and systematic responses by the schools to deaths that affect students. *All* schools should have policies and plans to deal with crises.

In addition to programs in crisis management, schools can provide education that is future oriented and preventive as well as interventive.

AIDS Education as Prevention

One recent effort toward classroom-based preventive education is AIDS education. With each new report from the Centers for Disease Control, other agencies, or the press, we are shocked and frightened about the seriousness of this disease. But there is also a great deal of denial and complacency. There are even voices suggesting that the problem is exaggerated. Whatever politics surround the issue, there can be no argument with data, and recent statistics *are* cause for concern. Thousands of adolescents, more than ever before, are at risk of contracting the human immunodeficiency virus (HIV) that causes AIDS (Cowley & Hager, 1993) because they engage in risky sexual behavior or use drugs, or both. Most adolescents have important misconceptions about the disease and methods of its prevention. One fifth of the people with AIDS are in their twenties, many of them having contracted the disease in adolescence (American School Health Association et al., 1988). According to the most recent statistics released by the Centers for Disease Control, an alarming increase in AIDS can be expected for the near future among women of childbearing ages, 15–44, African Americans, and adolescents (Cowley & Hager,1993).

Various health officials, commissions and committees, at federal and state levels, and professional associations have recommended that schools provide instruction about AIDS as part of a comprehensive health education program for all grade levels. Fortunately most state education departments are now mandating it. The U.S. Department of Health and Human Services in collaboration with the Centers for Disease Control and other health agencies and professional organizations (1988) has developed guidelines for such programs. At the local level, the medical community and school officials and parents have worked together to develop such programs. More than half of the public schools provide some sort of instruction about AIDS at least at the upper grade levels (Wass, Miller, & Thornton, 1990b), and, perhaps surprisingly, nearly all the parents in those schools support such education.

These developments show that agencies and organizations can mobilize and collaborate effectively to introduce programs in the schools that benefit children and society, as long as the need for such education is clearly perceived. What we need now are similar preventive efforts in the areas of violence, drug abuse, alcoholism, smoking, overeating, and other behaviors and habits that threaten health and life.

Long-term Preparation

There has been significant progress in crisis intervention in schools. Such programs need to be expanded at all levels, as do programs aimed at prevention. But, in addition, we need *long-term systematic education* about dying, death, and grief. Schools are logical places for such education. Next to the family they are the most important agents for socializing and educating the young in all aspects of life, to prepare them for a future of personal well-being and responsible social behavior.

Schools are probably the most effective vehicle for public education about death in the long term. The public is being educated about death in various forums, through books, pamphlets, the press, the electronic media, through seminars, workshops, and other communication by word of mouth. However, such education is not systematic or comprehensive. It can become so through the processes and mechanisms of our public schools.

Formal death education can perhaps serve as an effective antidote to the sort of death education, orientations, and attitudes that children receive through the popular culture in which death is explosive, graphic, and quick, and in which emotions receive scant attention. When schools teach about life and death they complement and underscore the family's efforts.

Goals

The goals for preparatory death education are essentially those articulated by Leviton and others in the 1960s and 1970s. They are to inform and help the child gain insights and understanding; to help him or her develop constructive views and values by learning to weigh issues based on observation, reason, and compassion; to help the child develop coping and helping skills, and, most of all, caring attitudes and behaviors toward himself or herself, others, and life. These goals reflect society's needs as well as those of the individual child. They address the three major domains, cognitive, affective, and behavioral, that psychologists have identified for learning.

To accomplish these goals we need to expand existing programs of counseling and support following a death and any continuing or follow-up efforts that are made afterwards.

Teachers need to accept the importance of discussing death in the classroom when external events make it necessary. Although such education is informal in the strict sense of the term, it can be made systematic through school policy and general preparedness and sensitivity.

A dramatic incident exemplifying how teachers may have to deal with death in the classroom unexpectedly was the explosion of the U.S.

space shuttle *Challenger* that killed seven astronauts. Several million school children watched the liftoff and witnessed the explosion on TV in their classrooms because one of the astronauts, Christa McAuliffe, a teacher, was among the crew and was to broadcast lessons from space. It would be difficult to ignore such a catastrophe. At such a time the best pedagogy may fail and the only thing for teachers to do is simply to respond as human beings. In this case most teachers apparently stopped regular class activity, talked about the events, allowed children to talk and share their shock and their feelings.

Death as Part of Regular Studies

Most of all, we need to begin the difficult but important process of incorporating the subject of death, dying, and grief into the regular curriculum in subject areas where it fits naturally. Such death education need not stand out or apart or in any way dominate the scene. It does not take much time and does not counter the main cognitive objectives of the schools. We can still prepare children to become scientists and engineers, and nurses and doctors. When schools attend to human and social needs, children will become better professionals, technicians, parents, and citizens.

In this approach death topics are discussed in many areas such as history, social studies, health sciences, family planning, biology, earth sciences, literature, and art. For instance, in *art* class the teacher might encourage students to choose subjects for painting projects such as grief, suffering, and death. In art appreciation the teacher can point to some of the famous art works created through the centuries that treat death. After all, many artists have chosen this fundamental experience as a theme for their work and millions of people have been enriched by seeing such creations.

One of the students in my class on childhood and death teaches *literature* in a high school. Not too long ago as the students were studying Shakespeare's "Romeo and Juliet" she challenged them. She said: "Suppose Romeo were Rick and Juliet were Stacy and they were both eleventh graders living in Jacksonville. Would they feel the same way or different? What could they do? How could they get help? Do *you* ever have suicidal thoughts and impulses?" The discussion that followed was an eye opener for the teacher. She was surprised about how deeply her students felt and how interested they were in the discussion. Several months previously one of the students at another high school had committed suicide.

Obvious subjects for incorporating death-related information and discussion and concern are *health sciences* and *health education*. The threat of death can be a powerful motivator for adopting healthy habits of eating, sleeping, exercising, and personal hygiene and for avoiding activities, no matter how tempting, that threaten health and life. It can also be the place for discussing problems that concern the health of the globe as Dan Leviton suggests (1991). Here or in the study of the *earth sciences* students can learn how industrialization and unchecked population growth are causing the slow but steady deterioration of the earth such as the destruction of rain forests, pollution of air, land, and water, and the depletion of the ozone layer. They can also learn that means and measures to halt this process are available.

A natural topic for the *life sciences* would be to study not only the life cycle of plants and small animals such as the butterfly, but that of humans as well, from conception, birth, growth, and maturity, to old age and death.

Psychology or *family planning* are natural subjects for discussing how people respond to the crisis of dying and death, what feelings, thoughts, and behaviors such experiences evoke, and how one can cope and transcend them, and support others in this process. Psychology or social studies might also be fitting subjects in which to discuss the dynamics of frustration and anger and to teach skills for their management, for the management of interpersonal conflicts as well as the skills of tolerance, empathy, and cooperation.

At the *elementary level* teachers can fit death-related topics in their teaching even more easily. Because they have more time with the students, they have a wider range of possibilities and options. In the study of the community, for example, younger students often are taken on field trips to city hall, the fire station, hospital, supermarket, the museum. They could also visit the cemetery and the funeral home in this context. The possibilities are numerous. Thoughtful teachers who are comfortable with the subject, and have basic knowledge about it, find ways to incorporate it naturally into their teaching.

There are several advantages of long-term preparatory death education. For one thing, the topic is embedded in a larger context rather than separated from it, and thus less likely to be distorted. Then, too, the long-term approach is a developmental approach in which the child learns death-related matters in ways that are appropriate to his or her developmental level, learns it from different perspectives, in small doses at a time. Because it is foresighted rather than reactive, the preparatory approach is likely to be more low-keyed and less stressful and emotionally taxing. Because of these factors, this approach may be more acceptable to parents and school officials.

Health professionals and others in the helping professions can assist in many different ways through their work, organizations, and especially at the community level to make death education more acceptable in the schools. For instance, they can help by offering consulting services to the schools, by helping with training and preparing teachers, and informing the public, school administrators, and others. They can also serve on school boards.

When family, schools, and other community agencies work together to help the young develop knowledge and skills for coping and transcending, and to instill in them motivations and values of caring and compassion, there may be a future of full humanity for all.

References

American School Health Association, et al. (1988). National adolescent student health survey. *Health Education, 19* (August/September), 4–8.

Associated Press. (1993). Top executives promise less violence on TV. *Daytona Beach News Journal*, May 22, 3A.

Bender, D. L., Szumski, B., Biskup, M. D., & Cozic, C. P. (Eds.). (1992). *Youth violence*. San Diego: Greenhaven Press.

Cowley, G., & Hager, M. (1993). What if a cure is far off? *Newsweek*. June 21, 70.

Crase, D. R., & Crase, D. (1984). Death education in the schools. In H. Wass and C. A. Corr (Eds.). *Childhood and death* (pp. 345–363). New York: Hemisphere.

Curran, D. K. (1987). *Adolescent suicidal behavior*. Washington, DC: Hemisphere.

Feifel, H. (1959). *The meaning of death*. New York: McGraw-Hill.

Gentry, J., & Eron, L. D. (1993). American Psychological Association Commission on Violence and Youth. *American Psycholologist, 48*, 2, 89.

Gordon, A. K., & Klass, D. (1979). *They need to know: How to teach children about death*. Englewood Cliffs, NJ: Prentice-Hall.

Grollman, E. (1990). *Talking about death: A dialogue between parent and child*, 3d ed. Boston: Beacon.

Hefner, P., & Karlak, P. (1993). When violence entertains. *Gainesville Sun*, July 5.

Kantrowitz, B. (1993). Teen violence: Wild in the streets. *Newsweek*, August 2, 40–49.

Leenaars, A. A., & Wenckstern, S. (Eds.). (1991). *Suicide prevention in schools*. New York: Hemisphere.

Leviton, D. (1969). The need for education on death and suicide. *Journal of School Health, 39*, 270–274.

Leviton, D. (Ed.). (1991). *Horrendous death, health, and well-being*. New York: Hemisphere.

Lore, R. K., & Schultz, L. A. (1993). Control of human aggression. *American Psychologist, 48*, 1, 16–25.

Naylor, R. (1993). Rising violence in schools worries teachers, pupils. *Gainesville Sun*, July 5.

Pearl, D., Bouthilet, L., & Lazar, J. (Eds.). (1982). *Television and behavior: Ten years of scientific progress and implications for the eighties: Vol. 1. Summary report*. Washington, DC: US Government Printing Office.

Pine, V. R. (1986). The age of maturity for death education: A socio-historical portrait of the era 1976–1985. *Death Studies, 10,* 209–231.

Stillion, J. M., McDowell, E. E., & May, J. H. (1989). *Suicide across the life span: Premature exits*. New York: Hemisphere.

Surgeon General's Scientific Advisory Committee Report on Television and Social Behavior. (1972). *Television and growing up: The impact of televised violence*. Washington, DC: US Government Printing Office.

Uniform Crime Reports, 1990. (1991). Washington, DC: US Department of Justice, US Government Printing Office.

US Department of Health and Human Services, Public Health Service, Centers for Disease Control, & Center for Health Promotion and Education. (1988). Guidelines for effective school health education to prevent the spread of AIDS. *Health Education, 19,* 6–12.

Wass, H. (1984a). Concepts of death: A developmental perspective. In H. Wass & C. A. Corr (Eds.). *Childhood and death* (pp. 3–24). New York: Hemisphere and McGraw-Hill International.

Wass, H. (1984b). Parents, teachers, and health professionals as helpers. In H. Wass & C. A. Corr (Eds.). *Helping children cope with death, second edition,* (pp. 75–130). New York: Hemisphere McGraw-Hill,

Wass, H. (1984c). Books for children: An annotated bibliography. In H. Wass & C. A. Corr (Eds.). *Helping children cope with death, second edition* (pp. 373–376). New York: Hemisphere and McGraw-Hill International.

Wass, H. (1992). Disseminating our thanatology knowledge. In E. J. Clark (Ed.). *The Thanatology community and the needs of the movement* (pp. 37–49). New York: Haworth.

Wass, H., & Cason, L. (1984). Fears and anxieties about death. In H. Wass & C. A. Corr (Eds.). *Childhood and death* (pp. 25–45). New York: Hemisphere and McGraw-Hill International.

Wass, H., & Corr, C. A. (1984). *Helping children cope with death, second edition*. New York: Hemisphere.

Wass, H., Corr, C. A., Pacholski, R. A., & Forfar, C. S. (1985). *Death education: An annotated resource guide, volume II*. New York: Hemisphere and McGraw-Hill International.

Wass, H., Corr, C. A., Pacholski, R. A., & Sanders, C. M. (1980). *Death education: An annotated resource guide*. New York: Hemisphere and McGraw-Hill International.

Wass, H., Miller, M. D., & Thornton, G. (1990a). *Death education and grief/ suicide intervention in the public schools*. *Death Studies, 14*(3), 253–268.

Wass, H., Miller, M. D., & Thornton, G. (1990b). AIDS Education in the U.S. Public Schools. *AIDS Education and Prevention, 2*(3), 213–219.

Wass, H., & Stillion, J. (1988). Death in the lives of children and adolescents. In H. Wass, F. M. Berardo, & R. A. Neimeyer (Eds.). *Dying—Facing the facts, 2nd edition* (pp. 201–228). New York: Hemisphere/Harper & Row.

Twenty-three

Death Education
for Adults

Charles A. Corr

Charles A. Corr is a professor at the School of Humanities, Southern Illinois University at Edwardsville, and a volunteer with Hospice of Madison County in Illinois.

Dr. Corr has been a member of the boards of directors of the Association for Death Education and Counseling (1980–1983), the Illinois State Hospice Organization (1981–1984), and the International Work Group on Death, Dying, and Bereavement (1987–1993; chairperson, 1989–1993), as well as the Professional Advisory Board, Madison County Chapter, The Compassionate Friends (1980–present), the Scientific Review Board, Children's Hospice International (1988–present), the Honorary Board, The Dougy Center, Portland, Oregon (1988–present), and the National Donor Family Council, National Kidney Foundation (1992–present).

In addition to more than 50 articles and chapters, Dr. Corr's publications include: Death Education: An Annotated Resource Guide *(Hemisphere, Vol. I = 1980; Vol. II = 1985);* Hospice Care: Principles and Practice *(Springer, 1983);* Helping Children Cope with Death: Guidelines and Resources *(2nd ed., Hemisphere, 1984);* Childhood and Death *(Hemisphere, 1984);* Hospice Approaches to Pediatric Care *(Springer, 1985);* Adolescence and Death *(Springer, 1986);* Sudden Infant Death Syndrome: Who Can Help and How *(Springer, 1991); and* Death and Dying, Life and Living *(Brooks/Cole, 1994).*

Dr. Corr's professional work has been recognized by awards from the Association for Death Education and Counseling (1988) and Children's Hospice International (1989); Honorary Membership in the Society of Palliative Care (Towarzystwo Opieki Paliatywnej) in Poznan, Poland (1990); five Book-of-theYear Awards from the American Journal of Nursing; and Research Scholar (1990), Outstanding Scholar (1991), and Kimmel Community Service Awards (1994) from his university.

In the late 1950s and early 1960s, it was common to say that death was a taboo topic (Feifel, 1963). Gorer (1965) went so far as to say that death had changed places with sex, and that death was the "new pornography." This did not mean that issues related to dying, death, and bereavement had gone completely without discussion. To mention just one example, Plato's famous portraits of the trial, imprisonment, and death of Socrates in the *Apology, Crito,* and *Phaedo* are classics of western literature, and they include Socrates' observation that the whole of philosophy or human wisdom can be construed as a preparation for death (Phaedo, 67e).

But at the middle of the twentieth century, research and writing on dying, death, and bereavement were limited, and there were few educational opportunities in this field. In this context, Feifel's book, *The Meaning of Death* (1959), is a landmark that helped to encourage behavioral scientists, clinicians, and humanists to direct attention to these topics, study and do research, write articles and books, found journals and organizations, and engage in education of all sorts (Pine, 1977). That has led to educational programs for preschool and church-school groups, children and adolescents in elementary and secondary schools, college and preprofessional students, postgraduate and professional audiences, and hospice volunteers, members of support groups, and the general public (Wass, et al., 1980, 1985).

Important historical developments in the field of death education have been reviewed by Pine (1977, 1986) in two concise, informed, and effective articles. Our task is to understand the phenomenon of death education—that is, education specifically concerned with death-related issues. In order to do this, we need to think first about societal relationships with and attitudes toward death. Much of this applies to all of society's citizens—children, adolescents, adults, and the elderly—but our specific concern in this chapter is education for adults.

Societal Death Systems

Every society has its own *death system* (Kastenbaum, 1972). That is, every society develops ways in which, as an organized entity, it deals with the implications of dying, death, and bereavement. In technical terms, a death system is the "sociophysical network by which we mediate and express our relationship to mortality" (p. 310). In other words, in response to the implications of death, every society seeks to organize itself in various ways, on behalf of both the collective entity and its individual members. It does this by erecting a functional structure that it puts between death and its implications, on the one hand, and itself and its members, on the other hand, and that interprets the former to the latter.

One society's death system might be formally or explicitly organized in some or all of its respects. By contrast, another death system might be informally expressed in the ways in which the society conducts its everyday affairs. In practice, most death systems are likely to combine formal and informal elements.

Until recently, not much attention had been paid to the overall structure and patterns of societal death systems. But when individuals are asked to reflect on their own society's death system, they usually can easily identify its components and recognize ways in which they function. This suggests that most of us are familiar with the workings of our own society's death system, although we may not have thought of it in those terms.

Elements of a death system include: (1) people—individuals defined by their more-or-less permanent or stable roles in the death system, such as funeral directors, lawyers, florists, and life insurance agents; (2) places—specific locations that have assumed a death-related character, such as cemeteries, funeral homes, health-care institutions, and the "hallowed ground" of a battlefield or disaster; (3) times—occasions which are associated with death, such as Memorial Day, Good Friday, or the anniversary of a death; (4) objects—things whose character is somehow linked to death, such as death certificates, hearses, obituaries and death notices in the newspaper, weapons, tombstones, a gallows, or an electric chair; and (5) symbols—things that have come to signify death, such as a black armband, a skull and crossbones, certain solemn organ music, and certain words or phrases.

Functions of a death system are: (1) to give warnings and predictions, as in the case of civil defense sirens; (2) to prevent death, as in the case of emergency medical care; (3) to care for the dying, as in the case of modern hospice programs; (4) to dispose of the dead, as in the case of funeral directors, cemeteries, and crematories; (5) to work toward social consolidation after death, as in the case of funeral ritual or self-help groups for the bereaved; (6) to help make sense of death, as in the case of certain religious or philosophical systems; and (7) to bring about socially sanctioned killing, as in the case of some aspects of police protection, training for war, and capital punishment.

The important point about the notion of a death system is that such a system will be found in some form in every society. No society is without a system for coping with the fundamental realities that death presents to human existence. Much can therefore be learned about any society by considering the nature of its death system and the ways in which it functions.

A Death-denying Society?

Some have argued that the death system in our society functions largely to deny the presence of death, to exile or exclude death as a social or public reality (e.g., Kübler-Ross, 1969). Many things can be said in support of that view. For example, through a process of institutionalization, professionalization, and specialization, we have tended in our society to move death away from the mainstream of living. And we are often unwilling to speak openly or directly about death, preferring to employ oblique, evasive, or euphemistic language instead. Surely, it is true that the death system in our society functions in many important ways to keep death at a distance from the mainstream of life and to gloss over many of its harsh aspects.

That may be either good or bad (or perhaps a bit of both), but it is too simple to say that ours is solely a death-denying society. It is that, in many respects, but it is also more than that. Death is. It cannot be denied or avoided everywhere and at all times. Life, death, and societies are more complex than they are made to appear in the slogan of a "death-denying society." For that matter, denial and acceptance are themselves complicated phenomena that can coexist in individuals and in societies by functioning on several levels at the same time (Dumont & Foss, 1972; Weisman, 1972).

We need not think only of a contrast between acceptance or denial when we seek to characterize the death system in any society. We will do better to think of the many—often different, sometimes contrasting or contradictory—ways in which a given society relates to the many-sided issues associated with dying, death, and bereavement. If so, we will ask ourselves questions of the following sort: What is the nature of our death system? How does it function? How well does it serve our needs?

Societal Groups, Their Members, and Protection

One judgment about death systems in the modern, developed societies of North America and Western Europe is the following: "We have created systems which protect us in the aggregate from facing up to the very things that as individuals we most need to know" (Evans, 1971, p. 83). There are two important elements in this judgment: the interests of the aggregate against those of the individual, and the theme of "protection."

Groups do tend to serve their own interests. They will argue that this is done so that they can serve the interests of the largest number of their members. Or they will say that serving the interests of its members is achieved through serving the interests of the group. This is a noble ideal. It is often true. But not always. Conflicts do arise, as when society exercises powers of eminent domain to take private property of individuals for public (group) purposes, or when society sends its youth abroad to fight and die in wars on behalf of communal rather than individual interests. So we need to inquire whether our death system maintains an appropriate balance between the interests of the society and of the individual.

How will we judge the value of the desire to "protect" people from the realities of dying, death, and bereavement? Many years ago, the French essayist, La Rochefoucauld (1868, I, 41), said that "one can no more look steadily at death than at the sun." This is certainly true. To gaze directly and without filters at the sun is to run the risk of loss of one's vision, just as immersion in death without some redeeming perspective can numb and overwhelm vitality in living. But we do live our lives in the warmth and light of the sun, and we inspect it, often obliquely or through some sort of screen. Similarly, it is the privilege and obligation of human beings to be able to conduct their lives with an awareness of their own mortality. We cannot expect to cope effectively with loss, grief, and death when they break into our lives if we have not prepared ourselves to do so. Too much protection or protection of the wrong sorts may not be conducive to maximizing quality in living.

Society and Education

All of the mediating and expressive functions of a societal death system involve education. To give warnings and predictions about death or to try to prevent death is to alert people to the dangers of death and to advise them how to behave to minimize those dangers. To care for the dying and to support the bereaved is to draw attention to the needs of vulnerable people and to emphasize both how and why others should help. To dispose of the dead is to acknowledge that the corpse is no longer a living person, but still remains an object for special treatment. To help make sense of death and to sanction certain sorts of killings is to affirm an intellectual and value framework within which both life and death find their appropriate places.

Death systems are not neutral. They reflect attitudes and express positions through which messages are conveyed. Through its death system, a society says: This is how we ought to cope with death; this is how we will cope with death. Individuals are free to accept and internalize these messages, or to resist and reject them. But it is foolish to ignore or remain ignorant of them. The death system in our society is the milieu in which we live. Its messages are powerful and omnipresent.

Education for Adults: Four Levels

Education for adults in the field of dying, death, and bereavement is conducted at four distinguishable levels: the cognitive, the affective, the behavioral, and the valuational. Death education is a *cognitive* or intellectual enterprise in the sense that it provides information about death-related experiences and aids in understanding those experiences. Information of this sort takes many forms. For example, it is important to know that towards the end of the 1980s lung cancer surpassed breast cancer as the leading cancer cause of death for women. This tragic fact is clearly related to patterns of smoking and is, in part, an ironic outcome of cigarette advertising that tells women "you've come a long way, baby." Similarly, during the early 1980s it was the recognition of an unusually high incidence in young males of a relatively rare form of skin cancer, Kaposi's sarcoma, which had hitherto been confined largely to elderly males of Mediterranean descent, that helped to identify a new cause of death, acquired immune deficiency syndrome (AIDS).

The cognitive dimensions of death education run parallel to similar dimensions in all academic or classroom education, although these are not the only ways such dimensions can be addressed. In addition to facts, this dimension of education includes new ways of organizing or interpreting the data of our experience. In the field of thanatology, for example, Elisabeth Kübler-Ross (1969) and Maria Nagy (1948) are both well known for stage-based theories they advanced to explicate coping with dying (in the case of Kübler-Ross) and cognitive development in children (in the case of Nagy). Each of these theories has its limits and its critics; each has also helped draw attention to and illuminate an important field of study.

The *affective* dimensions of death education have to do with feelings and emotions about dying, death, and bereavement. A wide range of feelings, for example, are involved in experiences of loss and bereavement. Research and education in this area helps to sensitize the non-bereaved to the depth, intensity, duration, and complexities of grief following a death. Much of this has yet to be communicated to the public at large, which may still wrongly tend to think that a few days or weeks may be more than adequate to "forget" or "get over" the death of an important person in one's life (Osterweis, Solomon, & Green, 1984). In fact, mourning is far more like ongoing adaptation or learning to live with one's loss than it is like ending a process or resolving a problem, and recent research has suggested that it is important for at least some bereaved persons to maintain the "empty space" and not "finish grieving" (McClowry, et al., 1987).

In its affective dimensions, death education seeks to appreciate the feelings of those who have been affected by death, as well as the feelings of those who have not been so affected. For example, we have learned that it is always wrong for someone who has not been bereaved to say to a bereaved person, "I know how you feel." Not only is this impossible, but bereaved persons have told us how arrogant it appears to them and how it seems to diminish the uniqueness and poignancy of their loss. Instead of dismissing grief associated with miscarriage or stillbirth, on the false assumption that no bonding had yet occurred, we have learned to appreciate the many forms of bonding during pregnancy and the legitimacy of parental grief in cases of perinatal death (Lamb, 1988). This has led to widespread recognition in professional pediatric circles of the value of permitting parents to see and hold the dead infant as a means of completing the bonding process and laying the foundation for healthy mourning. In the light of realistic education, what might have seemed ghoulish or repugnant to the uninformed can now be seen as part of a healthy process.

The third important dimension of death education has to do with *behavioral* considerations. Why do people act as they do in death-related situations? How should or could people act in such situations? Behavior is the outward expression of what we feel and believe. In our society, much behavior, both public and private, seeks to avoid contact with dying, death, and bereavement. Often, that is because people do not know what to say or what to do in such situations. They pull back from contact with the dying or the bereaved, leaving the latter alone and without support or companionship at a time when sharing and solace are most needed (Klass, 1988). Similarly, many people hesitate to mention the name of a deceased person, leaving survivors to feel the double loss of both the presence and the memory of that person.

In contrast to all of this, the hospice movement in recent years has taught us how very much can be done to help people cope with dying (Corr & Corr, 1983), much as research on funeral ritual (Fulton, 1988) and on self-help groups (Lieberman & Borman, 1979) has shown the way to assist people coping with bereavement. Such education affirms the very great value to be found in the presence of a caring person and it directs us not so much to speak as to practice active listening. Sometimes it gives us confidence to be comfortable when we are only sitting quietly with our discomfort. For many, it has led to the development of skills in interacting. None of this eliminates the sadness of death, but it can help to recreate the caring communities that all vulnerable people need but that seem too frequently to have atrophied in many modern societies.

The fourth or *valuational* dimension of death education lies in its role in helping us to identify, articulate, and affirm the basic values that govern our lives. The only life we know in this world is inextricably bound up with death. We would not have *this* life if death were not one of its essential parts—and we struggle in our imaginations to conceive what any sort of life without death might be like. Life and death, living and dying, happiness and sadness, attachments and loss—neither pole in these and many other similar dyads stands alone in our experience. For this reason, the perspective of death is an essential one (but not the only one) in helping us to achieve an adequate understanding of life.

Many of the things already mentioned point towards what we value: vulnerability, resilience, temporality, finitude, community. But perhaps our values come to the fore most sharply when we are asked what shall we tell our children about death and how shall we respond to the moral problems of our time? Shall we hide death from children and beguile them with tales of an unending journey without shadows or tears? Can we sustain such a charade for long? And will it enable our children to cope with life on their own when we are gone (dead?) or unavailable? Or shall we introduce children to the realities of death in ways that are appropriate to their developmental level and capacities, and with the support of mature values that enable us to live life and cope with death (Wass & Corr, 1984a, 1984b)?

Death-related values arise in many of the moral problems of our time: nuclear warfare, epidemic, famine and malnutrition, dislocation of populations, capital punishment, and all of the quandaries posed by modern medicine and its complex technologies. For example, is life the ultimate value? I think not. Others might disagree. Certainly, human life is a value and for the most part an important one. This is part of what is meant by saying that life is sacred. But that is not the same as the assertion that life is absolute. I might sacrifice my life for the sake of the lives of others or perhaps for some transcendent value. And although I might act to sustain life when the life itself retained the potential to engage in human relationships and when its sustenance required no more than my presence and ordinary modes of care, would I do so when there was no longer the potential for any human relationship and when its sustenance depended on extraordinary interventions of medical technology?

Is there a "right to die"? Or is that only a popular slogan, so vague as to encompass a diverse range of situations, from a right to expect appropriate treatment when I am dying, to a right to refuse unwanted and unproductive interventions, to a right to end my own life?

Education for Adults: Goals

Our fundamental goals in death education for adults are of three general sorts. The first has to do with individuals themselves; the second concerns individuals in their personal transactions with society; and the third concerns individuals in their public roles as citizens within the society. First, education about dying, death, and bereavement is intended *to enrich the personal the lives* of those to whom it is directed. It helps them understand themselves, to appreciate their strengths and their limitations as finite human beings. Most of us wish to control every aspect of our lives. That is not a wish we can expect to achieve. Instead, only realistically hope to influence those aspects of our lives that fall within the scope of our autonomy. That may not seem like enough; we want more. But although accidents (mostly involving automobiles) are the fourth leading cause of death in our society and even though we cannot prevent our deaths in accidents, it is nevertheless important to fasten our seatbelts and drive defensively whenever we are on the road.

There is a self-help group called "Make Today Count" (Kelly, 1975) for those who have a life-threatening illness. Its members are living under the threat of death. Is that not true in some sense for all of us? In response to this realization, members of Make Today Count chapters find meaning and fulfillment in each day they are alive. Against this, think how many people are merely "killing time." Death education encourages every individual to make each day of his or her life as satisfying as it can be. This is not a hedonism of the moment, which gives no thought to the consequences of one's actions. That sort of hedonism is blind to the future, in just the way that so much living for the future is blind to the passing present. When we make today count we do not exclude memories from the past or hopes for the future, but we emphasize that the past is gone, the future may not come, and the present is all that we really have right now to treasure and enjoy.

The second goal of death education is *to inform and guide individuals in their personal transactions with society*. For our purposes, this goal can be illustrated by considering transactions with two major components of our societal death system: health-care services and the funeral industry. From birth to death, we are all consumers of health care, but statistics show that we draw upon such services most during the last six months of our lives. Care of those who have far-advanced illnesses, who are chronically ill and unable to take care of themselves, or who are terminally ill is big business in modern societies.

In recent years, the death awareness movement has drawn attention to the fact that even those who are within days or hours of death are alive. Dying patients, we have come to realize, are living human beings. As such, dying persons and their family members need to be informed about services that are available to them and options they might select. Should one continue to seek a cure to forestall death or is it appropriate to place greater emphasis on the management of distressing symptoms? Who should provide services and where should they be provided, e.g., at home or in an institution? Education acquaints us with alternatives and enables us to select for ourselves those that most satisfy the needs and preferences of the individuals involved.

Similarly, education speaks to the importance of funeral ritual as a means to achieve a number of important functions: *incorporation* of the corpse into the world of the dead; *separation* of the living from the dead, and of the living from their former roles, which have been altered by the death; and *integration* of the living back into society in their new roles (Fulton, 1988). But different societies and individuals address these functions in different ways. In our own society, one may embalm and view the body, bury the corpse under ground or entomb it in a mausoleum, cremate and dispose of the remains in various ways (burial, entombment, inurnment, or scattering of ashes), donate the body to science, and/or conduct a memorial service in the absence of a body. Each of these options has served the needs of some people at some time; any one of them may be unsatisfactory to a particular person or group. Education in this area is intended to inform people about alternatives and to assist them to choose which best serve their needs.

It is frequently said that a funeral represents the third largest expenditure (after the costs of a house and an automobile) that most individuals will make in their lives. And health care towards the end of life is also a major expense, although its burden may be amortized by federal funding and private insurance over many years of premiums and income from a group of beneficiaries. If death education only resulted in an informed consumer in these two areas, it would have done much to improve the ways in which individuals relate to their societies.

The third goal of death education is *to prepare individuals for their public roles as citizens within a society.* Once upon a time, when questions were raised about the legal meaning of death, society turned to "common law," the common body of knowledge and wisdom about any subject. Common law was often represented by a legal dictionary, such as Black's Law Dictionary (Black, 1979, p. 360), which defined death as "the cessation of life." Such a definition is true enough, but it seems to lack specificity and is not very explicit in its guidance. Recognizing that, the dictionary went on to offer a further explication of the concept of death as "permanent cessations of all vital functions and signs." The vital functions in question were usually identified as involving the respiratory and circulatory systems, and the signs were typically expressed in terms of bodily fluids, that is, air (or, more specifically, oxygen) and blood.

Some difficulties arose with the introduction of mechanical devices like the respirator, which forced air into and out of the lungs and which could often in this way stimulate the action of the heart. Was this "flow of vital bodily fluids" (and thus, life), or was it merely ventilation and the mimicry of such vitality? When these questions arose in civil or criminal litigation, judges and juries were forced to make decisions that led to case law. In the absence of legal rule or precedent, such decisions were not always consistent.

The natural progression of things leads to the enactment of legislation on such difficult points in order to guide the courts. Such legislation may take into account the views of various experts, but in the end it is the work of a political process on the part of those who represent the people. Clearly, when the populace and its representatives are informed and articulate, one might have a better basis on which to hope for sound public policy. The task of education is to contribute to policy making on issues like definition of death, natural death or living wills, durable power of attorney in health-care matters, organ transplantation, euthanasia, capital punishment, and a variety of other matters. No one can expect a democratic system to function effectively when its educational underpinnings are inadequate.

Adult Audiences for Death Education

Kalish (1989, p. 75) has described four types of concern in individuals who express interest in death education: "(1) personal concern because of some previous experience that has not been resolved; (2) personal concern because of some ongoing experience, such as the critical illness or very recent death of a close family member; (3) involvement with a relevant form of work, such as nursing, medicine, social work, the ministry, or volunteer service through a hospice organization; or (4) a wish to understand better what death means or how to cope more effectively with one's own death or the death or grief of others."

People with each of these types of concern can readily be identified in classes, workshops, or presentations on dying, death, or bereavement. Those who are dealing with a current death-related experience or with the aftermath of an unresolved death-related experience deserve special sensitivity. They may be very tender in their feelings and vulnerable to added pain. Many have chosen to come to an educational forum in order to use the information and other resources it provides in coping with their own experiences. But it is important to keep in mind the distinctions between education, support, and therapy, and to be alert to individuals who need intervention beyond education or simple support.

Two examples come to mind in this connection. The first was a young man who enrolled in our college course on children and death. In introducing himself, he explained that he had been planning to marry a divorced woman with three young boys. She died accidentally, and the boys were returned to the custody of their natural father. Our student explained that he felt a tie to these boys and had enrolled in this course to learn how he might help them, but as the class went on it became clear that his own needs were also salient. A second example was a young woman who enrolled in our college course on death and dying. After the first class, she talked to the two instructors and told them that her sister's fiancé had been killed in an auto accident just one week earlier. We asked her to consider whether she might wish to withdraw from this class at this time. Had she selected that option, we promised to arrange for her enrollment in another term. In the end, she chose to stay in the course, but did not find that an easy decision with which to live. She managed to get through the term only because she was very determined and because she sought the help of several private conferences with the instructors during which she was free to cry and express her feelings.

Individuals who enroll in death-related educational offerings for vocational reasons usually express their desire to improve their competencies to help those whom they serve, as patients or clients. For example, it was nurses who first flocked to seminars in this field offered by Dr. Elisabeth Kübler-Ross (1969), because they knew that they needed assistance and that they would likely be the ones who would find themselves alone in the middle of the night with a dying person. Some who link death education to their work speak only of what the education will mean for their clients. Others realize that it also applies to them, both as professionals in coping with their work-related responsibilities and as persons in their own right. With Kübler-Ross (1969), death education seeks to show its relevance in all of these ways: to the client who is coping with dying or bereavement, to the helper in his or her work-related role, and to the helper as a person in his or her own right. As Shneidman (1978) has noted, death-related interactions are the only ones of which it can never be said that the problems being faced by the client are not also problems to be faced by the helper.

A fourth group of people turn to death education for a different sort of reason. They do not have the immediate pressure of a past or present experience, nor are they primarily associated with work-related concerns. Rather, their motivation involves curiosity about the subject, which may be combined with a desire to prepare themselves for personal experiences that might arise in the future. Sometimes people like this will say, "No one important to me in my life has yet died. But my grandparents are getting pretty old." These individuals are pro-active, and prefer to act ahead of time to prepare themselves (insofar as that is possible), and not just wait until events demand a reaction. Individuals of this sort have benefited from the longer average life expectancies of the "death-free generation," but they are sufficiently alert to realize that their advantage cannot be endless and that no human life is "death-free."

Conclusion

During the seventeenth century, Francis Bacon (1620; 1960) described three kinds of philosophers. His description is relevant here because he meant by *philosopher* a person who seeks wisdom, a combination of knowledge and practical relevance. For his model, Bacon proposed that philosophers were like ants, spiders, or bees. We can think of these images as suggesting three views of death education for adults.

Ants are empiricists who gather lots of raw materials, but often without much selectiveness and without modifying what they have gathered for constructive exploitation. The caricature of this is the idiot savant, who retains and can recall huge masses of information about some limited or arcane subject, e.g., baseball batting averages. At best, the empiricist ant acts only to acquire information and then to produce it when required. But that is the end of the process. In this model, education might be described in terms of writing on a blank tablet or filling up an empty vessel. If this is so, then learners are essentially passive; their education is primarily determined by the nature of the external forces that act upon them.

According to Bacon, spiders represent philosophers of a different sort who spin theories of marvelous ingenuity and formal perfection out of their own innards. Here, one simply offers opinions without any foundation in the external world. This reflects a popular view of philosophy as the mere dreaming up of plausible theories, but it also describes a large group of people in our society who base their attitudes on their feelings, rather than on information or evidence. Such people take action to state their views, but they are essentially uneducated because, even when their theories are cleverly constructed, they lack effective links to the realities of life.

By contrast with ants and spiders, Bacon reminds us that bees both gather materials and transform them in satisfying and productive ways. Without the pollen gathered by worker bees who venture out of the hive into the countryside, there would be no honey. But it is equally true that without the contribution of the bees' internal organs, even the nectar of the sweetest flower would never be transformed into honey. Humans who proceed in the manner of bees both gather data obtained through their encounters with the world, and reflect upon it in ways that convert it from a brute given to an intelligent aspect of a larger mosaic of knowledge and appreciation.

In all of its many forms, death education for adults is intended to provide the materials, to suggest insights, and to guide the reflective self-understanding that help us to cope in more effective ways as individuals, as consumers, and as citizens with our own death, with the deaths of those close to us, and with all of the other implications of death throughout our lives. To the degree that this process is successful, our lives, our societies, and our death systems will be energized and enriched.

References

Bacon, F. (1620; 1960). *The new organon and related writings.* Ed. F. H. Anderson. New York: Bobbs-Merrill.

Black, H. C. (1979). *Black's Law Dictionary* (5th ed.). St. Paul: West.

Corr, C. A., & Corr, D. M. (Eds.). (1983). *Hospice care: Principles and practice.* New York: Springer.

Dumont, R., & Foss, D. (1972). *The American view of death: Acceptance or denial?* Cambridge, MA: Schenkman.

Evans, J. (1971). *Living with a man who is dying.* New York: Taplinger.

Feifel, H. (Ed.). (1959). *The meaning of death.* New York: McGraw-Hill.

Feifel, H. (1963). Death. In N. L. Farberow (Ed.), *Taboo topics* (pp. 8–21). New York: Atherton.

Fulton, R. (1988). The funeral in contemporary society. In H. Wass, F. M. Berardo, & R. A. Neimeyer (Eds.), *Dying: Facing the facts* (2nd ed.; pp. 257–277). Washington, DC: Hemisphere.

Gorer, G. (1965). The pornography of death. In G. Gorer, *Death, grief, and mourning* (pp. 192–199). Garden City, NY: Doubleday. [Originally in *Encounter*, Oct. 1955, 5(4), 49–52.]

Kalish, R. A. (1989). Death education. In R. Kastenbaum & B. Kastenbaum (Eds.), *Encyclopedia of death* (pp. 75–79). Phoenix, AZ: Oryx.

Kastenbaum, R. (1972). On the future of death: Some images and options. *Omega, 3,* 306–318.

Kelly, O. (1975). *Make today count.* New York: Delacorte.

Klass, D. (1988). *Parental grief: Solace and resolution.* New York: Springer.

Kübler-Ross, E. (1969). *On death and dying.* New York: Macmillan.

Lamb, Sr., J. M. (Ed.). (1988). *Bittersweet...hellogoodbye: A resource in planning farewell rituals when a baby dies.* Belleville, IL: SHARE National Office.

La Rochefoucauld (1868–1881). Réflexions ou sentences et maximes morales, #26. In his *Oeuvres,* Ed. D. Gilbert & J. Gourdault (3 vols.; I, 41). Paris: Hachette.

Lieberman. M. A., & Borman, L. (1979). *Self-help groups for coping with crisis.* San Francisco: Jossey-Bass.

McClowry, S., Davies, E. B., May, K. A., Kulenkamp, E. J., & Martinson, I. M. (1987). The empty space phenomenon: The process of grief in the bereaved family. *Death Studies, 11,* 361–374.

Nagy, M. (1948). The child's theories concerning death. *The Journal of Genetic Psychology, 73,* 3–27.

Osterweis, M., Solomon, F., & Green, M. (Eds.). (1984). *Bereavement: Reactions, consequences, and care.* Washington, DC: National Academy.

Pine, V. R. (1977). A socio-historical portrait of death education. *Death Education, 1*, 57–84.

Pine, V. R. (1986). The age of maturity for death education: A sociohistorical portrait of the era 1976-1985. *Death Studies, 10*, 209–231.

Plato. (1961). The collected dialogues of Plato including the letters. Edited by E. Hamilton & H. Cairus. New York: Bollingen Foundation.

Shneidman, E. S. (1978). Some aspects of psychotherapy with dying persons. In C. A. Garfield (Ed.), *Psychosocial care of the dying patient* (pp. 201–218). New York: McGraw-Hill.

Wass, H., & Corr, C. A. (1984a). *Childhood and death.* Washington, DC: Hemisphere.

Wass, H., & Corr, C. A. (1984b). *Helping children cope with death: Guidelines and resources* (2nd ed.). Washington, DC: Hemisphere.

Wass, H., Corr, C. A., Pacholski, R. A., & Sanders, C. M. (1980). *Death education: An annotated resource guide.* Washington, DC: Hemisphere.

Wass, H., Corr, C. A., Pacholski, R. A., & Forfar, C. S. (1985). *Death education II. An annotated resource guide.* Washington, DC: Hemisphere.

Weisman, A. (1972). *On dying and denying: A psychiatric study of terminality.* New York: Behavioral Publications.

Twenty-four

Thanatology: Its End and Future (with Special Reference to Euthanasia)

Larry R. Churchill

Larry R. Churchill is professor and chair of Social Medicine and adjunct professor of Religious Studies at the University of North Carolina at Chapel Hill. Professor Churchill teaches medical and social ethics in an interdisciplinary curriculum in the U.N.C. School of Medicine. A past president of the Society for Health and Human Values, Churchill was recently elected to the Institute of Medicine. He currently holds a Charles E. Culpeper Foundation Fellowship in the Medical Humanities. Churchill is the author of Rationing Health Care in America *(1987), and coauthor of* Professional Ethics and Primary Care Medicine *(1986), and has published widely in professional and medical ethics. His chief intellectual interest is the relationship of ethical theory to human experience.*

> Every art and every inquiry, and similarly every action and pursuit, is thought to aim at some good.
>
> Aristotle, *Nicomachean Ethics*

The End of Thanatology

Thanatology can be defined as the study of the phenomena of death and the attendant psychological strategies employed to cope with them.[1] Such studies are very useful to health-care practitioners, family, and friends of the terminally ill, and to the dying themselves—indeed, to anyone engaged with human finitude. The achievements of the past several decades in thanatology, to which this volume is additional witness, are great. But great past achievements do not guarantee a great future, or even any future at all. In fact, the factors that created the need for thanatology as a modern field of study are perhaps stronger than ever and the diversions to which the field is susceptible are more powerful.

The factors that created the need for thanatology are well known. In the broadest sense, they are the forces of modern industrial and post-industrial urbanization and mobility. A mobile, urban population is one uprooted from the land, from intimacy with the rhythms of nature, and from the witness to the life cycles evident in intergenerational households. The result is an acquisitive-possessive individualism, a notion of the good life as largely equivalent to consumption of material commodities. In such a social ethos both dying and aging are out of place and the dying and aged are perceived as alien. The identification of self with material goods (or the ability to command them) leads, of course, to a truncated and stunted assessment of human abilities, so that reliance on experts of all sorts is increased. This is no less true for dealing with terminal illness than in the rest of life.

Yet my major concern is not with these cultural and psychological forces of death-denial. My chief concern is with the transformation of thanatology into a set of beliefs, techniques, and practices that will divert its true purpose and thereby assure its demise. My worry is not that thanatology will fail because of a frontal attack on its agenda, but because its agenda will be coopted and subsumed under other forces.

This essay is concerned with ends—in a dual sense. First, has thanatology reached its end, or *finis?* Is it finished? Is thanatology dead, or will it become so because it is (or may become) subsumed under the current enthusiasm for euthanasia, or cost-containment, or geriatrics, or some other cause related but extrinsic to it? But this sort of talk presupposes the more important question: What is the end of thanatology, where "end" means purpose or aim *(telos)*? What should those who study and practice thanatology be striving to do? Being clear about the answer is essential. Otherwise, thanatology will forsake its end *(telos)* and becomes merely a means, and this I argue, will spell its end *(finis)*.

The task of identifying the purpose of thanatology is not a difficult one. The purpose of thanatology is to better understand human dying *in order to serve the dying.* Without the moral impetus of this agenda, thanatology becomes voyeurism, necromancy, or a tool of various professional and social agendas.

One type of diversion involves using the dying to serve our needs rather using our work to serve theirs. A classic case is the use made of the work of Elisabeth Kübler-Ross, whose "stages" of dying (denial, anger, bargaining, depression, acceptance) have too frequently become normative expectations that health professionals place on patients. In this professionalized, lock-step progression, the stages do not answer the needs of the dying but rather are responses to the anxiety of caretakers to have intellectual and social control, and thereby emotional control as well.[2] A second and more disturbing slippage occurs when thanatology changes from pursuit of knowledge about dying to pursuit of death. Here the temptation is to see active euthanasia as a form of caring for patients *in extremis*. Because this diversion is so powerfully before us, I will spend this essay addressing it. Resisting the equation of a "good death" with mercy killing may be the most important task ahead for assuring that thanatology has a future.

The Reduction of Thanatology to Euthanasia

Marcia Angell, an editor of the *New England Journal of Medicine*, said that doctors should prepare themselves to debate the issue of active euthanasia once more.[3] There is evidence everywhere that she is right.

In California an effort to place a proposed euthanasia law on the fall, 1988, ballot failed for what most believe were organizational, not substantive, problems.[4] The sponsoring organization, Americans Against Human Suffering—a branch of the Hemlock Society—may succeed on their next try.

In the Netherlands euthanasia is still officially a criminal act, but it is widely practiced and apparently widely supported by the public. Between 6,000 and 10,000 persons are euthanized annually in the Netherlands.[5] Four conditions must be met. The patient must be competent, must be suffering beyond tolerance, must request euthanasia repeatedly and consistently, and the act must be performed by a physician in consultation with another physician not involved in the case.

Public opinion polls show that a majority of Americans favor the legalization of euthanasia under certain circumstances.[6] Dr. Angell also cites a survey which indicates that a majority of doctors also favor legalizing euthanasia, though roughly one-half of those who favor its legalization also indicated that they would not perform it.

If morality were merely a matter of sociology, that is, a description of what values people hold, then the debate would be over when the surveys are complete. But of course the ethical question is not, Do people favor euthanasia? but, *Should* they?

Yet my primary interest here is not in debating the merits of active euthanasia but in noting how the preoccupation with it may come to overshadow the study of and care for the dying. If this occurs euthanasia may be presented as an answer to the "problem" of dying, and the "management" of the incurable patient. The chances that this will occur were in fact enhanced with the publication of a horrific tale of active euthanasia reported without attribution in the *Journal of American Medical Association* and entitled "It's Over, Debbie."[7]

"It's Over, Debbie" is a bad case for debating euthanasia but a paradigmatic case for how the pursuit of death as its own end can engulf the proper goal of thanatology—service to the dying person.

The call came in the middle of the night. As a gynecology resident rotating through a large, private hospital, I had come to detest telephone calls, because invariably I would be up for several hours and would not feel good the next day. However, duty called, so I answered the phone. A nurse informed me that a patient was having difficulty getting rest, could I please see her. She was on 3 North. That was the gynecologic-oncology unit, not my usual duty station. As I trudged along, bumping sleepily against walls and corners and not believing I was up again, I tried to imagine what I might find at the end of my walk. Maybe an elderly woman with an anxiety reaction, or perhaps something particularly horrible.

I grabbed the chart from the nurses station on my way to the patient's room, and the nurse gave me some hurried details: a 20-year-old girl named Debbie was dying of ovarian cancer. She was having unrelenting vomiting apparently as the result of an alcohol drip administered for sedation. Hmmm, I thought. Very sad. As I approached the room I could hear loud labored breathing. I entered and saw an emaciated, dark-haired woman who appeared much older than 20. She was receiving nasal oxygen, had an IV, and was sitting in bed suffering from what was obviously severe air hunger. The chart noted her weight at 80 pounds. A second woman, also dark-haired but of middle age, stood at her right, holding her hand. Both looked up as I entered. The room seemed filled with the patient's desperate effort to survive. Her eyes were hollow, and she had suprasternal and intercostal retractions with rapid inspirations. She had not eaten or slept in two days. She had not responded to chemotherapy and was being given supportive care only. It was a gallows scene, a cruel mockery of her youth and unfulfilled potential. Her only words to me were, "Let's get this over with."

I retreated with my thoughts to the nurses station. The patient was tired and needed rest. I could not give her health, but I could give her rest. I asked the nurse to draw 20 mg of morphine sulfate into a syringe. Enough, I thought, to do the job. I took the syringe into the room and told the two women I was going to give Debbie something that would let her rest and to say good-bye. Debbie looked at the syringe, then laid her head on the pillow with her eyes open, watching what was left of the world. I injected the morphine intravenously and watched to see if my calculations on its effects would be correct. Within seconds her breathing slowed to a normal rate, her eyes closed, and her features softened as she seemed restful at last. The older woman stroked the hair of the now sleeping patient. I waited for the inevitable next effect of depressing the respiratory drive. With clocklike certainty, within four minutes the breathing rate slowed even more, then became irregular, then ceased. The dark-haired woman stood erect and seemed relieved.

It's over, Debbie.

Note first the time of day, namely , the middle of the night—not a great time to consider weighty choices. Note that the physician is a physician-in-training, a resident, likely a junior resident since he is on call. He is, as are most residents, sleep-deprived, impatient, dreading his call but dutifully obedient to it. The patient is unknown to him, and he gathers a short biological, but not a social or personal history, from the nurse. His affective response is extremely truncated. He thinks only, "Very sad." We know that he identifies with this young woman's "unfulfilled potential." Her current state he describes as a "gallows scene...a cruel mockery."

Note that he takes a highly ambiguous request as a wish to be mercifully killed, and he announces his own intentions in an equivocal way to the patient and her female attendant. There is no move to clarify this patient's wishes, or to otherwise relieve pain. There is only a highly egocentric consideration of options, all from the perspective of what the physician could and could not do. With a moral sovereignty usually only attributed to deities, the physician describes himself as retreating to the nursing station with his thoughts. Note here the absence of an essential ingredient in ethics—conversation, explicit, deliberative reasoning, public discourse. The resident retreated to a solipsistic self-sufficiency, which doomed him to moral clumsiness and callousness from the very beginning. No doubt he felt vindicated when, after he killed the patient, everyone "seemed relieved."

Missing Agency

Others have commented on the haste, ignorance, and ineptness that mark this case. And these are all important. Yet there is something else more central here. It is the lack of self-conscious, moral agency. The case is described from an administrative posture, as if the resident were looking down upon and depicting his own acts in an impersonal way—as if for the medical record. But the medical record does not constitute a moral record or a human record in which the dying person is central.

The administrative posture is one in which actions are treated as occurrences, that is, as having happened, but without disclosing the interiority of the actor. We actually know very little about what this resident thought or felt. There is, to be sure, first-person language, but it describes eventlike actions, not personal assessment postures. "I answered the phone...I grabbed the chart...I asked the nurse...I took the syringe...I injected the morphine...I waited." This is a marvelous physical topography of events, but it discloses little of the moral psyche of the

actor. It reads like Caesar's regal summation: "I came, I saw, I conquered."[8] Indeed, conquest may be precisely the right metaphor, as I will
discuss later. But at least "I conquered" tells us what Caesar thought he
was doing in a way "I injected" does not and cannot.

In short, this is a case bereft of moral agency, a case, if you will, of a
missing agent. So the question we must put to the resident is "What did
you think you were doing when you injected this woman with a lethal
dose?"—in various senses of that question. For acknowledging explicitly
what we think we are doing as we do things is what separates us as moral
beings from the rest of the animal kingdom. Acknowledging what we are
doing as we act is how we can know what ends we seek, and whether our
actions are true to those ends.

I mean to suggest that this is a bad case in several senses. It is "bad"
in the sense of "morally wrong," because it describes acts that are
unthinking, hasty, callous, morally clumsy, and criminal. It is also
"bad" in the sense of "inadequate" because it tells us next to nothing
about *who* did these acts. It is, in this latter sense, a very poor case to
rekindle the euthanasia debate, but an illuminating case to exhibit the
reduction of care of the dying to killing the dying.

If we are to read accounts of physicians who have killed their patients
from motives of mercy, I hope we will find in those accounts recitations
of anguish, conflictedness, stress, deep worries about their character,
detailed discussions with patients, families, colleagues, and others, profound ambivalence, lack of certainty, citation of authorities on all sides of
the issue, accounts of courage, or perhaps regret and, overall, a quality of
reflection worthy of the act. Anything less is demeaning to both patients
and physicians alike. Anything less illustrates that death has become the
end sought, rather than service to the dying.

Sovereignty

The one time we are privy to the deliberations of this resident he is
focused on a choice centered on his own capabilities: "I could not give
her health," he reflects, "but I could give her rest." What is revealed here
is a fallacy couched in a euphemism. The euphemism perpetrated by this
physician on his readers, and perhaps on himself, is that "rest" is a proxy
for *death*. So it should read, "I could not give her health, but I could give
her death." The fallacy is black-and-white thinking. It's *either* health *or*
rest, that is, health *or* death.

What is disclosed here is a picture of a frustrated physician, a physician held captive by his powerlessness, his inability to help. What is
depicted are two persons in suffering and in need of mercy, one the
patient who suffers physically and the other the physician who is tor-
tured psychologically by his lack of control and inability to relieve pain.
Couched in the rhetoric of pain relief, or rest, he offers the only thing he

has—death. So like Caesar, the resident came, saw, and conquered, not the patient's disease, but the patient's suffering. But to do so, he conquered the patient as well. Killing this patient was, I submit, an act comprehensible as an attempt to redeem frustrated sovereignty, an act calculated to wrest control from the enemy. When restoration to health is impossible and pain control difficult, one can still offer death. Only death is not here offered, but foisted on the patient as a way to relieve the doctor. Euthanasia is then a continuation of medicine's conquest motif. If patients cannot be cured, they can at least be killed. Killing a patient, rather than letting her die a painful death retains control. It is a way of remaining sovereign, of being active rather than (helplessly) passive, it is a way of avoiding defeat. For just at the point of being vanquished by disease, physicians can seize the initiative and proclaim mastery over their adversary. Thus is killing patients seen as an act of great courageousness. It is, unfortunately, the courage of a bungler and a fool, an agent who has not acted but *reacted* with simplistic and egoistic ineptness. This physician has covered the pain of *his* inadequacies by dispatching the patient, the object of his suffering, and everyone, we are reassured, "seemed relieved." The physician retained his sovereignty but at a heavy price, an essential part of which is moral self-deception.

Brutalization

A moral agent who does not acknowledge personal presence in his actions, and who entertains a need for sovereignty over his actions is particularly susceptible to being brutalized by them. Brutalization is, in fact, the natural outcome of postures of sovereignty. Aristotle, wiser than most who have followed him, said that human beings are made for social interaction and those who do not have it are either brutes, or gods.[9] Human beings need conviviality, fellowship, social ties, and conversation. This is especially so in ethics, and it is no accident that Aristotle thought of ethical reflection as a dimension of social life, a branch of politics, of life together in a political order, not as a free standing discipline.

We can pretend to a godlike sovereignty if we wish, but we are human beings and the desire to be like gods leads us to be like brutes, to brutalization, in the most rudimentary sense—our moral sensibilities become no better than (perhaps worse than) those of animals.

The posture of sovereignty I have been attributing to the resident in the Debbie case is a form of psychological distancing. It is a way of being removed and remote from full moral awareness of one's acts; it is the assumption of an administrative posture, orchestrating and observing from above. The result can be seen in the factlike recitation we noted previously: "I retreated with my thoughts...I injected...I waited."

I refer to the result as "brutalization" to invoke Aristotle and his notion of ethical reflection as irreducibly social, not exercised by either brute animals (who lack a convivial order) or gods (who are sovereign). Moreover, I suggest that the moral retreat and distancing frequently associated with killing is a desire for sovereignty, that is, a desire for the sort of unrestrained power over events associated with gods. Human beings, however, being human, fail at sovereignty and the result is we become like brutes, or if you will, brutalized. Montaigne put it somewhat differently, but was emphasizing the same dynamic. "Two things I have always observed to be in singular accord," he says, "supercelestial thoughts and subterranean conduct." Montaigne continues:

> We seek other conditions because we do not understand the use of our own, and go outside of ourselves because we do not know what it is like inside. Yet there is no use our mounting on stilts, for on stilts we must still walk on our own legs. And on the loftiest throne in the world we are still sitting only on our own rump.[10]

The Future of Thanatology

If we are to resist the temptation to reduce thanatology to euthanasia we will have to be clear about what thanatology stands for. If we are to be convincing that killing patients mercifully perverts its purposes, we will have to say what the true purposes are.

Here it will be helpful to remember that thanatology—the study of dying—is essentially a humanities discipline. It, of course, uses a variety of tools drawn from social science disciplines and health-care fields, but these are all instrumentalities in the service of what is fundamentally a humanistic enterprise.

The humanities are the study of the human situation through the sustained effort to hear, record, and faithfully interpret the human voice. Humanities disciplines—philosophy, literature, the classics, history, religion—are the formalized efforts to do so. But no less important are the neighboring fields of study that undertake their work in a less canonized but no less important way. Thanatology is one of those neighboring, adjacent fields of study. The methods and traditions are perhaps more eclectic but the mission—the hearing, recording, and faithful interpretation of the human voice—is the same. In thanatology the task is more specialized, because the voices to be heard are largely voices in crisis and voices of loss, but the driving impetus to engage is no different. In thanatology the study is often preliminary, a first step to taking action to improve the lot of the dying and their caregivers. But what motivates the study is the same as what drives students and teachers of Shakespeare, Plato, Cicero, William Carlos Williams, Martin Luther King, Jr., or Toni Morrison. It is the passion to hear the authentically human, the remarkable, varied, and novel stories of human beings living their lives. Thanatology simply does this in a more specialized way.

It is of the essence of humanistic inquiry that these voices are, as much as possible, allowed to speak for themselves. The sustaining characteristic of the humanities is its effort to let be—on its own terms, and for its own sake—the human realities it studies. The first hint of techniques of manipulation, of "using" the voices for one's own purposes, to make a point, or to make a career, or to boost professional standing, or remove a troubling problem, or further a political agenda, subverts the task of attending.

The reduction of thanatology to mercy killing (or to the political effort to legalize euthanasia) is nowhere more vividly portrayed than in the Debbie case. The voice of the dying patient is completely subsumed under professional preoccupations. What I earlier characterized as the loss of agency, the effort at sovereignty, and the resulting brutalization are all ways of expressing this reduction. The reduction is not just of a field of study. It is a diminishment of the humanity of those involved. In this gruesome scenario, where all actions were performed in the name of mercy, both doctor and patient were belittled as human beings.

It follows from this that the end or purpose of thanatology must include ingredients that were absent or distorted in the Debbie case: first, an explicit claim of our own moral and intellectual agency in our interaction with the dying; second, a humility in studying the dying and their experiences that will obviate the need to control them or "fix the problem;" in thanatology we are always studying something beyond ourselves, problems we can only partially grasp; and third, a sustained recognition of the self-deception and brutalization involved in killing the dying.

These three items do not, of course, exhaust the ingredients that make thanatology what it is or ought to be. So these items are not sufficient, but they are necessary. I offer them as part of the agenda of thanatology for the future, as ingredients that will give intellectual clarity and moral impetus to the tasks ahead.

Notes

1. *Webster's Ninth New Collegiate Dictionary* (Springfield, MA) : Merriam-Webster, 1985), entry under 'thanatology.'

2. See Larry R. Churchill, Interpretations of dying: Ethical implications for patient care, *Ethics in Science and Medicine*, vol. 6, no. 4, 1979, 211–222.
3. Marcia Angell, Euthanasia, *New England Journal of Medicine*, 1988, vol. 319, 1348–1350.
4. Ibid.
5. T. Harper, Where euthanasia is a way of death, *Medical Economics*. Nov. 23, 1987, 23–28.
6. Roper Organization of New York City. The 1988 Roper poll on attitudes toward active voluntary euthanasia. Los Angeles: National Hemlock Society, 1988.
7. It's Over, Debbie, *Journal of the American Medical Association*, 1988, vol. 259, p. 272.
8. Gaius Suetonius Tranquillus, *The twelve Caesars*, transl. Robert Graves (London: Penguin, 1957), p. 30.
9. Aristotle, *Politics*, Bk. I, Ch. 2, 1253a, transl. W. D. Ross, Richard McKeon (Ed.), *The basic works of Aristotle* (New York: Random House, 1941), p. 935.
10. Michel de Montaigne, *The complete essays of Montaigne*, transl. Donald Frame (Stanford, CA: Stanford Univ. Press, 1965), p. 856.

Twenty-five

The Future of Palliative Care

Derek Doyle

Dr. Doyle qualified in medicine at Edinburgh University in 1955 and then served as a medical missionary in South Africa from 1957–1966, finally being accredited as a specialist in chest medicine. Between 1967 and 1977, he was in family practice in Edinburgh and responsible for one hundred and twenty beds in a teaching hospital.

In 1977, he was appointed first medical director of St. Columba's Hospice, the first modern hospice in Scotland, and continues in that post as well as being an honorary consultant physician in the National Health Service and a member of the Clinical Teaching Staff, Department of Medicine, University of Edinburgh.

He has been awarded the O.B.E. by Queen Elizabeth and is a Fellow of the Royal College of Surgeons, a Fellow of the Royal College of Physicians, and a Fellow of the Royal College of General Practitioners. He was the first chairman of the Association for Palliative Medicine of Great Britain and Ireland, first editor-in-chief of Palliative Medicine, first vice-chairman of the European Association for Palliative Care, and is currently vice-chairman of the National Council for Hospice and Specialist Palliative Care Services of Great Britain.

His books and writings have covered many aspects of palliative care, professional education, and the needs of relatives.

He has lectured extensively in Canada, Australia, New Zealand, South Africa, Israel, Europe, Saudi Arabia, and Hong Kong.

He is married with four children, two of whom are nurses, one a veterinary surgeon, and another a doctor.

What Do We Mean by Palliative Care?

The English philosopher, C. E. M. Joad, used to be a popular if somewhat incomprehensible member of radio discussion panels in postwar Britain. He became famous for his regular prefacing of every answer with, "It all depends on what you mean by...." We must preface this chapter with that same question and then attempt to define its origins, its strengths, and its weaknesses before starting to think about its future.

It is probably true to say that *palliative care, hospice care,* and *terminal care* are interchangeable terms all meaning one and the same thing. Some rebelled against *terminal care* because it seemed to denote the last few days of life, while others baulked at *hospice care,* which they took to mean residential care to the exclusion of domiciliary care. While many would claim that *palliative care* is more acceptable and self-explanatory, it takes only a moment's reflection to appreciate that it too is an ambiguous term. If, according to the dictionary, the meaning of *palliation* is "the relief of suffering when cure is unrealistic or unattainable," then most of the care given by the world's doctors and nurses is "palliative care!"

Professor Joad would insist that we must explain ourselves and therefore in this chapter we shall use the term as it has become to be accepted by common usage, that is, "the care of people with active, progressive and far-advanced disease." Perhaps the definition of the new British medical specialty, *palliative medicine,* can help us: "The study and management of patients in whom the prognosis is limited and the focus of care is the quality of life." This definition does away with pathological terms and misunderstandings about hospices. It saves us attempting to set a time limit and directs our attention to the central core of all care—the *quality* of life rather than its *quantity.* It reaffirms living rather than focusing on dying.

What Are the Origins of Palliative Care?

Palliative care is a product of our times. Our forefathers, who had none of our diagnostic technology and therapeutic armamentarium, would be amazed that we should give a name to what, after all, was all they sought to do every day of their working lives. The advances in cancer care, and in particular those of surgery, radiotherapy, and chemotherapeutic oncology, enabled us if not to cure all our cancer patients, certainly to offer them extra years of life and often long-term remissions. As such care became not only more promising and successful but also more active and intensive, so less attention seemed to be devoted to those beyond cure, especially in the final months of life. Reluctant as their doctors might be to admit it, such patients came to be seen as medical failures and defeats. Their suffering, whether physical, emotional, social, or spiritual, seemed scarcely to be noticed. Reports began to appear of appalling, unrelieved pain in spite of means being readily available to control it. Further reports followed on other symptoms, on previously unrecognized fears, on autonomy and dignity being taken from them, on relatives being ignored, and on medical intervention that depersonalized the patient whose life was fast ebbing.

Palliative care was born, or rediscovered to be more precise, to meet this challenge. It set out to control pain and other symptoms while leaving the patients alert, in possession of most of their faculties, in control of their lives and their environments. It asked how the needs of loving relatives can be met? How, in the face of loss, suffering, and pain of body and mind, can dignity be assured and life still have a meaning and a value? How can this be done without in any way denying or negating the very real advances of modern medicine? How can it be done *within* a modern health-care system, rather than as an alternative to it? The answer has been palliative care, the subject of this chapter.

The pioneers in this field to whom we owe such a debt were ortho-dox doctors and nurses, encouraged by an increasingly involved and vocal public. That point must be made at the outset. The public often perceived the need before the professionals and showed its concern and commitment by helping to found and then fund hospices but, even in this consumer-powered age, we would not be where we are today had there not been ordinary doctors and nurses prepared to dedicate their professional lives to this philosophy of care. Many times in this chapter will it be stressed that the strengths of palliative care, and the future healthy development of it, are contingent on it being and continuing to be a feature of mainstream caring. The fact that it grew out of disquiet about the direction such care was taking does not mean that it must be allowed to grow into alternative or confrontational care.

Palliation, as has already been said, has long been a noble and an honourable aim of all carers. If its importance was temporarily obscured in the new-found excitement of modern high-technology medicine, it was never lost. The challenge is to rediscover it, redesign it and re-inject it into modern care systems, not to allow it to develop in parallel. After all, parallel lines do not meet!

In its short life as a respectable discipline, palliative care has encoun-tered many threats, some predictable but others surprising. A brief re-view of them may help us when we look into the future and the chal-lenges palliative care will face.

Initially it was not well received by the medical establishment, always conservative and cautious and at times resistant to change. It saw this philosophy as an implied indictment of its standards and, it has to be admitted, there was indeed a basis for this reaction. Had patient care been all it could have been, there would not have been expressed either consumer or professional disquiet. It must, however, be remembered that most medical "advances" and most professional pioneers had been received with less than warm enthusiasm until the importance and relevance of their work was slowly recognised. One has only to read the history of anaesthesia or antisepsis to be reminded how conservative is the medical profession. To those who doubt if palliative care will ever be accepted as a respected and credible discipline, let the British experience be the answer. There it is now a full specialty with its own specialist training programme, attracting young physicians of high calibre.

Born of consumer dissatisfaction and fuelled by "public power," it was inevitable that its growth has often been unplanned and uncoordinated with little evidence of strategic planning and thought about the availability of resources. Hospice-type units and services have proliferated in response to public pressure, often insufficiently tempered by professional advice and responsible constraint. In some parts of the world they have become the ideal of each little community, a memorial to the energy and enthusiasm of some local dignitary, without any thought having been given to finding suitable or adequate professional staff, particularly doctors. Sadly, at times this has been intentional, not accidental—a deliberate move to demedicalize patient care, at others an equally deliberate initiative to capitalize on the good name of "hospice" for financial gain. The future of palliative care lies neither in deprofessionalizing and deinstitutionalizing nor in financial exploitation.

For some, palliative care was an attempt to eradicate the mystique and taboos surrounding death. "Bring it out into the open, show how suffering can be relieved, dignity and peace be restored, and death will lose its ugliness and sting," they seem to say. Before long, such protagonists were speaking as though dying could not only be eased but death itself always made a happy and beautiful event. They were wrong. One cannot sanitize dying any more than one can anaesthetize grieving. Many will indeed die at peace but many may die without pain, yet also die without happiness. There is no such thing as a model death, an ideal universally achievable in palliative care units.

Such sentimental, romanticized idealism has already done harm. Paradoxically, the evolution of palliative care as a special discipline has created as many problems as it has solved. Doctors and nurses in general hospitals, often working in inadequate surroundings with insufficient resources yet with the highest of ideals, have come to feel that they can never achieve the standards which they are led to believe are universal in palliative care units. Hearing that all is perfect in that world, and that the knowledge base in palliative care is so vast as to call for specialists in the subject, they feel discouraged from trying, so unachievable do these ideals seem to be in every day medical and nursing practice. Such a reaction is understandable but tragic.

Palliative care workers need to retain professional honesty and integrity, tempered by humility and self-audit! It is too tempting for them to bask in public adulation when they should be subjecting themselves and their work to the critical gaze of their professional peers, so many of whom have the same ideals but are less studied and appreciated by a public so selectively critical.

Some speak as though palliative care pioneers discovered holistic care! Others as though it is a uniquely Christian concept. Neither is true. Palliative care embodies holistic concepts and cannot be practised without due respect for mind and body and soul, but many have understood this for centuries. What has happened is that palliative care has reaffirmed the importance of holism and, as it were, given encouragement to others to practise it more openly. It has given pastoral care its rightful place and, in so doing, learned that Christianity gives meaning to both life and death. It rewards compassion but has no monopoly on it.

It will be obvious to the reader that palliative care by its nature, its youth, and its openness to change and need, is capable of absorbing and adapting many differing influences. This is evident in the way it permits the most exciting developments in nursing, without in any way threatening or endangering the role of the physician. Rather are they learning greater mutual respect and healthy interdependence. So too are social workers, therapists, and clergy finding their rightful places. The defining of roles is often difficult, the loss of autonomy or supremacy painful, but the end result is a degree of satisfaction seldom found in other professional settings. Such is one of its strengths—partnership in caring based on profound mutual respect without the domination or the diminution of any one (professional) discipline. It is therefore all the more sad that a few articulate and dominant people have attempted to hijack palliative care in order to further the development of their own professional group at the expense of many others who have chosen to be less assertive and ambitious.

A problem is that some would use palliative care as a proving ground for pet theories and therapies that have failed to stand up to scientific or critical evaluation. Noninvasive and innocuous they may seem, but it is no more ethically right for them to be used with such patients than it is acceptable for a pharmacological or physical regimen to be tested and used, unless under the most strict surveillance of a professional ethics committee. Palliative care must never be allowed to become a testing ground for protocols unacceptable in general medicine, nor must it be allowed to be taken over by those who would make it into a cult, a new "ism." We have enough of these already!

Health service administrators and managers must strive to provide high-quality care in the most economical way. Inevitably they have looked at palliative care to see if it is a cheaper alternative and found that, costly as it certainly is, it is modestly less expensive than care in a general hospital with its expensive diagnostic and operating room facilities. It must, however, be emphasized that it is expensive to provide because it is based on a high staff/patient ratio and staff salaries will always account for close on 85 percent of expenses. Attempts to reduce establishment to effect economies would be a false economy.

Volunteers have long had a role in hospice care for a variety of reasons. They have brought to it a homeliness and an informality that is often sadly lacking in general hospitals. They have sometimes released professional staff for more direct patient contact. Some would say that the deployment of volunteers helps to effect economies. Those with many years of experience in hospices will join the author in paying tribute to the contribution of volunteers but will probably understand why, at least in Britain, fewer and fewer volunteers are being recruited in spite of their clamouring to do this work. It is difficult, if not impossible, to employ many of them appropriately in direct patient care when at the heart of palliative care there has to be continuity, high-quality communication, and professional cohesion. In the view of the author, volunteers have an unquestionable role in bringing an added dimension to the environment and the ambience and can be indispensable in such services as the children's crèche, coffee rooms, car services, bereavement follow-up, fund-raising, gardening, as aides in the day centre, and in appeal organizations. They should not be employed to replace professional staff with the aim of effecting financial economies any more that they should be offered work to help them in their grief or other need. A palliative care unit must *always* be supportive for its staff but never become a therapeutic community for staff or volunteers.

Palliative Care Today

Worldwide, palliative care is provided in three different but interrelated ways: inpatient units, domiciliary care (often with an associated day hospice), and symptom relief teams working in general hospitals. Each meets different needs in different ways. They are not comparable, though many have been foolish enough to attempt comparisons. What matters is that local needs are met appropriately—the needs of patients, the needs of relatives, and the needs of fellow professionals.

An inpatient unit will provide high-quality care for those who cannot be cared for at home for some reason or another. What it must not do is to deprive a person of the chance to remain, or even die, at home if that is his or her wish. Neither must it inadvertently deskill colleagues in the community or in hospitals, nor lead them to feel that such caring is beyond their skills. Every inpatient unit from its commissioning must be prepared to share every skill and insight with all who share its ideal of compassionate, positive caring for those with mortal illness.

Those who would elect to remain at home should have available to them specialist nurses and doctors who understand and are trained in the unique disciplines of domiciliary care, but who must have the deepest respect for their professional colleagues working in the community. In

Britain—with its long tradition of high-quality family medicine and home visiting, supported by an army of specialist community nurses, "home-helps" (homemakers), therapists, and others—still only 30 percent die at home of whatever cause. Though 90 percent of the final year of life is spent at home, inevitably family physicians have few opportunities to practise and develop their skills in symptom control in the dying. What is needed is not a replacement for the family physician, nor a guaranteed admission to a hospice inpatient facility, but a team that can advise and support such a physician by sympathetic sharing in the care, a true partnership but not a takeover.

So long as some domiciliary palliative care services behave as though they had not only all the attributes but also the monopoly of concern and commitment, they will rightly be viewed with suspicion or resentment by many doctors. The answer lies, as in all professional work, in mutual respect, often hard-earned and humbly nurtured. In a real sense, palliative care workers should be servants to patient and colleagues.

If in Britain 65 percent and in North America more than 80 percent of people die in hospital, it must be asked how best both to improve *their* care today and guarantee improved standards for the future. Perhaps the answer lies in symptom relief (or as they are sometimes called symptom support) teams based in major general hospitals, responding to the calls of medical and nursing staff responsible for them. The benefits would seem so obvious but experience shows that they have major problems. Often the environment is not conducive to good palliative care; the whole ethos of the unit is cure orientated, the staffing numbers and training inadequate, and their support systems nonexistent. Death is seen as a medical defeat and the dying patient an embarrassment. Priority is given to those who may recover and cost-conscious management would often prefer to have beds occupied by patients undergoing high-profile care than by the dying who do not come back to vote.

Staff in such support teams report professional frustration at seeing what could be achieved yet not having the means to bring it about as they would wish, particularly when they have no designated beds at their disposal. What most certainly *can* be achieved, is a new heightened professional awareness of the goals of good care, improved confidence and skill in symptom control, and a reduced embarrassment in being with the dying. Some workers in symptom relief teams fear they may be deskilling others who too readily abrogate responsibility to the anonymous members of the peripatetic support team.

Increasingly in Britain and in Canada, palliative medicine physicians are being invited to sit in on "combined clinics" with physicians, surgeons, oncologists, and others sharing in the care of cancer patients. Specialist palliative care nurses are doing the same in nursing teams, both in hospitals and in the community, suggesting, supporting and, when the occasion arises, offering their own services, so developing a continuum of care to replace the fragmentation often seen in the past. Is this one area where palliative care will develop in the future?

Palliative Care in the Future

There always has been, and there always will be, a need for palliative care. No one will ever win a Nobel Prize for discovering the secret of immortality. Human beings will always have to face death but, we hope, not a death diminished by pain and fear and loneliness and degradation.

Today we stand at a crossroads. We may either develop palliative care, and hospices in particular, as an option for the privileged few or we may reintroduce its principles into mainstream medical care. We may permit it to develop as a cult and a testing ground for pet theories of alternative care or we may channel our energies into helping every doctor and nurse in the world to care with the same enthusiasm and skill they bring to their curable patients today. We may allow palliative care to develop as a feature of expensive western medical care or we may share its philosophy and its benefits with the millions of Africa and Asia who never dare dream of the luxury of cure. The choice is ours and must surely be obvious.

Let us look at some of the factors that will affect its development.

Relationship with Mainstream Health Care

Adoption of its principles by our colleagues (few if any of whom would find them new or strange) demands that palliative care workers be professionally respectable and credible, men and women of the highest professional standing and integrity, using no gimmicks, subjecting all they do to critical review and audit by their peers and academic colleagues.

This will necessitate the recruitment into this work of full-time doctors, nurses, and others, with qualifications and credentials comparable to those for any other discipline or specialty. It will call for critical evaluation of all we do, whether it be pain control, nursing care, or the type of relaxed, informal, homely environment we associate with the name "hospice." Anecdotes will no longer suffice. Public "consumer satisfaction" may encourage us but can never replace scientific evaluation. Nothing is too small or too trivial to study if it holds a promise of better care.

Public demands for more "bricks and mortar" units will need to be resisted as we experiment with designated beds in general hospitals and peripatetic symptom relief teams staffed by palliative care specialists. It is immediately obvious that worldwide we must move from part-time to full-time occupants of these posts, something long recognized in the United Kingdom but only recently in Canada, Australia, and New Zealand.

Education in Palliative Care

Today's palliative care systems will deserve to be relegated to the history books of the future if nothing is done to bring their principles within the spectrum of skills of doctors and nurses as a matter of urgency. The final year of life liberated from unnecessary suffering and usefully spent with loved ones cannot ever be regarded as an optional extra but only as a basic human right. Only by using the present palliative care workers as educationalists and catalysts will this be achieved. Is there any reason that every medical and nursing school should not have palliative care as a subject in its curriculum? Can it not become an examinable subject, taught at all stages and skilfully demonstrated in the wards as well as in the lecture rooms? The present insatiable demand for training and education in the subject is adequate proof that it is indeed regarded as important and also is evidence that the present "specialists" in palliative care are those expected to do the training. No one else will shoulder this daunting responsibility. Here, too, is another reason we must look to fulltimers rather than part-timers.

Sadly, there are many of them clinically skilled but without teaching experience, and little is being done to rectify this deficiency. Likewise, palliative care systems and units continue to be established without any provision, in terms of physical facilities, personnel, or resources, for educational work. It is sad enough that in most countries (except Britain), palliative care is not a specialty with its own training programmes, but even sadder when so little thought is given to the documented needs of local colleagues. The answer lies first in it being granted the status of a full specialty, then in developing training programmes to attract doctors and nurses of the highest calibre, and finally in their energetic and inspired influence in universities and colleges.

Research in Palliative Care

If a subject is worth studying, it is worth researching. If it claims to be a specialty it must, by definition, have a defined knowledge base, kept under review and regularly added to. It might be argued that the so-called hospice movement began not with the first hospice but when Dame Cicely Saunders put the work onto a scientific basis, her therapeutic regimes carefully researched and shown to be replicable.

Hundreds have followed her into this work but very few have researched as they might have done. It is almost as though some would see research as incompatible with compassionate patient-centred care, yet this is not so. One can study patients and their needs, treatment regimes and their outcomes without in any way endangering the dignity, the autonomy, or the privacy of a dying patient. Research is not experimentation, nor need it be depersonalizing. It is constantly asking "why" and then setting out to find the answers.

One has only to see the changes that have come about by recognizing nonnociceptive pain as an entity and appreciating that it is not sensitive to morphine to realize how patients have benefitted from a simple observation. There must be thousands of other areas—physical, emotional, social, and even spiritual—waiting to be looked at. There will be little future for palliative care if we stop asking "why." Professional credibility and, to some extent, patient confidence cannot be built on a foundation of sentimental anecdotes.

Adaptability of Palliative Care

It is easy to see why palliative care grew out of cancer care. It is relatively easy to define the end-stage when all the options of surgery, irradiation, and chemotherapy have been exhausted. The same might be said, with a little less certainty, about AIDS.

Likewise it is easy to explain why palliative care developed in western or westernized countries where health care is more sophisticated, the public more expectant and articulate, the resources more readily available. It would be wrong, in the author's view, to equate this too closely with Christianity. Rather was the development based on economic and sociological grounds that coexisted in a Judeo-Christian culture. Need it continue to develop in such an exclusive way? If, as we have said, palliative care is the relief of suffering with due and equal attention to the total needs of patient and relatives, why should it not be practised in Africa and in India where people die in just as much need but often without ever having had the slightest hope of cure no matter what their illness?

A child dying of kwashiorkor with super-added infection in rural Africa needs palliative care as much as someone dying of cancer in New York. The tuberculotic African in a South African township, the leper in India, and the Polish miner dying of silicosis all need palliative care. They know the horror of pain and the anticipation of fear. They know the anguish of wasting and the sense of being a burden on caring, but often impoverished, loved ones.

Today, palliative care is synonymous with end-stage cancer and AIDS. Tomorrow is should be the right of all who suffer and die; but whether that will happen depends on the palliative care workers of today! It is no accident that the World Health Organization has gone to such pains to have its analgesic ladder adopted and adequate opioids made available worldwide. In the next few decades we can never hope to have radiotherapy equipment in every major city of Africa and India, any more than we can hope to see body scanners, diagnostic laboratories and the specialists to use them in all the countries that need them. We *can* hope to see doctors and nurses well able to control pain, relatives shown how to nurse with the most meagre resources, and governments made willing to finance such low-cost, high-benefit caring.

There is little evidence that palliative care is being taken into these countries with the same evangelical vigour that characterized its dissemination in the western world. Why do we not release senior staff to work alongside colleagues in Africa for limited periods or find a place for them to come and work alongside us in the palliative care units of Europe and North America? If we fail to meet this challenge it will, with some justification, be said that palliative care is just another luxury to be found only in the affluent western countries who do not really care about the third world and its peoples.

At the very heart of palliative care is the recognition of and respect for personhood and the human need to be at peace within oneself, with family and neighbours, and with one's God. Such peace is founded on more than friendship and faith. It requires trust and respect, tolerance and the grace to forgive. The mystery of dying and death is that such peace can be achieved when, in worldly terms, all is disaster and loss. As strength ebbs from a body, a man or woman may grow in emotional and spiritual stature *if* the opportunity is given, *if* the caring environment is right. Palliative care workers have all seen families reconciled round a deathbed, or bitter cantankerous people blossom into men or women whom it is a positive delight to know.

The reason is not the drugs used nor any religious formula. It is because of the unembarrassed unleashing of love and compassion, which can overcome pain and despair and bring a new meaning not only to death but to life.

It is no accident that palliative care is blossoming at the same time that East and West are being reconciled, at the time when, worldwide, there is peace-making and soul-searching, at a time when such words as *care, concern,* and *love* are again acceptable away from the church or Hollywood.

We shall soon see spiritual as well as pharmacological initiatives coming out of palliative care units. With inspired doctors, nurses, and clergy we can hope to see reconciliation between white and black, between rich and poor, through this ministry to the dying—a ministry that can be seen almost as a sacrament. Everywhere there is a dynamic palliative care unit, there is reported new life in the local religious community and in the local social environment. Out of pain and dying can come life.

Integration into Acute Care Systems

As we have seen, palliative care has become identified with "end-stage disease," that, is the relief of suffering when cure is not deemed possible. Whereas until recently such patients were told, "There is no more that can be done," they may now be advised, "Though there's no cure, there's still much that can be done."

This seems to imply two things. First is that when cure is a realistic possibility there is less need for such measures as pain control, symptom relief, emotional support based on good communication, information-sharing and empathic care for the family—all basic tenets of good palliative care. This is transparently untrue. Even when an operation will cure a condition and consequently relieve suffering, there is still an obligation to guarantee freedom from pain before and after the surgical procedure, as well as a moral duty to provide skilled emotional support for patients and family alike. Pain of body or mind is not necessarily any less because the condition is curable.

The second implication, already alluded to, is that "acute hospitals" are for curing. Managers and administrators are happiest when bed occupancy is maximal, patient throughput rapid, and mean length of stay as short as possible. Those patients whose conditions militate against such administrative ideals are less welcome, and every attempt is made either to deter their admission to prestigious acute hospitals or to facilitate their transfer elsewhere as soon as possible, particularly if they have a mortal illness. As a result, though many might deny it, priority is given to curative procedures and therapeutic regimes to the exclusion of palliative symptom-relieving regimes, which by their very existence suggest incurability or medical defeat, something unacceptable in many academic centres of excellence.

Palliative care workers are therefore challenged to find ways of integrating their principles into acute, cure-orientated, care systems. The obstacles to this may appear insurmountable, particularly if acute and chronic care are seen as opposites, but surely they are not. Some illustrations may assist us here.

There is abundant evidence that postoperative pain control is as poorly achieved in many hospitals as cancer pain control was until recently. Equally there is evidence that the better the postoperative analgesia, the earlier can a patient be mobilized and discharged home, thus freeing a precious bed. Similarly, a patient is more comfortable, sleeps and eats better, and is more motivated to cooperate in a convalescent or rehabilitation programme when he or she is in full possession of all the facts about the condition, is involved in decision making and treated as an equal rather than as an inferior by his physician or surgeon. Once again, he or she may go home sooner, the care team can feel pleased with their work, and the managers feel proud of their patient throughput. Though, by our original definition, this was not strictly palliative care, nevertheless the results were achieved by the marriage of cure-orientated principles and those of palliation.

They could be achieved in several ways.

First, the skills of palliative medicine specialists within the hospital should be utilized, their skills with pain and fear and in rehabilitation, with curable as well as incurable patients. Second, studies should continue to be conducted (as they have so effectively been done to demonstrate the need for improved terminal care) on patients' and relatives' perceptions of acute hospitals, looking at such crucial issues as pain, comfort, sense of dignity and respect, information sharing, and recognition of the needs of relatives. When administrators and managers are confronted with consumer reports that acknowledge the cures but find fault in these other areas, they will undoubtedly permit and even encourage change.

Those who can most effectively bring about change in acute wards are those who so often see the problem and grieve for their patients but then protest their inability to change the system. I refer to the nurses!

They can press for adequate and appropriate analgesia. They can demonstrate levels of pain by using pain charts when the patient might otherwise be too frightened to report it to the surgeon. They can not only observe and record other distresses, but report them and offer to cooperate with doctors in finding relief for them, skilfully demonstrating that what to a patient is important may, to the doctor, seem trivial. They can offer to sit in with doctors when relatives are interviewed, can set up family conferences, and train their nursing staff in grief counselling. Even the author has to admit that for generations there has been medical domination, but those days are gone. In a good care system—whether acute, chronic, or palliative—there is no place for domination, no place for prima donnas, and always a place for mutual respect and sharing.

So far we have looked, some might say overoptimistically, at the integration of palliative care into acute care for those who will be cured. What of those who will not be cured who are now in the late stages of their illness and find themselves in an acute ward? What is their fate?

The author sees many such people, often lonely, frightened, and feeling out of place in such a unit. They were happy there in earlier days when active treatment was being given but now.... The concern of the nurses is real and touching but they always give the same reason for not giving them the type of care they need—"We simply haven't the time." Is this true?

Such people do not need *quantity* but *quality* of time. It takes no more time to answer their questions or dispel their fears than it takes to chat about inconsequential trivia when beds are being made and procedures being done. Every few days a senior nurse or junior doctor can sit on their bed and have their well-earned coffee rather than taking it in the office. Such a simple act says more than words. It speaks about empathy, understanding, companionship, touch, and intimacy.

It is a total myth that palliative care/terminal care requires abundant time—hours and hours of anguished, tear-soaked communications about dying, death, funerals, Heaven, and Hell. Palliative care is about human companionship, sensitivity to unspoken feelings or fears, attention to fine detail. All of those are at the heart of *all* good nursing and can be made available, almost as easily in an acute unit as in a specialist unit for the dying. Visiting hours can be made more flexible, more volunteers be brought in to create homeliness, outings be arranged.... Hospital rules are surely for the good of the patient and not for the professionals. In that respect, rules are there for changing.

The real problem surely is that of a change in attitudes. When the secret is found of reminding all concerned that at the heart of medical and nursing work is the goal of care, occasionally the reward of cure, then palliative medicine will have become integrated into acute care.

Palliative care has come about because of, and for, the dying. It is up to us to ensure that the legacy of the dying shall be the integration of its cardinal features into all care systems.

So far in this chapter we have looked at where and why palliative care came into being and seen some of the influences that have affected or challenged its development. Let us close by attempting to be positive to the point of provocativeness.

There always has and always will be a need for palliation. It always was, and should return to being, part of everyday orthodox medical care—holistic, compassionate, but still scientific and capable of being evaluated and replicated. Its future lies there and not in the realm of well-intentioned amateurism nor in the world of pseudoscientific alternative medicine. It has a well-established scientific base, a rapidly growing bibliography, and defined educational objectives and training programme. It is appropriate and relevant for millions more people than currently have access to it and none of its practitioners needs to oversell their wares for it to be recognised. Neither should they make and propagate false claims about "perfect deaths," "total freedom from pain for all," "death with a smile." Much good would come to palliative care if all its practitioners sought humility rather than honour and so remained happy to be mere mortals even when their satisfied consumers treated them as gods.

Let there now be a moratorium on hospice building, a fresh look at domiciliary care, and every effort to develop symptom relief teams in every major hospital, guided by regional palliative medicine specialists/

consultants—men and women equipped and prepared both to be clinicians and also dynamic members of faculty and hospital committees so that their influence may permeate laterally.

Finally, a goal to which we might aspire. By the year 2000, may palliative care be an examinable subject in every medical school, such an accepted and inspiringly taught subject that the doctors and nurses of the future cannot imagine a time when it was not taught. By then we should have doctors studying the subject alongside nurses and clergy, clergy being welcomed into care systems, and all brought together in a World Association of Palliative Care. By 2030, may its principles be practised worldwide even where the first oncologist, the first radiotherapist, and the first radiologist, has yet to set foot.

We began by searching for a definition. We close realizing that palliative care means even more than caring for the dying, and yet that is challenging and daunting enough. If a society cares sufficiently to honour and respect its dying, it will learn how to love and care for all its less fortunate. Out of palliative care may yet come the means for human beings to know peace—within ourselves, with our neighbours and with a God—a universal need that lies at the heart of life as well as death.

Reprise

Mary A. Pittman

Mary A. Pittman, Dr.P.H., is president of the Hospital and Research Education Trust of the American Hospital Association and former president and chief executive officer of the California Association of Public Hospitals. She received her master's degree from University of California, Berkeley, in public health and city and regional planning, and her doctorate from University of California, Berkeley, in public health. She has worked in the areas of public health hospital administration and health policy for more than fifteen years, and served for eight years as the Director of Planning and Evaluation for the San Francisco Department of Public Health. She has served on a number of national and state advisory panels, including the National Association of Public Hospital Research, Quality and Productivity, and AIDS Committees, the California Joint Legislative Task Force on AIDS, the San Francisco Women's Health Committee, the Bay Area Health Care Task Force, and the Public Hospital Caucus of the American Public Health Association (chair of program committee, 1991). Dr. Pittman co-edited the book AIDS: Principles, Practices and Politics, *which has received wide attention in the academic and lay press. She is currently involved in public policy, health services research, and health planning and program development related to public hospitals. She is principal investigator of several health services research studies and evaluations, including a Robert Wood Johnson Foundation Quality of Care and Quality Assurance Project. Dr. Pittman recently chaired the 6th National Aids Update Conference in San Francisco. She provides technical assistance to numerous policy-making bodies and service providers both nationally and internationally on AIDS, health-care organization, and administration.*

A reprise is an opportunity to recapitulate some of the ideas presented previously. I will take this opportunity to place some of these ideas in the context of public health. Death and dying is not only a topic for scholars and clinicians. Media attention is directed to the deaths of prominent public figures, particularly those of political, entertainment, and sports giants; the details of whose deaths and funerals are telecast or published around the world. An example of this is given in the *Postlude* by Corless.

Whether as a result of natural causes or due to an accident associated with alcohol, overdose of drugs, an assassin's bullet, famine, a devastating natural disaster, or the ravages of wars, our attention is focused on death scenes in a way that is different due to the immediacy given by the electronic media. The question of how we deal with what I would call the armchair experience of death and incorporate death imagery, influences how we deal with death in our everyday lives.

"Scared to death, deathly ill, death threat, death wish, death of cold, dead wrong, dead beat, dead wood, dead end, a dead issue, death mask, death house, dead as a door nail, death rate... " These phrases represent but a short list of common death-related terms redolent of a language and culture that incorporates the concept of death into the speech of everyday life while maintaining an adolescent-like distance.

Although rarely examined, except by scholars, the following motifs are richly amplified as common themes coursing through the chapters in this book—the search for the truth of living and the fear and anxiety of dying, the attempts to study thanatological issues and to understand death's meaning for life, the models for caring, and the personal experiences and expressions of death, dying, and bereavement. One is always left with a question at the end of the chapter or a call for further study and inquiry or an admonition, for example, to insist on the quality of living as having equal valence with aggressive therapies (Preston & McCorkle).

Many chapters in this book propose ways to bolster and reinforce the support network, to train and support the professional, and to explore the spiritual streams arising from death and grief. Although the papers, for the most part, are concerned with the individual, the public-health professional may also benefit from the thoughtful works presented. The health and medical community with which I have worked deal with death every day in ways described by Silverman as "stigmatized" or "spoiled." (See Silverman's chapter in *Death, Dying, and Bereavement: Theoretical Perspectives and Other Ways of Knowing*, edited by Corless, Gemino, and Pittman.) The concept of self is important in this context because the loss associated with death and the process of grieving is intrinsically linked to the transition to a new role which sheds the experience of social isolation and stigma.

Public health bridges the tough social questions that manifest themselves in medical terms. What happens to the person whose life experience is constantly associated with social stigma? What happens to the homeless drug abuser who appears in the emergency room in cardiac arrest? Who is responsible for the family whose everyday life experience incorporates traumatic death events resulting in complicated mourning that engenders feelings of vulnerability, powerlessness, guilt, and anxiety? How does one help the grieving family whose social support network is absent or experiencing the same level of distress?

Public health has at its foundation the incorporation of education, the prevention of the social problems affecting the dis-ease of the individual, and the promotion of "health." Public health's roots stem from the plagues and the major "killers" in society. Following the taming of the major communicable diseases in industrialized countries and until the Human Immunodeficiency Virus (HIV)/Acquired Immunodeficiency Syndrome (AIDS) epidemic, most public-health interventions have not focused on death per se, but on the antecedents to death.

Cancer and HIV disease have heightened the awareness of the general public to hospice and other alternatives to dying in a hospital, both from the perspective of the quality of life and the preferred death scene as well as from the perspective of the economic and social costs. In part, as a result of the aging of the population, individuals in a persistent vegetative state being kept alive by technology, and more recently, gay men living with HIV disease who wanted control over their deaths, there has been a concerted effort to develop and to inform individuals of the range of options in care during a terminal illness. The chapter by Degner discusses the new roles for caregivers when a disease cannot be cured and the help needed is compensatory for the resources the individual no longer commands personally. As Corless states in Chapter Six, "The ultimate contribution of hospice to how living and dying are viewed in our society may be to facilitate a greater appreciation for living as the humane possibilities for dying are actualized."

The public-health professional looks at disease patterns and the spread of disease with death as a marker, a rate, an index of where the prevention and education efforts have fallen short. One key indicator of the public's health is the rate of infant mortality. Our conflict in public health over death and dying is most often presented by the disparity in mortality rates between those who have and those who have not, the rich and the poor, the white and the black, the deserving and the undeserving.

An article on infant mortality in Washington, DC, highlighted this conflict in the city where U.S. health policy is made and directed (*Washington Post*, 27 October 1991). The article describes the way that a hospital helps the mother accept the death of her baby—a picture, a piece of the blanket the baby was wrapped in, a snippet of the hair, a sympathy card, and a rose, all placed in a basket called a *grief basket*. Such attempts by caregivers to help individuals deal with loss is an area of concern to scholars in the field of death and dying.

The public-health professional, on the other hand, working on an aggregate level focuses on the systematic exclusion of some people from basic health care. This is underscored by noting that the death rates for infants and children in developing nations are not dissimilar to those of Washington, DC. As startling as these statistics should be, as a society, we've become inured to the reality of each personal loss. The 1993 infant (0–1 year) mortality statistics for Washington, DC, indicated that there were 16.7 deaths per 1000 births, more than double the national rate of 8.2 per thousand, and well above the rate of most industrialized nations.

Health policy in the United States is heavily influenced by economics and the demographics of the population. Economic factors have been influential in identifying, segregating, and separating the so-called deserving from the undeserving for health care and social support. The demography of the population in the United States and other industrialized nations is indicative of the aging population. As a result, questions related to the quality of living in later years will focus more attention on options for dying, including attention to legislation for active voluntary euthanasia.

Qvarnstrøm's chapter discusses the difficulty of a multidisciplinary and cross-cultural group of professionals coming to consensus on the procedures for health professionals to participate in euthanasia. These professionals were able to agree on four commonly accepted norms for medical ethics which provide a foundation for the discussion of this issue. The responsibility of health professionals and scholars is to explore all four principles and particularly the last mentioned—justice—as well as to further explore our models of caring, support, grieving, and our terms for selecting acceptable versus unacceptable deaths. These deliberations are essential for the development of a more widespread societal discourse and clearly are the basis for creating and accepting legislation in this area. It would be ironic were we to give everyone equal access to voluntary assistance with death before we gave them the same access to life.

Postlude

And When Famous People Die...

Inge B. Corless

The death of Jacqueline Bouvier Kennedy Onassis evoked sorrow in the hearts of many who knew her only from afar. Whatever their social backgrounds, many persons were moved to tears by the death of the former First Lady. This interesting phenomenon of a loss perceived as that of a family member or close friend elicited my curiosity. By contrast, when infamous people die there is something more like a collective sigh of relief—we can put this behind us. Interestingly, a similar sentiment is experienced when a loved one dies after a prolonged period of suffering, though the latter is mixed with grief.

Thus there appear to be two elements of particular significance in the collective response to Mrs. Onassis's death. The first is the perception of the untimeliness of the death. A widow too young, her death too soon. In this aspect, Mrs. Onassis appeared to be too young. In the revision of our collective thinking about age, the "sixties" are now middle adult or young old age and thus Mrs. Onassis died too soon.

There is another sense of timeliness, namely that we, the general public, were not aware of the extent of her illness and thus were not prepared for her death. The lack of preparation contributes to the perception of the suddenness of her dying and death and thus the untimeliness.

Tragedy affecting the famous brings into public discussion unresolved issues of personal concern. The living will, cessation of cure-oriented medical treatment, breast cancer, and substance abuse all received national attention when presidential families were affected. Thus, we employ famous people as proxies to bring into the realm of public discourse the dilemmas that are often expressed behind closed doors.

Our collective grief is also related to what Terry Bard, a chaplain and colleague in Boston, has termed *transferred imagination.* By this he means we invest certain famous people with our collective hopes. And so it is when that individual dies we feel bereft not only of the person in our national scene but also all that individual represented with regard to our national and personal aspirations—a very difficult loss.

The death of Mrs. Onassis has been said to bring to a close the era of Camelot, a time of optimism, youth, and promise. In our national history it was a time when the promise of opportunity, equality, and justice for all seemed within reach. With the death of President John F. Kennedy our collective hopes were diminished.

Events affecting the famous often serve as hallmarks for our personal lives. And to the degree that occurs, tragedy affecting the famous evokes affective remembrances of our own losses—the deaths of our beloved persons. And our own unresolved grief. The manner in which Mrs. Kennedy grieved publicly provided boundaries and structure for our personal and national grief.

Jacqueline Kennedy, in an essay about the death of her husband, also wrote about the death of a leader and the meaning of such a loss for the nation. Bereaved persons often speak of the "first everything" without the beloved deceased—the first spring, the first time the plant that s(he) planted blooms. Mrs. Kennedy wrote about the "last everything" in her poignant essay about her husband. Wistfully, she may have also written with a view to history.

As we completed preparations for the publication of this book with its emphasis on issues in the field of death and dying, it seemed appropriate to once again, as we did in the first volume (*Dying, Death, and Bereavement: Theoretical Perspectives and Other Ways of Knowing*) conclude with the knowing of first-hand experience. We are privileged to end this volume with the words of a woman who respected words and their power to show respect; who used symbols to enshrine her husband as legend when she could no longer have him as man.

A Memoir

It is nearly a year since he has been gone.

On so many days—his birthday, an anniversary, watching his children running to sea—I have thought, "But this day last year was his last to see that." He was so full of love and life on all those days. He seems so vulnerable now, when you think that each one was a last time.

Soon the final day will come around again—as inexorably as it did last year. But expected this time.

It will find some of us different people than we were a year ago. Learning to accept what was unthinkable when he was alive, changes you.

I don't think there is any consolation. What was lost cannot be replaced.

"A Memoir" by Jacqueline Kennedy is reprinted with permission of H. & C. Communications, Inc., Houston, Texas.

Someone who loved President Kennedy, but who had never known him, wrote to me this winter: "The hero comes when he is needed. When our belief gets pale and weak, there comes a man out of that need who is shining—and everyone living reflects a little of that light—and stores some up against the time when he is gone."

Now I think that I should have known that he was magic all along. I did know it—but I should have guessed it could not last. I should have known that it was asking too much to dream that I might have grown old with him and see our children grow up together.

So now he is a legend when he would have preferred to be a man. I must believe that he does not share our suffering now. I think for him— at least he will never know whatever sadness might have lain ahead. He knew such a share of it in his life that it always made you so happy whenever you saw him enjoying himself. But now he will never know more—not age, nor stagnation, nor despair, nor crippling illness, nor loss of any more people he loved. His high noon kept all the freshness of the morning—and he died then, never knowing disillusionment.

...He has gone...
Among the radiant, ever venturing on,
Somewhere, with morning, as such
spirits will.

(from John Masefield's "On the Finish of the Sailing Ship Race")

He is free and we must live. Those who love him most know that "the death you have dealt is more than the death which has swallowed you."

Jacqueline Kennedy

Index